The Art and Practice of
Ancient Hindu Astrology

Other Books by James Braha

Ancient Hindu Astrology for the Modern Western Astrologer

Astro-Logos; Revelations of a Hindu Astrologer

How to Be a Great Astrologer; The Planetary Aspects Explained

How to Predict Your Future; Secrets of Eastern and Western Astrology

THE ART AND PRACTICE OF ANCIENT HINDU ASTROLOGY

Nine Intimate Sessions
Between Teacher and Student

BY JAMES BRAHA

HERMETICIAN PRESS

Hermetician Press
P.O. Box 195
Longboat Key, Fla. 34228

The Art and Practice of Ancient Hindu Astrology; Nine Intimate Sessions Between Student and Teacher
Copyright © 2001 by James Braha

All rights reserved. No part of this text may be reproduced or used in any form or by any means — graphic, electronic, or mechanical, including photocopying, mimeographing, or information storage and retrieval systems — without written permission from the publisher. A reviewer may quote passages.

Cover Design by Amy Sprouse

Head shot and back cover photo by Barbara Banks

Page design and graphics by Vashti Braha

ISBN 0-935895-09-4

Library of Congress Catalogue Card Number: 00-111450

Printed in Hong Kong by Liang Yu Printing Factory, Ltd.
Mr. Eric Hui (852) 2560-4453

First Printing
1 2 3 4 5 6 7 8 9 10 15 20 25

LONDON BOROUGH OF CAMDEN	
Browns Books	03/01/08
ANF	24.50
B	

For Julian

ACKNOWLEDGMENTS

There are many people to whom I am indebted for their help and support on this project. First, I would like to thank Martin Timmons, my student and indispensable partner in this endeavor. Martin approached his role as student with enthusiasm and sincerity of purpose. He consistently asked important and penetrating questions and urged me at every turn to include information that he felt would be helpful to fellow students of Hindu astrology. Beyond this, he read and re-read the text of our classes over and over during a three year period — to alleviate areas of confusion and anything that he believed would make the book better. I must also salute Martin for his generosity in allowing sensitive details of his life to be included in this text. Never once did he accept my offers to remove material that was sensitive and/or potentially invasive to his privacy. In all, Martin was a pleasure to work with.

I would also like to thank my editor, Anthony Salveggi, who went to great lengths to make my text readable and clear. I consider it a stroke of excellent fortune to have found Anthony, since one of my most difficult tasks was to locate an editor with the talents necessary for a dialogue-based text. Anthony's critical attention to detail along with his sensitivity to my "voice" was a gift for which I will always be grateful.

I am indebted to Dr. David Goldstein for reviewing the text and providing encouragement when it was sorely needed. Never have I written a text that took so long and was so difficult to finish. David encouraged me and impressed upon me the importance of completing this book as soon as possible. His helpful insights and important suggestions were greatly appreciated.

The horoscopes in this book were generated from a Western and Eastern astrology computer program called <u>Solar Fire</u>. I would like to thank the maker of the program, Graham Dawson, for use of the program as well as all his help and technical support.

I am also grateful to the students and friends who have allowed their horoscopes to be included in this book. They are: Kerry Breitbart, Rajesh Naz, Annie O'Connell, Deborah Brown, and Emmett Walz. A book such as this, based entirely on personal experience, could not have been written were it not for the many thousands of clients, students, friends, and peers who have allowed me the privilege of looking into their lives via their horoscopes. To all these individuals, I am deeply thankful.

For many years now, the founders and members of the American Council of Vedic Astrology (ACVA) based in Sedona, Arizona have done tremendous work for the cause of Eastern astrology. Aside from organizing intensive

Vedic astrology conferences every year, they have fostered a remarkable attitude of tolerance regarding the differing viewpoints that make up this vast field. Further, ACVA has worked hard to build a *community* of Hindu astrologers within the United States. I am very grateful to ACVA and pray that in my endeavor to discover and promote astrological truths I have not stretched the boundaries of traditional knowledge too far or offended any of my peers. It is certainly not my intention to upset anyone, and if I have inadvertently done so, I sincerely apologize.

Finally, to Vashti — my love, my life, my everything — I am eternally grateful. Aside from caring for my happiness and well-being, Vashti has assisted me in every possible way on this project. She made *invaluable* suggestions throughout, typeset this book, and did everything possible to provide time for my writing — a daunting task after the birth of our son Julian. Most of all, I am grateful for Vashti's never-ending encouragement and reassurance. Writing a text like this, based entirely on personal experience, brought up constant fears, doubts, and insecurities. Vashti insisted that regardless of whether my findings disagreed with those of other authorities, dedicated students deserved to know my true feelings. Vashti fought tooth-and-nail for fellow astrology students and for the cause of astrological knowledge. Without her input, this text would not be as it is. Without her presence I would be lost. I love her eternally.

Table Of Contents

Introduction   1

How to Use This Book   7

Note to Beginners   10

Note to Experienced Students and Astrologers   11

Class One – Analyzing the *Muhurta* Chart for This Project   13

>What is a *muhurta*, "Hindu astrology" versus "Vedic astrology," analysis of the Gemini ascendant of the *muhurta*, the differences between Hindu and Western Astrology, planets in detriment, planetary aspects, the two zodiacs, subtleties of planetary aspects, dispelling mistakes of the intellect, malefics in *upachaya* houses, malefics in exalted and own signs, Rahu and Ketu well-placed in Gemini and Virgo, Moon in the 8th house of our *muhurta*, when planets in 8th and 12th houses give good results, other *muhurtas* that were considered for this project, how malefic planets affect *upachaya* houses.

Class Two – Analysis of Martin's Horoscope   43

>Why there are so many different *Jyotish* viewpoints, Shiva's curse on astrologers, why ancient texts are cryptic, transits considered from the Moon versus the ascendant, functional benefics and malefics, James Braha's horoscope, planetary friendships and enemies, using *karakas* to assess each horoscope, *neechabhanaga* and *vargottama*, Martin's natal and *dasamsa* charts, astrology and genetics, Raj's businessman chart, *Parivartana Yoga* or mutual reception in Martin's and Ram Das' horoscopes, interpreting "mixed" charts and "wild card" influences, planets receiving fallen aspects, planets as deities, analysis of *dasa* and *bhukti* planets in "mixed" condition, Mercury retrograde effects, the importance of the Moon's nodes in Western astrology.

Class Three – How to Prioritize Horoscope Features, and Retrograde Planets in a Horoscope   93

>Daily planetary rulerships, Mercury retrograde periods, **List** of effects of retrograde planets ruling houses, retrograde planets in houses, retrograde benefics and malefics, retrograde planetary aspects, Roberto's horoscope with exalted Jupiter conjunct fallen

Mars, applying versus separating aspects, the responsibility of an astrologer, **list** of priorities of positive planetary positions, Robert De Niro's *varga* chart summary, **list** of priorities of negative planetary positions, **list** of what makes a house well-disposed, **list** of what makes a house afflicted, proper use of the *ashtaka varga* system, **list** of what makes a chart well-disposed, what makes a chart weak and afflicted, how to analyze a conjunction involving one exalted planet and one fallen planet, Bill Clinton's horoscope, the importance of planetary orbs.

Class Four – Stationary Planets, *Sade Sati, Panoti Yoga,* and *Prasna* Charts   131

Introduction to *Sade Sati*, the power of stationary planets, John Kennedy's horoscope containing two stationary planets, Tipper Gore's horoscope with stationary Jupiter, what happens when benefics ruling bad houses throw aspects, Robert De Niro's horoscope, Deborah's stationary Mars, using *prasna* charts, interpreting *kujadosha* or *mangaldosha* properly, Hank Aaron's horoscope with stationary Jupiter, analyzing planets that receive very "mixed" aspects, John Kennedy's extremely "mixed" Mercury, how to use *Panoti Yoga* to properly judge *Sade Sati*, three *Sade Sati* and *Panoti Yoga* examples from James Braha's horoscope, how to use *marakas* properly, why the *ayanamsa* is critical for *Panoti Yoga*, examples of *Panoti Yoga* using B.V. Raman's and Sri Yuketeswar's *ayanamsas*, the story of Rahu and Ketu, Kerry's chart with 11th house ruler conjunct Ketu, how malefic planetary energy can be used wisely, effects of equinoxes and solstices on people's health, using the horoscope to determine a person's spiritual path, the difference between readings given by Westerners and Indian *Jyotishis*, the story of Lord Ganesh.

Class Five – Subtleties and Often Ignored Significations of the First Six Houses   183

Why memorizing accurate meanings of the houses is critical, common pitfalls of house misinterpretations, astrologers who "mix and match" house meanings, the need to question astrological authorities, the importance of the Sun and Moon, why an afflicted Sun or Moon can still give good effects, the Sun as *atmakaraka*, details of houses one through six, Al Gore's chart, Fidel Castro's chart.

Class Six – Subtleties and Often Ignored Significations of the Last Six Houses   213

Intuition in astrological practice, *karakamsa* horoscopes, details of houses six through nine, John Lennon's horoscope and the difference of opinions over his accurate birthtime, Vashti's horoscope, how astrologers misuse *marakas*, details of houses ten through twelve, David Stockman's chart..

Class Seven – Analyzing Natal Horoscopes and *Varga* Charts for Career, Health, and Marriage   251

How to determine whether a *varga* chart is reliable, how to analyze *varga* charts, Deborah's *navamsa* chart, a **list** of key points to be used when analyzing career, importance of Moon and ascendant ruler, a **list** of houses as they relate to career, a **list** of key points to be used when analyzing health, a **list** of houses as they relate to health, a **list** of key points to be used when analyzing marriage, natal and *varga* charts of Henry, John, and Annie. How to determine a waxing or waning Moon.

Class Eight – The Problems with *Neechabhanga Rajayoga* and *Vargottama*, and Confusing Conjunctions Analyzed   307

Neechabhanga fails to work in the charts of Al Pacino, Werner Erhard, Francis Coppola, and Charles Braha, four *Vargottama* planets that are ineffective in James Braha's chart, planets in their highest degree of exaltation, planets in their worst degree of fall, example charts of Jack Nicholson, Albert Einstein, and Mick Jagger, what happens when Venus in Libra is tightly conjunct exalted Saturn, Orson Welles' chart containing exalted Venus tightly conjunct malefic Mars, why the *condition* of a malefic planet has nothing to do with the aspect it *throws*, what happens to planets conjunct Ketu.

Class Nine – *Upayes*. Gemstones, Mantras, and *Yagyas*. Wedding *Muhurtas*, Compatibility Charts, and How to Analyze a Stellium of Planets.   337

Why there is no agreement on prescribing gems, the purpose of a gemstone and how it works, four points about prescribing gems that are traditionally agreed upon, a **list** of "secondary" stones, James Braha's rules for prescribing gems, how mantras and *yagyas* work, why there is no such thing as wrong mantra chanting or a wrong *yagya*, why mantras or *yagyas* should be performed in cases where a gemstone could produce harm, explanation of *Brighu* readings and how every *Brighu* reading contains a *yagya* prescription, a **list** of astrological concerns when choosing a wedding *muhurta*, the wedding *muhurta* for James and Vashti, compatibility and synastry charts, why the *kuta* method of compatibility is ineffective for Westerners, how to analyze a stellium of planets in one house of a horoscope.

FINAL SUMMARY 373

APPENDIX A – FUNDAMENTALS 375

Hindu astrology primer for beginners.

APPENDIX B 417

All Horoscopes of this book drawn in North Indian Method.

GLOSSARY OF HINDU TERMS 425

SERVICES OF JAMES BRAHA AND HERMETICIAN PRESS 429-430

Computerized Hindu astrology birthchart reports, personalized full-life Hindu astrology readings by James Braha, James Braha's books, Hindu astrology computer program, address and phone number of American Council of Vedic Astrology, how and where to order remedial *yagyas*, contact for purchasing gemstones, where to find the best catalogue of Hindu astrology texts, where to order computer calculated Hindu horoscopes, where to find an excellent horary astrologer.

INTRODUCTION

The greatest obstacle facing Western practitioners of Hindu astrology, also known as Vedic astrology or *Jyotish*, is the lack of experienced teachers in local areas. This text is my endeavor to help improve the situation. For about four months, I sat with a student and friend named Martin Timmons and taught him Hindu astrology with the intent of producing this book.

In 1993, after completing my fourth text, I decided to give up writing because the financial gain was not worth the time, effort, and mental stress. I concluded that until I had the freedom to write without having to continue my private astrology practice, the strain would be too much.

In the middle of 1996, my wife Vashti ordered a seven-day Mercury *yagya* to help in her college endeavors and ease her mental tensions. A *yagya* is a Hindu ritualistic ceremony where about twenty priests chant mantras, or prayers, for seven days, eight hours per day for a person's well-being. The effects are often quite powerful. Perhaps because married couples are karmically entwined or perhaps because the photo we provided the Hindu priests in India was a wedding photo with both my wife and I in it, Vashti's Mercury *yagya* had a strong impact on me. During the week of the *yagya*, I found myself replacing all our stereo and taping equipment (significations of Mercury), something that needed to be done years earlier. More importantly, I had a thought that perhaps I *could* write the *Jyotish* text that I considered next in line without having to sit for a year alone in a room with my computer. The idea was to teach a student, tape record the sessions, and transcribe the tapes.

Now that the project is over, I am deeply indebted to the priests who performed the *yagya* that gave me the impetus to write this book. I am at heart an astrology teacher. That is why I always feel compelled to write. On the other hand, the project was not as easy as I had envisioned. After having ten or so of the astrological sessions transcribed, I found that I was unable leave the transcriptions alone. During the editing process, I quickly switched into "writing mode" and began adding material that Martin and I may have actually discussed in different sessions. I also spent a great deal of time reorganizing and restructuring the information. And, as the years have passed, I have occasionally written about events out that occurred long after our formal classes ended. For example, in Class Two, I have made references to my son who was born in 1999. In another class, I have written about the Bill Clinton-Monica Lewinsky scandal of 1999. So, while the material you are about to read is a result of our classes together, it is not actually a transcription. It is a "dialogue" based on our conversations.

In the end, our weekly three-hour astrology classes — that lasted about four months — became a writing project has taken over three years. The reason for this is that when I realized I was once again facing the long arduous task of writing a detailed astrology book, I had the good sense not to put the rest of my life on hold as I did during my other writing projects. The writing occurred only in spare time, while I fully continued my private practice, lecturing and workshops, and other astrology projects.

The teachings in this book are based, as much as humanly possible, on my experience. I tried to teach Martin, the student in the following nine lessons, the same way my second mentor P.M. Padia taught me. Mr. Padia was a practicing astrologer, not a scholar as was my first teacher, the late author/translator R. Santhanam. Most of what Padia taught me he had thoroughly tested through his lengthy professional practice. I remember that whenever Padia said something that contradicted textbook teachings or other astrologers, and was challenged about it, he would always make the same reply: "You take it from me. I have marked this (noticed this)!" If I protested further, as I often did, he would simply repeat emphatically "You take it from me. I have marked this!"

I quickly learned to trust Padia, for his predictions were so often accurate. And in time, as my own professional practice blossomed, I profoundly appreciated the knowledge Padia gave me that I would never have found in textbooks. Knowledge that had taken him years of trial and error to discover. For example, Padia explained that he had noticed that whenever a connection existed between the 3rd house and the 6th house in a person's horoscope, the person was either involved in the medical arts or had healing talent. He taught me that despite ancient seer Parasara's proclamation regarding *Rahu* being exalted in Taurus, both *Rahu* and *Ketu* function better in Mercury's signs Gemini and Virgo. He taught me that the older, more traditional house system (known as "whole sign houses") is more essential and consistently accurate than the newer one, *Sri Pati*, which I had been using for about a year before meeting him. He taught me that the second marriage can be seen from the 9th house, something rarely mentioned because ancient Hindus almost never re-married.

One day Padia said that he had realized that since Hindu life is divided into four essential functions, *dharma, artha, kama,* and *moksha* (duty or purpose, money, desires, and enlightenment), each person's horoscope must reflect the fact. After much consideration, he had determined that the four different elements, fire, earth, air, and water, correspond perfectly to the four different functions. Thus, he taught me that the fire houses, one, five, and nine, correspond to *dharma* houses. The earth houses, two, six, and ten, correspond to the *artha* houses, and the air houses, three, seven, and eleven, correspond to *kama* houses. The water houses, four, eight, and twelve, correspond to *moksha* houses. Such teachings I could never have learned from any book, and such teachings I have passed on to others through my books and lectures. This was the benefit of studying with someone who had practiced astrology for a paying public day after day for years on end. And this was the difference between studying with someone completely committed to his experience of astrology versus my first teacher, Mr. Santhanam, who was a translator of ancient astrological texts and whose purpose was to promote such traditional teachings.

On the other hand, Padia was not infallible just because he followed his experience. Whenever Padia taught me a technique that I felt did not work in my astrological practice, which I must admit was rare, I simply refused to use the teaching. And of course, because the field of astrology is so vast and so complicated, there were times when Padia and I disagreed. For example, being from North India, Padia had never even heard of the concept that the 9th house represents the father. He had not lived in Southern India where astrologers take the 9th house as the father, because in South India fathers act as gurus to their children and gurus are governed by the 9th house. Padia was taught that the 10th house represents the father. And so it goes. Each astrologer learns from his or her own teachers and refines the knowledge as much as possible through practical experience. While Padia was masterful at predicting certain features within a horoscope, he was fallible at others. Nevertheless, I am forever indebted to him, as I also am to my first mentor, R. Santhanam.

I have now been a full-time practicing astrologer for nearly twenty years. Much of what I teach in this text should be helpful because my findings have been tested over time. That is the point of the book. On the other hand, I too am fallible. Astrology is a vast and complicated subject, so vast it is unlikely to ever be perfectly mastered by one person. Readers must keep in mind that just because my experience has borne out certain truths, it does not necessarily mean that these truths will also work for you. For example, whenever I see a client with a heavily afflicted 9th house, there is inevitably some form of trouble within the session. Either the person is rude, shows up late, doesn't send in payment on time, or reading the birthchart is extraordinarily difficult. Although this has been my consistent experience during twenty years of practice, does it necessarily follow that other astrologers will also have the same problem? Could it not be that this happens to me because I am a typical 9th house person, and clients with afflicted 9th houses simply have trouble dealing with religious or spiritual types? After all, I did spend the 1970's pursuing enlightenment and have been practicing daily meditation for over twenty-five years.

In my own horoscope, eclipses have no impact whatsoever. For years, I have challenged astrologers who swear by eclipses to make a significant prediction about the effects of upcoming eclipses in my horoscope, and for years these astrologers have failed. Does this mean eclipses have no effects on others? Knowledge born of experience is a wonderful thing, but it is not everything. Therefore, although I now give you my honest experiences of many fundamental Hindu astrological techniques, it is your responsibility to determine whether my findings are accurate and whether they work for you.

One of my strongest intents within this project is to try and clarify, and in some cases disprove, astrological techniques that are traditionally accepted and promoted, but which function inconsistently at best, and at worst not at all. Astrologers with strong commitments to all ancient techniques must therefore expect to be offended or upset by some of my teachings. While I believe that this text contains plenty of pearls of wisdom, I have no doubt there is something in every chapter for astrologers to disagree with and argue about. This, I confess, is a strong point of the text. Too many Hindu astrology precepts are accepted blindly, without healthy skepticism and testing. Too many astrologers believe that the astrological techniques that worked for ancient Indian astrologers must still be relevant today.

On the other hand, putting my personal findings into print, which do not always agree with other authorities, either ancient or modern, leaves me in quite a vulnerable position. While I am willing to become a lightning rod for astrological purposes, I am sensitive about my reputation and standing within the Hindu/Vedic astrological community. It is one thing to disagree with other astrological authorities in a private classroom. It is another to put one's findings and opinions in print for all to see, not to mention that my printed words will be read for years and years, while my opinions could change at any time. In any event, rest assured that it is not my intent to offend anyone, particularly my peers for whom I have great respect.

What you are about to read is not a textbook of traditional astrological teachings. It is a nine-session series of distinctions, based on my personal experience, involving all kinds of astrological techniques that are either confusing to many or harmful to predictive accuracy due to their inefficiency. I therefore humbly ask readers to be mindful and sensitive to the process now put before you. When one of my findings flies in the face of your knowledge and experience, please bear in mind that my sole purpose is simply to share what I have found to work in my astrological practice. Although I cannot guarantee that every one of my findings is the unassailable astrological truth, I sincerely believe that the teachings in this text will be helpful to all astrologers, beginners and advanced.

As difficult or controversial issues are confronted and discussed within this text, some of my findings will resonate with the reader and some will not. The best strategy to take with the material is, I believe, a "live and let live" attitude. Use whichever truths and distinctions appeal to you and ignore the rest. Do not get bogged down in negative reactions if, or when, any of my teachings offend your sensibilities. This, unfortunately, may be easier said than done. Those of you who cheer out loud when I demonstrate *neechabhanga rajayoga* to be so inconsistent as to be nearly useless, may become quite upset when I assert that the *Vimsottari dasa* system, wonderful as it is, is fallible in a certain number of horoscopes. Those who are ecstatic when I state that the *kuta* numerical compatibility system does not work for Westerners (because the kind of compatibility ancient Hindus were looking for bears no resemblance to what modern Westerners are seeking), may get angry when I refute a common misunderstanding about "functional benefics" and "functional malefics." (A functional benefic is a malefic natured planet, such as Mars or Saturn, that takes on <u>some</u> beneficial energy because it happens to rule good houses, such as the 5th or 9th. A functional malefic is a benefic natured planet, such as Venus or Jupiter, that takes on <u>some</u> damaging energy because it happens to rule bad houses, such as the 8th or 12th.) When malefics like Mars and Saturn become functional benefics, they <u>do not</u> suddenly and miraculously lose their mean and destructive nature. They carry <u>both</u> extreme good and extreme bad energy. Likewise, when benefics like Venus and Jupiter become functional malefics because they happen to rule bad houses, they do not suddenly relinquish their essential benefic nature and lose all positive qualities.

Beginners who have no particular opinion about, or attachment to, which traditional techniques work well and which do not will obviously have the easiest time with this text. Wherever I have made statements that are radical, or contradictory to traditional textbooks, I have noted this fact so that each reader can make his or her own final judgements. Veteran astrologers who can temporarily put aside long-held beliefs in order to <u>seriously</u> consider and perhaps even test certain distinctions that are initially upsetting will also fare well. My advice, then, is to keep an open mind. Then, you may agree with some of my findings, disagree with others, and still enjoy peeking into the intimate astrology sessions between myself and Martin.

I am more confident in the accuracy and usefulness of the material in this book than that of my earlier writings, which were more theoretical. During the sixteen years that have passed since I wrote my first book, <u>Ancient Hindu Astrology for the Modern Western Astrologer</u>, I have analyzed thousands upon thousands of horoscopes. I have now been a professional astrologer for about the same length of time as P.M. Padia was in 1984, when he tutored me privately. As each year passes, I better understand the weight and profundity of his recurrent statement, "You take it from me, I have marked this." If some of my teachings in this book appear too emphatic, you now understand the reason. I am reminded of the occasions when Padia used to say to me, "James, I have given you all my secrets." He had.

I hope you will take my secrets seriously. If what you are about to read is half as beneficial to you as my sessions with Padia were, I can say two things with surety. First, your level of predictive accuracy is about to be dramatically improved. Second, get out a brand new highlighter — you are in for a treat.

HOW TO USE THIS BOOK

In this text, I focus mainly on *Jyotish* (Hindu astrology) fundamentals. I do this for several reasons. First, the best astrological readings I have received were from astrologers who were both intuitive and had mastered — truly mastered — the fundamentals. Second, astrology is a mirror of human existence. In the same way that there are fundamentals to life, so it is with *Jyotish*. The fundamentals of life (beyond food and shelter) are that we all need to be loved, we all want to experience ourselves as capable and successful, and we all want to feel that our lives matter — that we make a difference in the world. Without fulfilling such essentials, life goes awry and we suffer. Likewise, when we astrologers are imperfect or even haphazard with *Jyotish* fundamentals, predictive accuracy becomes impossible.

Finally, I have met too many students who report that they have memorized the varied rules and basics of *Jyotish*, but do not fully understand how to use them. Many have diligently studied the fundamentals and still, quite reasonably, have trouble with the complexity and the subtlety of this vast metaphysical art. This book is written with such students in mind. My intention, first and foremost, is to present examples of basic *Jyotish* techniques that will provide readers with a tangible experience of how *Jyotish* works, so that those who are merely hobbyists can become practicing astrologers.

In a field as complicated as Hindu astrology, a field containing hundreds of techniques and thousands of bits of information, it is all too easy to miss sight of the fact that the simplest techniques are actually the most important in contributing to predictive accuracy. It is easy to forget that the fundamental reasoning process of *Jyotish* is the core or nucleus of the system, while detailed arcane techniques exist mainly for refining purposes.

Unfortunately, it is natural to become bored with fundamentals and to crave more exotic and advanced astrological methods. Indeed, all of us hope, pray, and believe that one day a profound magical technique will appear and forever unlock the mysteries of predictive accuracy. Within my own studies, however, every time I have learned a so-called "wonder technique," it appears to have tremendous promise at first, but eventually reveals itself as yet another refining technique that works only occasionally. In the end, it is the fundamental reasoning process of *Jyotish* I return to, because it alone produces the real magic when used with <u>care and precision and consciousness</u>. While I also hope and pray that someday a great astrological guru will descend from the vast reaches of the Himalayan mountains and bless us with special ancient techniques, I prefer for now to try to master the techniques that work the best — the fundamentals.

Many astrology students have expressed a desire to see a textbook devoted solely to horoscope analysis. Although such a book would be enormously helpful, I do not think it would actually fill the gaps that most astrology students struggle with. Every basic *Jyotish* text written by a Westerner that I have seen (there are now at least six such books) contains a section of just such analysis. And yet students who have read all of those books complain that they still can only interpret horoscopes that are simple in their indications, and that they still desperately need a live teacher. I believe that many students are missing a profound, gut level understanding of each and every <u>basic</u> *Jyotish* technique. To my mind, the difference between presenting hundreds of analyzed horoscopes versus teaching the fundamentals <u>thoroughly</u>, is the difference between giving a person several fish versus teaching that person *how* to fish. I am far more grateful to my mentor P.M. Padia for teaching me the fundamentals and the underlying reasoning process of *Jyotish* than for the numerous tips and secrets he gave me. His tips and secrets were wonderful, but his perseverance with the fundamentals was infinitely more valuable.

In this book I do not deal extensively with astrological yogas. A yoga is a union, or combination, of planetary influences that is said to indicate a <u>specific</u> predictable result. Although yogas are considered by many to be fundamental *Jyotish* techniques, to me they are not. I consider yogas to be advanced because there is often no observable logic to them. For example, in natal horoscope analysis, wealth is indicated if the 2nd house (money from daily earnings) and the 11th house (money from side ventures) are strong and well disposed. In contrast, wealth is harmed if these houses are weak and afflicted. This is logical. On the other hand, *Laxmi Yoga* (pronounced lock-shmee), dictates that a person will be wealthy if planets occupy all of the following houses: the 2nd, 6th, 8th, and 12th houses. Where is the logic? Furthermore, *Laxmi Yoga* does not work consistently. Like all yogas, it works sometimes but not every time. These features keep it, and the many thousands of other yogas like it, out of the realm of fundamentals.

Although I have never found <u>any</u> astrological feature, basic or advanced, Eastern or Western, to work with one-hundred percent consistency, using yogas in one's daily practice requires a <u>pronounced</u> sense of intuition. The best astrologers I met in India had memorized hundreds of astrological techniques as well as thousands of yogas and then let their intuition be their guide as to which techniques to use for each horoscope. As I mention in Class Six, this method of filling one's head with an encyclopedic amount of astrological information and then allowing intuition to dictate when a yoga will work and when it will not, works well for Indians but is often difficult for Westerners. Indians have been raised in a profoundly mystical and metaphysical culture; conversely, Westerners have practiced the ways of science and linear thinking. Learning which yogas create positive effects and which ones create negative effects is extremely important. But learning which yoga produces a king, which one indicates a "mellifluous voice," which one specifies that a person will own elephants, and so on, is relatively futile. There is a saying in spiritual circles, "You can't get enough of what will never make you happy." The astrological equivalent is, "You can't learn enough (advanced information) of what will never make you a great astrologer." So, this book deals little with yogas, except to mention certain ones that produce good results, certain ones that produce bad results, certain ones that are overrated in terms of accuracy, and those that are commonly misunderstood or misused.

I cannot overstate the case for learning the essential reasoning process of *Jyotish* with utmost precision. Because I constantly meet astrologers who are lazy or haphazard with fundamentals, and because I suspect that advanced astrologers may question my obsession with the basics, I would like to offer a personal anecdote that will help clarify my approach and hopefully encourage others to follow.

As a child, I was a huge baseball fan who observed some of the most exciting years of the sport. Mickey Mantle hit the longest home runs imaginable, both right- and left-handed. Willie Mays made the most spectacular outfield catches and throws. And Maury Wills stole bases with lightning speed. But my favorite player by far was a quiet, unassuming outfielder who was consistently excellent in hitting, fielding, and base running, but who was often ignored by the press and fans for his talents. This man did not hit home runs one-hundred and fifty feet past the outfield wall, he did not dramatically tumble all over the field in order to make his outfield catches, and when he stole a base, he stole it gracefully. When he hit home runs, he did not wave to the fans, and he never, ever looked directly at the pitcher, the opponent he had just humiliated, as he unassumingly rounded the bases. After seventeen or so years of play, the sports world suddenly awoke to find that Hank Aaron was closing in on the most formidable of all baseball records — the lifetime home run record held by Babe Ruth (Ruth hit 714 home runs).

In the end, Aaron, who had clearly mastered the <u>fundamentals</u> of the game, surpassed Ruth by a mighty forty-one home runs. More importantly, Hammerin' Hank covered more bases than any player in history. When statisticians add up the bases every baseball player has covered in terms of distance (i.e. ninety feet per base), Aaron leads all other players by over <u>one mile</u>! And he did it without glitz or fanfare. Just innate talent combined with extraordinary commitment to fundamentals.

As astrologers, we do not need to dazzle our clients with spectacular predictions of what scars or birthmarks exist on their bodies. We do not have to predict some odd occurrence that is destined to happen to a person's cousin or uncle. We <u>do</u> have to be relatively and consistently accurate regarding our clients' health, career, married life, financial state, and general well-being. We also must follow up with our clients to find out which predictions we made have proved true, in order to determine which astrological techniques work well and which ones work poorly. When we astrologers invest the bulk of our time studying and researching the core truths of *Jyotish* fundamentals, and mastering the essential reasoning process of *Jyotish,* then — and only then — do we truly become great astrologers.

Note To Beginners

As mentioned in the introduction, this book is not a traditional Hindu astrology manual. Instead, it is a nine-session series of Hindu astrology distinctions, based on my personal experience, and involving many of the most basic astrological techniques. For beginners who are unfamiliar with Hindu astrology, also known as *Jyotish* or Vedic astrology, I have provided a 42 page introductory section titled <u>Appendix A - Fundamentals</u>, which begins on page 375. Once you have read and studied the section, you are ready to begin reading this text from the beginning. I have also tried to help by explaining many of the most fundamental *Jyotish* concepts in Class One. After that point, however, do not hesitate to refer to <u>Appendix A</u> whenever the need arises. And for those who are very serious about learning *Jyotish*, I suggest my first book, <u>Ancient Hindu Astrology for the Modern Western Astrologer</u>, which deals extensively with *Jyotish* fundamentals.

Please bear in mind that Hindu astrology is a complex subject, and what you are about to read is the <u>practical application</u> of the art. In other words, you are about to step into the world of Hindu astrology as it is <u>actually</u> practiced. Therefore, the less you are familiar with the subject, the more this book will approximate studying a foreign language through what is known as the "immersion method." In the immersion method, a person enters a classroom with a teacher of a foreign language and <u>only</u> the foreign language is spoken during the entire class.

While this text is certainly easier than the immersion method, because I give explanations throughout, beginners are bound to experience confusion within certain areas. Therefore, I have some suggestions. First, after reading <u>Appendix A</u>, go to the glossary (which begins on page 425) and read it in its entirety. Then, whenever confusion arises, refer to <u>Appendix A</u> as a guide. Finally, read the text calmly and mindfully, but <u>do not strain to understand</u>. Instead, remain in forward motion, keep a steady pace, and plan to re-read the text at least a second or third time. Bear in mind that even students who have studied Hindu astrology for years will likely read this book, or at least certain chapters, several times. The main instruction, therefore, is to continue reading and take what you get. Allow the information to seep in subconsciously, even if it is not fully understood at first. In time and with more study, the distinctions taught will not only be valuable to your predictive accuracy, they may save you considerable time, effort, and frustration.

Note To Experienced Students and Astrologers

Please read this book patiently. Keep an open mind and be willing to re-think — and above all, re-test — astrological techniques that you may have learned many years ago. If you have already read my introduction, go back and read it one more time, <u>slowly</u>. If you have not yet read the introduction, please read it once normally, and one more time, <u>slowly</u>. Those who do not fully comprehend the introduction will almost certainly miss the point of this book and have a less than enjoyable time with the text.

Also, when you read this text keep at least ten or twenty horoscopes (more if you can) of friends and relatives <u>whose lives you know very well</u>. Use these charts to test the techniques taught in this book. If some of my teachings contradict what you were initially led to believe, but actually prove to be more accurate, then you will have gained some insight.

CLASS ONE

James: The first thing we're going to do is analyze the *muhurta* chart for the project we're now beginning. A *muhurta* is a horoscope of the moment. Whenever you begin an important endeavor, it's crucial to pick a good starting time. If you pick a good starting time, the rest of the undertaking will go well. This is because the energy that begins any project — the breaking ground so to speak — will continue throughout the entire project. Ronald Reagan was known to use *muhurtas* all the time when he was President, but he was using Western astrology so the process was called electional astrology. It is said that when he was Governor of California he used to schedule his inaugurations at very odd times, even after midnight if the astrologer so advised. He did this to ensure that his term in office would go well.

As we discuss the *muhurta*, or "electional" chart, other astrological issues may come up that we can talk about and try to clarify. At some point in a later class, I'll come back to *muhurtas* and show you the chart Vashti (my wife) and I chose for our wedding (page 361). When you see the horoscope for that occasion, you'll understand why we got married at 10:50 P.M. on a Tuesday night. We picked a very good horoscope for married life; for love purposes. Consequently, the wedding was very beautiful and our married life has been strengthened.

In this first class, I'm going to try and fully explain even the most basic points that I mention. After this class, I'm going to assume you know the basics.

Martin: I already know most of the basics from reading your other books.

James: That's fine. But there will be readers of our classes who are beginners, and I want the first class to be easy for them. (After Class One, beginners should refer to Appendix A, whenever confusion arises.)

In our second class, I'm going to briefly analyze your natal horoscope and explain why, out of all the clients and astrology students available, I chose you as my student for this project. I did not choose you randomly, that's for sure.

Martin: I was wondering.

James: Your horoscope is excellent for a life in metaphysics or astrology. Astrology is a perfect *dharma* (life purpose) for you.

Before we begin analyzing, let's get our terms straight. Some astrologers use the term "Hindu astrology," some say "Vedic astrology," and some say "*Jyotish*." I generally use the terms "Hindu astrology" and "*Jyotish*" interchangeably. I almost never say "Vedic astrology" because I don't believe today's astrology of India is very similar to the astrology that was practiced many thousands of years ago, during Vedic civilization. This is a controversial matter.

In my opinion, there are simply too many fundamental *Jyotish* terms (*kendra*, *trikona*, *apoklima*, *hora*), that are actually Greek and have no meaning whatsoever in Sanskrit, the language of the Vedas. What can it possibly mean when many of the most basic terms of Hindu astrology are Greek?

Martin: It means that Indian astrology was influenced by invading cultures.

James: That's my point. Also, Vedic civilization was an enlightened society. *The purpose of Vedic knowledge was to produce enlightened, or self-realized souls.* Therefore, Vedic astrology had to be fundamentally concerned with helping each person realize enlightenment. This means the Vedic horoscope at the least revealed each person's particular evolutionary process and spiritual path. Today's *Jyotish* doesn't even mention which spiritual path a person should follow!

Martin: James, when you read my chart about a year ago, you said that my path was related to Lord Vishnu, the God of discrimination (i.e. evolution from Zen, the Bible, and intellectual techniques). Weren't you reading my path from the chart?

James: Yes, but that was quite general. That simply distinguished you from Shaivites, those who worship Lord Shiva (i.e. evolution from meditation, austerity, fasting, and so on), and those who worship Lord Krishna (i.e. evolution from devotion, prayer, chanting the name of Krishna, and so forth). I believe that in ancient Vedic astrology the horoscope revealed whether a person should practice *hatha yoga* (physical yoga), *gnana yoga* (yoga of discrimination), *karma yoga* (yoga of action), *bhakti yoga* (yoga of devotion), *raja yoga* (yoga of the senses), and so on. These are more specific and more important than simply revealing which God a person worships.

On top of all this, there's the problem of *nakshatras*. *Nakshatras* are the only bit of India's astrology that everyone agrees is exclusively Indian. And the real knowledge of *nakshatras* is completely lost. All we have now from very select ancient texts is a few short sentences to explain each one. The vast majority of books don't even mention *nakshatras*, let alone explain their meanings.

Martin: The books you loaned me haven't mentioned *nakshatra*s. Are those classic texts?

James: I'd say so. *Phaladeepika, Saravali, Hora Sara, Jataka Parijata, Satya Jatakam, Prasna Marga*. They're all classics. In any case, according to my teacher in India, P.M. Padia, *nakshatra*s are an entire system of astrology, not a slight adjunct to be added onto a chart reading with an extra two or three sentences. Dennis Harness has recently written a very good book on the subject, titled *Nakshatras; The Lunar Mansions Of Vedic Astrology*. But I still believe that what is known about *nakshatra*s today is barely related to how they were used in ancient Vedic culture. I intuitively felt this way within the first few weeks of studying *Jyotish* in India, and I've seen nothing yet that changes my mind. I'm not a historian by any means, but common sense tells me today's *Jyotish* is not Vedic.

Martin: James, is it possible that there are some astrologers in India who still have the knowledge of *nakshatra*s, but just haven't brought it out? I always hear stories of Indian saints that are several hundred years old living in the Himalayas.

James: It's anybody's guess. I'd love to believe that we'll eventually get the *nakshatra* system back. My guess is that it will re-surface if world consciousness ever rises to a high level.

What particularly upsets me about modern day use of *nakshatras*, by the way, is that I believe *nakshatras* were the heart and soul of ancient Vedic astrology, which was nothing if not a predictive system. Virtually everything you read today in terms of *nakshatra* descriptions is the opposite of predictive! Every text that describes *nakshatras* reads like Western astrology.

Martin: Psychological.

James: Psychological and behavioral and having to do with temperament. Typical *nakshatra* descriptions in Hindu astrology books available today (modern or ancient) go something like this: "The person with such and such *nakshatra* is learned, attracted to females, virtuous, brave, and proud." Or, "The a person will be irritable, hot-tempered, truthful, possessing leadership abilities, and politically inclined." These are predominantly *personality* traits and are, in my view, the antithesis of the Vedic use of *nakshatras*. Ancient Vedic astrologers would turn over in their graves if they saw how today's astrologers use them.

Anyway, aside from all that, please pronounce the term *Jyotish* properly. It is pronounced "joe-tish," not "joy-tish."

Now, look at the time I chose for the *muhurta*, the electional chart for this project. We are starting at six o'clock p.m. on December 14, 1996 in Longboat Key, Florida.

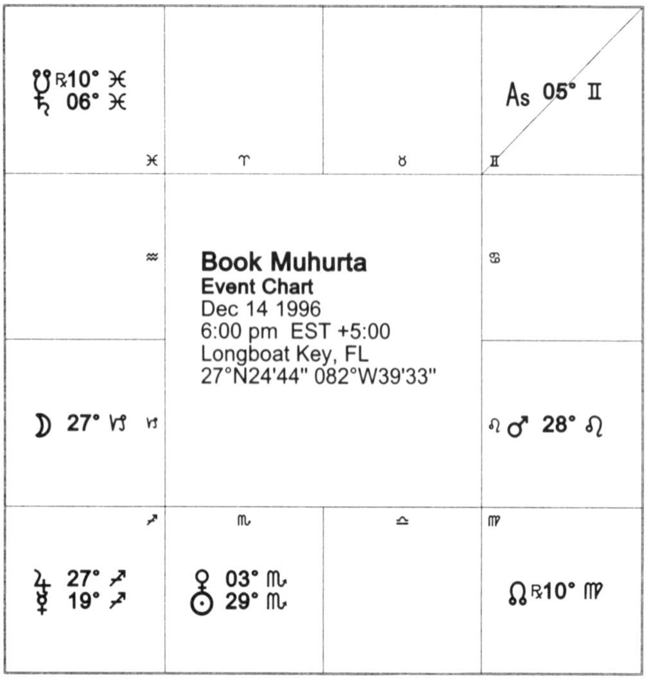
☋ ℞10° ♓
♄ 06° ♓
♓
♈
♉
♊
As 05° ♊
♒
♋
Book Muhurta
Event Chart
Dec 14 1996
6:00 pm EST +5:00
Longboat Key, FL
27°N24'44" 082°W39'33"
☽ 27° ♑
♑
♌ ♂ 28° ♌
♐
♏
♎
♍
♃ 27° ♐
☿ 19° ♐
♀ 03° ♏
☉ 29° ♏
☊ ℞10° ♍

South Indian Style

For North Indian, see Appendix B.

planets.pts

Pt	Name	Hs	Rules
☽	Moon	8	2
☉	Sun	6	3
☿	Mercury	7	1, 4
♀	Venus	6	5, 12
♂	Mars	3	6, 11
♃	Jupiter	7	7, 10
♄	Saturn	10	8, 9
☊	North Node	4	-
☋	South Node	10	-
As	Ascendant	1	-

Sg	Name
♈	Aries
♉	Taurus
♊	Gemini
♋	Cancer
♌	Leo
♍	Virgo
♎	Libra
♏	Scorpio
♐	Sagittarius
♑	Capricorn
♒	Aquarius
♓	Pisces

Normally, I would not have chosen to start in December, during the busy Christmas season and at a time when you're so busy with college exams. We are somewhat forced into this date because if we waited another few weeks, bad astrological forces would be in effect. Mercury would have started its retrograde motion. If you check the ephemeris, the book listing the motion of the planets, you'll see that Mercury goes retrograde from December 23rd, 1996 until January 12th, 1997.

Three times a year, Mercury goes retrograde for about three weeks. When Mercury goes backwards, it's good for certain effects and bad for others. It's good for focusing your attention on past activities that you may have neglected. I believe that's the ultimate purpose of Mercury retrograde — taking care of mail that has piled up, fixing appliances that have needed repair for some time, working on business details that have been on your mind, and so on. Mercury retrograde is the time to handle issues you were previously too busy to deal with. It's good for cleaning up all those little messes that have gradually accumulated.

Martin: Like when machinery breaks.

James: That's right. Machinery breaks during Mercury retrograde. If you have television sets, radios, or computers that are not in good working order, they stop working and you must fix them. But Mercury retrograde is a terrible time to begin any new project, because when Mercury is going backwards, communications are impaired. You should never sign a contract or make an agreement when Mercury is retrograde. If you do, the agreement usually comes apart or you make serious mistakes that come back to haunt you. The other astrological reason we need to start now is that around the last week in December, Jupiter enters Capricorn in the sidereal zodiac, which is the zodiac we use for Hindu astrology. Capricorn is the fallen sign, or worst sign, for Jupiter. Every planet has a sign where it functions best and that is called the exaltation sign. Likewise, each planet has one fallen sign, where the planet operates in an extremely weak or ineffectual way.

Martin: Jupiter must be important for this project because it rules religion, philosophy, and spiritual matters, right?

James: Absolutely. Since we're working on astrology, which is a subject that encompasses spiritual and philosophical issues, I don't want the *muhurta* chart of our beginning to contain a fallen Jupiter. Anyway, if we didn't start the project before Jupiter enters Capricorn, we would have had to wait a full year until Jupiter leaves that sign.

In picking a *muhurta*, I was looking mainly for a chart that would be excellent for knowledge. We could then transcribe these sessions and spread the word to everybody who is interested. So the knowledge, or information, feature of the horoscope had to be good. Knowledge is ruled by the 2nd house. Next, I wanted to create a strong connection between us. Since I have created this project, I am represented by the 1st house of the *muhurta*. As my partner in this project, you are indicated by the 7th house. (As my student, you are represented by the 5th house.) If, for example, Mars were to occupy the 7th house in the *muhurta*, we would constantly be arguing or fighting. So, I made sure that the chart includes a well-disposed 7th house as well as a strong connection between the 1st and 7th houses.

Finally, I wanted a horoscope that would be strong as a whole, particularly regarding the 10th house and the 1st house. Because we want to reach the public with this teaching, the 10th house needs to be powerful. The 10th house represents career, the public, honor, and status. If the 10th house is weak, the book would not be respected or honored, and critics might give negative reviews.

Martin: That's not good.

James: No, it's not. Now, the 1st house is, generally, the most important house in a horoscope. It is the essence, or nucleus, of the chart. If this *muhurta* we're looking at was the horoscope of a human, the 1st house would tell us specifically about the person — the body, the appearance, etc. So our project — my teaching you, as well as the book we're creating — is represented more than anything by the 1st house of the *muhurta*. Naturally then, the 1st house has to be excellent.

In our *muhurta* chart, the ascendant is Gemini. Gemini is the sign of teachers, writers, and communicators, because Gemini is ruled by Mercury, the planet of intellectual matters.

Martin: So the chart as a whole is geared toward knowledge and information?

James: Exactly. That's just what we want, right? Now notice that the ruler of the 1st house (Mercury) occupies the 7th house and is conjunct Jupiter, the ruler of the 7th house. This means that there will clearly be a powerful bond or connection between the two of us.

To give you an idea of how this works, imagine, for example, that a person calls an astrologer and says, "my wife has been kidnapped"; or, "My wife has left me." "Will we ever be together again?" The astrologer would draw a *prasna* chart (known as a horary chart in Western astrology). The chart would be drawn for the exact moment the question was asked. The time, date, and place of the caller would be recorded. Now, if in that *prasna* horoscope, the ruler of the 1st house and the ruler of the 7th house were together in any house, the answer is yes. (Note: In certain horary systems, the degrees of planets and whether the planets are applying or separating may be crucial.) This is because there is a connection between the person asking the question (represented by the 1st house) and the "other person," the spouse (represented by the 7th house).

In our *muhurta*, not only are the rulers of the 1st and 7th houses conjunct, but they occupy the 7th house — the house of partnership.

Martin: The connection is doubly strong!

James: That's right. The connection between you and me is doubly strong. By the way, in Hindu astrology, house rulers are also called house "lords." You know what house rulers are?

Martin: Yes. Each house is connected to a sign, and that sign is connected to a planet. (Rulerships are discussed in Appendix A on page 380.)

James: Correct. In our *muhurta*, the first house is Gemini. Gemini is always ruled by Mercury. So Mercury is the ruler, or the lord, of the 1st house. The 7th house of our *muhurta* chart is Sagittarius. Sagittarius is always ruled by Jupiter, so Jupiter is the ruler, or lord, of the 7th house.

Martin: Is there any reason Gemini would be a better ascendant sign than Virgo, since both are ruled by Mercury?

James: That's an excellent question. Actually, either of Mercury's signs would be great ascendants for this project, for disseminating information. The difference between Virgo and Gemini is that Virgo energy is very organizational. It has more depth, more "weighing" of words. Gemini tends toward the superficial or lighthearted. Gemini will help me to give information out in a much easier way, without the incredible angst and burden and tediousness that writing books usually entails. If you watch people with Gemini sun signs, they talk and talk and talk. They're always excited and talking about something.

When I thought about this project, my main concern was how much information I could bring out, and how to bring it out in a way different from my other textbooks. An easier way, a more enjoyable way. So it's interesting that Gemini, rather than Virgo, would come up as the ascendant, because I specifically don't want much Virgo energy in this work.

Martin: You've done so much organizing already, James.

James: Don't remind me. My other texts are extremely Virgonian. I can't tell you how many people, over the years, have thanked me for organizing Hindu astrology so well in my first book that they could finally begin to understand the Hindu system. But this project is about disseminating the knowledge in a way that is more flowing, more practical, and hopefully easier to grasp and less painful to study.

Martin: Isn't that why you stopped writing after your last book? Because it was too tedious?

James: Yes. The writing process was too demanding and too stressful. But I've always wanted to write a book analyzing Hindu horoscopes and teaching what I've learned through experience, rather than just the classic fundamental techniques and all.

Martin: Did you consciously pick the Gemini ascendant?

James: No, I didn't. It just happened that way. I was concerned mainly with choosing a chart with a powerful 1st house (the project as a whole), a powerful 2nd house (information and knowledge), and a powerful 10th house (honor and recognition of the project). I think the Gemini ascendant came naturally, as a result of my desire that the work be easy, flowing, and exciting.

Notice how strong the 1st house of the *muhurta* chart is. The ruler of the 1st house, Mercury, is conjunct Jupiter, and Jupiter is a great benefic, which in this case occupies its own sign — Sagittarius. Mercury is conjunct Jupiter within approximately eight degrees.

Martin: In Hindu astrology, conjunctions occur if two planets are in the same sign, so this Jupiter-Mercury aspect is pretty strong, right?

James: Yes. If Jupiter was twenty degrees away from Mercury, while still in the same sign, it would be good for Mercury. But the closer Jupiter gets to Mercury, the stronger the aspect and the stronger the benefit.

On top of this, when Mercury occupies the 7th house, it throws its glance, or aspect, onto the 1st house. In this particular horoscope, the 1st house is Gemini - Mercury's own sign. Whenever a planet aspects its own sign, as

Mercury is doing in our *muhurta*, the results are excellent. Because the ruler of the 1st house and the 1st house itself, are so powerful and well-aspected, our sessions together should be effective and the book we produce should be successful.

Martin: Full of knowledge.

James: Yes, that's the point. Normally, Mercury in Sagittarius is not a good placement because Sagittarius is the sign opposite Mercury's own sign (Gemini). In other words, one of the best places for Mercury is it's own sign, Gemini. The opposite sign from Gemini is therefore a bad placement for Mercury.

Martin: Isn't that called "detriment" in the West?

James: Yes, but the Hindus generally ignore what we call detriments. They use the term "detriment" to mean "fallen."

Martin: "Detriment" and "fallen" are interchangeable terms for Hindus?

James: Yes. For example: in *Jyotish*, Mercury is "fallen" in Pisces (as opposed to Mercury being "fallen" in Leo in the West). Hindu astrologers would say Mercury is *neecha*, or fallen in Pisces, but they sometimes say Mercury is in its detriment in Pisces. As I said, Hindus generally ignore what we call detriments. But this is a big mistake, because detriments (planets in signs opposite their rulership or own signs) are definitely harmful placements in astrological practice.

Martin: Isn't it odd that they would miss the harm caused by planets opposite their own sign?

James: There's a lot that Hindus miss because of their ignorance of Western astrology, and there's a lot that Westerners miss by not knowing *Jyotish*. That's why from the beginning I've strongly advocated using both systems for each horoscope reading. But you have to keep the purity — the integrity — of each system intact. You cannot haphazardly "mix" the systems or everything will be ruined. You can use the information you get from both systems, but not the techniques.

Martin: But aren't you mixing the systems if you use the concept of Western detriments in Hindu astrology?

James: Well, yes and no. See, I didn't set out to use Western detriments in Hindu horoscope analysis. I simply noticed early on in my practice of *Jyotish* that planets in the sign opposite their own signs functioned significantly worse than they should. When that happened, I began to wonder why, and it was not hard to determine. If you know both systems, you're going to find lots of places where the systems overlap, and knowledge from one system aids in the operation of the other. Just be careful not to haphazardly mix the systems. Here's another example.

Planetary aspects in Hindu astrology are completely different from those of the Western system (See page 386 for a description of planetary aspects in *Jyotish*). In *Jyotish*, planets don't "square" each other as they do in Western astrology (a square is a ninety degree aspect between two planets that creates problems, struggle, and tension). If you notice a ninety degree aspect between two planets, say Mercury and Jupiter, you must not consider these planets to be afflicted in the Hindu horoscope. They won't be. You may consider the meaning of the aspect in terms of Western analysis to be accurate, and you may tell your client the information you know about that Western aspect if you like.

Martin: Because if the ninety degree aspect exists in the Hindu chart it also exists in the Western chart?

James: Yes. The aspect has important meaning from the Western perspective, even though it has no meaning in the Hindu chart. What you cannot do, however, is consider Jupiter and Mercury afflicted in the Hindu chart, because, if you do, you will be dead wrong.

Martin: But why does the aspect have meaning in one system and not in another?

James: Because *Jyotish* is more concerned with prediction, and Western astrology is more concerned with psychology and behavior. The fact that a person exaggerates, talks a lot, and is fuzzy in his or her communications, which is what Mercury square Jupiter indicates, doesn't really help a *Jyotishi* (Hindu astrologer) make a prediction about the person's events and circumstances in life.

I'll give you a better example. In *Jyotish*, Saturn aspects the 3rd, 7th, and 10th houses from itself (count Saturn's house position as the 1st house and continue counting from there). Saturn's 3rd house aspect is, of course, similar to the "sextile" aspect in Western astrology. The difference, however, is that in Western astrology this Saturn sextile is good, whereas Saturn aspects in *Jyotish* are always harmful. In Western astrology, a Saturn sextile will lend discipline and staying power to the planet Saturn aspects. That's good.

In *Jyotish* charts, however, I have seen Saturn's 3rd house aspect cause divorce over and over again when the aspect is to the 7th house or even the ruler of the 7th house.

Martin: Even though the Saturn sextile in that person's Western horoscope causes good effects?

James: Yes. I've seen it hundreds of times. You just can't mix the systems haphazardly or your results will be damaged. Do you know that in Western astrology, Saturn is considered my most afflicted planet in a rating system called "astrodines?" But in *Jyotish*, Saturn is by far my strongest planet. It gives better results than any other planet in my chart.

Martin: So, I can mix the information I get from both systems, but not the techniques?

James: Yes. As long as the information the client gets is accurate, he or she doesn't care where you get it from. And believe me, it helps to know both Hindu and Western astrology. There are plenty of times I see *Jyotish* charts that are so confusing, my eyes cross. In those cases, I praise God that I can look at the person's Western chart and discover more useful information.

Oh, by the way, what I've just told you is controversial to some Westerners who practice Hindu astrology. There are some people who practice *Jyotish* who think that anything Eastern is wonderful and perfect, while anything Western is ugly and tainted.

Martin: Why is that?

James: Almost always, these are Westerners in Indian spiritual movements. Indian astrologers, at least all the ones I met in India, use any astrological information they can get their hands on. They don't care whose knowledge it is, as long as it's accurate. But too many of the Westerners in Eastern spiritual movements consider *Jyotish* part of their religion, so they get dogmatic and narrow minded about it. To each his own, of course. But I'm warning you because you are likely to meet some Westerners practicing *Jyotish* who will look down on you for using Western astrology, or merely respecting it.

Martin: For respecting it?

James: It's just ignorance. It's just a misunderstanding. I don't think there's any mean spirit behind their perspective. See, most people in these Eastern spiritual movements (not all, but most) only came upon astrology because it's part of the Indian culture and part of the Vedas. So all they know is one system, the Eastern system. They aren't aware that the tropical zodiac (the one mainly used in Western astrology) is based on the spring equinox, rather than the actual constellations employed in the sidereal (Hindu) zodiac. Because the tropical zodiac ignores the precession of the equinoxes, which is critical in determining the placements of actual constellations, they conclude that the tropical zodiac is faulty. (See the chapter titled *The Two Zodiacs*, on page 391 for a full explanation.)

Martin: That's odd. They're totally off base on that.

James: Yes, they are. But as the years go by, many of these disciples are learning the truth of the two zodiacs and how they differ. For the more "hard core" types, as I call them, we simply have to wait until the Indian gurus who lead these spiritual movements learn about Western techniques and inform their disciples. I'm sure it'll happen eventually, because truth always prevails.

Martin: I agree.

James: Oh, that reminds me. There are also some people who are aware of the difference between the sidereal and tropical zodiacs, but who also believe that there can only be one zodiac. This is so absurd I barely know how to address it. The concept of a zodiac was created by humans, so why can't there be many different ways of creating one? The people who believe only one zodiac is possible should go to Burma and experience Burmese astrology, where their system (called Mahabote) uses neither a sidereal nor a tropical zodiac and yet is extremely accurate in making event-oriented predictions. Maybe someone should go tell the Burmese people who have been practicing astrology successfully for centuries that their astrology is fake because they don't use our zodiac!

Anyway, let's get back to our *muhurta* before we alienate an entire segment of Western *Jyotishis*.

Martin: You mean you're going to put everything you just said in your book?

James: Yes, probably. The field of astrology can benefit tremendously from the spiritual disciples of Eastern religions who have trouble with the tropical zodiac. Their upside is that they are developing consciousness, and consciousness is what it's all about. Spiritual disciples can usually become excellent astrologers really fast. Their downside, in my view, is dogmatic thinking and vulnerability to authorities (i.e. gullibility).

Martin: I have one more question. Didn't you say something in one of your lectures about each zodiac being used for different purposes?

James: What I said was that according to Robert Schmidt of Project Hindsight (a project committed to translating all ancient Greek astrological texts), there appears to be evidence that in the days of the great ancient astrologer/author Ptolemy, the tropical zodiac was used to analyze horoscopes of individuals, and the sidereal zodiac was used for mundane astrology.

Martin: What's mundane astrology?

James: Predicting the weather and wars and occurrences within nations, and so on.

Now, regarding our *muhurta*. As I said earlier, normally I would not want Mercury to be in Sagittarius, where it is opposite its own sign (detrimented). Why do I consider it okay in this case? I consider it okay because Mercury is tremendously strengthened by being conjunct (in the same sign as) Jupiter. Jupiter is a great benefic that causes any planet it aspects to expand and flourish. And this is not just an ordinary benefic Jupiter. This is Jupiter in its own sign, which means that it's functioning better than usual. Therefore any planet conjunct Jupiter will benefit even greater than usual by absorbing Jupiter's extraordinary benefic vibrations.

Now, I need to make a crucial distinction here. And it's something I'll be mentioning over and over throughout our lessons, because if you're like the other students I have taught, you'll need plenty of exposure to this concept. We know that because Jupiter is functioning better than usual by occupying its own sign in this chart, any planet near Jupiter receives even greater benefit than normal by absorbing Jupiter's rays. That is how conjunctions work in terms of aspects. However, when you consider the other *drishtis*, the other aspects, please don't assume that Jupiter will be throwing better aspects than usual.

Martin: You mean when Jupiter's throws its aspects to the 5th, 7th, and 9th houses?

James: Right. When Jupiter throws aspects to other houses, it simply throws very positive energy. It won't throw better than usual energy just because it is strengthened by being in its own sign.

Martin: James, some of the books that you told me to read say the opposite. They say a planet that is exalted or in its own sign throws a particularly good aspect. And they say a weak planet doesn't have much strength to throw a good aspect.

James: I know that. So, we're now into a controversial matter again. Get used to this, because this is probably going to happen in every one of our sessions. I'm telling you what my experience has been with these techniques during all my years of practice, and your job is to consider my teachings as well as what the other astrologers say, and then make your own decision.

Martin: But that's so annoying, James. Why hasn't someone figured out how astrology works by now?

James: All I can tell you is to get used to the disagreements as soon as you can. If it's too bothersome, get out of the practice. That's all I can say, because I doubt it's ever going to stop. Astrology is too complicated, too vast.

In the first few years of my practice, I believed exactly what you read regarding strong planets throwing powerful aspects and weak or afflicted planets throwing feeble aspects. I thought, for example, that my Jupiter (Jupiter in my horoscope) threw better aspects than usual because it occupies its own sign, Pisces. The concept sounds completely reasonable and logical.

Martin: Yes, it does.

James: Strong, well disposed planets should throw better aspects than ordinary or weak planets. But in my experience, they do not. I don't know why they don't, I just know they don't. After years of practicing and analyzing thousands of charts, my experience is that the condition of a planet has nothing to do with the aspects that planet throws. I find that benefics (Jupiter, Venus, Moon, and Mercury) that are fallen throw just as much positive energy as well-disposed benefics. That is my experience. I can only say to you what my teacher (Padia) constantly said to me, "You take it from me, I have marked this!"

Martin: But if a planet is <u>conjunct</u> a well-disposed benefic planet, it receives better vibrations than just being conjunct an ordinary-placed benefic?

James: That's how it works. If a planet is conjunct Mars or Saturn, natural malefics, that planet will be quite harmed. But if that planet is conjunct <u>fallen</u> Mars or fallen Saturn, you better believe that the harm will be multiplied exponentially.

Martin: And you're saying that fallen Mars and fallen Saturn will not throw extra bad aspects or extra weak aspects to other houses?

James: That's right. Those malefics will simply throw harmful aspects because as natural malefics, that's their job.

I find that one of the problems today facing Westerners learning *Jyotish* is properly understanding the positive or negative natures of planets throwing aspects. If you misapply the aspects of benefics like Jupiter, Venus, Moon, and Mercury, there's not much consequence. What's the harm if you tell a client that Jupiter aspects a house and causes excellent results, when in fact it causes very good results.

Martin: You're in the ballpark of positive energy.

James: Exactly. But if you misapply the aspects of malefics, you're going to be dead wrong on a regular basis. Do you know how often I've heard astrologers say something like, "Saturn is aspecting your 7th house, but it is not a harmful aspect because Saturn occupies Libra, its exaltation sign, and therefore throws good energy." Or, "Mars throws only good aspects in your horoscope because it is the *Rajayoga-karaka* planet, the planet ruling the best houses." (In Hindu astrology, certain houses are "good" and certain houses are bad.) This is utter nonsense. If Saturn aspects the 7th house, divorce is nearly certain — and I don't care if Saturn is exalted, well-aspected, or forming a *rajayoga* because of the houses it rules!

Of course if it rules good houses, Saturn will ALSO throw some good energy as well as bad energy. That's the benefit of being a *rajayoga* planet, a planet ruling good houses. But don't think for a second that the malefic planet involved has lost its essential malefic nature or you'll find yourself making faulty predictions all over the place.

Martin: So a malefic planet that rules good houses throws both good and bad energy.

James: That's right. Saturn doesn't just suddenly transform into Jupiter because it rules good houses, and Jupiter doesn't just transform into Saturn because it rules bad houses. These planets maintain their essential nature and they take on some of the positive or negative energy of the houses they rule. If you can remember what I've just taught you, you'll be ahead of seventy percent of the *Jyotish* students I meet at workshops and conferences.

Martin: So, no matter how well-disposed Mars or Saturn are, if either one aspects the 5th house (children), the likelihood of abortions increases?

James: Increases dramatically. Or, if Mars or Saturn aspect the 9th house, troubles with gurus are likely, and so on. Forget any philosophy about well-disposed planets; forget how you hope or believe planets ruling good houses should throw aspects. Just observe what does happen when these malefics throw their aspects. If you take the time to observe what happens, you won't go wrong. Astrology is experiential and observational. Experience, observe, and test what I'm saying.

The issue of "functional benefics" and "functional malefics," that is, planets whose nature are altered by the houses they rule, is so critical that we'll talk a lot more about this in later classes. I'll give examples to back up my statements. But before we move on, I want to mention something that will affect the strength or weakness and the positive or negative energy thrown by an aspecting planet.

Anytime a planet throws an aspect onto its own or exaltation sign, or onto its fallen or detriment sign, that aspect is affected for better or for worse. For example, if Jupiter happens to aspect Cancer — Jupiter's exaltation sign — the aspect will be better than usual because the house and sign of Cancer is receiving "Jupitarian exaltation energy." On the other hand, if Jupiter throws its aspect onto Capricorn (Jupiter's fallen sign) or Virgo — an unfriendly sign to Jupiter, and Jupiter's detriment sign — then those houses and signs would be receiving Jupitarian energy that would not be nearly as beneficial. They would still be receiving positive energy, but not nearly as good as Jupiter's aspect onto some ordinary or neutral sign.

Likewise, if Mars aspects a house, that house is significantly damaged. But if Mars aspects the Cancer house of the birthchart (the fallen sign of Mars), look out. The results are terrible. When Saturn aspects Aries — its fallen sign — the results are much worse than Saturn's normally malefic aspects.

Martin: James, I don't really understand why this works. You've said that Jupiter aspects are always good, no matter how Jupiter is disposed, and you've said that Saturn aspects are generally bad, no matter how Saturn is disposed. Why should it matter which sign Jupiter or Saturn throws its energy onto?

James: It works almost the same way as planets in houses. Jupiter is going to bring very good energy onto most any house it occupies, except Capricorn, where it is fallen. Right?

Martin: Right.

James: Well, out of all twelve signs/houses, what signs would make Jupiter's house placement even better than average?

Martin: Jupiter's own signs, Sagittarius and Pisces. And Jupiter's exaltation sign, Cancer.

James: That's right. And that is exactly how the aspects work. For example, in my chart Jupiter throws an aspect onto Cancer (Jupiter's exaltation sign), and that means that the house of Cancer, which is receiving Jupiter's energy, benefits more than usual. Likewise, if Saturn aspects any sign/house, that house will be damaged. But if Saturn aspects Aries, that house is extremely damaged because Aries hates Saturn energy.

Martin: Oh. So, this is like a two-way relationship. In the same way that Jupiter likes the sign of Pisces, the sign of Pisces likes the planet Jupiter.

James: Yes. And in the same way that Mars hates the sign of Cancer, the sign of Cancer hates Mars. This is a very important condition that you will see over and over, so don't forget what I'm telling you now.

Martin: Okay. Let's hear about the *muhurta* chart.

James: In picking a good starting time, a major concern of mine was the fact that two first-class malefic planets, Saturn and Ketu, are conjunct. These two malefics have to occupy some house, and that could be pretty tricky. Also, Saturn is harmed by being near Ketu. Well, there was no way to avoid this conjunction unless we waited several months, and at that point Jupiter would occupy Capricorn, its fallen sign.

Martin: Which would be terrible.

James: Right. So what I did was pick a time that would put the two malefics, Saturn and Ketu, in an *upachaya* house, where malefics are welcome and cause overall (not entirely, but overall) good effects. The *upachaya* houses are the 3rd, 6th, 10th and 11th houses. They are known as "growing houses," because planets occupying *upachayas* grow stronger as a person ages.

Martin: So Saturn and Ketu in the 10th house of our *muhurta* chart are good?

James: Better than good — they're excellent. They indicate successful career activities. If an individual has Saturn in the 10th house, it indicates a big career, a career that impacts thousands and thousands of people. If an individual has Ketu in the 10th house, it signifies excellent career success and accomplishment. Because my intention regarding this project is to reach readers around the country, or even globally, having these malefics in the 10th house is wonderful. Further, Ketu is the planet of metaphysics and psychic phenomenon. This is a perfect placement for an astrological or spiritual endeavor.

Martin: Excellent.

James: The ruler of the 10th house of this *muhurta* chart is Jupiter, a spiritual and religious planet, and in this case it occupies it own sign — Sagittarius. So the ruler of the house is somewhat strong. I say "somewhat" because Jupiter also happens to be aspected by malefic Saturn. (Aspects are discussed in detail in Appendix A.)

Martin: So Jupiter is in mixed condition.

James: Exactly. The ruler of the 10th house is mixed but definitely has some positive energy, and the malefic planets in the 10th house give strength. This is good.

The *muhurta* chart also indicates a wonderful "healing" influence, which is excellent for you and me. In a personal horoscope, the 3rd house represents one's hands and "own efforts." The 6th house is the house of health and healing. Whenever there is a connection between the 3rd house and the 6th house, it means that your hands and/or your efforts are being used for healing.

Martin: Does this also mean that anyone with an Aries ascendant has healing ability because one planet (Mercury) rules both the 3rd and 6th houses?

James: No, not necessarily. The healing talent only occurs if the rulers of the 3rd and 6th house are conjunct, or the ruler of the 3rd house occupies the 6th, or vice versa. People with Libra ascendants also have one planet (Jupiter) ruling the 3rd and 6th houses and that fact alone is meaningless, in terms of healing.

In the *muhurta*, the ruler of the 3rd house (the Sun) occupies the 6th house. And the ruler of the 6th house (Mars) occupies the 3rd house. This is called exchange of signs or *Parivartana Yoga*. In Western astrology, it's known as "mutual reception." This means that there will be a lot of healing taking place in our sessions. As you learn more about your horoscope during our sessions, some healing will take place.

Martin: How so?

James: Healing through *Jyotish* means dispelling "mistakes of the intellect." A mistake of intellect occurs when a person perceives information in a way that is harmful. Or, a mistake of the intellect occurs because a person believes faulty information that has an impact on the person's well-being. For example, if a person's *dharma* — duty or life purpose — is to be an artist, but he or she has been convinced by parents, or whomever, that the proper path is law or medicine, then a mistake of the intellect has occurred. As an astrologer, you'll be dispelling mistakes of the intellect in nearly every astrological session. But sometimes it's complicated. It can be difficult to dispel someone's mistake of the intellect if it is caused by religious belief.

Martin: Like the disciples who believe Western astrology is faulty because it doesn't come from the East?

James: Exactly. You could show a disciple with that misunderstanding case after case of documented brilliant predictions made by Western astrologers, and it will have no impact at all if that person's mistake of intellect is too strong.

A common "mistake of intellect" occurs when a person has a connection between the 10th house and the 12th house. By this I mean the ruler of the 10th house occupies the 12th house, or vice versa. Or, if the ruler of the 12th house aspects the 10th house, or if it aspects the 10th house ruler within a fairly tight orb, say within ten or twelve degrees.

Martin: What does that indicate?

James: That the person has career debts from past lives and will suffer career difficulties, or have trouble finding one career. When you tell a client who has this feature not to waste time and energy looking for one specific career destiny, it dispel's the person's mistake about their *dharma* and takes off enormous pressure.

Martin: Because the person is like a mouse in a maze chasing cheese that will never be there?

James: Exactly. Now that the person knows it is his or her destiny, he or she can actually begin enjoying having many different careers, instead of lamenting that fact. So, dispelling a person's mistake of intellect is very powerful.

Another typical example I see a lot occurs when a spiritual disciple or highly religious person has the North Node in Taurus or in the 2nd house in the Western horoscope.

Martin: But not the Hindu chart?

James: Not the Hindu chart. When I analyze a person's horoscope, I always look at the Western chart. I generally don't discuss it, because most of my clients come to me specifically to learn about their Hindu chart. But the Western horoscope is important because it tells me quickly who the person is and about their psychology and behavior.

What I do mention from the Western chart, actually in every single session, is the North Node position. The North Node position of the Western chart indicates the purpose of the incarnation. It reveals specifically what the person has come to earth to learn.

Martin: So what does the North Node in Taurus or the 2nd house mean?

James: That the person has incarnated to learn about money, possessions, and earthly pleasures. The person will gain greater fulfillment and experience evolutionary growth by pursuing money, possessions, and earthly pleasures.

Martin: The root of all evil to someone who believes in the Bible.

James: Exactly. But the reason the person needs to do this is because in past lives earthly pleasures were ignored and now the person is imbalanced in that realm. In most cases, as soon as the person learns the meaning of the North Node in Taurus or the 2nd house, the information resonates as truth and a mistake of the intellect has been dispelled forever.

Martin: Freedom!

James: Yes, freedom. You've heard the statement, "The truth shall set you free"? Well, that's what dispelling the mistake of the intellect is all about.

My eldest brother has the North Node in Gemini, the sign opposite Sagittarius. This means that he is supposed to learn to be discriminating, picky, and skeptical. Religion and philosophy are essentially a dead-end for him. Well, when I was teaching meditation, I believed that everyone should learn to meditate. I was indoctrinated into that mind set by my guru. Well, guess what? When I taught my brother to meditate, he wasn't really interested. His evolution and fulfillment doesn't come from spiritual and religious endeavors. It comes from mental and intellectual activities.

Martin: Like Zen?

James: Actually, he loves psychology. He loves Freud and Carl Jung, and analyzing dreams, and so on. When I was teaching meditation, I was taught that everyone should meditate, and that psychology and psychotherapy were completely useless. Stirring up mud in a glass of water was the analogy my guru used to describe psychology. Well, that was a mistake that I fully embraced because it came from my guru, and it was only dispelled when I learned the meaning of the North Node in Gemini (or the 3rd house) in the Western chart. (For the meanings of all Western North Node positions, read my book _How to be a Great Astrologer_.)

Now this mistake didn't have great impact on me, because I have little interest in psychology. But can you imagine what happens to a spiritual disciple with North Node in Gemini or the 3rd house who believes that psychology and other kinds of intellectual analysis is useless? It's actually damaging to the person's evolution and well-being.

Martin: James, this makes astrology sound so important. We're not just dealing with people's karma; we're helping them with their spiritual evolution.

James: That's why I'm spending so much time explaining what I mean by dispelling the mistake of the intellect. So you can appreciate the full value of practicing astrology.

Martin: Could the healing feature of our *muhurta* chart also mean that we are healing *Jyotish* students with all the information that will come out in this book?

James: I hope so. This project is about teaching students how to practice Hindu astrology. Everyone knows the techniques by now. What they are having trouble with is putting the techniques into practice. So I certainly intend for some healing to take place.

In our *muhurta* chart, we're lucky to have chosen a horoscope where all the malefic planets in the chart except one, Rahu, occupy *upachaya* houses. Remember when I said malefic planets in *upachaya* houses produce good results? This means that even though Saturn, Ketu, Sun, and Mars still maintain their fundamental negative natures, they do not cause problems to the houses they occupy. They still throw harmful aspects onto other planets and houses, but they are well-placed by house position.

Martin: That's great. That means that so many houses that could have been harmed by malefic planets won't be.

James: That's right. On top of that, the one malefic planet that does not occupy an *upachaya* house, Rahu, happens to be exalted — occupying its best sign, Virgo!

Martin: But that's controversial, right?

James: Yes, The ancient Hindu sages disagreed on Rahu and Ketu's exaltation and ownership signs, so there are different opinions floating around. My teachers, and most of the astrologers I met in India, consider both "shadowy planets," to be best placed in Virgo and second best in Gemini. Having analyzed thousands of horoscopes, I absolutely agree with them. Parasara, the originator of the astrological system we are practicing, said that Rahu was exalted in Taurus, but Rahu in Taurus does not function nearly as well as Rahu in Virgo. Rahu in Taurus is okay, but it's nothing special in my experience.

Martin: James, does a malefic planet that is in an *upachaya* house function like it occupies its own or exaltation sign?

James: No. A planet in its own or exaltation sign is much better.

Martin: Why?

James: Because it not only produces excellent results in the house it occupies, but it also strengthens the houses it rules. In other words, a malefic planet in an *upachaya* house isn't particularly strengthened. It's just that its energy helps support or enhance the house it occupies. For example, if Mars is exalted in Capricorn in a chart with a Libra ascendant, then the exalted Mars helps the 4th house (the Capricorn house), while also strengthening the 2nd and 7th houses, the houses of Scorpio and Aries.

Martin: Because Mars rules those houses?

James: Yes. But if Saturn occupies an *upachaya* house like the 3rd, it will help the 3rd house in certain ways. But the houses that Saturn rules are not helped by 3rd house energy. There's nothing special about the 3rd house. Actually, I consider the 3rd to be a mildly harmful house.

Martin: James, some of the authors of the books you recommended to me say the 3rd house is a *dusthana*, a grief-producing house.

James: That's true. But I never heard my teachers brand any houses *dusthanas* except the 6th, 8th, and 12th. And I definitely haven't experienced the 3rd house to be anything more than slightly harmful. The 6th, 8th, and 12th houses can be pretty nasty, so I'm reluctant to include the 3rd house in that category.

On the other hand, I have to clarify what I mean when I say I find the 3rd house to be "mildly harmful." If, for example, I see the ruler of the 7th house occupying the 6th, 8th, or 12th house (*dusthanas*), I expect divorce to occur in about seven out of ten cases. But if the ruler of the 7th house occupies the 3rd house, I expect divorce to occur in about three or four out of ten cases. Now, the three or four poor souls who have gotten divorced because of 3rd house energy might say that the 3rd house certainly wasn't mildly harmful. But if I see a chart with the ruler of the 7th in the 3rd, I wouldn't expect divorce from that aspect alone. I would go looking for other 7th house or Venus (planet of love) afflictions for confirmation.

Martin: Whereas, if the ruler of the 7th was in a dusthana house, you would expect divorce no matter what.

James: Well, almost no matter what. If the ruler of the 7th is in the 6th, 8th, or 12th house in its own sign, I would not expect divorce. If the ruler of the 7th occupies the 8th in its own sign, I expect the person to marry a metaphysician and have a happy marriage. If the ruler of the 7th occupies the 12th in its own sign, I expect the person to marry a spiritual seeker. On the other hand, if the ruler of the 7th is in a *dusthana* and is not otherwise well-disposed, I would expect at least one divorce. And I wouldn't have to look for confirmation from other chart features.

Regarding our *muhurta* chart, I mentioned the fact that Rahu is exalted in the 4th house.

Martin: That should be helpful to us in terms of our surroundings, right?

James: Yes. The 4th house rules land, homes, and real estate. So here we are studying in a house on Longboat Key, which is a beautiful, stress-free, barrier island off the Gulf of Mexico. I would say the symbolism of exalted Rahu in the 4th house fits our situation pretty well. And being near water is excellent for psychic work, by the way.

Martin: How so?

James: It helps with intuition. So we can be thankful for exalted Rahu in the 4th house. Now regarding malefics that are exalted or in their own signs, I must warn you to be careful about making predictions. These kinds of placements aren't always as good as expected.

Martin: Why is that?

James: Because certain houses simply can't use malefic energy, even if the malefic planet involved is on its absolute best behavior. It has to do with the personal or impersonal nature of certain significations of the house.

Martin: Come again?

James: For example, the 7th house is a highly personal house. It has to do with a person.

Martin: You mean the spouse?

James: Yes. If either Mars or Saturn is exalted or in its own sign in the 7th house, divorce is going to occur in the vast majority of cases.

Martin: So you're saying that Saturn in Libra, Capricorn, or Aquarius in the 7th house indicates divorce?

James: Yes. The same goes for Mars in Capricorn, Aries, or Scorpio in the 7th house. In seventy or eighty percent of the cases, divorce will occur. The 7th house doesn't utilize malefic energy well as far as relationships go. This may contradict certain textbooks and it may go against your instincts of what should occur. But I'm telling you, if you practice in the Western world, these placements will indicate divorce quite consistently. Now, in other cultures, divorce is not always an option, but the placements would still cause marital problems. (We'll talk about how cultural factors affect horoscope interpretation in another session.)

Let's discuss the Moon in the 8th house in the *muhurta* chart. You know that the 6th, 8th, and 12th houses are called *dusthana* or "grief-producing" houses. You know that it's terrible for a planet to occupy the 6th, 8th or 12th house, and out of the three *dusthanas*, the 8th and the 12th are worst. (The 6th house is less problematic because it is an *upachaya* or a growing house, where planets are initially harmed but can improve with time and concentrated effort.)

Because Hindu astrology is a lunar-based system, the Moon is the most important planet in the horoscope, although it does share this honor with the ascendant ruler. If the Moon is the most important planet, and the 8th house is so terrible, then obviously the Moon in the 8th house is a terrible placement, yes? Were the Moon to occupy the 8th house in a person's horoscope, that individual would experience a great deal of suffering and emotional pain throughout life. So why would I pick a *muhurta* chart with such a critical Moon house placement as this? Can you guess?

Martin: Time constraints?

James: No. The Moon travels so fast in its orbit that we could have waited one more day, and the Moon would have changed its sign and house placement. The Moon would then occupy the 9th house of our *muhurta*, and the 9th house is the best house of a horoscope. In the same way the 6th, 8th, and 12th houses are grief-producing, the 5th and 9th houses are the best houses.

There are a few reasons I allowed the placement of the Moon in the 8th house. One is because the 8th house represents astrology, metaphysics, and psychic phenomenon, which is exactly what our project is about. In the same way that the ascendant (the 1st house, known as *lagna* in Indian terminology) and ascendant ruler represent our project, so does the Moon.

Martin: Because Hindu astrology is a lunar-based system?

James: Exactly. The Moon, ascendant, and ascendant ruler are critical factors in any Hindu horoscope you are analyzing. What could be more appropriate than having the Moon in the 8th house for our *Jyotish* project? Our energy and focus will be entirely intuitive and metaphysical.

As my mentor, P.M. Padia, always used to advise me, you must try to understand the reasoning behind the principles. What makes the 8th and 12th houses the worst houses in a horoscope? It is precisely the fact that 8th and 12th house energy is "otherworldly." How can otherworldly energy give good results to activities operating in the physical world? How can Jupiter, planet of luck and religion, function well if it is posited in an otherworldly house? How can Venus, which represents love and happiness, function well in a mysterious, alien, and otherworldly house?

Martin: It can't.

James: But if you are trying to function on the psychic, astral, otherworldly plane, you are in great shape with 8th or 12th house planets.

Martin: I see.

James: One of the hardest concepts for beginning astrologers to comprehend is that almost everyone who is metaphysical or spiritual is going to have one or more significant planets in a *dusthana* house like the 8th or 12th, and it doesn't always signify terrible things. A lot of people have the Sun, Moon, or ascendant ruler in the 8th or 12th house, and beginning astrologers always believe this means the person's life is incredibly harmed.

Martin: And it's not necessarily so?

James: Not at all. It is possible for 8th and 12th house planets to be well disposed if — and this of course is one big if — the planet involved is in its own or exaltation sign, or if the planet is receiving strong aspects from benefic planets.

Martin: What do you mean by "strong aspects"?

James: I mean an aspect from a benefic within a tight orb. Say, a person has Moon in the 8th or 12th house, and that Moon is aspected within three or four degrees of benefic Jupiter or Venus. That Moon may actually produce excellent results. Placements like these will lead a person towards enlightenment and metaphysical subjects. So will the Sun in Leo (its own sign) in the 12th, or Jupiter in Cancer in the 12th, or any planet in the 12th in its own or exaltation sign. These are excellent placements for spiritual seekers.

Of course, if 8th or 12th house planets are not well-placed in this way, major problems will exist. No question about it. But it's faulty judgement to simply condemn 8th or 12th house planets without carefully analyzing everything influencing them. I always hear astrology students cursing 8th and 12th house planets, but without these placements there would be no spiritual seekers or metaphysicians on the earth.

Martin: So you're saying that you wouldn't be upset if you had a planet in the 8th or 12th house in your horoscope, as long as it's in a good sign?

James: Absolutely, but you have to know what you're talking about when you say a planet in a good sign. I wouldn't want a planet in a *dusthana* house simply in a "friendly" sign. (See page 416 for the listing of planets in friends and enemy signs.) That would still create huge problems. The distinction of being in a friendly sign isn't dramatic enough to alter the intense negativity of the 8th or 12th house.

Another reason I allowed the Moon to be in the 8th house of our *muhurta* chart is because I like the aspect that the Moon in the 8th house throws onto the 2nd house, the house of knowledge and information. As a natural benefic, the Moon throws good aspects. But in our *muhurta*, the Moon's aspect onto the 2nd house is even better than usual because the Moon is aspecting Cancer, its ownership sign. The *muhurta* chart is already excellent for knowledge due to the close Mercury-Jupiter conjunction, the Gemini ascendant, and the fact that Jupiter and Mercury are throwing their aspects onto the Gemini ascendant.

Martin: So, the Moon's aspect onto its ownership sign 2nd house is just frosting on the cake. James, doesn't the 2nd house also represent money?

James: Yes, good point. Money is the most obvious signification of the 2nd house. So this *muhurta* could mean that the book project will be financially successful. I wasn't thinking about finances regarding this *muhurta* though.

Martin: Why not?

James: Because after writing and publishing four other astrology books, I'm fairly convinced there's not much money in this business.

Martin: James, in the *muhurta* chart I noticed that the Moon is in

Capricorn, the sign opposite Cancer (the Moon's own sign). Isn't that bad?

James: Yes, it is bad for the Moon to be in Capricorn. In fact, I would prefer that the Moon occupy a sign more favorable to its well-being. But you can never find a perfect chart, and you almost always have to make some compromises. I'm not too bothered by the placement though, because this is a *muhurta* chart, not a person's chart. For a person, the Moon in Capricorn would be much too serious, tedious, and laborious. The person's feelings and emotions (significations of the Moon) would be negatively affected.

In our case, the *muhurta* chart might cause us to be overly serious, businesslike, and goal-oriented, but I don't think that will be disastrous. And it could even be somewhat good. But as I said, I would still prefer the Moon not be in the sign of Capricorn.

Martin: So why didn't you just wait one or two days until the Moon entered the 9th house and got out of Capricorn?

James: Because of *Chandra lagna*. You've heard of *Chandra lagna*, "Moon ascendant."

Martin: That's when you view the house placements of the planets from the point of view of the Moon, rather than from the ascendant?

James: Yes. Notice that if the Moon were in Aquarius in the 9th house in the *muhurta,*, then Mars, which is in Leo in the 3rd house, would be in the 7th house from the Moon. Guess what that would cause? Arguing, fighting, and friction between you and me. You and I are partners, and having a first-class malefic in the 7th house from the Moon would harm our partnership.

Now, I have to be honest here. I'm not always as mindful as I could be about *Chandra lagna*. There are so many techniques in *Jyotish* that you have to be selective about which ones you are going to use for every single horoscope you analyze. But I never ignore a planet in the 7th house from the Moon because it tells you so much about a person's relationships — in natal horoscopes, of course.

Now, I want to show you another *muhurta* chart that I was considering, but decided against.

Remember I told you that my main concern was to bring out as much information and knowledge as possible in this project? Well, knowledge is signified by the 2nd house, and look at the 2nd house in this *muhurta*. Jupiter occupies its own sign (Sagittarius) in the 2nd house, along with Mercury, the planet of knowledge.

Martin: Wow, that's a better 2nd house than the chart we're using.

James: Yes, it is. I also love the fact that there is an exchange of signs

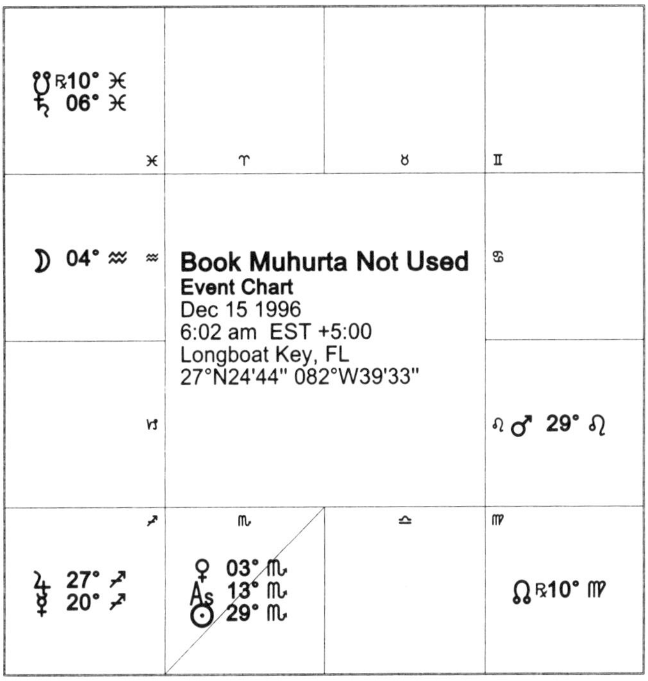
☋ ℞10° ♓
♄ 06° ♓
♓
♈
♉
♊
☽ 04° ♒
♒
Book Muhurta Not Used
Event Chart
Dec 15 1996
6:02 am EST +5:00
Longboat Key, FL
27°N24'44" 082°W39'33"
♋
♑
♌ ♂ 29° ♌
♐
♏
♎
♍
♃ 27° ♐
☿ 20° ♐
♀ 03° ♏
As 13° ♏
☉ 29° ♏
☊ ℞10° ♍

South Indian Style

For North Indian, see Appendix B.

planets.pts

Pt	Name	Hs	Rules
☽	Moon	4	9
☉	Sun	1	10
☿	Mercury	2	8, 11
♀	Venus	1	7, 12
♂	Mars	10	1, 6
♃	Jupiter	2	2, 5
♄	Saturn	5	3, 4
☊	North Node	11	-
☋	South Node	5	-
As	Ascendant	1	-

Sg	Name
♈	Aries
♉	Taurus
♊	Gemini
♋	Cancer
♌	Leo
♍	Virgo
♎	Libra
♏	Scorpio
♐	Sagittarius
♑	Capricorn
♒	Aquarius
♓	Pisces

between Mars and the Sun that involves the 1st and 10th houses (in the *muhurta* we chose, the Mars-Sun planetary exchange involves the 3rd and 6th houses). This is an incredibly good exchange because the 1st and 10th houses are so crucial to the success of any horoscope. The 1st house represents the "essence" of a chart, and the 10th house represents career, honor, and status.

Martin: And activities that affect the public, right?

James: Yes. So these features are all excellent, aren't they? But there are two big problems with this *muhurta*. First of all, Mars would have been in the 7th house from the Moon, as I already explained. Second, Saturn and Ketu, two malefics, occupy the 5th house, the house representing the mind. Whenever there are two malefics in one house, that house will be rather devastated.

Martin: Unless the house is an *upachaya* where malefics are welcome?

James: Yes. In this case Saturn and Ketu occupy the 5th house, the house of the mind and creativity. This could have made our project pretty depressing.

There's nothing good, incidentally, about the 5th house of the *muhurta* we actually chose, but it's not nearly as severe as the December 15th chart. In the *muhurta* chart we chose, the ruler of the 5th house is Venus, and Venus is definitely afflicted. Venus occupies the 6th house, a *dusthana*, and is in Scorpio, the sign opposite its own sign (Taurus).

Martin: It's also aspected by Mars (a malefic) and conjunct the Sun (another malefic).

James: That's right. The aspects you mentioned are not too intense because of the wide degree orbs, but they certainly don't help matters. In the end, even the *muhurta* we chose will create some difficult mental energy. But even looking at the 5th house in the second *muhurta* hurt my eyes.

Martin: James, in the December 14th *muhurta* chart, wouldn't the Sun and Venus in the 6th house help with the detail work that astrology requires?

James: I think so, yes. Astrology is an extremely detailed craft. If you look at charts of individuals, you'll see that anyone who has Venus in the 6th house is generally excellent at detail work. In fact, the person might also be a mathematician. I can't tell you how many horoscopes I've done for accountants who have Venus in the 6th house.

Martin: That seems odd. Wouldn't the logical conclusion be artistic work? Venus rules art and the 6th house governs daily work.

James: Your reasoning is sound. But you'll find in your practice that Venus in the 6th house produces an awful lot of accountants.

Martin: Are you saying that Venus in the 6th house does not indicate an artist?

James: No. I'm just saying that I've seen so many accountants with Venus in the 6th house that I always consider that possibility as well as artistic work. In terms of artists, if I see Venus in the 6th house I want to find some other corroborating artistic features.

Martin: Such as?

James: A very activated 3rd house or 5th house.

Martin: Activated means the house either has planets in it or planets aspecting it?

James: Either. But they should be benefics. Mars and Saturn in the 3rd or 5th don't do much for the arts unless they rule the ascendant (the person) or the 10th house (career). And I would be more inclined to think "artist" by an activated 3rd house rather than the 5th.

Martin: Because the 5th house is art in general, whereas the 3rd is music, dance, and drama?

James: Exactly.

In any case, the Venus-Sun conjunction in the 6th house of our *muhurta* will help us to probe the details and nuances of the horoscopes we analyze in this project. The Sun, incidentally, is very well-placed in the *upachaya* 6th house of our *muhurta*. The Sun represents the "soul" in an individual's horoscope. How can we lose if the soul of our efforts relates to technicalities and detail work?

In terms of the negative features of our *muhurta*, the biggest deficiencies appear to be the 5th and the 9th houses; and I've already mentioned potential mental difficulties (or mental strain) due to 5th house afflictions.

By the way, do you know that in both *muhurtas* I showed you (as well as a third choice I haven't shown you) the 5th house was afflicted? This is a common occurrence, finding the same type of problem arising in all the *muhurtas* available for a particular endeavor. It especially happens when I'm looking for marriage *muhurtas* for couples.

Martin: Why is that?

James: Well, let's say that a couple who want to marry come to you for a *muhurta* chart and let's say that their relationship is excellent for everything except religion.

Martin: Different religious beliefs.

James: Anything like that. Maybe one person has very strong faith in God, while the other person is atheistic because of having been deceived by some religious teacher. The likelihood is that when you try to find favorable marriage times, every chart you look at has a weak or afflicted 9th house (house of religion).

Martin: You mean all the *muhurta* charts you find with a good 7th house have a bad 9th house?

James: Exactly. Or Jupiter, the planet of religion, will be extremely weak and afflicted. And when you try to alter the situation by looking for charts with well-disposed Jupiters and 9th houses, then of course the 7th houses keep being heavily afflicted. It's interesting, but extremely annoying.

Martin: That's bizarre. Why does that happen?

James: Because the two people have serious problems in their religious compatibility. So they come to you and ask for a marriage time, when the possibility of finding a chart that is well-disposed for marriage and religion is near impossible. If they were capable of coming to you at a time when the heavens indicate good love connections and good religious harmony, they wouldn't have had religious problems to start with.

Martin: So what do you do?

James: You work hard and try to find the best *muhurta* you can. Sometimes the couple has to wait six months or a year to find a truly good *muhurta*.

Martin: Are most people willing to wait that long?

James: Some are, some aren't. Vashti and I got married at 10:50 P.M. on a Tuesday night in January. It was certainly a strange time for a wedding, but the chart was good so we went for it. If you tell some clients to get married at a time like that they'll look at you like you've lost your mind.

When you're choosing a *muhurta*, by the way, you always have to accept some compromises. There's no such thing as a perfect chart. There are going to be some planets and houses that are weak or afflicted. The task is to make sure that these afflicted planets and houses are not the significant influences regarding the success of the particular project.

Martin: I don't follow.

James: If the *muhurta* is for starting a writing or teaching project, the chart needs a good 2nd house (education), but it isn't terribly harmful if the 11th house (friends and side ventures) is weak. If the project is for some kind of health business or health endeavor, the 6th house (health) needs to be strong, and it doesn't much matter if the 5th house (children and the mind) is weak. Like that.

Martin: I see.

James: In our *muhurta* chart for this project, the 9th house is afflicted. This means that some of the material in this book could upset foreigners or religious people. Or, it could mean that you and I have religious or philosophical disagreements. But generally, I'm not concerned about a weak 9th house for our project. This is a teaching project that involves astrology. So my main concerns were the 2nd house (education) and the 8th house (astrology), as well as the planets ruling these significations.

Martin: Mercury for knowledge, and Jupiter and Ketu for astrology?

James: Yes, and I would include Mercury for astrology. Astrology is such a mental subject. Aside from making sure these houses and planets were in good shape, I had to be also be aware of the essentials.

Martin: What essentials?

James: The 1st house represents the essence or nucleus of any chart, *muhurta* or natal. Also, the 10th house is critical because it represents fame and status. In a *muhurta* for any business or public venture, it needs to be powerful.

Martin: What are the 9th house afflictions in our *muhurta*?

James: They're pretty obvious. First, malefic Mars aspects the 9th house. Next, the ruler of the 9th house, Saturn, is closely conjunct Ketu. Ketu (the South Node) represents everything that is metaphysical, astral, other worldly. Whenever a planet gets near Ketu, that planet is sort of "swallowed up" into a black hole, because Ketu represents everything otherworldly. The energy of any planet near Ketu functions in a strange, unconscious, or uncontrollable way.

Another affliction to the 9th house is the fact that the 9th house ruler (Saturn) is aspected by malefic Mars. So this a pretty afflicted 9th house, yes?

Martin: If Mars is aspecting Saturn, that means Mars also aspects the 10th house, because Saturn occupies that house. Will the Mars aspect onto the 10th house hurt the career energy or fame of this project?

James: That's a difficult question for me to answer because I'm not sure. I definitely wouldn't worry much about a malefic planet aspecting an *upachaya* house, because *upachaya* houses can use malefic energy. Remember, malefics are well-placed in *upachaya* houses?

Martin: So the aspect is not harmful.

James: Well, I'm not sure about that. I'm sure that the house will be energized by the aspect because *upachayas* welcome malefic planetary energy. But it may also be that the malefic planet causes some destruction as well. If Mars or Saturn or any malefic planet has to aspect a house, I'd prefer that the aspect is thrown onto an *upachaya* house. But that doesn't mean that the house doesn't also receive some harm.

Martin: What kind of harm?

James: A Mars aspect onto the 10th house of a natal chart could mean that the person gets into arguments or fights with career bosses. A Saturn aspect onto a natal chart 10th house could cause some restriction or obstacles to the person's career. But I have to tell you that even after nearly twenty years of practice, I still don't know for sure. It's a subtlety that I have found hard to pin down.

I know that many astrologers consider aspects of malefic planets thrown onto *upachaya* houses fine and dandy. But so many of the astrologers I have met over the years aren't discriminating enough. In my view, too many astrologers accept textbook teachings without enough investigation.

Martin: So I'll have to draw my own conclusions on this?

James: That's right.

Martin: This is frustrating.

James: Welcome to *Jyotish*. We all want to take textbook teachings at their word, but the subject is so complex, so incredibly vast. And the texts, which are already so detailed, almost never spell out issues in the completeness that is required. Let me give you an example. Astrology texts state unequivocally that malefic planets are well-placed in the *upachaya* houses, or that malefic planets belong in *upachaya* houses. The texts never state in the same paragraph that a malefic planet in the *upachaya* 3rd house will also harm certain features of that house, namely younger bothers and sisters. By not specifically stating that malefics in the 3rd house are excellent but dramatically harm siblings, the reader assumes malefic planets in the 3rd house are excellent for every feature of that house. This is not so, not by a long shot.

Martin: Because of the personal nature of the 3rd house?

James: That's right. A person who has a chart with Mars, Saturn, or Ketu in the 3rd house is not going to get along well with younger siblings. A person with malefics in the 11th house, another *upachaya* house that welcomes malefics, does not have luck and fortune with his or her eldest sibling, nor with friends. That is simply how it works, so don't forget what I'm telling you now.

Martin: But if a malefic planet is in one of those houses in its own or exaltation sign, the problems wouldn't occur?

James: That's right. If Mars is in the 3rd house, well disposed, then the younger sibling might be successful in sports or something like that. If Saturn is well disposed in the 11th, the eldest sibling might be an authority figure. So even though the textbooks say malefics in *upachayas* are good, you have to notice the actual effects and think for yourself.

Martin: Why don't the textbooks say what you just said?

James: I've written four books, and it's hard — I mean really hard — to get all the subtleties into print. That's why there's actually a need for *Jyotish* to be both oral and written. There are things I can teach orally that are very hard to put on paper. You'll find this out if you ever write an astrology book.

I'll give you another example of a malefic planet in an *upachaya* house that is wonderful in theory but not so wonderful in practice: Saturn in the 10th house. Although many people with this placement create very powerful careers, others with the same position can't get out of their own way. They just are as restrictive as they can be about their professional lives. I never consider Saturn in the 10th house to be a good position in a chart unless the rest of the horoscope is strong and well-disposed. If the chart is weak or average — and most of the charts I see are average — you can bet that the person with Saturn in the 10th house has career problems. These are the subtleties you learn by analyzing thousands of horoscopes over the years. I believe we've come to the end of our first class. Bas (pronounced "buzz").

Martin: What's "bas?"

James: That's what Santhanam, my first mentor, used to say to end our sessions. Bas.

Martin: Okay. Bas.

CLASS TWO

James: Today we're going to look at your horoscope, Martin, so I can show you why I chose you as my student. I'm not going to analyze the entire chart, just the features that indicate why you would make an excellent astrologer.

Martin: Okay.

James: But first I want to address the issue of why there are so many different opinions about Hindu astrological techniques.

Martin: Great. Because I've read several books written by Westerners — your books and the ones you've recommended — and there are some significant disagreements.

James: I know. There are different opinions about mathematical calculations, the best placements for Rahu and Ketu, the efficiency of yogas (planetary unions), and on and on.

Martin: It makes it hard for beginners.

James: Well, that's exactly why I'm doing this project — to try and clarify some of these disputes. Of course, you'll still have to decide for yourself whose opinion is correct, but I'll try to bring up as many conflicting issues as possible and explain what I have found to work in my many years of practice.

Martin: So ultimately I have to test everything I read or hear.

James: In my view, there is no other way. Every astrology teacher who has an opinion swears that it is based on his or her experience. You have to find your own way. Most of *Jyotish* is pretty straightforward, but the subject is so enormous that there have to be disagreements and different opinions.

Martin: That's the nature of life, isn't it? Different viewpoints?

James: Yes. And my advice is that you accept the problem of different opinions in *Jyotish*, because it's unlikely to ever disappear. As far as I'm concerned, there are two important explanations.

First, according to Hart deFouw (co-author of the book <u>Light on Life</u>), there is a story in the ancient *puranas* (Vedic scriptures) about Lord Shiva testing the astrologers of the day to see if they were accurate in their predictions.

Martin: Were they?

James: Yes. But because Lord Shiva felt that his astrologers were somehow interfering with free will, he put a curse on them. Essentially, he declared that from the time of his edict astrologers would never agree with each other. I don't know much about curses, and I don't know whether the story is to be taken literally or symbolically, but when I heard this account I was impressed. The extent of disagreement amongst astrologers, in my opinion, is mind-boggling. Not only within *Jyotish*, but within the entire field of astrology. For me, Shiva's curse is one explanation, metaphysical as it is.

The second point is that *Jyotish* is an oral tradition, not a written one. And it is an oral tradition, I believe, for good reasons. *Jyotish* is metaphysical knowledge. That means it is necessarily hidden and cryptic. It is not for everyone to learn. Therefore, ancient Indian astrological gurus didn't give out their knowledge to every Tom, Dick, and Harry.

Martin: You mean any Patel, Sharma, or Krishnan?

James: I believe that in ancient times Indian gurus only gave out metaphysical knowledge to disciples who proved their worth, character, and dedication. *Jyotish* was taught orally from master to disciple, not from book to student. And there are huge ramifications from this fact.

Martin: Is this why *Jyotish* books written by Indians are so hard to work with?

James: I believe so. And I believe there's a correlation between the poorly written Hindu texts and many of the discrepancies in our field. Now I know there are astrologers who greatly enjoy and respect the Hindu texts, and I don't mean to offend anyone. But I believe if you are well-trained in *Jyotish* and you examine most Indian texts, you'll conclude that the authors have little intention of sharing their *interpretive* knowledge. For a long time, I thought that the authors — at least the modern ones — wanted to keep their wisdom secret for selfish reasons, so that other astrologers couldn't supersede them.

Martin: But what about ancient texts like <u>Parasara Hora Shastra</u> and other classics?

James: The ancient texts make it obvious that *Jyotish* is an oral convention, not a written one. These books teach the techniques of astrology openly — the mathematical calculations and general techniques and all. But the interpretive knowledge is given in a very peculiar, fairly unusable manner.

Martin: So the technical information is perfect and the interpretive information is flawed?

James: Yes. Anyone with enough diligence can learn the technical information in these books with complete accuracy. But if you take the interpretive information and use it in a <u>literal</u> fashion, you'll sound foolish. This almost certainly means that, although the authors wanted to record astrology in written form to some extent, they didn't want every ignorant soul on earth to have access to the powerful and profound knowledge of *Jyotish*.

Martin: Are you saying that the interpretive information in the ancient texts is practically useless?

James: Not at all. I'm saying you have to approach the material with an awareness of the real intention of the ancient sages and seers.

Martin: Which was?

James: To give the knowledge out in a way that would weed out the uninformed.

Martin: Like the way Christ spoke in parables?

James: Exactly. Except parables could be decoded by intelligent people, whereas the astrological interpretive information requires a very high degree of intuition.

Let me give you two examples from *Phaladeepika*, one of my favorite ancient texts. These are typical interpretations, by the way:

1) "If Mars be in the 2nd house, the person concerned will be adverse or ugly faced, devoid of learning and wealth, and will be dependent on bad people."

2) "If Saturn should be posited in the 5th house, the person born will be roaming about, will have lost his reason, will be bereft of children, wealth, and happiness."

Martin: These are big exaggerations, right?

James: Yes, but the author of this book was not stupid. The technical matter in his book reveals a great intellect. The sage didn't have to exaggerate. He could have easily made accurate interpretations by simply modifying his statements. He could have said, for example, "If Saturn is in the 5th house, the person will be overly serious and have few children, or he will have children late in life."

He could easily have said, "Mars in the 2nd house causes roughness in schooling, financial problems, and facial scars." Instead, he makes rash, over-the-top, declarations that cause any astrologer who takes them literally to fall on his or her face.

Martin: I see.

James: If you want to know how effective the sages were in keeping *Jyotish* from the masses, consider this: Western astrologers avoided the subject for so many generations because whenever they read the textbooks, the interpretations were patently ridiculous. In the late seventies, when I read Hindu astrology texts before going to India, I came face to face with the problem.

Martin: This was when you already knew Western astrology?

James: Yes. I knew people with Mars in the 2nd house who were not ugly faced or dependent on bad people. I knew people with Saturn in the 5th house (myself included!) who hadn't lost all reason and were not constantly roaming about devoid of all happiness.

Martin: So the authors were successful. They hid their knowledge from everyone except those who had been instructed orally.

James: Exactly. A person who had already received some knowledge from a teacher could easily follow the interpretations and conclude that they are accurate but deceptively exaggerated. The two explanations above from *Phaladeepika* aren't worthless unless the reader is starting from scratch, in which case he or she is effectively shut out of *Jyotish*.

Now, the reason I've brought up the matter of the oral tradition is because I believe the cryptic *Jyotish* writings are a core reason for many of our misunderstandings.

Martin: How so?

James: When you read Indian authors, especially the ancient ones, you have to try to read them with the awareness of what was _not_ being said. Obviously, you can only do this if you have already been initiated to some extent by a live, successful, practicing astrologer.

If you simply take the writings literally and precisely, watch what happens. I'll give you some examples.

In many *Jyotish* texts, it says that transits should be considered from the Moon. They don't say that transits should be considered from both the Moon and the ascendant, and yet that is actually how transits work. The vast majority of Indian astrologers first consider transits in relationship to the ascendant and secondarily in relationship to the Moon.

Martin: So why do the authors do this?

James: Good question. Are they careless? Are they being cryptic? It's hard to say for sure; but what you need to notice is that what is left out of the instruction is the obvious. Indian authors very often leave out certain pieces of information that they expect every student to have learned orally from master to disciple.

Martin: This must cause all kinds of problems.

James: It does. I've actually met astrologers, even some Indians, who only use transits in relationship to the Moon.

Martin: Maybe they learned *Jyotish* from books.

James: Probably so. In any case, can you see why it's obvious that transits are more essential when considered from the ascendant rather than the Moon? It's because transits from the ascendant are much more specific to a horoscope than transits from the Moon. And in astrology we are always trying to become more specific, not more general.

Martin: Why are transits from the ascendant more specific?

James: Because on any given day there are a possibility of twelve different ascendants, while the Moon can occupy at most two different signs. In many cases, the Moon stays in one sign the entire day. This means that if 50,000 persons are born on a particular day, either all 50,000 people have the exact same transits from the Moon their entire lives, or there will be two groups of people within the 50,000 each having the same transits.

Martin: In my case, the Moon occupies Pisces. So you're saying that probably all the people born on my birthday have the Moon in Pisces, and therefore, when Saturn transits Aries, we all have Saturn transiting the 2nd house?

James: Exactly. And when Saturn transits Virgo, everyone born on your birthday has Saturn transiting the 7th house. This is way too general in a field that necessarily has to be specific. In order to cover the entire population, astrology has to be as specific and individualized as possible. Each person has his or her own specific karma.

On the other hand, if you look at the ascendants of all the people born on your birthday, there are going to be twelve different ones. Therefore, the transits will be more specific to each person. For a person born on your birthday who has a Gemini ascendant, Saturn transiting Virgo would be passing through the 4th house. For a person born on your birthday who has a Leo ascendant, Saturn transiting Virgo would be passing through the 2nd house.

Martin: I see.

James: Let's take another textbook problem — the issue of "functional benefics" and "functional malefics," or, the good or bad energy each planet takes on by virtue of the house or houses that it rules. For my ascendant (Taurus), Saturn, which is a malefic planet, takes on some very positive and beneficial energy because it rules the 9th and 10th houses (see the graph on page 381 which shows the good and bad planets for each ascendant by virtue of rulership).

Martin: So that makes it a functional benefic?

James: Yes, exactly. But when a textbook makes reference to Saturn as a functional benefic, what it doesn't mention is that Saturn as a natural malefic must also give some negative results.

Martin: Which is obvious, right?

James: Yes. The text doesn't have to mention that Saturn will produce

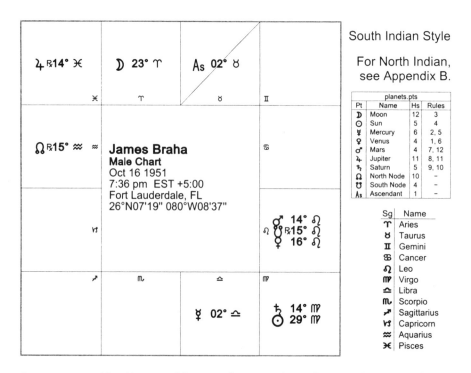

damage even if ruling good houses, because it is obvious. Everyone knows that Saturn is a mean, grief-producing planet. Saturn doesn't suddenly lose its malefic energy just because it also carries some good energy by its rulerships. And Jupiter doesn't suddenly lose its benevolence and expansiveness just because it happens to rule a bad house (8th or 12th) and becomes a functional malefic.

Martin: So the functional benefics and functional malefics always retain their essential nature while at the same time carrying some good or bad energy from the houses they rule?

James: Yes. This isn't a difficult concept, by the way, when you understand that in India planets are considered deities, living beings. If people can be mixed in their positive and negative traits, can't the planetary deities carry both positive and negative energy simultaneously?

I'm emphatic about this issue because we are now laying the foundation for *Jyotish* in the West, and I have met so many students at workshops and conferences who misunderstand functional benefics and malefics. It's a huge problem that needs to be addressed.

Many astrologers also have a problem understanding the meaning of the friendships and enemies of planets (graph on page 416). They think that if planets are friends they can't hurt each other. Well, talk to some astrologers who have tight Venus-Saturn conjunctions (Venus and Saturn are friends) and they'll tell you how these conjunctions have caused tremendous problems. Or, talk to astrologers who have close Mars-Jupiter conjunctions, and see how spoiled their luck is because of the affliction Jupiter receives from malefic Mars. Friendships between planets have some significance, <u>but they don't cancel out the essential natures of the planetary energies.</u>

Martin: Which is obvious.

James: Yes. And if astrologers would go by their experience, rather than textbook teachings, these problems wouldn't be as prevalent.

Martin: Or, if we were learning *Jyotish* orally from a master there wouldn't be a problem.

James: That's exactly right.

Martin: James, in my chart Mars becomes a functional benefic because it rules the 5th and 10th houses (good houses). Doesn't it therefore give some definite benefits?

James: Yes, in your case Mars gives some excellent energy due to its rulerships. Not only is it considered a good planet, it's considered a *rajayoga-karaka* — a royal union maker — or, "the best planet for your chart." <u>But that doesn't mean that Mars stops acting Mars-like</u>. Mars still has an accident-prone nature, and creates friction and tension even though it rules good houses. It still throws bad aspects on any planet it conjuncts or aspects while simultaneously giving some significant benefits. When Mars becomes a functional benefic, it doesn't suddenly act like the Moon or Venus.

In my horoscope, Saturn is the *rajayoga-karaka*, the best planet in the chart by virtue of rulership.

Martin: Because it rules the 9th and 10th houses?

James: Yes. Those are excellent houses. Therefore, Saturn brings some very good energy to the house it occupies (the 5th) and onto the houses and planets its aspects. But it also simultaneously harms the same planets and houses that it aspects and occupies in my chart. For example, as a malefic planet aspecting the marriage house, it caused divorce and relationship problems. But because it rules good houses, the women I've been in relationships with have been quite special. They have been spiritual and talented and beautiful.

As a first-class malefic, Saturn in the 5th house (the mind) has caused my mind to work very slowly. During my early years, I had a lot of trouble in school because of this. And my mind still works more slowly than that of most people. But the fact that Saturn is the *rajayoga-karaka* gives depth, logic, and profundity to my thought process. Some good effects and some bad effects.

The *rajayoga-karaka* Saturn in the 5th house has also clearly had a good and bad effect on children in my life. First, there have been unwanted

	☽ 19° ♓		☋ ℞07° ♉
♂℞22° ≈	**Martin Timmons** Event Chart Sep 21 1956 2:20 am PDT +7:00 Los Angeles, CA 34°N03'08" 118°W14'34"		As 10° ♋ ☿ 20° ♋
			☊ ♃ 22° ♌
	♄ 05° ♏ ☊ ℞07° ♏		☉ 05° ♍ ♀ ℞15° ♍

South Indian Style

For North Indian, see Appendix B.

planets.pts			
Pt	Name	Hs	Rules
☽	Moon	9	1
☉	Sun	3	2
☿	Mercury	3	3, 12
♀	Venus	1	4, 11
♂	Mars	8	5, 10
♃	Jupiter	2	6, 9
♄	Saturn	5	7, 8
☊	North Node	5	-
☋	South Node	11	-
As	Ascendant	1	-

Sg	Name
♈	Aries
♉	Taurus
♊	Gemini
♋	Cancer
♌	Leo
♍	Virgo
♎	Libra
♏	Scorpio
♐	Sagittarius
♑	Capricorn
≈	Aquarius
♓	Pisces

pregnancies, which Saturn in the 5th often causes. Also, during my first marriage, from the age of twenty-three to twenty-eight, I never even considered having children

Martin: Because Saturn delays kids?

James: Exactly. Saturn didn't suddenly function like some great benefic just because it rules excellent houses. Then, after I got married the second time at the age of forty-one, Vashti and I were infertile for four years, which was very frustrating and upsetting. Now that I finally was ready for children, I couldn't have them. It was awful. But because Saturn is the *rajayoga-karaka*, not only did we finally have a child, we had a very special child.

Martin: Julian!

James: Every father feels his child is special, but in this case I'm referring to his horoscope, which in certain ways is extremely special. In his chart, the Sun occupies the auspicious 9th house in the sign of Pisces and is conjunct Jupiter within five degrees! He will have good luck and fortune his entire life because of the Sun being so close to the Jupiter.

Martin: But not so close that it will destroy Jupiter.

James: Right. Technically, Jupiter is combust, or burned, by the Sun. But the aspect has an orb of five degrees, which is not extremely close; on top of which Jupiter gains strength by being in its own sign, Pisces, and in the best house of the chart — the 9th.

Martin: He'll also be very spiritual.

James: Right. He'll be spiritual and lucky his whole life. Also, the Sun in his chart, which is the *atma-karaka*, or indicator of the soul, is right at the zenith of the horoscope. It is in the exact same degree as the midheaven, which is an extraordinary position. (Not all Hindu astrologers use the midheaven, but those who do are aware of its power.) This is one powerful Sun, being near Jupiter in Jupiter's own sign and exactly at the midheaven.

I've just given you an example of how my 5th house has been dramatically harmed by Saturn, while also being powerfully benefitted by the *rajayoga-karaka* factor.

Martin: You've had some good effects and some bad effects.

James: Yes, and that's the way life works. Sometimes certain realms of life are only positive or only negative, but most of the time we experience a mixture of good and bad. And sometimes, the mixture of good and bad comes in extremes. I'll give you a good example from your own chart.

Mars, which is a first class malefic by nature, and the *rajayoga-karaka* in your chart, throws an exact aspect (an aspect within a one degree orb) onto Jupiter in your horoscope. On one hand, Jupiter, which rules the 6th and 9th houses, will receive some great benefit because it is aspected by Mars as the ruler of good houses (5th and 10th). This has resulted in your having lots of knowledge about health and healing, and Chinese medicine and acupuncture, and so on.

Martin: Because Jupiter rules the 6th house?

James: Yes. And as the ruler of the 9th house, Jupiter and the aspect it gets from *rajayoga-karaka* Mars has given lots of interest in religion and philosophy. Now, I promise you that Jupiter and the houses that it rules are also going to be seriously damaged by this Mars aspect, even though Mars rules good houses. My prediction would be problems with religious or spiritual teachers (significations of Jupiter and the 9th house), and/or serious problems with health or enemies (6th house significations), and/or serious problems with your father (9th house signification). I'm talking about obvious problems. We're not "fudging" and we're not going on a fishing expedition, understand? Now, what is the story about these realms of life in your case?

Martin: I've had lots of health problems that have pretty much dominated my life. My father is an alcoholic and I haven't talked to him in fifteen years. Basically, he's dysfunctional. So you're right about all these realms being damaged.

James: How about gurus?

Martin: I've been ripped off by them.

James: You mean deceived with false knowledge?

Martin: I've been financially cheated by spiritual teachers. More than once.

James: So, you see the damage that the tight Mars aspect onto your Jupiter has caused, even though Mars is the ruler of wonderful houses.

Martin: One hundred percent.

James: Usually, only a few of the significations of an afflicted planet will be devastated. In your case, it looks like nearly everything ruled by Jupiter is taking a beating.

Martin: Is it ever possible to know which significations ruled by a damaged planet will be hurt?

James: It's very hard. The best thing to do is first look at the significations of the planet, then the significations of the houses that the planet rules, and then see if the *karaka*, or natural indicator of those significations, is also afflicted.

For example, if the Sun is afflicted and it rules the 5th house, you begin to think that the person may have problems with children, sports, politics, speculations, *poorvapunya* (past life credit), and so on. The next thing you do is to look at Jupiter, the *karaka* of children and speculations. If Jupiter is afflicted, then of course speculations and children are going to suffer.

Martin: As opposed to sports and politics?

James: Exactly. Except that in this case you know politics (and leadership) are hurt because those realms are ruled by the Sun, which we already said was afflicted. Regarding sports, you analyze Mars, and so on. This process of looking at *karakas* will definitely help you narrow matters down.

But let's be honest here. When you're with a client you've got to mention <u>potential</u> problems with <u>all</u> matters connected to the afflicted house ruler. Looking at *karakas* simply tells you which realms <u>must</u> be damaged.

Martin: So all house significations are vulnerable?

James: Yes. Now, I'll mention one more problem caused by ancient *Jyotish* texts, which is what we were talking about before I decided to spend so much time talking about functional benefics and functional malefics.

The texts state in no uncertain terms that if a planet is exalted, but also retrograde then it functions like it is fallen. They also say that if a planet is fallen, but retrograde, then it functions like it is exalted. These are gross exaggerations which will cause you to lose credibility if you advise your clients accordingly.

Martin: Are these techniques completely worthless or are they just more exaggerations?

James: More exaggerations, which is how the Indian astrology books usually work. Everything is exaggerated. In this case, what the authors actually mean is that an exalted planet, when retrograde, is <u>slightly weakened</u> from what you would expect of an exalted planet. It does not act like a fallen planet, but it is not as strong as a forward-moving exalted planet. You see?

Martin: Yes.

James: The same goes for a fallen planet that is retrograde. It does not suddenly function like an exalted planet, as the texts declare, but is it not quite as bad as a forward-moving fallen planet is.

Martin: So an exalted planet that is retrograde is very good, but not great, and a fallen planet that is retrograde is very bad, but not devastated.

James: Yes. The extent of excellence and the extent of damage are slightly mitigated.

I've just shown you three different astrological techniques that are sources of trouble to astrologers simply because of how textbooks describe them. Most astrologers who care about accuracy eventually notice that being retrograde doesn't completely transform exalted and fallen planets into their opposites. And most astrologers eventually notice that transits from the ascendant are at least as powerful, and probably more so, than those considered from the Moon. But it takes time, effort, and some mental agony.

Martin: I have to admit, James, this makes me kind of crazy. If I listen to other astrologers, they're probably going to contradict half of what you've just said. Why should I believe you?

James: You shouldn't necessarily believe me and you shouldn't necessarily believe other astrologers. You should test these issues on your own.

Martin: I guess anything that is written in *Jyotish* texts is suspect to some degree.

James: In my opinion the problem of functional benefics and functional malefics is the most critical threat facing Westerners trying to learn *Jyotish*. It's so fundamental and so important. If you get it wrong, your accuracy with predictions will be seriously marred. That's all I can tell you. The next worst problem is misunderstanding friendships and enemies (graph on page 416). They have some significance, but are greatly overrated. Saturn and Mars don't suddenly become agents of fortune when they throw aspects onto planets that happen to be friends.

Martin: But they do less harm to a friend than to an enemy.

James: Yes, but they still cause harm — serious harm. Likewise, even though Venus and the Sun are enemies, the Sun will always benefit from a conjunction to Venus because Venus is a natural benefic.

Martin: How does the Sun benefit?

James: A person who has a Sun-Venus conjunction that is fairly close — within eight or nine degrees — will be artistic, sensitive, and gentle. More importantly, that person will be happy and content, as well as protected from harm throughout all of life.

Martin: Even though Venus and Sun are enemies?

James: Absolutely. The essential nature of the planets <u>always</u> comes first. The Sun benefits from Venus' naturally benefic rays, while Venus is harmed from the Sun's naturally malefic rays. As far as I'm concerned, the friendship and enemy dynamic is more connected to the issue of whether a planet welcomes another planet into its house.

Martin: In other words, because the Sun and Venus are enemies, the Sun is not welcomed in Venus' signs, Taurus and Libra?

James: That's right. And Venus is not welcomed in Leo, the Sun's sign. We'll talk about friendships more as we go on, but they are not nearly as big a deal as most astrologers make them out to be.

Martin: Because the essential benefic or malefic energy of each planet comes first?

James: Exactly. Two other major *Jyotish* problems are *neechabhanga* and *vargottama*. And since I feel very strongly about these two techniques I'm going to devote plenty of time to them in a later class. For now, let me just say that *neechabhanga rajayoga* means "cancellation of debilitation," which is a condition that <u>supposedly</u> cancels out the destruction of a fallen planet. In my experience, however, *neechabhanga* is another gross exaggeration by Indian authors. For every ten people who have the condition, one or two of them find that their fallen planet gives good results. The other eight people are lucky if *neechabhanga* gives a five percent reduction of damage to the afflicted planet. I see people with *neechabhanga* planets in their charts constantly who get no good effects from those fallen planets at all.

As for *vargottama*, I find the technique utterly useless and can't figure out why any astrologer ever created the distinction. *Vargottama* is a condition that occurs when a planet occupies the same sign in the *rasi* (natal) chart as it does in the *navamsa* (marriage) chart. According to classic texts, a planet that is *vargottama* (also known as *vargothamamsa*) acts as good as a planet in *swakshetra*, a planet in its own sign. As I said, I have found *vargottama* to be a completely useless distinction. I have not found it to work <u>at all</u>, not even by accident.

Martin: Maybe the ancient sages had a sense of humor, and put it in there to throw off people who they didn't want learning astrology.

James: Actually, I once came up with a possible explanation. This may sound like a joke, but it's not. *Vargottama* is so useless that I once considered that maybe Parasara, the originator of the *Jyotish* system we're using, made up the distinction because he didn't want to offend some eminent guru or god who had a terrible horoscope that happened to have lots of *vargottama* planets.

What really gets my goat is when I discuss this issue with certain astrologers who use *vargottama* and say, "Well, I don't place too much importance on it, but I use it as one of a variety of factors." In other words, if a planet is well-aspected and well-placed <u>and</u> it is *vargottama,* then it is one more positive influence to throw into the mix. To these people, I always say the same thing — if a technique works, it must be able to stand on its own. Exalted and fallen planets work on their own. Planets in their own signs work on their own. *Vargottama* planets do not. I've never seen a *vargottama* planet act like it's occupying its own sign, and I've never seen a *vargottama* planet even slightly strengthened. As Padia used to say, "You take it from me. I have marked this!"

Although I feel strongly about *vargottama*, it's not a serious problem because the majority of experienced astrologers I've met have figured that *vargottama* is a sham early in their careers.

Martin: How did they figure it out?

James: It's pretty easy to figure out what works and what doesn't when people are paying you to do their charts. In my beginning days, whenever I saw a *vargottama* planet I told the person they would have some special results from that planet and of course they never did. I didn't like being wrong so I eventually kept my mouth shut about *vargottama*. Later on, when I asked other astrologers their findings about the technique, the ones who were experience-oriented felt the same way.

In any case, I would recommend that every astrologer find five or ten cases of *vargottama* planets, where the planet is in a relatively average condition other than being *vargottama*, and <u>then</u> see if that planet gains any strength by its supposedly special status.

Martin: What do you mean by "relatively average condition?"

James: Well, don't take a planet that is aspected by benefic Venus or Jupiter within four or five degrees to use as an example, because that planet is already in a tremendously powerful state. Take a planet that is in a mediocre condition, not terribly weak and not terribly strong. If it is *vargottama*, it is supposed to function like a planet in its own sign. I guarantee you it won't.

Of course, it may take you some years of study to be able to discern a planet that is actually in a mediocre condition to use as a test. Lots of Hindu astrologers don't even notice when a planet is stationary. Can you imagine looking at a *vargottama* planet that happens to be stationary, and thinking that its enormous power is coming from the *vargottama* status?

Martin: It probably happens a lot.

James: Probably so.

Anyway, it's time to look at your horoscope, Martin, and see why I chose you for this project.

Your chart is incredibly strong for practicing astrology, or any other metaphysical subject for that matter. The ruler of the 10th house is Mars. Mars occupies the 8th house, which rules astrology and metaphysical subjects. The 8th house is also, of course, a bad house, and this has caused difficulties in your ability to determine your career. This is why for so many years you've been unsure of your *dharma*, your purpose in life. But when a planet is well-aspected in a metaphysical house, as yours is, then a metaphysical career is perfect for one's *dharma*.

Notice that Mars, the ruler of the 10th house, is tightly aspected (within one degree) by Jupiter — the planet of religion and philosophy. This dramatically increases the odds that your career will be spiritual. When Jupiter occupies or aspects the 10th house or 10th house ruler, a person is always involved, or hoping to be involved, in some kind of consciousness-raising.

There is, incidentally, a distinct difference between a spiritual endeavor and metaphysical one. A spiritual career has to do with raising consciousness and bringing about wholeness or completeness, whereas a metaphysical career has to do with working with unseen, hidden forces and realities. As an astrologer, you must be very clear in your understanding about this distinction. Astrologers are constantly interpreting 8th, 9th, and 12th house matters interchangeably, when they are actually quite different.

Martin: Are you talking about the fact that the 8th house represents metaphysical endeavors, the 9th house religion, philosophy, and higher knowledge, while the 12th house rules enlightenment, evolutionary matters, and consciousness raising?

James: Exactly. These are three distinct significations, and you have to memorize the astrological significations precisely. When I went for my first astrology reading back in the late seventies, I thought the astrologer was too picky and precise and careful with the words she used. After I learned to practice, I realized that every good astrologer should be as picky as she had been.

At any rate, sometimes a person has both metaphysical and spiritual tendencies indicated in the horoscope, which is what you have.

Martin: The 10th house ruler is in the 8th house, so the career is metaphysical. And the 10th house ruler being aspected by Jupiter makes the career spiritual. Right?

James: Yes. Incidentally, whenever you see Mars-Jupiter connections in a horoscope, as you have in yours, you should begin perusing the horoscope for law. Mars is the planet of mechanical ability as well as <u>technical fields</u>. Technical professions include law, architecture, engineering, and drafting, etc. Jupiter, aside from ruling spiritual matters, also rules law, so whenever you see mutual aspects between Jupiter and Mars, you should always consider law a possible career for a person.

Martin: Even if Mars and Jupiter don't particularly relate to the 10th house?

James: Yes. When you are judging career, of course you look at the 10th house because that's the career house. But you must look at the entire horoscope. In fact, it's not simply Mars-Jupiter aspects that make lawyers. If Mars and Jupiter happen to stand out in the chart simply because they are both more powerful than all the other planets in the chart, you may be looking at the chart of a lawyer.

Martin: How would they have to stand out?

James: If they are angular or exalted or in their own signs. If they are aspected tightly by benefic planets. You'll get a sense of what makes planets strong as you practice more and more. Just remember that when Mars and Jupiter are <u>both</u> strong, the person will make a good lawyer <u>and</u> may be drawn to that profession. By the way, I see a lot of lawyers who have Venus-Mars conjunctions and Mercury-Mars conjunctions.

Martin: Because Mars becomes strong when aspected by benefics?

James: Yes. And a strong Mars leads a person to technical fields. So, have you ever considered becoming a lawyer?

Martin: No, but there are lawyers on my mother's side of the family and people constantly tell me I'd make an excellent lawyer.

James: Well, I'm not suggesting you become a lawyer, even though you have the talent. Your horoscope positively indicates a spiritual career. Not only is the *rasi* (natal) chart indicating a spiritual *dharma*, but so is the *dasamsa*, which is a divisional or *"varga"* chart, drawn specifically for career.

♃ ☊ ♓	 ♈	☽ ♉	☉ ♊
  ♒	Dasamsa for Martin Timmons		♋
  ♑		♌ ♄	
  ♐	 ♏	☿ ♎	♀ ♂ ☋ ♍

South Indian Style

For North Indian, see Appendix B.

planets.pts

Pt	Name	Hs	Rules
☽	Moon	10	2
☉	Sun	4	3
☿	Mercury	4	1, 4
♀	Venus	2	5, 12
♂	Mars	9	6, 11
♃	Jupiter	3	7, 10
♄	Saturn	6	8, 9
☊	North Node	6	-
☋	South Node	12	-
As	Ascendant	1	-

Sg	Name
♈	Aries
♉	Taurus
♊	Gemini
♋	Cancer
♌	Leo
♍	Virgo
♎	Libra
♏	Scorpio
♐	Sagittarius
♑	Capricorn
♒	Aquarius
♓	Pisces

I'm going to devote one class to analyzing divisional charts; not all fifteen of them, but the career chart and the marriage chart (Class Seven).

Martin: Why only those two?

James: Because those are the ones I regularly use in my practice. The others certainly could be used, but *vargas* are a bit of a problem because the birthtime must be accurate for them to be of any value. In India, almost everyone notes the proper birthtime because *Jyotish* is part of the culture. In the West, nurses in hospitals may wait four or five minutes before they look at the clock. On top of that, the clocks may be way off. I was in the hospital for my son's birth and the clocks were off by four minutes. I know they were four minutes off because I had set my watch perfectly in order to record Julian's birth. Now the point about *varga*, or divisional, charts is that the ascendants of *navamsa* (marriage) charts generally change every seventeen minutes or so, depending on the place of birth. The *dasamsa*, or career, chart generally changes every fifteen minutes, again, depending on the location of the birth.

Martin: But most birthtimes aren't off by fifteen minutes are they?

James: No, most birthtimes in the West are probably off by four or five minutes, or a little more. But if each ascendant changes by fifteen minutes, that means a seven-and-a-half minute discrepancy exists <u>on either side</u> of the clock, assuming the birth occurred <u>exactly</u> in the middle of the fifteen minutes.

Martin: Which is unlikely.

James: Very unlikely. If we take your chart as an example, you'll get an idea of how sensitive these divisional charts can be. I'm not going to go into the details of calculating *navamsa* and *dasamsa* charts now, because we'll do that in the class on *vargas*. But, in your case the *navamsa* ascendant is Libra, and it so happens that the <u>approximate</u> seventeen minute Libra ascendant lasted from about 2:19 AM until 2:36 AM.

Martin: I was born at 2:20 Am. That means if the nurses were wrong and I was actually born only one minute earlier, my *navamsa* ascendant would be Virgo.

James: That's right. And guess what? One minute is such a minuscule amount of time that aside from a nurse writing down a wrong birthtime, another issue comes into play. What should we use for the birthtime? The moment your head comes out of the womb? The moment you take your first breath? The moment your body touches the earth? All three of these are considered the moment of birth by different astrologers, believe it or not.

Martin: What do you use?

James: I go by the moment of the first breath. But guess what? When my son was born, I couldn't tell exactly when he took his first breath. I probably clocked his birthtime within twenty or thirty seconds.

Martin: So, does it look like my career chart is accurate?

James: There's a good chance that it is. Without getting on a computer to determine the exact timing of ascendants, the likelihood is that your *dasamsa* chart ascendant of Gemini occurred from <u>approximately</u> 2:14 A.M. to 2:30 A.M. Since your birthtime was recorded as 2:20, you have a six minute leeway on the earlier side and a 10 minute leeway on the later side. This makes it a fair bet that the *dasamsa* is accurate.

Martin: Can I check the exact times for that ascendant with a computer?

James: Yes. Just keep punching in the birthtime minute by minute, and check each *dasamsa* ascendant until Gemini is over and Cancer begins.

So, in analyzing your *dasamsa* chart, we see that the ruler of the 10th house is Jupiter, which is in its own sign, Pisces, in the 10th house. This is perfect symbolism indicating a spiritual career.

Martin: And what exactly is a spiritual career?

James: It is any profession that is involved in raising people's consciousness. Astrology, religion, philosophy, tarot, spiritually-based healing methods (ayurveda, herbology) certain forms of counseling, and so on.

Now notice that Ketu, or the South Node, also occupies the 10th house. Ketu represents everything astral, otherworldly, metaphysical, and spiritual. Remember the story of Rahu and Ketu from my books? In the beginning of creation, Lord Vishnu was giving a potion of immortality called *amrita* to the planetary beings to make them live forever. A *rakshasa,* or serpent demon, entered the room and swallowed a few drops of potion and became immortal. The Sun and Moon both saw the demon and alerted Lord Vishnu, who then cut it in half. The top of the serpent is called Rahu and it represents "insatiable cravings for power and materialistic benefits." The bottom half of the demon is called Ketu and it represents the opposite tendencies of Rahu. If Rahu signifies desires, cravings, and worldly power, then Ketu rules everything spiritual, metaphysical, and astral.

So, for someone with a horoscope that is spiritual and metaphysical <u>as a whole</u>, Ketu in the 10th house will certainly direct the person toward a career in alternative, or occult, healing systems such as acupuncture, herbology, Ayurveda (Indian health care), and Chinese medicine. The person is also drawn to occult, mystical, and metaphysical professions such as astrology, psychic work, Feng Shui, and interpreting omens.

Martin: So my natal chart and my *dasamsa* are good for astrology?

James: More than good. I'd say they're perfect.

Predicting someone's career, or careers, through a horoscope takes plenty of experience, by the way. The thing to remember is that you have to look at everything in the chart. Career is not simply a 10th house matter. Obviously, the 10th house is the most critical factor, but you have to analyze the chart as a whole and synthesize everything you see. In my practice, I pay special attention to Saturn as the *karaka*, or <u>indicator</u> of the 10th house. According to traditional texts, there are four *karakas* of the 10th house — Sun, Mercury, Jupiter, and Saturn. In practice, however, having four *karakas* for one house is too many.

Martin: Sounds like another way of saying "look at the whole chart."

James: Yes, I think so. But I definitely find that out of all the planets, Saturn has the most influence on a person's career.

Martin: So you look at Saturn's house placement for career hints?

James: Yes. I also look at the aspects to Saturn. If Saturn is aspected by Venus, I start looking at the rest of the chart to see if art is indicated. If Saturn is close to Ketu, I begin to look for a career in spiritual or metaphysical realms, or a career involving gas or oil. A Saturn-Mercury conjunction may give tendencies towards a literary or communications career.

Martin: James, this is so confusing. I thought that if Saturn aspects a planet, it harms that planet tremendously. That's what you told me. How could a person have a literary career if Mercury is devastated by Saturn?

James: This is where astrology gets difficult. This is where you have to have "a computer mind to practice astrology," as my teacher Padia used to say.

Yes, it is true that any planet that gets close to Saturn is seriously harmed. But you have to look at the chart as a whole; you have to look at everything. In the case you mentioned, Mercury could be very hurt and afflicted, and the person could still be in a Mercurial profession. The key here would be to find other corroborating factors.

Martin: Such as?

James: Well, let's say that the ruler of the 10th house occupies the 2nd, the house of education and writing. Or, say that there are very personal planets, like Sun, Moon, or ascendant ruler in the 2nd house.

Martin: Or if the Mercury-Saturn conjunction occupies the 2nd?

James: Yes. Then you have Saturn, which I consider the most important *karaka* (indicator) of career in the house of education as well as its being aspected by Mercury, the communication planet.

Another way to find corroboration is through the *dasamsa* chart. Let's say that Venus is conjunct or opposite Saturn in the natal chart, so you start thinking the person may have an artistic career. Well, if the ruler of the 10th house in the *dasamsa* chart occupies the 3rd house, the house of art, the case for an artistic career becomes very strong. Or if Venus, the planet of art, occupies the 10th house of the *dasamsa* chart, an artistic profession is very likely. But as I said, it takes a good deal of experience to predict career from a horoscope because there are so many factors to consider.

We'll talk about predicting careers later. Let's get back to your horoscope.

Martin: Is it important that Rahu and Ketu are retrograde in my chart?

James: I don't consider the retrogrades of Rahu and Ketu particularly meaningful, because the North and South Nodes (Rahu and Ketu) are going backwards most of the time. I believe they may be <u>slightly</u> stronger when they are in direct, or forward motion.

Martin: What about retrograde Mars in my chart?

James: Retrograde planets are very important, so important that I'm going to spend an entire class on them. I didn't explain them in enough detail in my first book (<u>Ancient Hindu Astrology for the Modern Western Astrologer</u>), and I've been paying the price for years. In my workshops, I always have to spend a lot of time on retrogrades because students don't understand them properly. It doesn't help that they work very differently from how they are explained in ancient texts, of course. The ancient texts say that retrograde planets are more powerful than direct planets, but this is not exactly accurate, to say the least. I'll explain retrogrades in our next class.

The retrograde feature of Mars in your chart is very significant because Mars rules such a prominent house — the 10th. The fact that it's retrograde means that its energy, is a little bit held back or a little bit latent. It isn't so much that Mars is afflicted or weakened or harmed, but that the energy does not manifest in the outer world so readily or so easily. The career will be slower to show itself and you have to make a concerted effort to get things moving in the professional realm, especially in your early years — up to approximately age 30. I say this because it is around the late twenties or early thirties that people become adults (astrologically) and begin using a significant amount of free will.

Martin: But the textbooks I've read say that retrograde planets are stronger than forward-moving planets, not weaker.

James: Yes, I know. And that is definitely not an accurate assessment. As I said, we'll spend an entire class discussing retrogrades, but for now I'll just say that a planet that is retrograde is stronger than a forward-moving planet in the sense that retrograde planets are closer to the earth than they normally would be. The effect is to make the energy of the planet strong in a psychological sense, but weaker in terms of manifesting its significations in the outer world. This is a complex subject, so let's put it on hold until we discuss it later, okay?

Now, aside from doing a spiritual and/or metaphysical career, it is also indicated that your career will, or at least can, be incredibly successful, and I mean *incredibly* successful. This is because the 10th house ruler, Mars, is aspected within one degree by benefic Jupiter. Mars occupies twenty-two degrees Leo, while Jupiter occupies twenty-two degrees Aquarius. This is tremendous. Your 10th house ruler is similar to my 10th house ruler, Saturn, which is aspected by Jupiter within one degree.

Of course, my 10th house is further energized by Rahu's placement in the 10th house, as well as receiving aspects from Venus and Mars. But as far as I am concerned, I consider the nearly exact aspect Jupiter throws onto my 10th house ruler to be the reason I have gained fame and recognition (or "name and fame" as the Indians say).

Martin: You also said that Saturn is the most important *karaka* for the 10th house in general.

James: That's right. That certainly doesn't hurt. It's similar to a person who has a great marriage because Venus, the planet of love, is exalted and well-placed, as well as ruling the 7th house, the marriage house.

In your chart, Martin, Mars rules the 5th house, the mind. So Jupiter's exact aspect onto Mars makes you brilliant. When I was deciding on who to choose for this project I wanted someone who could pick things up quickly. Your powerful 5th house ruler gives a quality mind.

Martin: But, what about Rahu and Saturn in the 5th?

James: In terms of intelligence, they intensify your brilliance. They don't make you happy-go-lucky and optimistic-minded, that's for sure! But Saturn is a planet of logic and practicality. So, even though Saturn can make you somewhat somber or depressed at times, it won't hurt your intelligence. And it will make you quite logical and practical minded, which is very important for an astrologer.

It's pretty much the same with your Rahu in the 5th house. Rahu will hurt your peace of mind, but it will intensify your thought process. But the fact that the ruler of your 5th house, Mars, is aspected to the degree by the great benefic Jupiter is a tremendous benefit for you.

Martin: And Jupiter rules the 9th house, the best house in the chart.

James: That's right. The best planet for the Cancer ascendant is Mars because it rules the 5th and 10th house, but Jupiter isn't far behind as the ruler of the 9th and 6th houses (see page 381 for the list of good and bad planets for each ascendant by virtue of rulership).

Now, let's look at Jupiter, which is in an extremely mixed condition. As I've mentioned earlier, Jupiter is severely hurt because it is aspected by a first-class malefic (Mars). But Jupiter is strengthened because Mars as the *rajayoga* planet also throws some excellent energy due to the good houses it rules (5th and 10th).

When I analyzed your horoscope for this project, I did have a concern about your ability to deal with higher knowledge as well as your ability to deal with a mentor. There's no way that your dealing with religious or spiritual teachers is going to be smooth when Jupiter in your chart is aspected so tightly by Mars.

Martin: When you read my chart a year ago, you said I should wear a big yellow sapphire for Jupiter.

James: That's right, and I also prescribed chanting the Jupiter mantra. I was very concerned about your health, because of Jupiter's rulership of the 6th house. Jupiter afflictions cause allergies and problems with the liver, gall bladder, and spleen.

But I was also concerned about skepticism. People with Jupiter afflictions have problems having faith. This can mean faith in God, or faith in the realms Jupiter signifies in the horoscope.

Martin: What do you mean?

James: For example, a person who has a fallen (or seriously afflicted in any other way) Jupiter that rules or occupies, say, the 7th house, may not trust their marriage, or the person may not trust their spouse.

Martin: Jealousy.

James: Yes, Jupiter rules faith. So, in your case, Jupiter could cause problems in your dealings with me as your mentor.

Martin: The hardest part of our sessions, James, is that you teach me one thing and the books you told me to read often say something different. This drives me crazy.

James: Yes, I know. And if I had realized what a problem this was going to be, I would have never told you to read the other authors. This was my mistake. I should have taught you my teachings and then, after you had practiced for a while, told you to read the other books.

Martin: Well, most of the knowledge is the same, but there's so many little subtleties that everyone seems to disagree about. It makes me angry.

James: Yes, well, the anger has to do with Jupiter being aspected by Mars. Mars rules friction, fighting, and anger. You will find yourself getting angry at gurus and spiritual teachers in general.

Actually, I have to tell you that when I noticed the Jupiter-Mars aspect in your chart I thought it could be a big help in your practice of *Jyotish*. The biggest problem with astrologers, both Eastern and Western, is that we are way too gullible and naive and "new agey." As far as I'm concerned, astrologers need to be as skeptical and discriminating as possible. This means going by your experience, not some theory or textbook teaching. It means admitting when you don't know what some feature in the chart indicates, and admitting to your clients that you simply can't answer certain questions. Too many astrologers are afraid to say the words "I don't know."

Martin: So you don't believe everything can be predicted from a horoscope?

James: Your question is moot. Because even if it is theoretically possible to predict everything, in practice it'll never happen. Astrology is too complex to ever be practiced with total accuracy. The best we can do is use our technical skills and our intuition and hope for the best. As I see it, astrology is a numbers game. You look at a chart and see what is likely to occur based on what has happened in the past when you've seen those similar features. Of course you also use intuition, but intuition is not perfect either, even for the most psychic or evolved souls.

In my view, the miracle of existence is that omniscience, and by this I mean total foresight, is impossible.

Martin: Even for enlightened beings?

James: Yes. I believe that God made creation in such a way that complete prediction is impossible.

Martin: There's also the issue of free will that complicates making perfect predictions.

James: I agree one hundred percent. There are plenty of people who believe that enlightened beings can know everything, but I strongly disagree with that.

Martin: Why?

James: For two reasons. The first is that I've heard so many predictions about worldly events made by famous gurus that have failed miserably. I pay attention to predictions made by gurus, and they all have a bad track record, at least regarding their public predictions. Second, my understanding of enlightenment is that it is about living in a continual state of <u>pure</u> awareness. Pure awareness means awareness of <u>infinity or spirit</u>, not awareness of any one particular detail or subject. Enlightenment is characterized by freedom from attachment, infinite bliss, various extra sensory perceptions which differ from person to person, and a state of everlasting contentedness. It is <u>not</u> characterized by knowing data or information. I know lots of spiritual disciples who may disagree, but that's how I see it.

Anyway, regarding skepticism and discrimination, the more you question astrological techniques and astrological theory and so on, the better astrologer you will be.

Martin: James, you must be skeptical because your Jupiter is aspected tightly by Saturn.

James: That's right. My Jupiter is also aspected by Mars, and that aspect is also exact (within one degree). There's another similarity between our charts, and that is that you and I both have Saturn in the 5th house, which gives the ability to think deeply and seriously.

The main reason I chose you for this project, however, was that through your horoscope I could see your natural receptivity and innate comfort with metaphysical subjects. When I saw that, I knew that my job of teaching you would be easy, smooth, and fulfilling. Simply put, metaphysics is genetically ingrained in you.

Martin: Genetically ingrained?

James: Yes. I'd say metaphysical interest is in your genes. It's funny, the idea of the horoscope revealing your genetics, but I believe it does. I'll give you an example of what I mean.

There are lots of times when I see a person's profession very clearly in the birthchart. But, sometimes the person is involved in that profession, and sometimes the person simply has no interest in that realm.

Martin: Your kidding?

James: Not at all. It's not a common occurrence, but it happens. In these circumstances, I ask the person if the profession indicated in the chart runs in the family.

Martin: Because the horoscope reveals genetics?

James: Yes. So, if you said you had no interest in metaphysical and spiritual subjects, while your horoscope so strongly indicates talent in these areas, I would have to ask if any of your closest relatives were highly spiritual or metaphysical.

Martin: Like when you saw law indicated in my horoscope, which runs in my family but is the last thing I'd want to do.

James: Exactly, the tight Mars-Jupiter opposition we spoke about.

I have a friend named Rajesh, whose chart looks extraordinary for business. He has the ruler of the 10th house (career) in the 7th. The 7th house rules marriage and partnerships, but it is also the most essential house for business.

Martin: Business?

James: Yes. You won't find it in many texts, but if a person has an active or energized 7th house, he or she loves to interact with people and therefore the person leans toward commerce or sales, where there is constant contact with people.

I analyzed Rajesh's chart many years ago, when I first met him as a client. I predicted that he was in business.

Martin: Because the ruler of his 10th occupies the 7th house?

James: Yes, but also because the 10th house ruler, Saturn, which happens to be in the 7th house <u>in its exaltation sign</u>, is conjunct Venus, <u>the 7th house ruler</u> in its own sign, Libra.

Martin: So, Saturn's tremendously strong because it is close to a benefic in its own sign, right?

James: That's right. I was certain I was looking at the chart of a businessman. Well, when I told him that, he laughed and said every psychic and astrologer he had met had said the same thing. In fact, he is a doctor.

Martin: Shock.

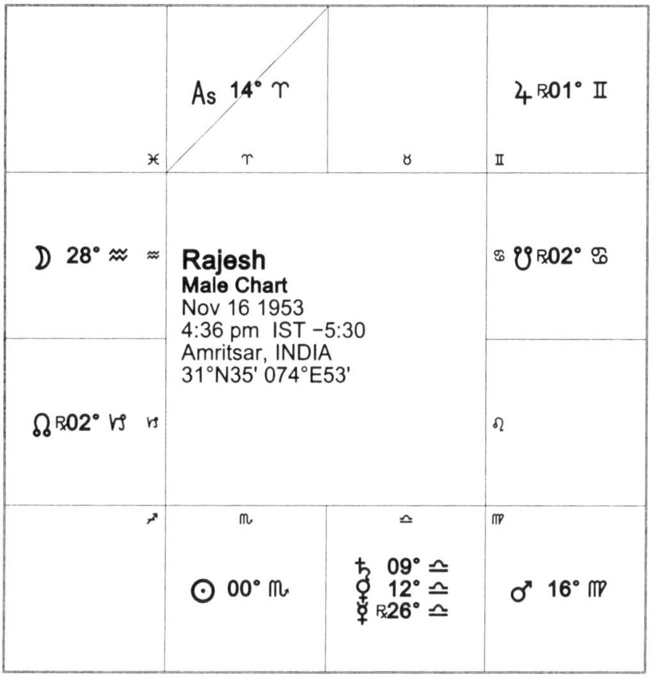

As 14° ♈
♃ ℞01° ♊
♓ ♈ ♉ ♊
☽ 28° ♒ ♒
Rajesh
Male Chart
Nov 16 1953
4:36 pm IST -5:30
Amritsar, INDIA
31°N35' 074°E53'
♋ ☋ ℞02° ♋
☊ ℞02° ♑ ♑
♌
♐ ♏ ♎ ♍
☉ 00° ♏
♄ 09° ♎
♀ 12° ♎
☿ ℞26° ♎
♂ 16° ♍

South Indian Style

For North Indian, see Appendix B.

planets.pts

Pt	Name	Hs	Rules
☽	Moon	11	4
☉	Sun	8	5
☿	Mercury	7	3, 6
♀	Venus	7	2, 7
♂	Mars	6	1, 8
♃	Jupiter	3	9, 12
♄	Saturn	7	10, 11
☊	North Node	10	-
☋	South Node	4	-
As	Ascendant	1	-

Sg	Name
♈	Aries
♉	Taurus
♊	Gemini
♋	Cancer
♌	Leo
♍	Virgo
♎	Libra
♏	Scorpio
♐	Sagittarius
♑	Capricorn
♒	Aquarius
♓	Pisces

James: Darn right I was shocked. The only feature in the chart that I could find indicating healing is the ascendant ruler, Mars, occupying the 6th house. On top of this, in the *dasamsa* chart, the career chart, the ruler of the 10th, which is Venus, occupies the 7th. We're going to talk about *vargas*, or divisional charts, in another class. But for now, I'll just tell you that when I look at a career chart (the *dasamsa*) I mainly look at the 10th house (career) of that chart. And I look at the ascendant (1st house or nucleus) of that chart. I know lots of astrologers look at the chart as a whole, but I don't. I find the divisional charts work much better when I look at the ascendant and the house connected to the symbolism of the *varga*.

Dasamsa

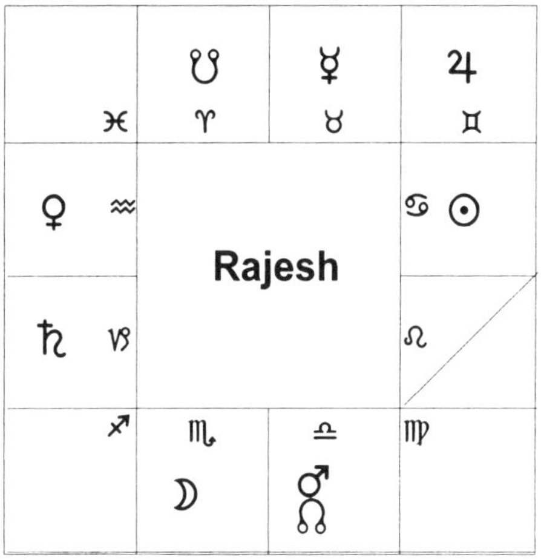

☋ ☿ ♃
♓ ♈ ♉ ♊
♀ ♒
♋ ☉
Rajesh
♄ ♑
♌
♐ ♏ ♎ ♍
☽ ♂ ☊

Martin: So for a *navamsa*, or marriage chart, you look at the 1st house and the 7th house?

James: Yes, and for the *saptamsa*, the chart for children, I look at the ascendant and the 5th house. Parasara (originator of the particular Hindu system of *Jyotish* we are using) and other ancient seers might be turning over in their graves when I say this, but in my experience, looking at the particular *varga* chart as a whole doesn't work nearly as well as looking at the ascendant and the house pertaining to the meaning of the *varga*. I told you from the start I would be telling you my experience rather than theory, so there you have it. But I'll give plenty of examples of how to analyze *varga* charts later on (see Class Seven).

In any case, in Rajesh's chart, everything clearly pointed to business. So what do you think he tells me a year or two <u>after</u> I read his chart, when he was finally a friend? He said that all his ancestors for about five or six generations were business people! Take my advice, when you have a situation where the chart indicates some interest or ability that the client says he or she doesn't relate to, ask the person if that talent runs in the family.

Martin: That way you don't look incompetent.

James: Exactly. Of course sometimes the person doesn't relate to what's in the chart because the <u>birthtime is wrong</u>, but I'm talking now about situations where the chart generally fits, and there's one huge, glaring inconsistency.

Regarding Rajesh's chart, by the way, can you see how successful he is? Saturn, as the 10th house ruler, is not only exalted but is aspected by every benefic in the chart except for the Moon. Saturn is aspected by Jupiter, Venus, and Mercury.

Martin: Is he at the top of his field?

James: The very top. He does medical research in a university and recently obtained a multi-million dollar grant. By the way, the fact that the 10th house ruler is conjunct Venus gives a hint that his career would involve females.

Martin: As a doctor?

James: He is a fertility doctor, and a good one at that.

Martin: James, do you ever see horoscopes where some profession is clearly indicated, and yet the person hasn't even considered that kind of career.

James: Yes. It happens every so often. I remember analyzing a chart for a wealthy Swiss man who was in Florida many years ago. His chart was so strong for art that I thought he was an artist, a painter. This was because he had a very strong Venus and a very strong 5th house. Maybe he had Venus in the 5th house, or something like that. I don't remember exactly. The 5th house represents crafts and painting and art <u>in general</u>, whereas the 3rd house specifically represents music, dance, and drama.

Well, this man had inherited hair salons from his father and had never even considered an artistic career. About five years later, I was visiting Switzerland, and this client heard I was in town and invited me to his home for dinner. At that point, I remembered nothing about his horoscope or what I had said to him five years earlier. Well, the man had a beautiful home, extremely luxurious, and there were beautiful paintings all over the house.

Martin: Nice ones?

James: Very nice. Eventually, I realized that he was the painter, and when I told him how nice the paintings were, he got a very puzzled look on his face. He said I was the one who told him he should paint! He had never held a paint brush before middle age. The next thing I know, he's asking me to look in his chart and tell him when would be a good time to put his work in a gallery. In the same way astrology is in your genes, art was in his.

Martin: So, astrology is in my genes?

James: Yes. Whether or not you want to learn astrology or practice it is up to you. But the ability is definitely there. What I haven't told you yet, believe it or not, is the strongest placement indicating your metaphysical talent. This has to do with rulerships. You have what is called an exchange of signs, or *Parivartana Yoga* (mutual reception) between Mars and Saturn, the rulers of the 5th house and the 8th house. Mars rules the 5th house, Scorpio, and it's in the 8th. Saturn rules the 8th house, Aquarius, and it's in the 5th. The 5th house is *poorvapunya*, or past life credit, and the 8th house is astrology and metaphysical subjects. Either one of these placements, ruler of the 5th in the 8th, or ruler of the 8th in the 5th, indicate that in this life you will learn metaphysical subjects because of your past life efforts. The exchange between the 5th and 8th house rulers simply intensifies the indication. You must have given out astrological knowledge in the past or helped out in a significant way this realm, and now the karma is returning to you.

Martin: So, if I want to know about a person's past lives, I look at the 5th house of the chart?

James: Well, it's a bit more complex than that. The entire chart is a result of your karma from past lives. The 5th house simply indicates past life credit <u>or debt</u> that <u>must</u> occur during this lifetime because the karma has building for so long without repayment. (There is a school of thought that the 9th house, not the 5th, represents *poorvapunya*, but that is not how I was taught.)

Poorvapunya always seems to come back in a very destined way incidentally. Look at what happened to you. You're going to college and living your life, and suddenly I call to ask if you'd like to learn Hindu astrology privately for free, so I can produce this book. Pretty good karma I'd say.

Martin: I guess there are a lot of people who would like to be tutored privately in *Jyotish*.

James: That's right. And the fact that you entered the Sun *dasa* a month ago is largely why you are getting so much knowledge now.

Martin: Because the Sun rules the 2nd house?

James: Yes, that's the house of knowledge and education. The Sun in your chart is extremely strong. It's aspected by the full Moon and by exalted Mercury. The Sun could hardly be more well-disposed. During your Sun *dasa* you're either going to make a lot of money (2nd house) or you're going to get a tremendous amount of information and knowledge.

Martin: Or both?

James: Right. So, the knowledge is already occurring. Money may be on the way soon. Let's wait and see.

Regarding your *Parivartana Yoga,* the exchange of signs between Mars and Saturn, as rulers of the 5th and 8th — I want to say something to clarify how this yoga works.

Martin: It's not good for my peace of mind, right?

James: That's right. Your 5th house (mind) is hurt by the 8th house energy it receives, while your 8th house benefits tremendously by the 5th house energy it receives. Any house or planet that associates with a *dusthana* house (6th, 8th, or 12th) or the ruler of a *dusthana* house gets harmed — significantly harmed. Any house or planet that associates with a *trikona* house (5th or 9th) gets an increase of luck and fortune.

Some astrologers believe that any exchange of signs is good, no matter what houses are involved, no matter what signs are involved, but this is utter nonsense in my experience. Experience aside, it doesn't even make sense in theory!

If the ruler of the 10th house exchanges signs with the 8th or 12th houses (*dusthana* houses), do you think this is good for career?

Martin: No.

James: Of course it isn't. The person's career will have all kinds of problems and obstacles. If the 1st house ruler exchanges signs with the 8th or 12th house ruler, how can this possibly be good for the person's confidence and ability to be recognized?

Martin: And you're saying that some astrologers don't know this?

James: That's right. Since *Parivartana Yoga* is considered a good yoga, they assume every exchange of signs is good. But if you ask clients who have exchanges that involve bad houses, you'll find they are quite harmful. Even more destructive than a *Parivartana Yoga* involving bad houses is an exchange of signs involving fallen planets. These are brutal. And still, believe it or not, I meet clients who were told by astrologers that the exchange between two fallen planets is good! Their reasoning is beyond me. Let me give you an example.

Look at the chart of Baba Ram Das (A.K.A. Richard Alpert – page 72.)

Martin: The associate of Timothy Leary at Harvard?

James: Yes, the man who experimented with LSD until he became involved in Eastern mysticism and wrote many wonderful books on the subject.

Notice that the Moon and Mars are both fallen and exchanging signs.

Martin: Mars is fallen in Cancer and the Moon is fallen in Scorpio.

James: That's right. In his case, Mars rules the 6th house and is fallen in the 2nd, while the Moon rules the 2nd house and is fallen in the 6th. Want to guess what happened in his Mars *dasa*? He had a stroke and lost the ability to speak! Rumor has it that the damage was not permanent.

Martin: Speech is ruled by the 2nd house.

James: Yes. In his Moon *dasa*, the worst subperiod had to be Mars. And in his Mars *dasa*, the worst *Bhukti* is that of the Moon. This is because the planets of the period and subperiod are both fallen. This is simple basic astrological reasoning, and the fact that the planets exchange signs in this case is bad, not good, for the 2nd and 6th houses. Is that not obvious?

Martin: It seems pretty basic.

James: It is. Now, these 2nd house afflictions, by the way, were responsible for all of Ram Das' drug use. Of course, almost everyone in college during the sixties took drugs, but Ram Das became famous for his drug use. The 2nd house rules the food that one eats, and when it's afflicted the person will eat bad foods, including alcohol or drugs. Incidentally, make sure you don't confuse appetite, which is a 6th house matter, and the food one eats, which is a 2nd house matter. I've met astrologers who get tripped up by this.

Martin: James, Ram Das was kicked out of Harvard when he taught there because of his drug experiments, wasn't he? Schooling is ruled by the 2nd house.

James: That's true. But I'd want to know the year that happened because it could also be related to the 9th house, which governs universities.

Martin: If Ram Das has such a bad 2nd house, how could he do so much teaching and public speaking?

James: Well, rule number one in astrology is that you have to look at a horoscope as a whole before passing any final judgement. God only knows how many errors I made in my first few years of practice because I didn't look at everything in the chart before speaking.

In Ram Das' case, I would be surprised if he didn't have serious trouble in school as a child because of the 2nd house afflictions. But ultimately, you have to give enormous weight to his Gemini ascendant. The most important

South Indian Style — For North Indian, see Appendix B.

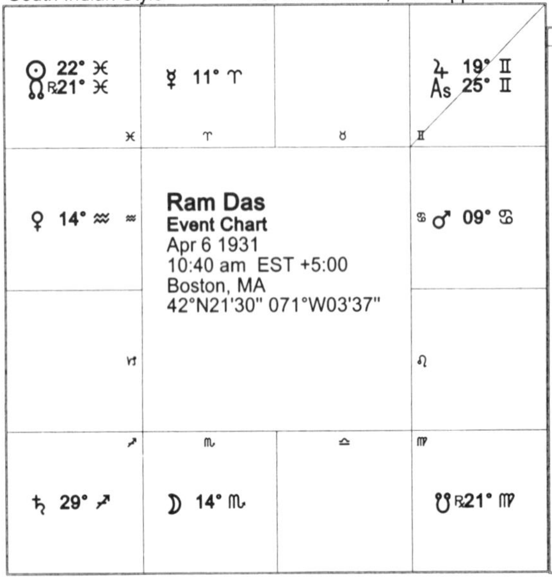
☉ 22° ♓
☊ ℞21° ♓
☿ 11° ♈
♃ 19° ♊
As 25° ♊
♓
♈
♉
♊
♀ 14° ♒
♒
Ram Das
Event Chart
Apr 6 1931
10:40 am EST +5:00
Boston, MA
42°N21'30" 071°W03'37"
♋ ♂ 09° ♋
♑
♌
♐
♏
♎
♍
♄ 29° ♐
☽ 14° ♏
☋ ℞21° ♍

DASA-BHUKTIS

DASAS & BHUKTIS - Lahiri Zodiac

♄ / ☊	Apr 6 1931	0.0	☉ / ☽	Sep 1 1978	47.4
♄ / ♃	Nov 1 1931	0.6	☉ / ♂	Mar 2 1979	47.9
☿	May 14 1934	3.1	☉ / ☊	Jul 8 1979	48.3
☿ / ☋	Oct 10 1936	5.5	☉ / ♃	Jun 1 1980	49.2
☿ / ♀	Oct 7 1937	6.5	☉ / ♄	Mar 20 1981	50.0
☿ / ☉	Aug 7 1940	9.3	☉ / ☿	Mar 2 1982	50.9
☿ / ☽	Jun 14 1941	10.2	☉ / ☋	Jan 6 1983	51.8
☿ / ♂	Nov 13 1942	11.6	☉ / ♀	May 14 1983	52.1
☿ / ☊	Nov 10 1943	12.6	☽	May 14 1984	53.1
☿ / ♃	May 30 1946	15.1	☽ / ♂	Mar 14 1985	53.9
☿ / ♄	Sep 3 1948	17.4	☽ / ☊	Oct 13 1985	54.5
☋	May 15 1951	20.1	☽ / ♃	Apr 14 1987	56.0
☋ / ♀	Oct 11 1951	20.5	☽ / ♄	Aug 13 1988	57.4
☋ / ☉	Dec 10 1952	21.7	☽ / ☿	Mar 14 1990	58.9
☋ / ☽	Apr 17 1953	22.0	☽ / ☋	Aug 14 1991	60.4
☋ / ♂	Nov 16 1953	22.6	☽ / ♀	Mar 14 1992	60.9
☋ / ☊	Apr 14 1954	23.0	☽ / ☉	Nov 12 1993	62.6
☋ / ♃	May 2 1955	24.1	♂	May 14 1994	63.1
☋ / ♄	Apr 7 1956	25.0	♂ / ☊	Oct 10 1994	63.5
☋ / ☿	May 17 1957	26.1	♂ / ♃	Oct 29 1995	64.6
♀	May 14 1958	27.1	♂ / ♄	Oct 3 1996	65.5
♀ / ☉	Sep 13 1961	30.4	♂ / ☿	Nov 12 1997	66.6
♀ / ☽	Sep 13 1962	31.4	♂ / ☋	Nov 10 1998	67.6
♀ / ♂	May 14 1964	33.1	♂ / ♀	Apr 8 1999	68.0
♀ / ☊	Jul 14 1965	34.3	♂ / ☉	Jun 7 2000	69.2
♀ / ♃	Jul 14 1968	37.3	♂ / ☽	Oct 13 2000	69.5
♀ / ♄	Mar 15 1971	39.9	☊	May 14 2001	70.1
♀ / ☿	May 14 1974	43.1	☊ / ♃	Jan 25 2004	72.8
♀ / ☋	Mar 14 1977	45.9	☊ / ♄	Jun 19 2006	75.2
☉	May 14 1978	47.1	☊ / ☿	Apr 25 2009	78.1

features of any horoscope are the ascendant, its ruler, and the Moon. And let me tell you that even though his Moon is fallen in the house of knowledge, the house holding the Moon becomes very important because it is so critical to a horoscope. In another session (Class Five), I'm going to focus on the importance of the Sun and Moon, and explain how even when they are afflicted they can produce some powerful and positive effects. Also, I'll explain how the Sun, which is definitely a malefic by nature in *Jyotish*, can create some very good effects regarding the house it occupies.

Martin: How so?

James: The lights (Sun and Moon) are so incredibly important to a horoscope that even when they are afflicted the person may eventually learn how to use their energies in a positive way. But let's leave that for later, when I can explain it in more depth (See Class Five).

Ram Das' teaching and speaking skills are indicated by the Mercury ruled Gemini ascendant. They are also indicated by Jupiter, the 10th house (career) ruler, occupying the sign of Gemini. And Mercury, the planet of communication, becomes more powerful every year for Ram Das because it occupies an *upachaya* house. *Upachaya* houses (3rd, 6th, 10th, and 11th) are "growing" houses, where planets grow stronger year by year.

Martin: Does it help that Mercury throws an aspect onto Ram Das' 5th house?

James: That gives him an excellent and objective mind.

Martin: I see.

James: Now, another problem that could occur because of Ram Das' afflicted 2nd house is rough family life. This means a lot of unhappiness with his parents and siblings, as well as major bickering and arguing with his love partners. When we get into analyzing marriage (Class Seven), you're going to see how complicated it can be to analyze that realm properly. So many astrological factors are involved.

You have to look at the conditions of Venus, the natal 7th house, the 7th house from the Moon, and the 1st and 7th houses of the *navamsa* (marriage chart). On top of all these factors, and what many astrologers forget, is that if you neglect to analyze the 2nd house to see the person's luck in family life, you can fail miserably in your love life predictions.

Martin: James, regarding Ram Das' afflicted 2nd house, you seem to be saying that every 2nd house signification could be harmed in his life. Does this mean if a particular house is weak or afflicted, I should mention every signification of that house as a potential problem to my client?

James: Yes, I would say so. In Ram Das' case, the 2nd house is so afflicted that if he were my client I would even have warned him about the health of his right eye, particularly in both the Moon and Mars *dasas*. Of course, I don't expect that all 2nd house significations would actually be hurt. But unless an astrologer is magnificently psychic, I doubt he or she is going to know exactly which 2nd house features will be harmed and which ones escape harm. In my practice, if I see a planet or a house seriously afflicted, I generally mention all the potential problems.

Martin: Better safe than sorry.

James: Yes. But remember to look at the chart as a whole, because there will sometimes be mitigating factors, depending on the significations you're addressing.

The way I was taught *Jyotish* was to memorize everything possible about the meanings of the houses and planets. If you only memorize the obvious significations of planets and houses, and ignore the seemingly trivial ones, you lose the ability to make certain predictions that may be important to your client. I discovered this when I returned from India, after my second journey.

My very first session was with a young woman whose birthchart indicated a medical or healing type of career. The chart also had a very prominent Mars — I believe it was Mars in its own sign (Scorpio or Aries) in the 10th house (career) or the 6th (daily work). So I told her, "You should become involved in medicine, but in a technical or mechanical way."

Martin: Because Mars represents technical or mechanical skills?

James: Exactly. I then became more specific and said, "Why don't you learn to practice surgery or acupuncture?" She got very excited and replied, "I want to be a surgical nurse!"

Then I noticed that her 3rd house was massively afflicted — I mean massively. Now the 3rd house represents a lot of things. It signifies brothers and sisters, daily desires, courage, artistic energy, the right ear, and on and on. So I started mentioning all the potential problems she might have due to the horrendous 3rd house. When I got to the signification of the "right ear," the woman became animated and said, "This is amazing. I have a hearing problem that doctors always blame on my left ear. I keep telling them that it's not my left ear (which, incidentally is ruled by the 12th house), but my right one. They don't want to believe me, but it is definitely my right ear that is weak."

Martin: What was so bad about her 3rd house?

James: Well, its been about fifteen years since that reading so I don't remember exactly. My best recollection is that there was a fallen Mars in the 3rd house (Mars in Cancer) and the ruler of the 3rd house (the Moon) was combust the Sun within one degree. So the 3rd house ruler was badly burned by the malefic Sun's hot rays.

Martin: Sounds like a really bad 3rd house.

James: It was. It's easy to make accurate predictions when a house or a planet is tremendously strong or tremendously afflicted. Unfortunately for astrologers, most features in horoscopes are mixed. We'll have to talk about mixed indications in detail later on because the subject is so important, but I will say this: if you don't learn how to make predictions about charts that are mixed, and astrological features that are mixed, you better forget about becoming an astrologer. Most charts, like most people, have lots of good conditions and lots of bad conditions simultaneously.

Martin: That's what I find so difficult, James. What do we do in these cases?

James: I will devote more time to this subject later. But, just to give you an idea of how I deal with it, let's take one feature in your horoscope that's clearly mixed. Look at the Moon in your chart (See page 51). Notice that the Moon is full (it is easy to notice a full Moon because the Moon is full when it is in the sign opposite the Sun). This is excellent. *Jyotish* is a lunar based system, and the brightness of the Moon is critical. The relative brightness of the Moon tells in a general sense whether a person may live a life abundance and well-being versus a life of poverty and misfortune. The Moon in your chart also occupies the 9th house, a *trikona* (trinal) house that signifies luck, and is considered the best house of a chart. All of this is excellent so far, right?

Martin: Yes, but what do you mean when you say the Moon governs abundance or poverty in a <u>general</u> sense?

James: Well, the Moon doesn't rule money and prosperity specifically, but if the Moon is very bright the person is usually going to be powerful and is going to attract attention in life. Being powerful and attracting attention <u>generally</u> leads to abundance and fortune. A person with a weak or dim Moon has a much harder time attracting attention and commanding power. This leads to less abundance and opportunity. This is a subtlety that you will get after analyzing hundreds of horoscopes. After a while, you begin to notice that people who have very strong charts <u>and</u> very bright Moons become successful much faster and easier than people whose charts are very strong but contain a very dim Moon. When I'm in the presence of someone who has a full Moon in their chart, I usually feel the person's power.

If you remember nothing else, remember this: The Moon is more than another planetary influence — it is like a second ascendant. If the Moon is very bright, that second ascendant is a major boon, a major advantage. If the Moon is very weak, the second ascendant is feeble or powerless.

Martin: Is it afflicted? Does it cause damage when it's dim?

James: Some astrologers believe it becomes malefic, but I don't agree with that. I find that a very dim Moon doesn't do anything to <u>help</u> a person. It makes a person "average," as opposed to a full or very bright Moon, which makes a person special or talented or favored. So, do you understand now why I say that the Moon rules abundance and fortune <u>in a general sense</u>?

Martin: Yes.

James: Now, back to your horoscope. Look at the negatives of the Moon. The Moon is aspected tightly (within about four degrees) by Mercury. Mercury, even though a generally benefic planet, happens to rule the *dusthana*, or grief-producing, 12th house. Far worse than that, Mercury is throwing its aspect onto the sign of Pisces, which is Mercury's <u>fallen</u> sign. This is real bad because Pisces hates Mercury energy. This condition substantially damages the Moon's disposition. On top of all this, malefic Rahu throws an aspect onto the Moon.

Martin: Wait. James, you say in your textbook that Rahu and Ketu don't throw aspects. What's the story?

James: Neither of my mentors used the aspects of Rahu and Ketu in their practice, even though Parasara, the originator of the system we are using, said that Rahu and Ketu aspect the 5th, 7th, and 9th houses from themselves.

In 1985, when I wrote my first text, I believed my teachers. But, after looking at thousands of charts, I eventually came to believe that Rahu and Ketu <u>do</u> throw aspects that are harmful. I don't have much to say about the <u>specific nature</u> of the aspects that they throw, because I haven't isolated their exact effects, other than noticing that they cause destruction and harm to any house or planet they aspect. I have also noticed that when a planet or house is aspected by either Rahu or Ketu <u>and</u> another malefic planet, serious damage definitely occurs. That is guaranteed.

Martin: So, you use aspects from the nodes even though both of your mentors didn't?

James: Yes. I don't blindly follow any astrological rules. I test them for myself, and I expect you to do the same. This doesn't guarantee that our findings will always be right, of course. But it is the only sane approach in a field as diverse, vast, and filled with disagreements as *Jyotish*. Each astrologer has to find his or her own way to accuracy. The key words here are <u>to accuracy</u>. And if you want to increase your accuracy, you have to follow up with clients to see what parts of your natal analysis were correct and what future predictions you made actually came true. Understand?

Martin: I do.

James: Now, regarding the Moon in your chart, there are some wonderful features and some terrible features. In other words, the Moon's condition is mixed.

Martin: So how do you handle this in a session with a client?

James: I tell the client that the Moon is in a mixed condition and <u>is most likely going to give both good and bad effects</u>. I don't commit myself to any prediction regarding the Moon, except to say that it will likely give mixed results, meaning good and bad effects simultaneously.

Martin: So one good aspect doesn't cancel out one bad aspect?

James: No. In the vast majority of cases, if there are two contradictory aspects <u>of equal weight, equal importance</u>, one does not cancel out the other. The good aspect will give good effects and the bad aspect will cause harm. But you have to know the difference between an intense and powerful aspect versus a minor aspect. For example, if the Sun is in the tenth degree of Aries — the Sun's <u>highest</u> point of exaltation — which is wonderful for the Sun (See Page 379 of Appendix A for a full explanation of exaltations and falls), and is also aspected within fifteen or twenty degrees by some malefic planet, say Mars or Saturn, which is bad for the Sun, these factors are not equal in intensity. In this case, the Sun will give good effects because the <u>extreme</u> exaltation of the Sun definitely outweighs the <u>moderately</u> bad aspect from the malefic planet that occurs within a relatively wide orb. Of course, the results would be even better without the malefic aspect the Sun is receiving, but the end result certainly will be positive.

I'll talk about mixed features in a birthchart quite a bit in later classes. But, let me warn you now that it takes years of experience to get a visceral feel for the weight and significance of each astrological feature.

Martin: That's what is so hard. There are so many features to try and synthesize.

James: Believe me, I know. Like every other astrologer, I'm still working on it. In any case, if a planet or house or *dasa* planet is in a mixed condition, meaning it receives one or two good aspects and one or two bad aspects of equal significance, then I tell the client to expect mixed results.

Martin: Does that satisfy the person?

James: Yes, because it's the truth. The more truth you speak, the more credibility you gain with the client. As astrologers, we generally have an urge to say something dramatic, something bold. But the truth always works better. And the truth is, that because life conditions are so often mixed in their positive and negative effects, most astrological conditions are also mixed.

But I want to make sure you get this concept, because it is very important. If a planet or a horoscope is mixed, tell the client that the effects in his or her life are also going to be mixed. I know it doesn't sound dramatic, but the effect it has on the person is dramatic because he or she has just found an astrologer who is accurate. Do you get it?

Martin: I do.

James: Now, this includes saying the words "I don't know," if the person is looking for a definitive "yes" or "no" to an issue surrounding a mixed planet, mixed house, mixed *dasa*, or whatever. Generally speaking, if an indication is clearly mixed and you give a definite "yes" or "no" answer, you are misrepresenting the horoscope. Most beginner astrologers, myself included (when I was a beginner), live with the misconception that every question a client asks can be answered definitively if only we were talented enough. You must let go of that concept. It's nonsense. Astrology is difficult enough when the horoscope indications are clear and dramatic and we have plenty of experience in the field. We simply must accept the fact that astrology is never going to be practiced with total accuracy. I've been in metaphysics for about twenty years now, and have never met anyone (psychic or astrologer) who practices with near total accuracy.

Martin: When the horoscope indications are mixed, it makes it that much harder to predict.

James: Exactly. If you want to give the person certainty about a mixed indication, tell them that the realm of life indicated by the mixed condition is going to give mixed results. You'll be amazed at how your accuracy rate will go up. Also, tell the person that their free will, the efforts they are willing to make, will have a significant impact on the results of the mixed planet, or *dasa* or whatever you are analyzing. It will.

Now, if a planet (or house, or *dasa*, or whatever) is in a condition that I call "a mixture of extremes." I explain that it becomes something of a "wild card." By "mixture of extremes" I mean that the planet involved has some <u>extremely</u> good features and some <u>extremely</u> bad features.

Martin: Like my Moon.

James: Like your Moon.

I'll give you two examples. A minute ago, I mentioned the Sun in its highest degree of exaltation (10th degree of Aries) and aspected by malefic Mars or Saturn within fifteen or twenty degrees. But, instead of these malefic aspects occurring within fifteen or twenty degrees, imagine that one of them is <u>within one degree</u>. That's a wild card! The Sun is both wonderfully strong and horribly afflicted. And if you think you're easily going to make an accurate prediction about how that Sun behaves natally and in its periods and subperiods, think again. It's just too mixed with extreme conditions.

The second example we'll take is your Moon. The brightness of your Moon in the best house of a chart is extremely good. The aspect that Mercury throws onto the Moon <u>in its fallen sign</u> is extremely bad. Your Moon is, in my vocabulary, a "wild card."

Martin: So what does that mean, in terms of results?

James: It means that although your Moon will <u>probably</u> give both <u>extreme good</u> results and <u>extreme bad</u> results, the effects are even harder to predict.

Martin: Why?

James: I'm not exactly sure. I can only tell you that my experience is that when an influence is mixed in very extreme ways, sometimes it gives mixed extreme results, sometimes it gives <u>only</u> extreme good effects, and sometimes it gives <u>only</u> extreme bad effects. Hence the term "wild card."

Martin: This is very annoying, James.

James: I know. It's unfair. Kind of like life, isn't it? Anyway, please test what I'm saying. I think you'll find this wild card concept useful.

Martin: How do I test this?

James: Well, here's one way. Find a bunch of charts where the Moon is full — a full Moon is one of the most auspicious influences possible — but is also <u>seriously</u> afflicted, say by occupying Scorpio, the fallen sign of the Moon. (Not two or three days away from full, but actually full. If the Sun and Moon are in opposite signs from each other, the Moon is full.) And watch what happens. Some clients with this placement will have <u>dramatically</u> mixed results from that natal Moon and <u>dramatically</u> mixed Moon *dasas* and Moon *bhuktis*. Some will have excellent natal results from that Moon as well as excellent Moon *dasas* and Moon *bhuktis*. Others will have terrible natal results from that Moon and terrible Moon *dasas* and Moon *bhuktis*. (Be aware, however, that the Moon in the first three degrees of Scorpio is a very bad placement, due to being so close to its most intense point of fall.)

Another test would be to find a bunch of charts that have a planet that is extremely well-disposed because it is very near (within one or two degrees) its highest point of exaltation (e.g. Mercury near the fifteenth degree of Virgo, or Jupiter near the fifth degree of Cancer, etc.) and also happens to be aspected within two or three degrees by malefic Saturn or Mars. I think you'll find that some people with these placements will have mixed extreme results (both natally and during periods and subperiods) with that planet, while others will get only extremely good or only extremely bad effects.

Martin: And what do you tell the client about this?

James: First of all, when I'm preparing the chart I try to get an intuitive feel for how the planet or mixed influence will operate. Then, in the session, I explain the wild card principle to the client and ask him or her exactly how the mixed influence has functioned in the past, both natally and in the periods and subperiods of the planet involved.

Martin: James, to a skeptic, this kind of "wild card" analysis could sound like bunk. You're saying anything is possible from a wild card planet. What good is that?

James: It's not bunk. Most planets in horoscopes give average results! A wild card influence gives only extreme results. Extreme good, extreme bad, or a mixture of extreme good or bad. There is a huge difference, and if you tell your client that the planet in question is likely to give extreme results, either positive or negative, or extreme positive and negative, I promise that person will relate to what you're saying. But please only use this wild card concept if a planet is mixed in extremely positive and negative ways. Don't use it just to let yourself off the hook because you don't know an answer to some astrological question a client has asked. That would be terrible. And don't forget what I said about questioning the client about how a planet that you find confusing has actually functioned in the past.

Martin: So, if a planet is in a mixed condition and the client says that the past periods and subperiods of that planet have been bad, then it's probably going to be a harmful influence in the future.

James: Yes. That doesn't mean it won't function well once in a while, but that would be very rare. I'll give you an example. This is not an example of a mixed planet, but an example of how a planet can give extremely bad results almost all the time and then suddenly turn around and give excellent results. Let's say that Mars occupies ten degrees of Leo, and Venus occupies eight degrees of Aquarius.

Martin: So the planets are opposite each other.

James: Right. Therefore the planets aspect each other. Let's also say that Saturn is in nine degrees of Sagittarius. This means that Saturn is aspecting Venus <u>tightly</u>, within one degree (due to Saturn's 3rd house aspect).

Martin: Venus is devastated.

James: Yes, a Venus like this is going to give terrible results. Venus is so maligned by tight aspects from <u>two</u> first class malefics that its house position and the houses that Venus rules are basically irrelevant (in terms of mitigating the negativity). Right?

Martin: Right.

James: So, how would you expect Venus periods and subperiods to be?

Martin: Very rough.

James: Exactly. But, the person may get extremely good results when running a Mars *dasa* and a Venus *bhukti*. This is because Mars as the *dasa* planet has precedence over the *bhukti* planet, and Mars benefits from the aspect it receives from benefic Venus.

Martin: Even though Venus is so afflicted?

James: Yes. Venus is terribly afflicted, but that's Venus' problem. Any planet <u>aspected</u> by Venus will benefit by Venus' naturally harmonious vibrations. So, there are times that an afflicted planet can give good results in a subperiod.

Martin: But this is rare?

James: Very rare. It generally only occurs if the afflicted planet is forming a tight aspect with another planet and the two are running a *dasa-bhukti* together.

Now regarding what I said about not misusing the term "wild card" with clients, I want to make myself clear. Please don't be tempted to use the phrase every time you're confused about something.

Martin: If I did, I would be using it every fifteen minutes.

James: I only use the term when <u>I am confident</u> that the planet or house or *dasa* involved is going to give <u>extreme</u> results, but the results could go either way because there are both extremely good and extremely bad features about the planet, and the intensity of the positive and negative features <u>appear about equal</u>. If you misuse the term, you'll just disempower yourself the same as when you render judgements about issues that you're totally confused about.

Now, before we talk about your Moon *dasa* that is coming up in 2002, which I expect will be a mixture of extremes, I need to clarify something I said about the main affliction of your Moon.

Martin: You mean the aspect that Mercury throws onto the Moon in Pisces (Mercury's fallen sign)?

James: Yes. I've already told you that when a planet aspects its fallen sign, it's throwing a very bad aspect. But there is an important subtlety to this matter that gets right to the heart of *Jyotish*. As a beginner, your tendency is simply to memorize astrological rules and leave it at that. But it's not always so simple. You must consider each planet as a deity or living being, with its own nature and personality. Since each planet has its own personality, each will react differently to the particular aspect it receives.

Martin: You mean some planets wouldn't be hurt by Mercury's fallen aspect?

James: I don't mean that. In fact, any planet receiving a "fallen" aspect will be hurt, but you have to consider the nature of <u>both</u> planets, the planet <u>throwing</u> the aspect and the planet <u>receiving</u> the aspect in order to understand the <u>nature</u> of the affliction. Some planets are very sensitive by nature, and that cannot be ignored. If I had a choice between hard-natured planets like Mars and Saturn receiving Mercury's fallen aspect, versus sensitive planets like Moon and Venus receiving the same aspect, I would definitely prefer Mars or Saturn receive the aspect.

Martin: If Mars or Saturn received the bad aspect, they would be hurt, but not as badly?

James: Yes. But don't get me wrong. Saturn or Mars would not benefit from a fallen Mercury aspect. They would definitely get hurt. But, because they are not quite as sensitive as Moon and Venus, they might be able to handle the affliction a bit easier. This is a real subtlety, something for you to think about on your own.

Martin: Why is it a subtlety?

James: Because it concerns the <u>degree</u> of harm each particular planet will receive. That's something that takes time to learn, to sense. Also, you have to understand that while the planets will have their own particular reaction to each aspect, the effects on the <u>houses ruled by the receiver</u> are all the same.

Martin: Say what?

James: If the fallen Mercury aspect in our example is thrown onto the ruler of the 7th house, <u>regardless of whether Saturn or Moon or Venus or Sun rules that 7th house</u>, the person's marriage is going to be damaged by mental instability.

Martin: Equally? No matter what planet rules the 7th house?

James: That's right. The person is going to choose partners who are a little crazy or mentally unstable, because the 7th house ruler is aspected by fallen Mercurial energy. Do you see the logic?

Martin: Well, I get the point about fallen Mercurial energy creating mental weakness or instability within the person's marriage *if* a fallen Mercury aspect is thrown onto the 7th house ruler. But, let me get this concept straight. You said malefic or hard-natured planets planet might handle the fallen Mercury energy differently from benefics, but the negative energy is received equally as far as the planets rulerships go. Am I understanding you right?

James: Yes, perfectly. It's just another subtlety.

Martin: How many subtleties are there, thousands?

James: Plenty. And I doubt anyone knows all of them. Most of the subtleties you have to learn from practical experience. The more charts you analyze, and the more feedback you get about your analysis, the more subtleties you will learn. As an astrologer, there is a point when the planets come alive for you, when they become more than symbols on a piece of paper.

Martin: When they become deities?

James: Yes, living beings. I once had an interesting conversation with Chaprapani Ullal that may shed some light on this matter. Chakrapani was one of the first Indians to come to America and practice *Jyotish* in the West. He lives in Los Angeles and has interpreted thousands upon thousands of horoscopes. He's also known to interpret four, five, even six charts a day.

Martin: Incredible.

James: Well, one day I sat down and asked him how it is that he doesn't burn out on doing charts. I mean, after a while, it can get quite tedious.

Martin: What did he say?

James: His face lit up, he got very animated, and said something to the effect of, "I'm always so fascinated by what the planets are doing, how they're behaving. I love watching what Saturn and Venus and Jupiter and everyone are doing." In other words, planets to him are not just symbolic representations. They are deities, living beings. When you perceive the planets as deities, or Lords of Karma, who have always existed and will always exist, that's when you begin to interpret properly. That's when *Jyotish* ceases to be a process of memorization, of merely considering a bunch of rules and technicalities. That's when it comes alive.

Now, so far we've talked about planets receiving fallen aspects. Actually, the main reason I brought up the matter of fallen aspects is to make a distinction about how different planets throwing fallen aspects create different results. Even though the results of such aspects are always negative, the nature of the problems that are caused vary, depending on the planet throwing the aspect. Let me explain.

If Mercury throws its fallen aspect (Mercury aspecting Pisces) onto the Moon, then the Moon is going to act a little crazy, a little mentally unbalanced because Mercury rules the mental process. And if Mercury throws its fallen aspect onto the Sun, the Sun is also going to act a little mentally unbalanced or a little crazy because it's receiving the fallen aspect of a mental planet.

But if Saturn is aspecting the Moon in Aries (Saturn's fallen sign), the Moon is going to be harmed in a radically different way. Saturn will damage the Moon in a Saturnian way. The person will have karmic emotional problems (Saturn rules karmic effects) or intense emotional suffering. The person's emotional confidence will be hurt, and the person will feel almost no sense of worthiness or deservedness at all. Do you see what I mean?

Martin: I think so. Saturn is a planet of restriction, so when it throws its aspect it causes restriction and limitation.

James: Yes. And if Jupiter throws its aspect onto a planet in Capricorn (Jupiter's fallen sign), that planet will be damaged because of problems that have their basis in bad philosophy, lack of faith, or religious misunderstandings. For example, a person who has Venus aspected by Jupiter in Capricorn (either Venus conjunct fallen Jupiter or Venus in Capricorn, opposite Jupiter) will likely have love problems (Venus) with jealousy because jealousy is a problem involving problems with faith.

Martin: Which is Jupiter's signification.

James: Yes. And the fallen Jupiter aspect is creating Jupitarian problems. Another dilemma that Jupiter's fallen aspect thrown onto Venus could create is a misguided philosophy about love.

Martin: Like what?

James: It could be anything. The person's religion or philosophy may dictate that all women should wear pink clothes, stay home, and have kids. Or that one gender is superior to the other.

Martin: Aristotle said that women don't have souls. Maybe his Venus received a fallen Jupiter aspect.

James: Actually, his sounds more like a fallen Jupiter aspect onto the Moon. The Moon rules women in general, whereas Venus rules your love partner. But, obviously you're getting the point. Fallen Jupiter energy creates religious and philosophical errors. Fallen Mercury energy creates mental imbalance.

But these are not simply features to be memorized. They are features to be reasoned and understood. I'm going to keep mentioning the fundamental reasoning process of *Jyotish*, because that is what you have to become comfortable with or you'll never make the jump from hobbyist to professional. Yes, you can dazzle a client who has Venus in Capricorn tightly aspected by Jupiter by predicting the kinds of problems I've just described. You can do the same with everything I've just said about Mercury's aspect onto the Moon or the 7th house ruler. But what happens when you see a planet receiving Venus' fallen vibrations?

Martin: I'd be lost. What would you say about that aspect, James?

James: First, I would tell you to think and reason out how Venus' fallen energy might affect a planet receiving negative or misguided Venusian energy.

Martin: Well, I see fallen Venus as causing a person to be promiscuous or unstable in love matters.

James: Yes, but we're trying to determine how that fallen or misguided Venusian energy would affect a planet that it throws an aspect onto. I would say that what makes a person promiscuous (when indicated by fallen Venus energy) is an underlying or fundamental self-indulgence or narcissism.

Martin: So a planet receiving Venus' fallen vibrations might function in a self-indulgent or narcissistic way.

James: Yes. And a planet receiving the Sun's fallen energy, aside from being badly burned, would lose any sense of confidence or dignity. A planet receiving the Moon's fallen energy might act irrationally or in an unstable, emotionally wavering manner.

Martin: What about a planet receiving Mars' fallen energy?

James: That planet would probably behave in a "whacked out" way. Anyway, these are subtleties of *Jyotish*. When you first begin practicing, all you know is that a planet tightly conjunct with a fallen planet, or a planet receiving another planet's fallen vibrations, is seriously damaged. And in a way, that is fine. Your clients will be impressed that you know which areas of life are strong and which are weak. But as you continue, as you analyze hundreds and hundreds of charts and you study the results of each person's life with a detective's thoroughness, you begin to grasp the finer points.

Martin: That sounds exciting.

James: It is. And the learning never stops, which is both wonderful and frustrating.

Martin: James, what about fallen Rahu and fallen Ketu? You didn't mention them.

James: I don't know of any fallen placements for the nodes.

Martin: What about Pisces and Sagittarius? Those are the signs opposite Virgo and Gemini, which you consider the best placements for Rahu and

Ketu.

James: They are fine in theory. But in practice, Rahu and Ketu work quite well in Jupiter's signs.

Martin: What about Ketu in Scorpio? Do the astrologers who believe what Parasara said about Rahu's exaltation in Taurus also believe that Ketu is fallen in Scorpio?

James: Believe me, I have seen Rahu in Taurus and Ketu in Scorpio hundreds of times, and I have never seen those placements produce anything out of the ordinary.

Martin: Either positive or negative?

James: That's right. Rahu's exaltation in Taurus strikes me pretty much the same as *vargottama*, a completely useless distinction. I have analyzed so many charts with these placements and asked the clients about the results, and have found nothing of worth. (*Vargottama* is discussed in detail in Class Eight).

Now, after everything I have said about planets receiving fallen aspects, I have some very bad news. When malefic planets throw aspects onto their fallen signs, the effects are consistently awful. When benefics throw their aspects onto their fallen signs, there is, in my experience, sometimes a wild card effect. In other words, I have seen lots of cases where a planet receiving a fallen Jupiter aspect functions very well and lots of cases where it functions very poorly. I have seen the same thing happen with planets receiving a fallen Venus aspect. (Some examples: Moon in Virgo conjunct fallen Venus in Virgo, Mercury in Capricorn conjunct fallen Jupiter in Capricorn, Venus in Capricorn receiving an aspect from Jupiter in Cancer, and so on.)

Martin: Why does this happen?

James: Because Jupiter and Venus as natural benefics may throw beneficial energy.

Martin: Even when they are aspecting their fallen sign?

James: I told you this was bad news. Theoretically, planets receiving these fallen aspects from benefics should be quite harmed. In my experience, however, sometimes they are dramatically hurt and sometimes they are dramatically benefitted.

Martin: No wonder you said this was bad news, James. How am I supposed to know what's going to happen to a planet receiving a fallen aspect from a benefic?

James: What I do is simply consider the aspect a wild card. I make very little commitment about the planet receiving the fallen aspect until I can ask the person how that planet has functioned natally and in its periods and subperiods. Usually, the person will say that the planet has given excellent results or terrible results.

I'm not happy about wild card effects either. But my experience is my experience. The logical conclusion of many astrologers is that the fallen aspect sometimes creates good energy instead of bad because the planet involved happens to rule good houses, or because it is aspecting a friend. But let me tell you straight out that these explanations haven't worked one bit for me. Maybe there's an explanation that some other astrologer has discovered, but I'm telling you how it is for me.

Martin: Which is all you can do.

James: Well, I could go on and on about astrological theory, but what good would that do? I know many astrologers would make a big deal about the friendship or enemy scheme (graph on page 416) regarding the two planets involved in the aspect. But, I've already told you that friendships and enemies are massively overrated. In my experience with thousands and thousands of horoscopes, friendships between planets are significant mainly in terms of whether one planet is welcomed in another planet's house.

Martin: You haven't found the conjunctions and aspects between friends and enemies to be terribly significant?

James: No, I have not. It sounds great in theory, but it doesn't work in practice.

Martin: But other astrologers make such a big deal about friendships, James.

James: Once again, please think of the planets as living beings. If you think of them this way, you'll find that the natural makeup of the planet takes precedence over everything else. If a planet is a benefic by nature, or a malefic by nature, that is the most significant factor. That is the bottom line.

Martin: But there are subtleties and mitigating influences, right?

James: Yes, of course. That is what is so demanding in this field, trying to weigh and judge each and every positive and negative feature, and then coming to a conclusion. But if you take nothing else from all of my classes, I would prefer that you remember this one point: The natures of the planets come first, the natures of the planets come first, the natures of the planets come first!

Bearing in mind that the planets are deities, living beings, let me give you an example that may help. Who is the nicest, sweetest person you know?

Martin: My mom.

James: Okay. Does your mom know people she doesn't like?

Martin: Of course.

James: Does she intentionally hurt these people? Does she go out of her way to insult them when she's in a room with them?

Martin: Inconceivable. She just ignores them.

James: She's too nice to hurt them. Her basic nature is nice and sweet. If she can't say or do something nice and sweet, she doesn't say or do anything.

Martin: Exactly.

James: That's the same way Venus, Moon, Jupiter, and to a large extent, Mercury behave!

Martin: Mercury is different?

James: Mercury is definitely benefic, but it's not <u>quite</u> as beneficial as the other benefics.

Now, does your mother invite enemies into her house for tea and crackers?

Martin: No. She's not hypocritical or two-faced.

James: Well, it's the same with planets. Planets don't invite enemy planets into their houses.

Now take the malefics — say Mars and Saturn. Essentially, they act like insensitive bullies. They hurt everyone they associate with, even their friends, because their basic nature is mean and rude and insensitive.

Martin: You're saying that bullies hurt their friends?

James: Of course they do. They may not hurt their friends intentionally, but they lead friends into all kinds of trouble. Hang out with a bad crowd and watch how you develop bad habits and spoil parts of your life.

Martin: If benefic planets are so good natured, then how can they hurt other planets when they are fallen?

James: The same way that sweet and nice people do harm when they are in a weakened or damaged state. My father was one of the nicest, sweetest, most compassionate people you could ever meet. But if a person upset him — I mean really hurt him — he'd start to drink. Guess what would happen then?

Martin: He'd blow?

James: That's right, he'd explode. And then the person who hurt him would get hurt back. Nice people hurt others when they are in a weakened state. It happens all the time.

Martin: This concept of the planets as deities or living beings sounds really important.

James: It is. I can't imagine becoming masterful at *Jyotish* without embracing that concept. And I certainly can't imagine practicing *Jyotish* without recommending mantras and *yagyas* regularly (discussed in Class Nine).

Martin: Because they are prayers to the planets?

James: That's right. The fact that the planets are deities, living beings, Lords of Karma, or whatever you want to call them is what makes *Jyotish* a living, breathing art. The planetary beings exist to influence our lives, to help us learn our lessons by giving us back our karma, so we can perfect ourselves. And to help us in any way they can when we properly appeal to them for grace. Astrology is not merely a train schedule, and the universe is not a machine. This becomes obvious when you use *Jyotish* fully, and the *upayes*; the ameliorating techniques of gemstones, mantras, and *yagyas* are the way to use *Jyotish* fully.

Martin: This is interesting, James, because it shows how the Lords of Karma are involved in both fate and free will, or can be used for both fate and free will.

James: That's exactly right. And we'll spend time on *upayes* later. But now, let's look at your Moon *dasa* that starts in 2002 (see following page).

The condition of the Moon in your chart is a mixture of extremes, as we've just seen. Therefore, it's functioning like a wild card. So, if your Moon *bhuktis* were very good, your Moon *dasa* will <u>very likely</u> also be good. If your Moon *bhuktis* were bad, I would expect the same in the *dasa*. And if the effects were mixed, I would also expect the same. You follow?

Martin: My Moon *dasa* will probably be pretty mixed, James, if it's similar to my last Moon *bhukti*. The one within Venus *dasa*. That was from March, 1981 until November, 1982.

James: What was that like?

Martin: Well, I traveled all over the United States. Is that because the Moon occupies the 9th house?

James: Yes.

Martin: So, the 9th house rules travel within the United States as well as to foreign countries?

James: Yes. The 9th house governs long distance travel, which certainly means travel outside of your state.

Martin: I also lived in great abundance part of that time, because I was taking care of my grandfather, who was living in a beautiful house on the water, with all kinds of luxuries.

James: This is really interesting, because grandparents are ruled by the

9th house. What I really want to know is — what was your confidence level? The Moon rules the 1st house, which is your confidence, general well-being, ability to be recognized, and so on. How were those areas affected?

MARTIN'S DASAS

DASAS & BHUKTIS – Lahiri Zodiac		
☿ / ♀ Sep 21 1956 0.0	♀ / ☊ Jan 2 1984 27.3	☽ / ☋ Feb 1 2010 53.4
☿ / ☉ Jan 27 1959 2.3	♀ / ♃ Jan 2 1987 30.3	☽ / ♀ Sep 2 2010 53.9
☿ / ☽ Dec 3 1959 3.2	♀ / ♄ Sep 2 1989 32.9	☽ / ☉ May 3 2012 55.6
☿ / ♂ May 3 1961 4.6	♀ / ☿ Nov 2 1992 36.1	♂ Nov 1 2012 56.1
☿ / ☊ May 1 1962 5.6	♀ / ☋ Sep 2 1995 38.9	♂ / ☊ Mar 31 2013 56.5
☿ / ♃ Nov 17 1964 8.2	☉ Nov 1 1996 40.1	♂ / ♃ Apr 18 2014 57.6
☿ / ♄ Feb 23 1967 10.4	☉ / ☽ Feb 19 1997 40.4	♂ / ♄ Mar 25 2015 58.5
☋ Nov 2 1969 13.1	☉ / ♂ Aug 21 1997 40.9	♂ / ☿ May 3 2016 59.6
☋ / ♀ Mar 31 1970 13.5	☉ / ☊ Dec 27 1997 41.3	♂ / ☋ Apr 30 2017 60.6
☋ / ☉ May 31 1971 14.7	☉ / ♃ Nov 20 1998 42.2	♂ / ♀ Sep 26 2017 61.0
☋ / ☽ Oct 6 1971 15.0	☉ / ♄ Sep 8 1999 43.0	♂ / ☉ Nov 26 2018 62.2
☋ / ♂ May 6 1972 15.6	☉ / ☿ Aug 20 2000 43.9	♂ / ☽ Apr 3 2019 62.5
☋ / ☊ Oct 2 1972 16.0	☉ / ☋ Jun 27 2001 44.8	☊ Nov 2 2019 63.1
☋ / ♃ Oct 21 1973 17.1	☉ / ♀ Nov 2 2001 45.1	☊ / ♃ Jul 15 2022 65.8
☋ / ♄ Sep 27 1974 18.0	☽ Nov 2 2002 46.1	☊ / ♄ Dec 8 2024 68.2
☋ / ☿ Nov 5 1975 19.1	☽ / ♂ Sep 2 2003 46.9	☊ / ☿ Oct 15 2027 71.1
♀ Nov 2 1976 20.1	☽ / ☊ Apr 2 2004 47.5	☊ / ☋ May 3 2030 73.6
♀ / ☉ Mar 3 1980 23.4	☽ / ♃ Oct 2 2005 49.0	☊ / ♀ May 22 2031 74.7
♀ / ☽ Mar 3 1981 24.4	☽ / ♄ Feb 1 2007 50.4	☊ / ☉ May 21 2034 77.7
♀ / ♂ Nov 2 1982 26.1	☽ / ☿ Sep 2 2008 51.9	☊ / ☽ Apr 15 2035 78.6

PLANET SYMBOLS
Pt	Name
☽	Moon
☉	Sun
☿	Mercury
♀	Venus
♂	Mars
♃	Jupiter
♄	Saturn
☊	North Node
☋	South Node
As	Ascendant

Martin: Very badly. I felt isolated taking care of my grandfather. Also, I was trying to heal my lifelong health problems through diet and I lost too much weight. That caused my peace of mind to be weakened.

James: How so?

Martin: I had a lot of anxiety and confusion.

James: So, can you see how that would be due to Mercury throwing its harmful aspect onto the Moon in Pisces, Mercury's fallen sign?

Martin: Yes. It was a very mixed period. There was a lot of good stuff that happened, but also a lot of pain.

James: So, you can see how these wild card influences work. Extreme good and extreme bad. We'll analyze mixed influences more as our classes progress.

In our next class, we're going to talk about retrograde planets. The next Mercury retrograde begins December 23rd, and I want you to watch the effects of it. Mercury retrogrades are always felt about eight or ten days before Mercury actually goes backwards (approximately eight or ten days before Mercury goes backwards and ten or twelve days after Mercury turns direct is known as the "shadow" of the retrograde), so you'll have plenty of time to observe.

Martin: The effects are felt before Mercury turns backwards?

James: Yes. As Mercury slows down and gets ready to go retrograde, it starts causing machinery breakdowns, scheduling problems, computer glitches, communication difficulties, and so on. Anything that's not in good working order starts to break. Also, in the next few weeks, watch how people start dealing with unfinished projects, old papers piled on desks, and things they have been putting off for months. And notice how people who have chronic health problems or physical weaknesses start having recurrences of their illnesses or disorders. Mercury retrograde periods are horrible for people with serious health problems.

As an astrologer remember to check your calculations <u>at least twice</u> during any Mercury retrograde.

Martin: Because it's easy to make mistakes?

James: Yes. And be diligent with clients who call to make appointments. Ask them where they got their birth data from, and if you have <u>any</u> doubt that their birth data is accurate, make them check it again. Otherwise, you may end up doing the chart twice. Also, always trust your intuition when your making appointments with clients. If, for no clear reason, you simply have a <u>feeling</u> that the person has wrong birth data, trust yourself. Tell the person to do a little research with parents or the Bureau of Vital Statistics, or whatever. Also, if someone is going to call the bureau of Vital Statistics, tell them to ask for a "vault copy." Sometimes the vault copy has a birthtime on it, while other copies may not.

Before we meet next week, I want you to watch how the days of the week are affected by the planets ruling them. I think you know the rulerships: Sunday is ruled by the Sun, Monday by the Moon, Tuesday by Mars, Wednesday by Mercury, Thursday by Jupiter, Friday by Venus, and Saturday by Saturn. See if you notice that on Wednesday (Mercury's day) you have more of a tendency to communicate or write or work on the computer. See if you notice people fighting more on Tuesday (Mars' day), and so on. Tell me your findings when we meet next week. Okay?

Martin: Yes. But I have one more question before we end. You talked earlier about the North Node of the Western horoscope relating to a person's purpose and destiny. Would you tell me a bit about mine?

James: Sure. In my chart readings, I speak mainly about the Hindu chart, but I always look at the person's Western chart for several reasons. One of those reasons is that in my opinion the most important feature in **all** of astrology, Western or Hindu, is the Western horoscope North Node placement.

Martin: Why is it so important?

James: Because it tells me what the person has come to Earth to learn. It doesn't tell me what a person will <u>do</u>, but it tells me what the person <u>should</u> do for happiness, evolution, and fulfillment. What could be more important?

Martin: Do I also look at Rahu (Hindu name of North Node) in the *Jyotish* chart for purpose and destiny?

James: No, absolutely not. Rahu in the Hindu chart essentially represents "insatiable worldly cravings and desires." Ketu signifies the opposite; it represents everything "otherworldly, metaphysical, spiritual, weird, strange, and astral." Within *Jyotish*, I would leave it at that.

I've given extensive explanations of Western Nodal positions in my book, *How To Be A Great Astrologer*. But, to answer your question, the North Node in your Western chart falls in the 5th house and the sign of Sagittarius. (Note: Because Western astrology uses a tropical, rather than sidereal, zodiac, Martin's Rahu and Ketu do not occupy the same signs as in his Hindu chart) Because the North and South Nodes are always <u>exactly</u> opposite each other, your North Node in the 5th house and Sagittarius means your South Node is in the 11th house in Gemini. The South Node position represents past-life activities that no longer hold any significant growth or fulfillment. So your South Node in Gemini means that in past lives you learned how to use your mind extensively, you've gained skill and proficiency in analytical, rational matters, and you've developed your powers of discrimination. Continuing these activities in this life will generally be a waste of time.

Martin: So, I should follow the indications of the North Node in Sagittarius?

James: Yes. This means cultivating as much faith as possible. Not just faith in religion, God, and spiritual matters, but maintaining faith all the time, faith as a general principle.

As for the South Node in your 11th house, it signifies that in past lives you learned how to be with friends and groups, and your activities were focused on the community at large. The new territory to follow, as indicated by the North Node in the 5th house, is to develop your own creativity, to focus on the creative or artistic side of life so that you can get in touch with the uniqueness of your individual spirit. Try to express that which makes you special and different from others.

Martin: I guess I do that as an artist.

James: Yes, you do. And you're lucky, because the realms you are supposed to go towards — creative endeavors and self expression — are very well-disposed in the Hindu chart. You are an extraordinarily gifted artist (painter) because Venus (planet of art) occupies your 1st house, and because the ruler of the 5th house, Mars, is aspected <u>tightly</u> by benefic Jupiter. Of course it doesn't hurt that your exalted Mercury, which has a lot to do with drawing, is aspected by a <u>full Moon</u> and is exalted in the 3rd house, the house of art (music, dance, and drama) and the house of the hands.

Martin: You're saying that my strong 3rd house gives me the ability to use my hands very well?

James: Absolutely. Not only is the 3rd house strong, but so is Mars — the *karaka*, or natural indicator, of the 3rd house. Mars is incredibly well-disposed because of the tight aspect it receives from Jupiter. Okay? Have I answered your questions?

Martin: Yes. But I also wanted to make a request for next week's class. The biggest trouble I'm having with *Jyotish* is that there are so many factors that make a planet strong and powerful or weak and afflicted. How do I prioritize? How do I know which feature is more significant than another feature?

James: Wow. You've just asked an extremely difficult question. The ability to prioritize is something that takes years of experience. It's a sense that you develop over time, and I'm not certain it's something that can be taught. Why don't you let me think about it?

Martin: Can you give me some kind of "pecking order," or a list of priorities? Otherwise, I'm lost when I try to analyze a horoscope.

James: Let me think about that. I'll see what I can come up with for next week. See you then.

Martin: Bas.

CLASS THREE

James: Today I'm going to do my best to answer your question about how to evaluate which horoscope features are more important than others. We'll examine a list of astrological priorities I've devised for planets, houses, and the chart as a whole.

Martin: Good. That's a big problem for me James — trying to figure out what influences take precedence.

James: It's a difficult subject, and not very easily answered. So be patient and don't hold my feet to the fire on this, okay?

Now, before we get to the priorities, I want to talk about an important subject that is often misunderstood — retrograde planets. First, we'll discuss the three week period of Mercury retrograde that occurs twice a year, and is happening right now. Then we'll discuss the meaning of retrograde planets in the natal horoscope.

Finally, I'm going to talk about what are called "orbs of influence." The orb of influence is the amount of degrees involved in a planetary aspect. There is a big difference between Saturn aspecting the Moon within twenty-two degrees versus Saturn aspecting the Moon within three or four degrees.

Martin: That makes sense.

James: Last week, I asked you to notice the planetary effects relating to each day of the week. Did you do that?

Martin: Yes. I noticed on Tuesday (Mars' day) that the students in my art class were irritable and grouchy.

James: That reminds me of an astrology class that I taught on Tuesdays. It felt very stressful. There was always some sort of friction going on. The easiest and smoothest day to teach, in my opinion, is Thursday, the day of Jupiter. Wednesday seems like a good teaching day, because it's ruled by Mercury. But I find that my nerves are too sensitive on Wednesdays. Also, people can also be a bit scattered on Mercury's day.

Martin: Well, I noticed that last Wednesday there were a lot of computer breakdowns and communication problems at school.

James: That's because on Wednesdays, Mercurial energies are intensified and we are now in a Mercury retrograde period.

Martin: So, that's a double whammy, no? On Thursday I stayed home and read astrology all day so I didn't notice much.

James: Perfect. Thursday is Jupiter's day. You didn't stay home reading science or math. You read a spiritual subject. Thursdays are great for "higher knowledge."

Martin: Friday I went to a Christmas party. People's spirits were pretty high.

James: Yes, well Friday is Venus' day. Good for dating and lovemaking.

Martin: So, is it important to use these daily influences?

James: I think it's a good idea to be aware of daily rulerships. I don't make too a big deal about them, but I definitely take them into account when people are in difficult *dasas* or *bhuktis*.

Martin: How?

James: If someone is in a rough period or subperiod of Venus, that person will most likely have very stressful Fridays. A person in a seriously afflicted Jupiter period, will have difficult Thursdays.

Martin: What should the person do?

James: During an afflicted Jupiter period, take Thursdays off. During an afflicted Moon period, take Mondays off. Keep the planetary day as a day of rest. Also, try to pray, meditate, chant mantras, fast, or take walks in the country. Anything that will relieve the strain, and anything that may appease the planet involved will help.

Martin: What if it's impossible to take the day off?

James: Just be aware that the day may be more stressful and try to do the bare minimum of hard work. When the workday is over, go straight home and jump in a hot bath or do whatever relaxes you. Indians often fast or drink juices on a day they are trying to ameliorate. At the least, they avoid alcohol or meat eating on that day.

Martin: What about Saturdays? When I was observing the days of the week in relation to their planetary rulers, I noticed that Saturday didn't feel Saturnian at all. Saturday felt great.

James: That's an interesting point and I think you're right. Saturdays don't feel very Saturnian to me either. My best guess is that both Saturday and Sunday are affected by cultural influences. Because our entire society stops working on weekends, both Saturday or Sunday seem to feel more easy and restful. But I can't say for sure. Cultural effects, of course, fit into the realm of free will.

Now, have you noticed any effects of the Mercury retrograde?

Martin: Absolutely. A friend told me that right after fixing the starter in her truck, she returned home and quickly blew a head gasket, which is now going to cost her over $1,000.

James: I had a typical Mercury retrograde experience the other day. A client called for her reading and I was late, so I told her I would call her back in about five minutes. After five minutes I called back, but her line was busy for the next thirty minutes. My blood was starting to boil. What could the lady have been thinking to talk on her phone for thirty minutes knowing full well I would be calling back so soon? Well, when I finally got her on the phone and asked her what happened, she said, "What do you mean what happened? I've been sitting next to the phone waiting patiently for your call." The phone lines were just messed up, typical Mercury retrograde.

Martin: That's funny. A couple days ago, I tried calling a friend and for some reason the phone lines wouldn't connect. I had to call her number about five or six times before the phone rang. Then when I finally reached her and was telling her to have her phone line checked out, the phone died.

James: If I ever wanted to try and prove that astrology works, I would quantify the effects of Mercury retrograde. They are so reliable.

The most important thing to advise clients about Mercury retrogrades is not to make <u>major</u> decisions or <u>major</u> purchases in the ten days preceding and during the retrograde. I would also wait until the Mercury retrograde is over for at least a week before making important decisions and signing contracts, and so on. Also, never, never, never let a person schedule surgery right before, or on, a Mercury retrograde if there's a choice. Aside from the fact that a mistake could be made, the healing process is horrendous. Mercury retrogrades dramatically slow down the body's ability to heal. It's very frustrating.

A friend of mine needed heart surgery a few years back, and he had to decide whether to have surgery just days before the Mercury retrograde or to wait over three weeks until it passed. If he waited, he was in danger of dying. If he went ahead with the surgery, he was going to heal very slowly.

Martin: What did he do?

James: He went ahead with the surgery. The healing process was torturous. He kept asking his doctor why he was so weak for so long. So advise your clients not to have surgery before a Mercury retrograde, if they can help it.

Now I'll tell you a story that will illustrate why you shouldn't make a major decision on a retrograde. My brother bought a house during the last retrograde, and when I asked him why he couldn't wait, he said he was sure the house was great and the price was great, and so on. I advised against it, but he was sure he found the right house.

Martin: What happened?

James: A few weeks later, after he had moved in, he discovered that he didn't like the floor plan at all. The reason he didn't realize it sooner was that on the day he decided to buy it he had just visited three or four houses that were so terrible it made the house he bought look like a mansion. Typical Mercury retrograde!

Now, let's go into detail about retrograde planets in the natal chart. My understanding and experience of retrogrades, as well as my mentors' teachings, differs radically from the teachings of traditional textbooks on this matter. This is an issue that you better pay very close attention to, otherwise you will wind up like the majority of astrologers — correct in Hindu astrological <u>theory</u> of retrogrades, but sorely lacking in predictive accuracy of them. In *Jyotish,* there is an intricate planetary weighting system called *Shad bala*, literally "six fold source of strength," which reveals the relative strength of every planet. *Shad bala* takes several hours of calculations, although a computer now does the process in a split second. In that system, a planet gets extra points (in its power weighting) for being retrograde. However, if you apply that concept literally in your horoscope analysis, you will miss the true meaning of retrogrades.

Martin: So, retrograde planets are not stronger than forward-moving planets, even though they are considered stronger in *shad bala*?

James: That's right. But I have to qualify my answer. A retrograde planet has <u>a certain kind of extra strength</u> because when a planet is retrograde, it is closer to the Earth. This causes the energy or vibrations of the retrograde planet to be <u>an underlying prevalent force</u> in the person's awareness and thinking process throughout his or her entire life. The statement that a retrograde planet is more powerful is misleading, however, if you expect that planet to readily and powerfully manifest its results in the outer world.

Martin: Then how does this underlying force of a retrograde planet affect a person?

James: Well, a person with a retrograde Venus, for example, spends his or her life constantly analyzing, processing, and thinking about love matters. A person with a retrograde Jupiter is continually approaching matters from a philosophical and ideological context.

Martin: So, the planet is more powerful on an internal level?

James: Yes. The energy of the retrograde planet is an intense force within the person's consciousness and internal processes. It creates a distinct psychological reality in the person.

On the outer level, the manifest level, a retrograde planet is never strong and active. It is neutral or passive. Of course, the planet has the potential to produce powerful effects if — and this is one large "if" — the person consciously decides to activate the energy of the planet. I'll give you some examples. And later on, you can test what I am teaching now. But don't do a test with only two or three charts. Use fifteen or so.

Let's say a person has an unafflicted benefic, like Venus or Jupiter, in the 5th house. You're thinking, "Wow, this person is going to have wonderful children." If the ruler of the 5th house is retrograde, however, having children is not a foregone conclusion. It's not that the retrograde 5th house ruler has prevented children or harmed the childbearing process, but that the 5th house energy is latent. The 5th house energy must be consciously activated.

Martin: So, the person can have children, but doesn't have to?

James: Exactly. The person has choice.

Martin: Whereas, if the person had a forward-moving 5th house ruler along with one or two benefics in the 5th house, he or she would definitely have a child?

James: Yes. Assuming, of course, that the 5th house ruler wasn't massively afflicted. And assuming that Jupiter, the *karaka* (indicator) of children wasn't massively afflicted.

As another example, take the placement of a retrograde 7th house ruler in a chart where the 7th house is otherwise well-disposed. First off, the person may not feel any need to get married. Second, a person with this placement who has been married and divorced once often feels no desire at all to marry again.

Martin: Would you predict that the person will not marry a second time?

James: No. Again, it's the person's choice. The person simply doesn't feel as compelled to enter a long term committed relationship if the ruler of the 7th house is retrograde.

I believe that a retrograde planet, more than any other feature, is nature's way of leaving a certain realm of life completely up to a person's free will.

Martin: More so than a realm that has mixed astrological indications?

James: Absolutely. In fact, it's through retrogrades that I'm able to determine whether a particular feature of life that is strong in the horoscope is more likely to be a hobby or a profession.

For example, take a horoscope that contains a powerful 3rd house, where two or three planets (mostly benefics) occupy the house, and perhaps one of those planets is in its own sign. In that case, the person will likely be involved in music, dance, or drama, or some action-oriented career like public relations.

Martin: Regardless of 10th house indications?

James: Yes, because the 3rd house is clearly dominating the chart. But, if the ruler of the 3rd house is retrograde, the 3rd house energy may manifest as a hobby during the person's first thirty years. After the age of thirty or so, the person has matured and starts using some free will rather than following every impulse and desire. Then the person consciously decides whether to make use of the artistic talent that was always apparent, but never acted upon due to the retrograde 3rd house ruler. You'll see how this works when we start analyzing horoscopes.

Martin: Can you give me examples of a retrograde planets ruling all twelve houses?

James: Yes, but this isn't something for you to memorize as much as it is a reasoning process that you consider on your own as you think about the meanings of all the houses.

If the 1st house ruler is retrograde, the person's outgoing tendencies are curtailed. The person is introspective or introverted, and has a harder time gaining recognition or fame. I actually consider a retrograde ruler of either the 1st or 10th house to be harmful, because the person is slower in actualizing his or her abilities and worldly power.

If the 2nd house ruler is retrograde, money comes in slower. If the person has literary or teaching talent, he or she probably won't want to write or teach until a later age.

Martin: After the late twenties?

James: Right. If the 3rd house ruler is retrograde, the person won't be overly ambitious. Desires will be less. There is less chance of having younger siblings, and less chance of pursuing music, dance, or drama.

Martin: But those could be hobbies in the early years?

James: Yes, but that's only if the chart indicates some propensity for the arts. If the 4th house ruler is retrograde, there is less chance of owning land or dabbling in real estate. Also, the person might have less desire to gain higher educational degrees.

Martin: Does that mean the person has problems gaining degrees?

James: Not at all. Remember that the retrograde status doesn't mean a planet is afflicted. It just indicates a latent or passive energy. If you start thinking of retrograde planets as afflicted, you're going to make an awful lot of mistakes in your practice.

If the 5th house ruler is retrograde, the person will not feel compelled to have children. Sports, politics, spiritual techniques, and other 5th house matters would probably remain hobbies until after the age of thirty. One thing I don't like about the 5th house ruler being retrograde is that it generally weakens the *poorvapunya* (past life credit) connected to that planet. In other words, if the ruler of the 5th house occupies the 10th house without affliction, it means there is past life credit connected to career. But if that 5th house ruler is retrograde, the *poorvapunya* factor is weakened or even nonexistent.

I don't see a 6th house ruler that is retrograde having a terribly significant effect. The only thing that might be held back for a time would be a healing or medical profession. I don't know that enemies or law suits are affected at all by the 6th house ruler being retrograde.

Other than what I've already said about the 7th house ruler being retrograde, the only thing I can think to add is that it could impede becoming a merchant or business person until the late twenties or early thirties.

If the 8th house ruler is retrograde, it could slow down the ability to get money from wills, legacies, insurance companies, and one's spouse.

Martin: Would it slow a person down from becoming an astrologer?

James: It could. Before the late twenties, the person might consider astrology or psychic practice as merely a hobby. My 8th house ruler is retrograde, and I knew nothing about astrology until my late twenties.

A retrograde 9th house ruler could lessen a person's desire for travel. The person might also consider religion and philosophy a hobby rather than a profession.

If the 10th house ruler is retrograde, the person is slower to <u>choose</u> a career and slower to <u>actualize</u> a career. This is one of my least favorite retrograde placements.

If the 11th house ruler is retrograde, there is less likelihood of having an older sibling. Friends and groups are not a high priority, and it may take a longer than usual for the person to realize his or her major goals and ambitions.

Like the placement of a 6th house ruler being retrograde, I can't think of any significant effect of a retrograde 12th house ruler. Maybe the person has less sexual desire and less desire to visit remote foreign countries.

Martin: What about less desire to pursue enlightenment?

James: Maybe. I'm not positive. At any rate, I trust that you get the concept that retrograde planets don't cause harm and they aren't afflicted. But they do slow things down and make for an introverted, rather than extroverted, energy.

Martin: What about retrograde planets in houses, James? I have trouble understanding how they work.

James: Let's talk about them. Since a retrograde planet functions in a more <u>latent or introspective</u> way, it can either help or hurt the house it occupies depending on its essential benefic or malefic nature. If a planet is benefic by nature, it almost always strengthens or benefits the house it occupies, correct?

Martin: Correct.

James: And if a planet is retrograde, it is a more latent, or introspective, influence. In other words, it is less action-oriented. So, what would you prefer to have in your chart, retrograde Jupiter or Venus in the 10th house, or forward-moving Jupiter or Venus in the 10th house?

Martin: Forward-moving.

James: Of course. Career luck is going to be wonderful with either Venus or Jupiter in the 10th house, but if Jupiter or Venus are retrograde they're not going to give their full effects to the career. Follow?

Martin: Yes.

James: These are already <u>good</u> placements, don't get me wrong. But they would be even <u>better</u> if they were in forward motion.

Martin: But, if retrograde Venus is in the 10th house, do you still predict that the person may have an artistic career?

James: Absolutely. The person has powerful Venusian energy in the career house, even though Venus would be stronger or more <u>active</u> if it were forward-moving. If Mercury is retrograde in the 10th house, I would expect the person to have a Mercurial career (writing, teaching, lecturing, and so on). So, even though a retrograde planet is more intense on a psychological or internal level, you can't ignore the fact that whatever house it occupies will be affected by its energy, its vibrations.

Martin: Then it's only the houses that the retrograde planet <u>rules</u> that are held back in the person's early years? Those are the realms that may become hobbies instead of professions?

James: Yes, only the houses that are ruled by a retrograde planet are extremely dependent on the person's desire, the person's free will.

Now let's consider a malefic planet that is retrograde in a house. If Mars or Saturn occupying the 4th house causes serious suffering to the mother, and retrograde planets are more latent and introspective, and less action-oriented, would you rather have these malefics in the 4th house retrograde or forward-moving?

Martin: Retrograde.

James: Of course. Will retrograde Mars or Saturn in the 4th house cause problems to the person's mother? You bet your life they will. But they will not be nearly as severe as they would if the planet was forward-moving.

Martin: So, what do tell a person with retrograde Saturn in, say, the 7th house?

James: I tell that person everything I would tell someone with forward-moving Saturn in the 7th, but I would lessen the intensity of my words because the person's love problems would not be as great. I tell the person he or she is paying back love debts from past lives and will have difficulties in marriage, will likely be divorced, will have to give more than receive in love matters, and will feel restricted and oppressed in marriage. But I also say that the suffering will not as intense as it could be and that the karma being paid back may not last an entire lifetime. The person clearly has a chance of creating a good marriage, after paying back karmic love debts, assuming there are no other 7th house or Venus afflictions.

Martin: On a scale of one to ten, ten being worst, how would you rate forward-moving Saturn in the 7th and retrograde Saturn in the 7th in terms of negative effects?

James: I would rate forward-moving Saturn in the 7th house as a ten and retrograde Saturn in the 7th house as a seven. But remember — I'm talking about these influences in *isolation*. A person could have Saturn in the 7th house, aspected by benefic Jupiter or Venus. This would alter matters a lot.

Martin: The 7th house becomes a mixture of good and bad?

James: Yes. I would most likely still predict divorce, because malefics in the 7th house cause major problems, no matter how well-disposed. But, I would also predict a happy marriage, <u>eventually</u>.

Martin: In other words, the karmic love problems wouldn't last a whole lifetime. James, what about Mars in the 7th house? How would you rate those positions, in their retrograde and forward motion?

James: Mars in the 7th is definitely not a good placement for marriage, but it's less severe than Saturn in the 7th. Of course, either Mars or Saturn in the 7th indicate divorce, but the person with Mars in the marriage house doesn't suffer so bad and for so long. A person with Saturn in the 7th is treated very unfairly and disrespectfully, and because Saturn gives staying power, the person may take the abuse for years and years.

A person with Mars in the 7th typically fights and argues for a few years and then gets a divorce. But I'd certainly prefer to have a retrograde Mars in the 7th as opposed to forward-moving Mars. I'd rate the level of suffering about a seven for forward-moving Mars in the 7th, and a five or six for retrograde Mars. If the person has retrograde Mars in the 7th, there's a good chance of eventually having a decent marriage. And if that retrograde Mars is well-aspected by some benefic, other than Moon or Venus, the person will almost certainly have a happy marriage, eventually.

Martin: Why are Moon and Venus exceptions?

James: Because if Mars is aspected by the Moon, it means that Mars is opposite the Moon, and that's like having Mars in the 7th house.

Martin: *Chandra lagna* (discussed in Class One).

James: That's right. Moon ascendant.

Martin: And if Venus aspects Mars, then Venus gets harmed by the aspect that Mars throws onto it.

James: Right. And Venus is the planet of love. So we don't want that.

Martin: James, what about retrograde malefics in *upachaya* houses (3rd, 6th, 10th, and 11th), where malefics are welcomed?

James: Malefics in *upachaya* houses are excellent. This is probably a judgement call, but I would prefer a retrograde malefic to occupy the 3rd or 11th house rather than a forward-moving malefic.

Martin: Why?

James: Remember when I said that although malefics are welcomed in the *upachaya* houses, they cause some harm there as well?

Martin: You said malefics hurt siblings if they occupy the 3rd or the 11th (11th being the <u>eldest</u> sibling).

James: That's right. Well, if a malefic planet is <u>retrograde</u> in the 3rd or the 11th, then it's harmful nature is subdued and siblings are not hurt at all. Or, if there is damage to siblings, it is extremely slight. As for the 10th house, I would prefer a retrograde Saturn in the 10th house because so many people with forward-moving Saturn in the 10th use the Saturnian energy to simply hold themselves back.

Martin: That wouldn't happen with a retrograde Saturn in the 10th?

James: No. Retrograde planets are always a latent, less action-oriented influence. The vast majority of people have trouble with forward-moving Saturn no matter where it exists in the horoscope. Retrograde Saturn is a blessing for most people.

Martin: Except that it holds back the power of the two houses that it rules.

James: That's true. You can't have everything, can you?

Martin: What about retrograde malefics aspecting other planets and houses?

James: An aspect that a retrograde malefic throws onto another house causes the *exact same* damage as a forward-moving malefic that throws its aspect. As far as aspects that a retrograde planet throws onto other <u>planets</u>, it causes the same damage as a forward-moving planet, but there are certain exceptions, which are interesting. When you see a retrograde planet aspecting another planet, you need to look at whether the aspect is applying or separating because this will often have a big effect.

Martin: What do you mean?

James: Say that there is a conjunction involving retrograde Mars and forward-moving Venus, that occurs within a three degree orb. If Mars is retrograding <u>away</u> from Venus, then the aspect is "separating," and Venus is not as badly harmed as it would be if the two planets were moving toward one another. For example, if Mars occupies five degrees of Gemini and is moving backwards, Venus would be better off in eight degrees of Gemini (i.e. past Mars) rather than, say, two degrees of Sagittarius (i.e. moving toward Mars).

If Venus occupies two degrees of Gemini, while retrograde Mars occupies five degrees of Gemini, then Mars is backing up toward Venus and Venus is approaching Mars, and the aspect is "applying"' which is greatly intensified for good or bad.

Martin: How could it ever be good?

James: Well, in this Venus-Mars example, the aspect is bad for Venus but wonderful for Mars. Mars is strengthened tremendously by being close to benefic Venus. So, an applying aspect here gives Mars even greater benefit.

I see cases all the time where a planet that is aspected by a retrograde malefic is not nearly as harmed as expected because the aspect it receives is separating. The places where it happens are almost exclusively with conjunctions and oppositions. I've seen many cases where retrograde Mars or retrograde Saturn is opposite Venus, within about four or five degrees, and the person doesn't have the typical damaged love life that these aspects indicate. Whenever this happens, it's always because the aspect is separating, rather than applying.

Martin: But this doesn't happen when Mars is throwing its 4th or 8th house aspects, or when Saturn is throwing its 3rd and 10th house aspects? (For details on planetary aspects, see Appendix A.)

James: I haven't noticed it have such a big impact there, but I can tell you that when it comes to conjunctions and oppositions, the effects are quite noticeable. Let me give you an example of a separating opposition aspect. If Jupiter occupies ten degrees of Taurus, and <u>retrograde</u> Saturn occupies fourteen degrees of Scorpio, then Saturn is backing up *towards* Jupiter.

Martin: Then, it's applying.

James: Yes, and therefore the aspect hurts Jupiter intensely <u>and</u> strengthens Saturn intensely (because Saturn receives the strong aspect from benefic Jupiter). If, however, Jupiter occupies twenty degrees of Taurus, while retrograde Saturn occupies fifteen degrees of Scorpio, then the aspect is separating and you may be surprised at how ineffectual the aspect is. So, try to remember this issue when you analyze charts with retrograde planets.

Another point I want to make about retrograde planets is something I learned from my first astrology teacher. A retrograde planet generally represents an energy that a person may have misused in a past lifetime. I'm not talking about abusing the energy in a way that was harmful or devastating to other people, because if that happened the planet would likely show up this lifetime in an extremely weak or afflicted condition. I'm talking about using a planetary energy in an imbalanced way.

Martin: Imbalanced?

James: Imbalanced, exaggerated, ignored. The person somehow misused the planetary energy, and the result is that in the current life he or she is constantly compelled to focus on the significations of that planet in a serious, rather consuming way.

Martin: Which occurs naturally because retrograde planets are closer to the Earth than other planets.

James: Yes. And the process of how this all-consuming focus comes about is interesting. A retrograde planet signifies a *latent* influence, an influence that is almost completely overlooked or neglected in the beginning stage of life. Later on, it comes to the forefront and stays there until the person dies. I'll give you two examples.

If Venus is retrograde at birth, then the child is simply unaware of the concept of romantic love in the earliest years. The child soon learns about parents, siblings, intellectual matters, homes, money, and so on. After encountering many different areas of existence, the child suddenly finds out about romantic love and because it has taken so long to discover that realm, because Venusian matters are so latent, it is somewhat shocking for the child. The person then spends the rest of his or her life making up for the initial loss. Then <u>everything</u> in life, all experiences really, are seen through the context of how they relate to, or how they affect, romantic love.

If Jupiter is retrograde, the child learns the concepts of religion, philosophy, and morals last. Because these matters were originally missing, it's shocking when they are finally noticed and the person spends the rest of his or her life filtering everything though philosophical eyes. All experiences are related to the meaning of life, religion, ethics, and so on. I've never done statistical research on retrograde planets, but I can't tell you how common it is for spiritual seekers to have a retrograde Jupiter.

Martin: When does this happen to a child?

James: Very early. Maybe in the first two to four years. This is not so much a rational process as an organic or instinctive one. If it was rational, a person probably wouldn't decide to spend an entire life focusing psychologically so heavily on one realm.

Also, I believe it is significant when a person runs the *dasa* of a retrograde planet later in life, say after the age of thirty-five or forty. Then, the person has the maturity to focus on the energy of that planet which was imbalanced in past lives and finally learn to get it straight. And when you are analyzing a person's *dasas*, I think it's important to look at them as a whole. In other words, take notice of the order of the realms of life that are going to be in focus, particularly after the age of thirty.

Martin: Why thirty?

James: Well, that's the age when people generally become adults, because of the "Saturn return." The Saturn return, as far as I know, is a Western astrological concept. It takes Saturn between twenty-nine and thirty-one-and-a-half years to transit all twelve houses. Once those houses are transited, you've learned at least some degree of all the possible lessons in life. That's when people start using some free will, rather than following every impulse and desire that happens to arise.

In the cases of spiritual disciples, I often see two or three *dasas* in a row that entail spiritual activities during adulthood. I think that's significant and I think it should be told to the client. In cases where the horoscope indicates a person has seriously misused, for example, love activities in past lifetimes, I often notice two or three *dasas* in a row that relate to love matters. This is very significant, because three *dasas* in a row takes up twenty-three years, if the periods are short (i.e. Sun, Moon and Mars), and fifty-two years if they are long (i.e. Jupiter, Saturn, and Mercury).

Martin: That gives the person a long time to learn the proper use of a particular realm.

James: Or, to suffer a long time while paying back the bad karma caused in past lives.

Martin: Is there a way to know which is happening, based on the horoscope?

James: Well, anything related to past lives is speculative. Since we have no provable experience of past lives, I'm a bit wary of making very definitive statements about those matters. But, I do believe that if a person has an extremely afflicted planet, he or she probably abused that realm of life in past lives.

Martin: Obviously.

James: No, not obviously. You and I are not experiencing our clients' past lives, we're looking at symbols on a piece of paper, so we don't know anything for sure. For all we know, the person may have a very afflicted 2nd house causing terrible money karma in this life simply because he or she has always had many "easy money lifetimes" and now wants to find out what it's like to be poor. When we predict details of someone's life, the person's life (in time) bears out whether we are right or wrong. The reasons for what happens to a person is simply our belief. No matter what our understanding of karma is, and how it works, it's pure speculation on our part.

With that in mind, I believe that if a person has badly misused, say, career energy in some past lifetime and has not yet paid back that debt, he or she will pay the price in the current life. One way the person could pay back a lot of career debt would be to run through several rough *dasas* connected to the career house during adulthood. Maybe the person runs the *dasa* of a planet that is fallen in the 10th house. That causes career problems for a good ten or twenty years, depending on the period. If that period is followed by a *dasa* of the ruler of the 10th house, and that ruler is tightly conjunct with, say, the malefic Sun or the ruler of the 12th house, that's good for another ten or twenty difficult years within career, depending on the *dasa* involved.

If you take the time to notice the realms activated by the *dasas* during the person's adult life, you'll sometimes — not always but sometimes — notice an important theme running through the person's life.

Martin: So I can look at the *dasas* not as separate, isolated periods, but as portions of a whole life, which may have a thread running through it?

James: Yes. Sometimes, you'll see the thread or the theme as plain as day. I definitely advise paying attention to this point.

Martin: Among the ten thousand other things I'm busy paying attention to?

James: See how simple it is?!!!

Now, let's talk about the question you asked last week regarding priorities. You asked how one goes about prioritizing the features that make a planet strong and powerful, or weak and afflicted. As I mentioned then, this is something that takes years of practical experience with horoscopes and I have serious doubts that it can be learned quickly.

Martin: What I'm looking for is some kind of pecking order. Like, in poker a royal straight flush beats everything. A flush beats a full house. A full house beats three of a kind. Can you do that with the astrological factors?

James: The problem is that *Jyotish* is filled with nuances and subtleties, upon more nuances and subtleties. Any prioritization system I give you has to be taken with great caution because there are always going to be mitigating aspects and extenuating circumstances. I'll try to help you, but don't take what I say as gospel. Very little of *Jyotish* should be taken as gospel anyway, because many paths can lead to the same goal. Many astrologers get excellent results using completely different systems or even using different "weighting" methods within the same system.

Martin: Is that why you told me to read so many books by other authors even though they don't always agree with you?

James: Yes. If you can't be open minded with *Jyotish*, you're in the wrong field. I respect anyone who achieves predictive accuracy in astrology, no matter what approach or techniques the person uses. What I don't respect is someone who masquerades psychic ability for astrological technique. That happens a lot and it gets my goat because it helps to muddy our field, which is muddy enough already.

So make sure you approach what I say as a <u>general</u> guide and don't be surprised if the list of items I cover is incomplete. Better yet, <u>expect</u> the list to be incomplete and don't be surprised if, or when, other astrologers disagree with my sense of priorities.

Martin: That's a fair disclaimer, James.

James: It's an emphatic disclaimer. In my opinion, you've asked an almost impossible question. And while we're on the subject of disclaimers, let me reiterate an important one that definitely applies now. Nothing in astrology is foolproof. I've seen every single astrological technique, fundamental or otherwise, fail at least a few times. And every single astrologer I've ever met, or heard about, has made wrong predictions. Every one. So, if I mention some feature that makes a planet magnificently powerful and you've seen <u>a few</u> horoscopes that contradict that fact, don't assume that what I've said is wrong. Always test <u>many</u> horoscopes before drawing conclusions.

Martin: Wait a minute, James. You're saying that no matter how long I study, or practice, I'm always going to be making mistakes. If that's true, how can I ever feel confident enough to charge money and practice professionally?

James: First of all, my guess is that <u>the best</u> astrologers have around a seventy percent accuracy rate, give or take ten percent. Second, if any client expects you to be one hundred percent accurate and accepts everything you say as gospel truth, that person needs some lessons in practicality. We're talking about divination, and divination is not a "closed science." We have to leave room for free will, prayer, the grace of God, and human error. I suggest that you constantly strive for predictive perfection, but use some common sense about what is and what isn't your responsibility as an astrologer. And remember that human error occurs in all humans, not just the ignorant or unlucky ones.

Martin: Isn't it my responsibility to be accurate in my chart analysis?

James: Yes, but if you consider it your responsibility to be accurate <u>all</u> the time, you better forget about ever practicing professionally. Or you can learn to massively rationalize, and ignore reality, which is what some astrologers do.

Martin: What do you mean?

James: Some astrologers believe not only that astrology can predict everything perfectly, but that their abilities with astrology is perfect.

Martin: That's ridiculous, isn't it?

James: Of course it is.

Martin: So, what is your definition of an astrologer's responsibility?

James: I see <u>the practice</u> of astrology as a probabilities, or percentage, game. I definitely don't consider it a "hard science." Therefore, if I see a bunch of horoscopes where Saturn occupies the 5th house and the overall majority of those people are childless, or have very few children, or only had children in their older years, then I will tell any client who has that same placement that he or she will probably have similar results.

Martin: Unless there are other astrological features contradicting that fact?

James: Of course. But, contrary to what many clients and astrology students think, I am not responsible for knowing everything about a person's life or that person's future. I'm only responsible for knowing the implications, the likelihoods, and the probabilities of much (definitely not all) of the person's life.

Martin: What if you come across some astrological feature that you've never seen?

James: If I see one or two dramatically unfamiliar features in a horoscope, I don't worry about it. I simply give the client my <u>opinion</u> about its meaning while clearly explaining that because that aspect is new to me, I can't be sure of what it will produce. Having one or two of these situations in a chart reading is not a problem because there is so much more to analyze and discuss.

Martin: But what if the unfamiliar aspect seems really important?

James: If the aspect seems incredibly significant and its meaning eludes me, I may tell the person to get other opinions. I even have a list of astrologers I use as referrals for clients who come to me for astrological work outside my expertise (investment astrology, kidnapping cases, law suits, and so on). If the unclear feature seems like it could be dangerous or life threatening, which sometimes happens, I will advise the person to see a good psychic, if they can find one. But I <u>never</u> take the position that I have to know <u>everything</u>. Each astrologer has his or her own specialty or expertise, and each astrologer has his or her own blind spots. I recognize this and am not uncomfortable saying the words "I don't know."

Now, a much bigger problem occurs when I see a horoscope which <u>as a whole</u> is unclear. That's a serious problem.

Martin: What do you do?

James: I tell the person straight out that their horoscope is very difficult to read. This usually occurs because the indications are extremely mixed, and I explain the meaning of "mixed indications." Most of the time, the person exclaims, "Well, that's exactly how my life is — mixed (or confused)!"

Martin: In which case you've scored a point on the accuracy meter?

James: Absolutely. I've immediately gained some trust from the client for speaking the truth of what I've seen. Then comes the hard part — reading the chart! Now, I tell the person that because the chart as whole is unclear or without definite themes, the best I can do is to interpret each and every aspect individually, and ask the client to help clarify how these features are actually functioning. I actually ask for help and I ask for the person to involve him- or herself in the reading.

Martin: So, you're actually asking the person to take some responsibility for getting a valuable reading?

James: That's a great way of putting it. Yes, I am. Please understand, however, that as an astrologer it is your responsibility to learn all the essentials of *Jyotish* <u>well</u>, and to have analyzed hundreds of horoscopes (of friends, relatives, and so on) and achieved a <u>good level of accuracy</u> before you call yourself a professional. But, as I said, I don't consider astrology a "hard science" — I consider it a game of probabilities and likelihoods, and I treat it like that. I consider perfection impossible because of the vastness and very nature of astrology. I leave omniscience to God, and only God.

I meet way too many astrology students who are capable enough to practice professionally, but won't do it because they believe they have to achieve perfection. These people have never achieved perfection in any other realm, so I have no idea what makes them think that astrology is any different. In one respect, it's fine to study astrology without practicing it. On the other hand, it makes no sense to hold back incredibly valuable knowledge because it feels uncomfortable to be imperfect. It's kind of like having water in a desert and watching people who are dying of thirst walk by and saying "I have some water here to quench your desperate thirst, but the water is a little murky so I'd prefer not to give it to you. Just keep starving."

Martin: So, what about a list of priorities, regarding those astrological features that take precedence?

James: Okay. I've made a list for you, but I want to say something about planets in exaltations, falls, and ownership signs <u>first</u>, because these are often misunderstood. A lot of people who see my list are going to wonder why the number one benefit of a planet is not its placement within its exaltation or own sign. Every time I give a workshop, I meet students who believe that the <u>most</u> powerful or <u>most</u> weakening effect a planet can have is the condition of exaltation or fall (e.g. the Moon is exalted in Taurus and fallen in Scorpio.). This is definitely false. This impression was partly created by the explanations in my first textbook. When I gave explanations for the planets in all of the houses, I didn't want the reader to think that, for example, Venus in the 7th house was <u>always</u> good or that planets in the 6th, 8th, or 12th houses (*dusthanas*) are <u>always</u> bad. So, I gave explanations of planets in exaltations, falls, and ownership signs. Because the explanations were so prevalent, because they took up so much space, they gave the mistaken impression of being of enormous significance to many readers, as if the benefits of an exalted planet couldn't be <u>seriously</u> mitigated by being tightly aspected by Mars or Saturn, or any other malefic.

Martin: But exaltations and falls are enormously significant, aren't they?

James: Yes, if — and this is one *huge* "if" — the <u>exalted</u> planet in question isn't tightly aspected by one or two malefics. Or, if the <u>fallen</u> planet in question isn't tightly aspected by one or two benefics. That would change the equation dramatically, and sometimes <u>completely</u>.

Martin: Completely?

James: Sometimes completely. When a planet is <u>tightly</u> aspected by another planet — within three or four degrees — the planet that is receiving the aspect is <u>intensely</u> affected, for better or worse, depending on the benefic or malefic <u>essential nature</u> of the planet throwing the aspect. I've analyzed so many charts where fallen Mars is tightly conjunct exalted Jupiter, and guess what happens? Exalted Jupiter is completely ruined, while fallen Mars becomes phenomenally powerful and well disposed because it is receiving not just Jupiter's <u>close</u> rays, but Jupiter's close <u>exalted</u> rays. In terms of priorities, a <u>tight</u> aspect received from a benefic or malefic planet is far and away more significant than the sign placement (exaltation, ownership, or fallen sign) of a planet.

Let me give you an example. Here is a chart of a man with exalted Jupiter conjunct fallen Mars (see following page).

In a case like this, many astrologers would predict good results from Jupiter because it is exalted and bad results from fallen Mars. In fact, the opposite is the case. This man, Roberto, reported that his 12th house and 7th house (the houses ruled by Mars) gave extraordinary results while Jupiter has caused nothing but pain.

Mars, as the ruler of the 12th house has given Roberto wonderful spiritual experiences. Meditation and pursuing enlightenment are his greatest pleasures. He has even traveled to India more than once for spiritual purposes.

Martin: Because the 12th house rules journeys to remote foreign countries?

James: Yes. His Mars is so powerful, due to receiving exalted Jupiter's rays, that he gets great benefits from such countries.

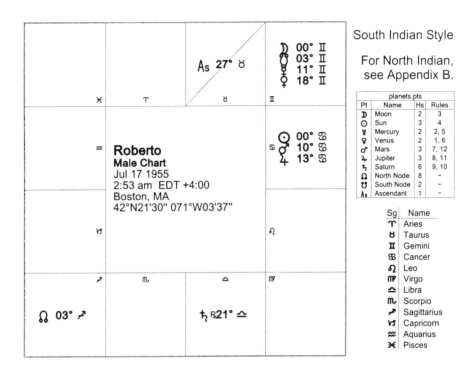

Martin: What about his wife, the other 7th house signification?

James: He met his wife at a spiritual retreat and they have been happily married for more than twenty years. The wife is extremely spiritual and rather well off financially. She is a typical Jupiterian person, which is exactly what you should expect when the ruler of the 7th house <u>closely</u> conjuncts exalted Jupiter. Mars becomes a very beneficial influence here.

Martin: What about Jupiter?

James: Do you want to guess what happened when this man went into Jupiter *dasa*?

Martin: Well, Jupiter is afflicted because it's so close to fallen Mars, and Jupiter rules the 8th and 11th houses. Did he have accidents (8th house) or problems with an eldest sibling (11th house)?

James: Roberto said that the Jupiter *dasa* was the worst period of his life. The only realm that didn't go sour was his marriage.

Martin: The signification of the house that Mars rules.

James: He even had problems with spiritual matters, because Jupiter rules gurus and spiritual teachers. The worst feature was that he couldn't fulfill any of his desires, even the smallest ones. Everything he touched seemed to go bad.

Martin: Because the *dasa* was so bad it hurt everything?

James: To some extent, that's true. But in this case, he would have to have troubles with desires because the terribly afflicted Jupiter occupies the 3rd house, which rules desires.

Also, the Jupiter-Mars *dasa-bhukti* was dangerous to longevity because Jupiter rules the 8th house and is taking a beating from fallen Mars. He could have died in such a period, and I would definitely have prescribed mantra chanting for Jupiter and several *yagyas* for Jupiter to protect him if I had seen him before that period and subperiod.

Now, let me finally show you the lists of priorities that I've made for you.

Martin: There's more than one?

James: I made a list prioritizing what makes a <u>planet</u> weak or strong, a list for what makes a <u>house</u> weak or strong, and a list showing what helps or hinders a chart as a <u>whole</u>.

First of all, bear these points in mind. Benefic planets are Jupiter, Venus, Moon, and Mercury. The brighter the Moon, the more benefic, and waxing also helps. Mercury is <u>somewhat</u> less benefic than Jupiter, Venus, and bright Moon, but <u>still</u> benefic. Malefic Planets are: Sun, Mars, Saturn, Rahu, and Ketu.

Planets conjunct Ketu are hurt <u>far worse</u> than planets conjunct Rahu (despite what many textbooks say). And <u>houses</u> are generally hurt more by the placement of Rahu than Ketu.

I don't acknowledge *neechabhanga* or *vargottama*, which I consider generally worthless and which will be explained in detail later on (see Class Eight). A fallen planet that is retrograde is less afflicted, but <u>still</u> quite bad. Likewise, an exalted retrograde planet is weakened, but is <u>still</u> good. So, here we go:

Positive Planetary Priorities

1) Stationary Direct or Stationary Retrograde — Beats everything. (Note: Stationary planets are so important that Class Four is devoted to a full explanation.)

2) Planet is conjunct, <u>within two or three degrees</u>, with Jupiter, Venus, Mercury or bright Moon, <u>where the benefic planet is occupying its exaltation or own sign</u>. (Note: Beware *dusthana* rulers.

If planet is conjunct a *dusthana* ruler, it will cause a "wild card" effect.)

3) Planet is aspected, <u>within two or three degrees</u>, by Jupiter, Venus, Mercury, or (bright) Moon. (Note: Beware *dusthana* rulers. If planet is conjunct a *dusthana* ruler, it will cause a "wild card" effect.)

4) Planet is within <u>two or three</u> degrees of its most intense exaltation <u>degree</u>. (Note: Once a planet is <u>past</u> its highest exaltation degree, it <u>quickly loses strength</u>.)

5) Moon within one or two days of full (<u>can</u> even mitigate <u>fallen</u> Moon — a Scorpio Moon).

6) <u>Planet</u> occupies exaltation or own sign <u>and</u> is well aspected by a benefic.

7) Planet occupies exaltation sign.

8) Planet occupies own sign.

9) Planet occupies the house of a benefic planet, and is aspected by the benefic <u>owning</u> or exalting the house (e.g. Mercury occupying Taurus, while aspected by Venus. Or, Moon occupying Virgo, while aspected by Mercury).

10) Planet is hemmed in by benefics, and not aspected by malefics.

> **(10a)** <u>Excellent</u> if it occurs within one sign (Example: in a case where Jupiter occupies the fifth degree of Leo, Mars occupies the tenth degree of Leo, and Venus occupies the fourteenth degree of Leo, then Mars — the planet in the middle — is "hemmed in" by benefics.)

> **(10b)** <u>Very good</u> if involving three signs. (Example: in a case where Moon occupies Leo, Saturn occupies Virgo, and Venus occupies Libra, then Saturn — the planet in the middle — is hemmed in by benefics.)

11) Planet occupies 5th or 9th house (*trikona* houses), <u>and</u> is well-aspected by a benefic.

12) Planet occupies house 1, 4, 7, or 10 (*kendra* houses) <u>and</u> is well-aspected by a benefic.

13) Planet is aspected by two benefic planets (<u>even</u> within a wide orb, say, 10-30 degrees), and no malefics.

14) Planet <u>rules</u> best houses, thereby becoming *Rajayoga-karaka*.

15) Planet <u>rules</u> good houses, thereby becoming *yogakaraka*.

16) Planet occupying *trikona* house (5th or 9th) becomes fortunate.

17) Planet occupying *kendra* house (1st, 4th, 7th, or 10th) becomes powerful.

James: So, this list is a general guide to how I see the power of planets. But, remember that some of these factors are so similar that it's hard to say definitively one is stronger than another.

Martin: Well, I can see how the first nine or ten on the list are far more powerful than the last ones.

James: Yes, that's true. The first nine or ten are extremely strong influences. Did you notice that a planet in its own or exaltation sign rated in the middle of the list, not right at the top? Beginning astrologers always think that a planet in such a placement is a phenomenal benefit. As good as it is, there are lots of other influences that make a planet stronger. Also, I constantly see charts where a planet is well placed by being in its own sign, but is otherwise very badly aspected. So, make sure you don't pronounce judgement on a planet too quickly. You have to consider all features before drawing a conclusion.

Martin: James, regarding number seven, I have a question. Do all aspects have the same strength? For example, Jupiter throws aspects onto the 5th, 7th, and 9th houses from itself. Are its 5th and 9th house aspects as strong as its 7th house aspect?

James: Generally, yes, I think so. It's kind of a hard question to answer because I think intuition comes into play here. You have to judge every horoscope individually. But generally, I would say the power of the aspects of each planet are the same. The only distinction I would make is with conjunctions. I find conjunctions to be somewhat more powerful than other aspects. The reason I say "somewhat" is because this distinction only becomes significant when a planet is aspected by more than one planet, and one of the aspects is a conjunction. I'll give you an example.

If, say, Venus is conjunct Mars within five degrees, and also receives an aspect from Jupiter in the opposite house within five degrees, I would give a bit more weight to the conjunction. This may be a personal preference of mine. I don't know whether other astrologers would agree or not. But to me, conjunctions are slightly more intense, more powerful than the other aspects.

Martin: Maybe that's why the texts say Jupiter aspects the 5th, 7th, and 9th, rather than the 1st, 5th, 7th, and 9th, and so forth.

James: Maybe so.

Martin: I have a question about numbers 16 and 17. Is there a difference between a planet gaining benefit and a planet gaining power? Is one better than the other?

James: That's a difficult question. The terms "benefit" and "power" are kind of used interchangeably, just like the terms "weak" and "afflicted." In the instances of numbers 16 and 17, where I define planets in *trikonas* (5th or 9th houses) as gaining "benefit" and planets in *kendras* (1st, 4th, 7th, or 10th houses) as giving "power," I personally would prefer a planet to occupy a *trikona* rather than a *kendra*. But both placements are excellent <u>for the planet involved</u>. I emphasize "for the planet involved" because no one in his or her right mind desires to have Saturn in the 1st, 4th, or 7th house. These are house placements that cause a lot of grief and pain.

Martin: But, Saturn becomes powerful by being in those angular houses?

James: Exactly.

Martin: If those are such bad house placements, then what good is it for Saturn to become powerful?

James: If Saturn is powerful, then the houses that Saturn rules become strengthened. If Saturn rules the 2nd house and occupies the 4th or 7th (or any angular house), then the person has more power to make money.

Of course I would prefer for Saturn to occupy either the 3rd or 6th house over the 1st, 4th, or 7th, because life would be far less painful. Saturn doesn't cause much suffering in *upachaya* houses (3rd, 6th, 10th, and 11th) where malefics are welcomed. But the houses that Saturn rules would actually be weak or afflicted by having that ruler in bad houses like the 3rd and 6th. Do you see?

Martin: Yes. Does this also mean that in a Saturn period or subperiod, the effects of Saturn would be more powerful if it's in an angular house natally?

James: Yes.

Martin: Okay. How do you rate the (natal) strength of a planet that happens to be in its own or exaltation sign in the *navamsa* (marriage chart)?

James: I give it a little weight, but not very much. I know that all the texts, mine included, say that a planet that is strong in the *navamsa* greatly strengthens that planet's power in the natal chart. But that hasn't been my experience. I imagine some other astrologers would disagree, but that's how it's been for me.

Martin: Also, you didn't mention the *varga* (divisional chart) summary. I've heard you mention in lectures that if a planet is in its own or exaltation sign in many of the divisional charts, then a planet becomes very strong.

James: Good point. There are sixteen *varga* charts, and although I believe Westerners should only use a few of them, because they are so sensitive to birthtime error, the planets in the <u>signs</u> of the *vargas* will be accurate regardless of minor birth<u>time</u> errors. I've noticed that if a planet occupies its own or exaltation sign, or a combination of the two, in about eight or nine *varga* charts, then that planet becomes strengthened in the natal chart. I haven't found that the planet becomes phenomenally strong, but its power is definitely increased. Likewise, if a planet is fallen or in its detriment sign (the sign opposite it's rulership sign) in many charts, then the planet is weakened in the natal chart. But it takes about seven or eight significant *varga* placements before I notice significant effects.

Robert De Niro's VARGA CHART SUMMARY

	Own Sign	Exalted	Fallen
Sun:	11	4	0
Moon:	2	1	0
Mercury:	3	2	0
Venus:	5	0	0
Mars:	2	1	1
Jupiter:	3	1	3
Saturn:	1	2	1
Rahu:	0	2	0
Ketu:	0	1	0

One of the most important things to be aware of regarding the *varga* chart summary is that sometimes — not always but sometimes — if a planet occupies a very weak degree, like the first or last few degrees of a sign, it may occupy the same sign in ten or fifteen *varga* charts, and that can make it quite powerful. Usually, planets in a very early or late degree are seriously weakened. But, occasionally there is this interesting "*varga* effect" that makes the planet strong. An example of this occurs with Robert De Niro's Sun in Leo. His Sun, which occupies the first degree of Leo, is in its own sign ten times and it is exalted twice (see De Niro's natal chart on page 140). If you start looking at *varga* chart summaries, which a computer can do in a second (I don't know if all *Jyotish* programs calculate the *varga* chart summary, but the one I use — *Haydn's Jyotish* — does) you'll see what I mean. Now, let's look at influences that harm a planet.

Negative Planetary Priorities

1) Planet is conjunct, <u>within two or three degrees</u>, of Saturn, Mars, or Sun, which are occupying their <u>fallen</u> signs. (Example: Venus conjunct fallen Mars in Cancer).

2) Planet is conjunct or aspected <u>within two or three degrees</u> by Saturn, Mars, Ketu, Rahu, or Sun. (conjunct with Saturn or Ketu is the worst).

3) Planet is within <u>two or three</u> degrees <u>before</u> its most intense fallen <u>degree.</u> (When the planet is past its worst degree of fall, it's affliction is <u>quickly</u> diminished.)

4) Planet occupies fallen sign <u>and</u> is aspected by a malefic.

5) Planet occupies the house of malefic's fallen sign placement and is aspected by that malefic (e.g. Moon in Aries, aspected by Saturn. Or, Mercury in Cancer, aspected by Mars.).

6) Planet occupies 6th, 8th, or 12th house (*dusthana*), <u>and</u> is aspected by a malefic.

7) Planet is aspected by <u>two</u> malefic planets (even within 10-30 degrees), and receives no benefic aspects.

8) Planet is in its fallen sign.

9) Planet is hemmed in by malefics, and not aspected by benefics:

   (9a) <u>Devastating</u> if this occurs within one sign.

   (9b) <u>Very bad</u> if involving three signs. (Example: Venus in Leo, flanked by Rahu in Cancer and Saturn in Virgo.)

10) Planet occupies the 8th or 12th house (*dusthanas*), and is not well aspected or in its <u>own</u> or <u>exaltation</u> sign (which is actually good).

11) Planet occupies 6th house (*dusthana*).

12) Moon is <u>very</u> dim (e.g. in same house as Sun, or in house preceding the Sun).

13) Planet is opposite its <u>own</u> sign (called detriment in the West).

14) Planet rules bad houses and becomes functional malefic (Note: Do not ignore <u>essential</u> nature of planet).

15) Retrograde planet is considered latent, or slow to produce outer effects.

16) Planet in either the first or last two or three degrees of a sign. (Note: Sometimes this is devastating, sometimes there is very little effect. Use intuition and look for corroborating factors.)

Martin: James, if a planet is stationary, which you say is the most powerful placement of all, and that planet is also afflicted or badly aspected, does the stationary status cancel out the negative effects of the afflictions?

James: No. As I told you before, planets that are mixed give mixed results. But if the planet is stationary, it will have some enormous power as well as whatever afflictions exist. You'll see how this works when we talk about stationary planets. Now let's look at the positive effects that can help a house.

HOUSES: Positive Elements

1) A *rajayoga* (royal union) involving <u>one</u> or two planets in a house.

2) Exalted planet in a house (near most intense degree of exaltation).

3) House occupied by two benefics (not aspected by any malefic).

4) Planet is in its *swakshetra* (own sign) in a house.

5) Ruler of a house <u>tightly</u> (within two or three degrees) conjunct a benefic, where that benefic is <u>exalted</u> or in <u>own</u> sign.

6) Ruler of a house <u>tightly</u> conjunct (within two or three degrees) with a benefic.

7) *Kendra Trikona Adipathi Yoga* in a house (a conjunction of a ruler of an angular house (1, 4, 7, 10) and a trinal house (5 and 9).

Martin: What about the *ashtaka varga* system, James? Some astrologers say that if a house has a lot of points, then it becomes very strong.

James: The *ashtaka varga* system is explained in my first book as a rating system where there is a total of 336 points (some astrologers use a system with a different total), so that the average rating is twenty-eight points per house. The way I was taught (and which I agree with) is that the *ashtaka varga* system is used to determine the power and benefit of planets <u>transiting</u> houses, not the power of the house in general. In other words, if a house has, say, thirty-seven points, which is quite a bit more than twenty-eight (the average), then the effects will be powerful <u>and beneficial</u> when a planet transits through that house.

Martin: Even when transited by malefics?

James: Yes. Now I don't mean that Saturn or Mars transiting a "high point house" will <u>only</u> produce good effects, but they will definitely give some significant benefits <u>that otherwise would not occur</u>.

Martin: But those malefics would still harm that house during the transit?

James: Usually, yes. The job of malefics is to cause problems and obstacles (so we grow and evolve, and so on). But if the points in the house are high, then the negative effects are <u>somewhat lessened</u>, and there will be some very good effects as well. I know some astrologers would make extreme statements, like — if the points are very high, there will only be good effects. And if the points are very low, say nineteen or twenty, that there will be only bad effects even when the house is transited by benefics like Venus and Jupiter. But in my experience these are exaggerations. And not accurate. *Ashtaka varga* is a <u>weighting</u> system for planets transiting houses. Maybe if there were sixty or seventy points in one house, the effects would only be good, but the most points I've ever seen was forty-something, and that's extremely rare. In my practice, a really strong house in the *ashtaka varga* has somewhere between thirty-five and forty points. Forty is incredibly high!

Now, all that being said, I must admit that any house that has a lot of *ashtaka varga* points does gain a certain general strength because planets will be transiting that house on and off for a whole lifetime. And a house with relatively few points will suffer because planets will be transiting that house throughout all of life, causing many problems, particularly when malefics transit that house. Let's look at how a house can be harmed.

HOUSES: Negative Elements

1) Fallen planet in a house, <u>near most intense degree of fall</u> (e.g. Venus near the twenty-seventh degree of Virgo or the Sun near the tenth degree of Libra).

2) <u>Ruler</u> of a house <u>tightly</u> conjunct a <u>fallen</u> malefic planet.

3) <u>Ruler</u> of a house <u>tightly</u> conjunct or aspected by a malefic planet (conjunct with Saturn or Ketu is the worst).

4) House occupied by one or two malefics, unless in *upachaya* house (3, 6, 10, & 11).

5) Malefic planet in the house opposite its own sign (e.g. Saturn in Cancer). (Note: A planet in an <u>enemy</u> sign is a weakness, but not of great significance.)

6) Ruler of a house is retrograde (this is not an "affliction," but it does hold back house significations during first thirty or so years).

7) Ruler of a house is in first or last two degrees of a sign. (Sometimes devastating, sometimes not. Use intuition and look for corroborating features.)

CHART AS A WHOLE — Negative

1) Both Moon and ascendant ruler are weak and afflicted.

2) Saturn <u>tightly</u> conjuncts <u>or</u> aspects ascendant ruler, Sun, or Moon.

3) Ketu <u>tightly</u> conjuncts ascendant ruler, Sun, or Moon.

4) Saturn sits very close to the ascendant degree.

5) All, or most, benefic planets in the chart are weak and afflicted (e.g. conjunct malefics, occupying *dusthana* houses or fallen signs, and so on).

6) Chart is completely devoid of <u>themes.</u> Planets seem isolated and have no relationship to each other. No one house appears to be strong.

7) Very early or very late ascendant degree (0, 1, or 28, 29).

8) Very afflicted 5th house (house of the mind) along with a very afflicted Moon or Mercury (planets of the mind).

James: Now, I want to make it clear that I do not consider a chart that has lots of planets in *dusthana* houses (6, 8, and 12) to necessarily be afflicted. I've already said that many planets in the 8th house make a person metaphysically oriented, while many planets in the 12th house make a person spiritual and interested in enlightenment.

Martin: Then many planets in the 6th house would make a person interested in health matters.

James: That's right. And remember that if there are many planets in the 8th house, then the 2nd house receives the aspects of those planets and becomes extremely energized. If there are many planets in the 12th house, then the 6th house receives the aspects of those planets and becomes energized. So even though planets occupying *dusthana* houses are harmed, don't assume that a chart <u>as a whole</u> is afflicted just because many planets occupy *dusthana* houses. It depends very much on how the planets in the bad houses are aspected and what signs they occupy.

Martin: James, in item number one you mentioned that a chart is damaged if the Moon is weak or afflicted. So, these terms "weak" and "afflicted" are used interchangeably? One isn't worse than the other? And what exactly is the difference?

James: As far as the difference, a weak planet is one that simply has no power, like one that occupies the very first or last degree of a sign, and is unaspected and isolated. An afflicted planet is one that is bombarded by a tight aspect from a malefic like Mars or Saturn or Ketu. Or, a planet tightly combust the Sun. Or a planet in its fallen sign. These are examples of afflicted planets.

I see planets that are weak cause major problems in people's lives and I see planets that are afflicted do the same. So I don't make much distinction between the two.

Martin: What's the story about number eight? I haven't heard you mention that one before.

James: I have seen a number of charts over the years where the chart as a whole is fine, but the 5th house <u>and</u> Moon or Mercury is afflicted, and the person is simply crazy. I'm not saying that the person is psychotic necessarily, but when I talk about the chart, or certain features of the person's life (marriage, career, and so on), I find that the person is simply not dealing with reality.

Martin: So, if the person isn't mentally stable, or mentally grounded, that ruins the whole chart?

James: In my opinion, it does. At the very least, it makes it impossible for me to work with the client. The person doesn't hear clearly what I am saying. And the responses the person gives to the questions I ask don't make sense. I'd say that's a major failing.

CHART AS A WHOLE — Positive

1) Both Moon and ascendant are extremely well-disposed.

2) Jupiter <u>tightly</u> aspects ascendant degree, ascendant ruler, Sun, or Moon.

3) All benefics in the chart are strong and well-disposed (e.g. occupying their own or exaltation signs, not aspected by malefics, not occupying *dusthana* houses, and so on).

4) Several benefic planets occupy *trikonas* (5th and 9th houses).

5) Many planets in *kendras* (angular houses 1, 4, 7, and 10).

6) Many of the malefics occupy *upachaya* houses (3, 6, 10, and 11).

Martin: In item number one, what do you mean by the ascendant being well-disposed?

James: This means that there are benefics occupying the ascendant, or benefics aspecting the ascendant. It means the ascendant ruler is exalted or in its own sign and not aspected by malefics. Conditions like that.

Martin: James, when you showed me Roberto's chart with the exalted

Jupiter in Cancer tightly conjunct fallen Mars in Cancer, I got the point that Jupiter would be devastated by being so close to a fallen malefic, and Mars would be tremendously strengthened by being so close to an exalted benefic. But, what happens when the aspect isn't tight. What if Mars is fallen in, say, ten degrees of Cancer while Jupiter is exalted in twenty degrees of Cancer?

James: That's when astrology becomes difficult. In my judgement, if fallen Mars has a ten or twenty degree aspect from exalted Jupiter, then it would <u>probably</u> produce problems in its periods and subperiods, and for the natal houses that Mars rules, because it's fallen. But, then again, it might not. It could possibly be saved by the positive aspect it receives from benefic Jupiter. It's really hard to say.

On the other hand, Jupiter, in the case you mentioned, might produce good effects in its periods and subperiods, and in terms of the natal houses it rules, but then again it might be hurt by the fallen Mars aspect. Again, it's very hard to say.

Martin: This is a really annoying "mixed" condition.

James: That's right. Conditions like these make it difficult to gain a sense of certainty about the precise results. If I see two or three of these situations in a horoscope, I usually tell the person at the start of the reading that their horoscope is difficult to interpret. I also tell the person that he or she is likely to get rather different interpretations from every astrologer who reads the chart.

Martin: Then I guess it's up to the client to try and figure out which astrologer has got it right, isn't it?

James: Absolutely. With charts that are hard to interpret, I always advise the client that regarding <u>future</u> predictions, the person should trust the predictions that are made by the astrologers who are most accurate in the interpretation of the <u>natal</u> chart. Of course, everyone wants to believe all the positive and happy predictions that are made, but that's foolish.

I get an awful lot of clients with conditions like close conjunctions of exalted Jupiter and fallen Mars who are told they are going to have tremendously good results in their Jupiter periods, and the exact opposite happens. I also see lots of clients with close conjunctions of fallen Sun (in Libra) conjunct Venus in its own sign who are told how happy they will be when their Venus period arrives. When that period comes, of course, the person's disappointment is very intense.

Martin: That's something I don't fully understand. If a person has Venus in Libra conjunct the fallen Sun in Libra, and the aspect is tight, will the entire Venus period be ruined, or just the Venus-Sun *dasa-bhukti* (period-subperiod)?

James: Difficult to answer. I would always warn a person with a <u>close</u>

aspect like the one you're describing that <u>all</u> Venus periods (or subperiods) are likely to be quite bad for the whole duration. I have to admit, however, that I do see plenty of cases where the Venus period is good, and only the Venus-Sun *dasa-bhukti* is horrendous.

Martin: So this is yet another wild card effect?

James: Yes.

Martin: There are too many wild cards, James.

James: I have three suggestions. One: Ask the person how their previous subperiods of Venus have been. That will clue you in on what to expect in future Venus periods. Two: Develop your psychic ability and you may be able to intuit what to expect. Three: Get out of metaphysics. Or, at least try not to forget that what you love about astrology is its vast, expansive, mystical, metaphysical nature! What were you expecting when you entered a field that is <u>necessarily</u> every bit as vast and mysterious as life itself?

Martin: This sounds like a love-hate relationship for me. I love making accurate predictions, but I hate making mistakes.

James: Excellent.

Martin: Why is that excellent?

James: Because astrology, in practice, is always going to be an imperfect science. If you're not frustrated with your lack of perfection in the field, it means either you don't care, or, far worse, you don't even notice your mistakes. I've told you over and over that one of the biggest problems in modern day astrology is astrologers not asking for feedback to see which of their predictions (natal and future) are accurate and which ones aren't.

Martin: Well, I must be doing great because I sure get frustrated a lot. James, regarding number two in the list of "Negative Planetary Influences," you say that when a planet is tightly conjunct a malefic, it is extremely hurt and damaged.

James: Correct.

Martin: Well, I know that your statement is true, but I've also seen horoscopes where planets are tightly conjunct a malefic and they aren't hurt. In Bill Clinton's chart, Mercury, the ruler of the ascendent and the 10th house, is tightly conjunct Saturn — and yet Clinton has a great career and a strong presence. What's the story? Why isn't his Mercury devastated?

James: Before I answer your question, I have to state that there is disagreement amongst astrologers about Bill Clinton's birthtime. I favor the birthtime that gives a Virgo (rather than Cancer) ascendant. Although neither Clinton chart works perfectly, hence all the disagreement amongst astrologers, the Virgo birthchart (see below) contains a close Venus-Mars conjunction in the 1st house, with Venus being fallen, which to me reveals

Clinton's personality perfectly. The Cancer ascendant, on the other hand, puts Saturn and Mercury in the 1st house, which I think is not only inaccurate, but absurd (see page 129).

I don't want to seem intolerant to those who believe in the Cancer ascendant, by the way. Some astrologers whom I respect argue for the Cancer ascendant.

Although I can definitely show you <u>some</u> damage that Mercury is causing in Clinton's life, my final conclusion is that Mercury has escaped the harm normally expected. In other words, basically, Clinton has beat the odds. I told you that nothing in astrology is foolproof and this demonstrates it. Every time I do a horoscope reading, there's one or two pieces that don't

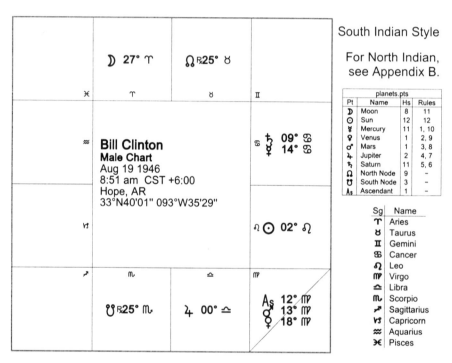

seem to fit. That's the nature of astrology. This becomes a serious problem, however, when a piece that doesn't fit is hugely important.

Martin: Like an eight-year president who has a weak ascendant and weak 10th house?

James: Damn right. I choked on Clinton's chart for quite a while when I saw it. But, there are plenty of other features of the chart that fit quite well.

Martin: James, if you use the Cancer ascendant, then Clinton has a great career, indicated by the ascendant ruler Moon in the 10th house, aspected by Jupiter.

James: Yes, but then he has Saturn and the 12th house ruler Mercury in the 1st house. This indicates an introspective, <u>extremely humble and responsible person</u>. In his personal life, and in answering legal questions, Clinton has probably acted more recklessly than any other president. Can you imagine Jimmy Carter, who has Saturn in the 1st house, acting in a remotely similar way? On top of that, consider the humiliating Monica Lewinsky affair that occurred while Saturn was transiting the house of Clinton's Moon (the transit occurred from April 1998 to June of 2,000). Does this seem like a Saturn transit of the Moon in the 10th house (Cancer ascendant) or a Saturn transit of the Moon in the 8th house (Virgo ascendant)?

Martin: Well, it sounds like Saturn transiting the 8th house in terms of all the embarrassment and shame Clinton went through. But it sounds like Saturn transiting the 10th house in terms of how badly it hurt his career.

James: I suppose it depends on how you perceive things, but in my view what ultimately happened to Clinton was a two-year devastating, <u>humiliating personal experience that occurred in front of the entire world</u>. People with 8th and 12th house Moons are constantly being humiliated. In the end, Clinton didn't lose his career like Richard Nixon did. What he lost was his dignity and his emotional well-being.

Martin: Moon in the 8th house.

James: I'd say it was a textbook example of an 8th (or 12th) house Moon getting hit by a particularly nasty transit.

Martin: But couldn't the personal humiliation could have occurred because the Moon rules the 1st house of the Cancer ascendant?

James: That's kind of irrelevant because the Moon is similar to the ascendant anyway. Remember *Chandra lagna*, Moon ascendant?

Martin: Oh, that's right.

James: Planets transiting the Moon have similar effects to planets transiting the ascendant. The difference is that transits to the Moon hit the emotional nature of the person.

I'll give you another very basic reason I think the Virgo ascendant fits. We're considering the Clinton scandal in terms of what happened to his career and personal well-being. But the love affair Clinton engaged in had to have a devastating effect on his marriage. Hillary was humiliated terribly, and Bill must have suffered and paid an enormous price over that. Guess what *dasa* the affair occurred in? Jupiter. Guess what house Jupiter rules if the ascendant is Virgo? The 7th.

Martin: Marriage.

James: Of course, the First Lady wasn't going to divorce Clinton while he was a sitting President, but I wouldn't be surprised if the marriage essentially ended over the affair. We'll have to wait and see whether Hillary divorces Clinton six months or a year after his presidency is over.

Martin: What subperiod was Clinton in when all this occurred?

James: His problems started in 1998 (during Saturn's transit of the 8th house Moon), while he was in Jupiter-Sun *dasa-bhukti* from 12/1997 to 9/1998. They got worse and worse after entering Jupiter-Moon on September 23, 1998. (For those who use the Krishnamurti *ayanamsa* — the only other *ayanamsa* I consider feasible — the Moon subperiod began September 8, 1998.)

Martin: So by the end of the whole mess he was in Jupiter-Moon, with Moon being transited by Saturn.

James: Yes. I don't want to be dogmatic about the Virgo ascendant. It's only my opinion, and if I'm wrong it wouldn't be the first time. But I do want to give you another reason I favor the Virgo ascendant. You're aware that Clinton plays the saxophone, right? But he only practices as a hobby. Well, the Cancer chart, with the ascendant ruler Moon in the 10th house, looks decidedly like that of a professional performer.

Martin: Where are you seeing the artistic talent in the Cancer chart?

James: In that chart, the 10th house ruler, Mars, occupies the 3rd house (music, dance, and drama) and is conjunct with Venus (planet of art).

Martin: But Venus is fallen.

James: Still, when the ruler of the 10th occupies the house of art, and is conjunct even a fallen Venus, and the person has the Moon in the 10th house, the quintessential placement of performers, the likelihood of being a professional performer is enormous. There's an old saying about astrology, "See an indication once, it's a possibility. See an indication twice, it's a probability. See an indication three times, and you can bet on it." I'd say that statement applies here.

Martin: Where do you see artistic talent in the other chart, the Virgo ascendant?

James: In that chart, he has Venus in the 1st house, which, even though fallen, may give artistic inclinations. More importantly, Mars, the ruler of the 3rd house (art), is occupying the 1st house and is conjunct Venus, the planet of art. Even though both charts give artistic ability, as I see it, one chart makes it a profession, the other a hobby.

Anyway, no matter which chart you use for Clinton, the horoscope is problematic.

Martin: It is?

James: Absolutely. That's why astrologers disagree strongly about the chart. Regarding your question "why Clinton hasn't fared worse in terms of his 1st and 10th house being ruled by such an afflicted Mercury," I believe the lesson here is that nothing in astrology is foolproof, and Clinton's chart is a good example of this point. Some people would say that Mercury became strong because it is conjunct (within about five degrees) Pluto, which I don't use in *Jyotish*. It's possible they're right. But I'm not sure that's the true reason for Mercury's strength.

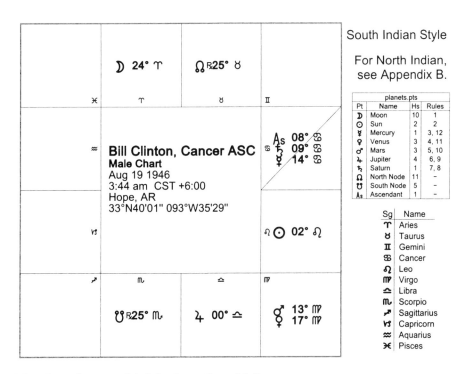

Martin: So, you think he beat the odds?

James: Probably. In seventy or eighty percent of cases where Mercury (or any planet) is <u>tightly</u> conjunct a malefic, <u>particularly Saturn</u>, Mercury is going to be quite wasted. But Clinton's isn't.

My other piece of advice is that this is the kind of case where your intuition as an astrologer needs to come into play.

Martin: Are you saying that some astrologers might see Clinton's afflicted Mercury and know intuitively that it is not as hurt as it appears?

James: I'm saying exactly that. There are lots of times when I see a chart where a planet is obviously afflicted, but I get a strong feeling that the person has escaped the harm. There are lots of times when I'm doing a chart and I suddenly get a feeling that the person is a doctor, but there's no clear emphasis on health matters in the chart.

Martin: What do you do?

James: I start looking for a medical profession in the chart <u>with a fine tooth comb</u>. Sometimes I find it and sometimes I don't. When my intuition comes in really strong, I'm usually accurate. The problem is that if I haven't been able to find in the chart what my intuition suggests, I am very hesitant to mention what I've felt. Then I feel foolish when it turns out my gut feeling was correct.

Martin: That's annoying.

James: I consider it a hazard of the field. Some astrologers are more comfortable with psychic phenomenon than others. I only want to rely on my intuition if I can confirm it through the birthchart.

Martin: But sometimes your intuition is accurate even though you can't confirm it in the chart?

James: Occasionally, yes.

Martin: That's not so good.

James: It is what it is.

Martin: James, another question. I notice that in a lot of *Jyotish* books written by Indians, the author never mentions the planetary orbs of aspects or conjunctions. The Indians I've read don't seem to care whether an aspect is tight by degree or not. Why is this?

James: First off, when Indians do that, it is a **big** mistake. Most of the Hindu *Jyotishis* I've met don't seem to even notice the orbs of aspects, although a few of them do. As I've taught you over and over already, there is a huge difference between an aspect that occurs within, say, three degrees and an aspect that occurs within, say, twenty-four degrees. In my opinion, there is no comparison at all.

I suspect that the reason Indians ignore the orbs is simply because of their style of drawing birthcharts.

Martin: Drawing birthcharts?

James: When Hindus draw a chart, they don't list the degrees of the planets inside the horoscope. They list the degrees <u>outside</u> of the map. On top of this, they list the "<u>sign</u> degree"; they list degrees numerically from 0 to 360. For example, if Mars occupies sixteen degrees of Taurus, they list Mars at forty-six degrees. If Jupiter occupies two degrees of Pisces, they list the planet as 332 degrees.

Martin: That's very confusing.

James: Especially in such a visual art as horoscope analysis. Sometimes

Westerners practicing *Jyotish* try to imitate the exact methods of Indians, but if they draw charts like Indians and can't notice the closeness of aspectual orbs, they are shooting themselves in the foot. But as I said, some Hindu astrologers do take note of the orbs.

I'll give you two examples of aspects from my own horoscope (see page 50) that show how dramatic tight orbs can be. First, my ascendant ruler, Venus, is conjunct <u>within one degree</u> of Ketu, giving me great metaphysical inclinations while just about completely ruining any sense of self. You can't imagine how shy and introverted I was as a child. And still am, essentially.

Martin: And that wouldn't be the case if Venus was ten or fifteen degrees away from Ketu?

James: The intensity would be dramatically lessened. Tendencies would be similar, but without nearly the same magnitude.

Another tight aspect in my chart is the Jupiter-Saturn opposition that occurs within one degree. Saturn rules the 10th house and is aspected by Jupiter, which even though ruling a bad house — the 8th — <u>is still a great benefic</u>. It is this tight Jupiter aspect onto my 10th house ruler Saturn that has given me fame in my profession. And it is the tight Jupiter aspect onto the 9th house ruler Saturn that has allowed me to be lucky in gaining higher knowledge. Jupiter is a very divine kind of influence, and I have had so many lucky and protective occurrences in the realms of higher knowledge and career that are blatantly Jupitarian, it makes me laugh.

My favorite one occurred when I was putting the finishing touches on my second book, <u>Astro-Logos, Revelations of a Hindu Astrologer</u>. I had read and re-read the book many times, and it had been professionally edited and proofread, and was ready to go to the printer that week. Even though I was certain the book was ready for the printer, a thought arose to let one of my students read the last two chapters as a final proofing.

Do you know what he found? The astrological mantra pronunciations were all wrong. Instead of writing out the mantra pronunciations myself, I tried to save time by simply lifting them from a computer file of my first book, which also gave all the mantras. The file, however, came from an unedited draft, and my proofreaders, not being Hindu astrologers, couldn't possibly have noticed the errors. Because they came from a computer file, I just assumed they were correct. But they weren't, and I nearly made a huge mistake. It was a stroke of pure luck that I asked my student to proofread the last two chapters.

Martin: Or divine intervention.

James: When this happened, I had the strongest feeling of being divinely protected in my career.

Martin: Which is the way Jupiter aspects work.

James: Well, it's the way <u>extremely tight</u> Jupiter aspects work. A person with a tight Jupiter aspect will always have lucky intuition in the realms governed by the planet (and the houses that planet rules) that is aspected by Jupiter.

Martin: And this wouldn't have occurred if the aspect was ten or twenty degrees?

James: There would be some luck connected to the aspect, but not nearly as much. When you think of aspects, imagine standing ten or twenty feet away from a fire versus standing a foot or two away. That's how aspects work. Any questions?

Martin: No, not yet. We've covered a lot today.

James: Bas.

CLASS FOUR

James: Today, our main focus will be two subjects. The first is stationary planets, which I've briefly mentioned in my other books, and the second is a technique called *Panoti Yoga* that isn't described in any textbooks in the West.

Martin: In the list of priorities you gave me last class, you said that a stationary planet is the most powerful condition a planet can have.

James: That's right. In my opinion, it is.

Martin: What is *Panoti Yoga*?

James: *Panoti* Yoga is a technique relating to *Sade Sati*, pronounced "sah-dee, sah-tee," which is a seven-and-a-half-year period when malefic Saturn transits the three signs closest to the Moon (the house preceding the Moon, the house containing the Moon, and the house following the Moon). *Sade Sati* is <u>mistakenly</u> considered a dreaded, grief-producing period where only bad effects can occur for seven-and-a-half years. The kicker is that *Sade Sati* occurs every seven-and-a-half years within Saturn's thirty-year cycle.

Martin: That's a long time.

James: That's right. *Sade Sati* encompasses one-fourth of our lives. And if you believe that everyone experiences non-stop grief and suffering for <u>at least</u> one fourth of their lives, regardless of the condition of each particular horoscope, you need to have your head examined.

Martin: You mean some astrologers believe that everyone suffers for one-fourth of their lives, on top of whatever other problems exist in the horoscope? That's crazy.

James: Astrology already has a bad name without astrologers perpetuating such nonsense. That's the main reason I'm teaching you *Panoti Yoga*. *Panoti Yoga* is a technique that reveals whether each particular *Sade Sati* period in your life will be good, bad, or terrible.

Martin: So, you're saying a person's *Sade Sati* can be good?

James: Indeed. *Panoti Yoga* reveals whether each *Sade Sati* period is good, bad, or terrible. But even if you don't know about *Panoti Yoga*, you still should pass the word to other Hindu astrologers that it is patently absurd to believe that one-fourth of everyone's life is going to be horrendous because of *Sade Sati*. It just doesn't make sense. If *Sade Sati* ruins one-fourth of a person's life right off the bat, can you imagine what would happen to poor souls like me whose horoscopes are more than partially afflicted, or who run a couple of rough *dasas*?

Martin: At least one out of every two days would be suffering! People would be committing suicide all over the place. Are there astrologers who really believe this?

James: It depends on how amateurish or unthinking the astrologer is. My guess is that if you visit five Hindu astrologers during a *Sade Sati*, at least two or three will try to scare you about it.

In any case, let's discuss stationary planets first and then we'll come back to *Sade Sati*. I've already explained the meaning of retrograde planets, now let's see what happens to a planet when it's not moving at all, or when it's moving <u>extremely</u> slowly.

Martin: James, planets don't ever actually stop moving and turn backwards, do they?

James: No. They only appear to, from our viewpoint. Since astrology is an observational art, the apparent motions are crucial.

Before a planet turns retrograde, it has to first slow down for several days or weeks. At the moment when the planet stops completely, just before it goes backwards, that planet is in an immensely powerful condition called "stationary retrograde."

After the planet goes retrograde for several weeks or months, it once again slows down and stops in order to resume its forward motion. This is also an immensely powerful condition known as "stationary direct." As I've already said, there is no condition stronger than a stationary planet. Or a planet that is extremely slow-moving, meaning a day or so before the stationary position.

Martin: Can you say why it's so strong?

James: Well, imagine that all the planets in the sky are moving — some slower, some faster; and one planet has stopped completely in its tracks, no movement at all. That planet becomes an intense point of <u>focus</u>. It stands out dramatically; it distinguishes itself.

Martin: In what way?

James: I'll give you a few examples. If Venus is stationary (stationary retrograde or stationary direct) in a person's horoscope, the person may become an artist.

Martin: Even if Venus is not in a house relating to career or work?

James: That's right. The person's chart might not look particularly artistic at all, and yet Venus is so powerful that it takes precedence over almost everything else.

If Mercury is stationary, the person may become a writer or lecturer, even if Mercury is not otherwise prominent, and <u>even</u> if Mercury isn't connected to work or career in the chart. If Jupiter is stationary, the person may become a lawyer or religious proponent.

Martin: That's pretty significant, James.

James: Now remember, I'm not saying that <u>everyone</u> with a stationary Venus is going to be an artist. Or that everyone with a stationary Mars is going to be an athlete. I <u>am</u> saying that the stationary planet is going to have an <u>extremely</u> important and <u>noticeable</u> effect in the person's life. Beyond question, if you fail to notice that a planet is stationary, or very close to stationary, you're going to miss important information.

Martin: Is it only the stationary planet that becomes strong, or do the houses that planet rules also become more powerful?

James: Both. I'll give you some examples. John Kennedy actually had two stationary planets, which is extremely rare.

Mercury was stationary direct while Uranus was stationary retrograde, and they were both <u>perfectly</u> stationary. By this I mean that Kennedy was born right on the day of the stations, not on the day before or the day after, which are also extraordinarily powerful. Mercury rules Kennedy's ascendant (personality, confidence, ability to be recognized, and the essence or nucleus of a horoscope) and his 10th house (career, fame, professional status).

Martin: So that's why he had such incredible charisma and such a big career.

James: It's also why he was known as the intellectual president, and why his speeches were so memorable.

Martin: Because Mercury was stationary?

James: Yes. Mercury is the planet of communications.

Now, what is so fascinating about Kennedy's Mercury, and the reason I always use his horoscope as an example of the power of stationary planets, is that his Mercury is so incredibly devastated and afflicted that if an astrologer didn't know that Mercury was stationary, he or she would have to predict nothing but problems relating to Mercury and the two houses it rules.

Martin: Because Mercury is devastated in the 8th house (a *dusthana*, or grief-producing house) and is also tightly conjunct with malefic Mars?

James: Yes, but Mars hurts Mercury even more because it rules the "evil" 8th house. The fact that Mercury is in the house of death, conjunct the ruler of the house of death (Mars), and conjunct the ruler of accidents (Mars) is why Kennedy was in pain and on crutches all of his life. And also, to some extent, why he died early.

Martin: And why he was read his last rites about five different times!

James: That's right. Death played a huge part in his life. According to some biographies, Kennedy lived recklessly because his health was so fragile, he never expected to live long.

Martin: So Kennedy's Mercury is a mixed influence? It gives some excellent effects because it's stationary, but some terrible effects because it's so afflicted.

James: Exactly. This is the kind of condition that drives every astrologer crazy. It's the old "wild card" rearing its ugly head again.

Martin: James, in terms of Kennedy's great speeches and his intellectual nature, does this also relate to the fact that his ascendant is Virgo and his 10th house is Gemini?

James: Of course it does. But I've analyzed hundreds of charts of people with Virgo ascendants who aren't fabulous orators and speechmakers. The combination of Kennedy's stationary Mercury and the fact that Mercury ruled 1st and 10th houses made the difference. Never underestimate the power of a stationary planet.

Martin: If Kennedy's Mercury wasn't stationary, how would you read it?

James: First of all, I would consider the possibility that Kennedy could've died much earlier than his forties. I would have expected horribly <u>dangerous</u> Mercury subperiods and would have recommended that *yagyas* be performed immediately after birth. I would expect health problems with lungs, intestines, or the nervous system early in life. If — and this is a very big "if" — he was able to make it to adulthood, I would have expected huge problems in career and in self-confidence, and almost no possibility of gaining recognition or fame. There would have been some career success due to Ketu in its own sign, Gemini, in the 10th house, but definitely not fame.

Martin: Are you saying that the <u>ruler</u> of the 10th house is more important than the <u>planet</u> in the 10th house? Is that why there would have been some career success, but not fame?

James: Well, the ruler of a house is <u>slightly</u> more important than a planet in a house. But it's a subtle distinction. I'm saying that because the 10th house ruler <u>and the all-important 1st house ruler</u> are so incredibly devastated, with no good influence to counteract the affliction to the ascendant, that the good placement of Ketu in the 10th probably wouldn't affect the situation in a major way.

As to as whether the ruler of a house is more influential than a planet in a house, most Indian astrologers dance around the question.

Martin: What do you mean?

James: I could never get a straight answer to that question when I was in India. It was only after practicing professionally for a few years that I drew my conclusion. Later on, I found that most other <u>Western</u> astrologers practicing *Jyotish* felt the same.

Now, regarding "mixed" influences like Kennedy's Mercury — when you're analyzing someone's chart and are trying to draw a conclusion about the functioning of a house that has extremely contradictory indications, you can sometimes get help by looking at the *dasa* or *bhukti* that is currently running. For example, if natal Venus is exalted in the 10th house and the ruler of the 10th house is a fallen Jupiter, you can fairly well count on Venus periods and subperiods being excellent for career, while Jupiter periods and subperiods are difficult for career.

Martin: I see. James, what about Kennedy's stationary Uranus? What effect did that have?

James: I think it probably helped get him killed. Aside from ruling originality, excitement, and inventiveness, Uranus also rules independence, rebelliousness, and revolutionary tendencies. Kennedy's attitude about trying to coexist peacefully with the Russians was a revolutionary idea during the cold war. It frightened a lot of people; especially, I imagine, the CIA and FBI chief J. Edgar Hoover.

Kennedy also behaved rather independently with the Mafia, according to most reports, by obtaining their help in getting him elected and then allowing his brother Bobby, who was Attorney General, to try and prosecute as many of them as he could. Pretty Uranian behavior.

Martin: I guess he was also somewhat of a revolutionary in terms of civil rights.

James: Ultimately, yes. Now, let's look at another chart with a stationary planet.

Martin: Wait. How do I know whether a planet is stationary?

James: Most (<u>but not all</u>) computer programs will note a stationary planet by placing a "D" next to the planet involved. But they will only do so in the case of a planet that is absolutely stationary and that is not good enough because a planet will be extremely powerful a day or two before it stations as well as a day or two after it stations. In fact, the outer planets — Uranus, Neptune, and Pluto — move so incredibly slowly that they will be powerful for several days around the exact station. You need to know if a planet is <u>close</u> to stationary. To determine the speed of the planet, you either have to get a computer program that tells you the speed of the planet (one of the programs I use, <u>Haydn's *Jyotish*</u>, does this. See "Services" in the back of this book for more information on that program) or you simply look in the ephemeris, the book listing the daily positions of the planets.

Now let's look at some other charts containing a stationary planet, or a planet close to stationary. Tipper Gore (Al Gore's wife) was born three days after Jupiter turned stationary direct (see following page). Although three days seems like a long time, if you look in the ephemeris you'll notice that Jupiter was only moving about four <u>seconds</u> on the day she was born. In the ephemeris, ten seconds equal one minute and sixty minutes equal one degree. When Jupiter is moving fast, it moves about twelve minutes, or 120 seconds per day.

SAMPLE EPHEMERIS LISTING FOR JUPITER

August 15, 1948	℞	19° ♐ 6' 1"
August 16, 1948	D	19° ♐ 6' 0"
August 17, 1948		19° ♐ 6' 1"
August 18, 1948		19° ♐ 6' 4"
August 19, 1948		19° ♐ 6' 8"

NOTE: D = *Direct*, ℞ = *Retrograde*

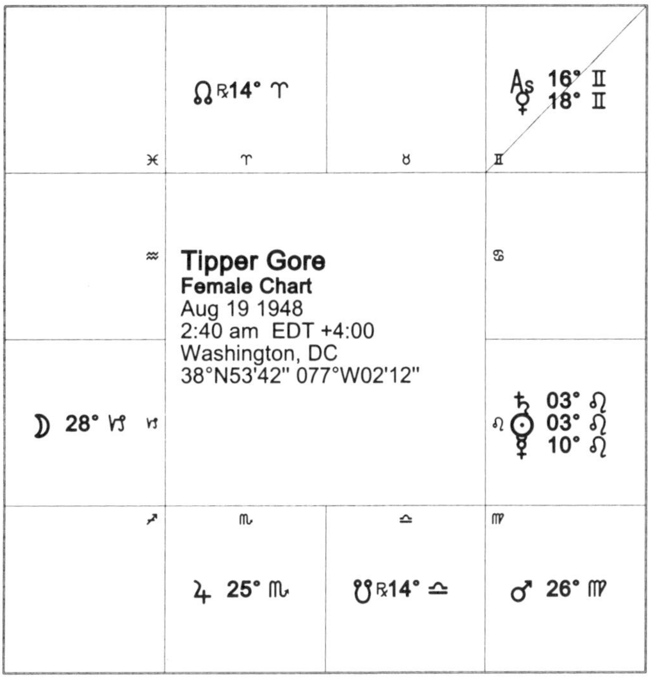

	☊ ℞14° ♈		As 16° ♊ ♀ 18° ♊
♓	♈	♉	♊
≈	**Tipper Gore** **Female Chart** Aug 19 1948 2:40 am EDT +4:00 Washington, DC 38°N53'42" 077°W02'12"		♋
☽ 28° ♑ ♑			♄ 03° ♌ ☊ ☉ 03° ♌ ☿ 10° ♌
♐	♏	♎	♍
	♃ 25° ♏	☋ ℞14° ♎	♂ 26° ♍

South Indian Style

For North Indian, see Appendix B.

planets.pts

Pt	Name	Hs	Rules
☽	Moon	8	2
☉	Sun	3	3
☿	Mercury	3	1, 4
♀	Venus	1	5, 12
♂	Mars	4	6, 11
♃	Jupiter	6	7, 10
♄	Saturn	3	8, 9
☊	North Node	11	–
☋	South Node	5	–
As	Ascendant	1	–

Sg	Name
♈	Aries
♉	Taurus
♊	Gemini
♋	Cancer
♌	Leo
♍	Virgo
♎	Libra
♏	Scorpio
♐	Sagittarius
♑	Capricorn
≈	Aquarius
♓	Pisces

Martin: So four seconds is really slow.

James: That's right. It's really slow, and therefore really strong.

Tipper has a near-stationary Jupiter as ruler of the 7th house, the house of marriage.

Martin: Which is why she has a special spouse?

James: Exactly. Now, her chart definitely indicates marriage problems, and the stationary 7th house ruler isn't going to cancel out the marriage problems that are indicated. But it does mean she gets a special, wealthy, or powerful spouse.

Martin: Where do you see the marriage problems?

James: Mars, the planet of friction, which is occupying the 4th house, is aspecting the 7th house. This creates *Kujadosha*, or Mars affliction, which harms married life (*Kujadosha* is also known as *Mangaldosha* or *Manglik*, and occurs if Mars occupies the 1st, 4th, 7th, 8th or 12th house). It also doesn't help that the Sun, which represents men in general, is <u>tightly</u> (within one degree) conjunct malefic Saturn.

Martin: What about the fact that the 7th house ruler (Jupiter) is occupying the *dusthana* (grief-producing) 6th house?

James: I wouldn't give it much weight because the Jupiter in the 6th house is near-stationary. In this case, I would say Tipper's near-stationary Jupiter occupying the 6th house shows that she would have good health, a very strong appetite, and not be bothered much by enemies. As the ruler of the 7th house occupying the 6th house, it also indicates the likelihood of obtaining a spouse who is interested in health or healing.

Martin: A doctor?

James: Yes. Now, we all know that Al Gore is a politician, not a doctor. But guess what? Gore has the Moon and Jupiter in Sagittarius in the 6th house of his own horoscope, which has created a major interest in health matters. Aside from trying to heal the planet ecologically through his books and politics, he was active in promoting health legislation during the 1980's and became the vice-chairman of Congress' Biomedical Ethics board. So, I wouldn't be bothered much about the *dusthana* 6th house harming Jupiter. Her near-stationary Jupiter is simply too strong to be harmed much by the 6th house.

Martin: Does it receive <u>any</u> harm from the 6th house?

James: Probably a little. But I think it is more responsible for indicating strong health and getting a partner interested in 6th house matters. This wouldn't be the case if Jupiter as ruler of the 7th were occupying the 6th house while moving at its normal speed (not nearly-stationary).

Martin: What would that cause?

James: Lots of things. First, there would be serious marital problems, maybe even divorce. Second, the spouse would be weak or have problems in life. Then, there would be some other effects that would greatly depend on whether the 6th house Jupiter was afflicted or strengthened through planetary aspects. If Jupiter was afflicted by planetary aspects, the spouse would have health problems. If Jupiter was well-aspected, the spouse would be successful in the field of health or healing.

Martin: What if this hypothetical Jupiter was not aspected at all? Would the spouse still be interested in health matters? Would the spouse have health problems?

James: You would have to use your intuition on that one. The answer to both questions is "maybe, but not definitely."

By the way, Tipper's near-stationary Jupiter rules the 10th house as well as the 7th, so she could clearly have tremendous career success.

Martin: The 10th house is also fortified by Jupiter aspecting its own house (Pisces).

James: That's right. Tipper must be an extraordinarily capable person. I don't doubt that she has some confidence problems, but with the near-stationary Jupiter in the house of work, while ruling the career house, this woman can accomplish a lot.

Martin: Are the confidence problems due to the tight Sun-Saturn conjunction?

James: Yes, but that's only one indication. The Moon occupies the *dusthana* 8th house, in a bad sign (Capricorn is the sign opposite the Moon's own sign — Cancer). Also, the 12th house ruler Venus is too close to the ascendant degree (the ascendant degree is sixteen and Venus' degree is eighteen).

Martin: Wait, James. I know Venus rules the 12th house, but it's also the *yogakaraka* (union indicator) — the best planet for a Gemini ascendant. Doesn't Venus, both as a natural benefic and a *yogakaraka*, give excellent effects?

James: It does. This excellent Venus in the 1st house makes Tipper attractive, artistic, kindhearted, and able to be recognized. But do you think we should just ignore the fact that Venus also rules the 12th house, one of the worst *dusthanas* there is? This is where astrology gets complicated, but you have to consider everything. You have to have a computer mind, as my mentor used to say.

In terms of Venus in the 1st house, I would not expect it to give any significant harmful 12th house effects to the personality if it were not so very close to the ascendant degree. But it is. So it is going to give both very good effects and some harmful effects to the ascendant.

This is similar to Robert De Niro's chart, where there is a tight Venus-Mercury conjunction in the 3rd house (see chart on the following page). Mercury rules De Niro's ascendant and is conjunct with benefic Venus, which is also the *yogakaraka*. So, this is good for fame, but it also means his confidence is seriously harmed because the ascendant ruler is too close to the 12th house ruler. In fact, if it weren't for the fact that the 10th house is so strong, his fame would not have been nearly as assured. I'm aware that the ascendant ruler, Mercury, is involved in a tight *rajayoga* with Venus (because Venus rules the 5th house and Mercury rules the 1st house). But Mercury is too close for comfort so near to the 12th house ruler. I've seen many charts where there is a tight (two or three degrees) *rajayoga* involving Mercury as ascendant ruler and Venus as the 12th house ruler, and almost always the person's confidence is harmed. There is some possibility of fame or recognition due to the ascendant ruler being in a *rajayoga*, but the person doesn't usually realize it unless the 10th house is also very powerful.

In terms of De Niro's strong 10th house, notice that the 10th house ruler (Jupiter) is exalted and is aspecting its own house.

Martin: What about it being closely conjunct Rahu?

James: First, you have to understand that Rahu doesn't hurt planets quite

		♂ 03° ♉	♄ 01° Ⅱ As 22° Ⅱ
☽ 21° ♒	\multicolumn{2}{l|}{**Robert De Niro** Male Chart Aug 17 1943 3:00 am EWT +4:00 Brooklyn, NY 40°N38' 073°W56'}	♃ 17° ♋ ☊ ℞22° ♋
☋ ℞22° ♑			☉ 00° ♌ ☿ 25° ♌ ♀ ℞27° ♌

South Indian Style

For North Indian, see Appendix B.

planets.pts

Pt	Name	Hs	Rules
☽	Moon	9	2
☉	Sun	3	3
☿	Mercury	3	1, 4
♀	Venus	3	5, 12
♂	Mars	12	6, 11
♃	Jupiter	2	7, 10
♄	Saturn	1	8, 9
☊	North Node	2	-
☋	South Node	8	-
As	Ascendant	1	-

Sg	Name
♈	Aries
♉	Taurus
Ⅱ	Gemini
♋	Cancer
♌	Leo
♍	Virgo
♎	Libra
♏	Scorpio
♐	Sagittarius
♑	Capricorn
♒	Aquarius
♓	Pisces

the same way as Ketu or the other malefics — I don't care what most textbooks say. In my experience, Rahu is generally not nearly as hard on a planet that it conjuncts as Mars, Saturn, Sun, or Ketu. Rahu *usually* only hurts a planet that it aspects in the sense that it delivers the qualities of intense cravings, materialistic power, and so on. For example, Rahu hurts De Niro's 7th house by being conjunct Jupiter (Jupiter rules the 7th house) because it makes the spouse intense, smothering, and materialistic, etc. These are not good qualities for a spouse (man or woman) to have. Who wants a domineering, smothering, bossy spouse? But cravings, intense desires, and a bossy nature in the career realm are generally helpful.

Martin: How close does a 12th house ruler that is a natural benefic have to be to spoil a planet it conjuncts or aspects?

James: This is a judgement call, but I only worry when the 12th house ruler (or 8th house ruler) is within two, three, or four degrees. That's my judgement, my experience.

Martin: So, if Tipper's Venus was six degrees away from the ascendant, you wouldn't expect that to hurt her confidence?

James: That's right. I would expect mainly very good effects. Remember that Venus has been deemed the *yogakaraka* even though it rules the evil 12th house. The sages who made the astrological rules determined that the rulership of the wonderful *trikona* (trinal) house outweighed the negative effects caused by the 12th house rulership. But I'm telling you from experience that if a benefic-natured *yogakaraka* planet (e.g. Venus or Jupiter) rules a *dusthana* house like the 12th, it needs to stay four or five degrees away from other planets and sensitive points in the chart, or serious damage will arise. I've sen this over and over and over. As Padia would say, "You take it from me. I have marked this!"

Martin: Let me ask you this, James. Venus, as a benefic and the *yogakaraka* in Tipper's 1st house, must be causing some very good effects, right?

James: Undoubtedly.

Martin: If you had a choice, would you want to have a placement like hers in your chart?

James: Well, that's hard to answer, because the influence is both good and bad. But, ultimately, Tipper's Venus is too close the ascendant. I would not want a 12th house ruler, benefic-natured or not, to aspect any planet or sensitive point in my chart within three or four degrees. Even though the effects would be both good and bad, the damage that would be created would certainly be undesirable.

Martin: James, you've told me over and over that the nature of a planet takes precedence over the houses that it rules. Are you contradicting that teaching?

James: Not at all. I'm not saying that anytime a benefic planet rules a bad house it gives more bad effects than good. I'm saying that when a benefic planet rules one or two bad houses it will have a searing effect <u>if it gets within a few degrees of another planet or a a sensitive point in the chart</u>. I might be wrong in saying that the damage becomes intense within three or four degrees. That's a judgement call. But if that *dusthana* ruler is within one or two degrees, it has to cause some serious harm.

The astrologers who consider house rulerships to take precedence over the essential natures of the planets (those who consider functional malefics and functional benefics <u>most</u> important) don't make any distinction at all about the degrees of aspects thrown by such planets. They say, for example, that Jupiter as the ruler of the 8th and 11 houses (Taurus ascendant) hurts any planet that it aspects, and any house that it occupies. And they don't acknowledge that it does any good at all. Or, if they are openminded, they say it does some tiny amount of good, but very little. As I've said over and over, based on my experience I vehemently disagree with that assessment.

Martin: But you're always talking about how you've gained career recognition because your 10th ruler Saturn is aspected *within one degree* by Jupiter, and Jupiter is the ruler of your 8th house. You always seem to be happy about that aspect. If what you've said about Tipper's 12th house Venus and De Niro's 12th house Venus causing problems is correct, then you must experience some problems because of your 12th house Jupiter aspecting your 9th and 10th house ruler Saturn, right?

James: That's right. Do you know how many careers I've had? I spent four intense years training at one of the finest drama schools in the country and then gave that up in an instant to pursue enlightenment and teach meditation. During the years I taught meditation, I made most of my money as a businessman. I gave up that career in an instant and haven't made any significant money since. As an astrologer, I thought I would pay my bills by the four books I've written. That never happened, not even close. In 1994, when I finally realized that making a living through book sales was impossible, I started looking for a different profession. I tried speculating in stocks and didn't do particularly well. By 1995, I was aching to stop doing horoscope readings for a living.

Martin: Really?

James: I was burned out from doing so many chart readings for so many years.

Martin: What happened?

James: I moved to Longboat Key and found that living in the middle of the ocean helped blow off the stress and psychic strain that had been mounting for so long. I actually began enjoying doing readings again.

Make no mistake, I've had plenty of problems due to the 8th house ruler tightly aspecting my 10th house ruler, and I've used the 8th house energy in as positive a way as possible by choosing an 8th house profession (astrology)!

Martin: So, Jupiter's exact aspect onto your Saturn is a mixed influence?

James: Absolutely. I wouldn't be affected much by the 8th house factor if the aspect wasn't so tight, but it is. Anyway, you've simply got to get this concept of mixed influences. Life is multi-dimensional and therefore *Jyotish* has to be also. You have to stop expecting astrological features to be simply black or white, good or bad. Life doesn't work that way.

Martin: And this means that you must have mixed results with 9th house significations, since Saturn also rules your 9th house too.

James: Of course. And, when you analyze my 9th house, you also have to notice that the planet of religion (Jupiter) is aspected by Saturn within one degree. So there are even more problems associated with higher knowledge than just the 8th house ruler Jupiter throwing its aspect onto my 9th house ruler.

Martin: This is interesting, James. Even the aspect that Saturn throws onto Jupiter is both good and bad because Saturn throws bad energy as a malefic and excellent energy as the *rajayoga karaka,* the ruler of good houses.

James: You're getting it. That's how *Jyotish* works. There are some features that are all good, some that are all bad, and some that are mixed, mixed, and more mixed!

Martin: So you have some great luck with higher knowledge and some terrible luck with higher knowledge.

James: That's right. The good features I've experienced within that realm are the knowledge I've gained about meditation, yoga, Hinduism, astrology, and so on. The bad features are that I've been disappointed and disillusioned by enlightened gurus and none of the disciples I know who have spent their lives pursuing higher consciousness have reached the goal. Worse yet, I've seen too many famous gurus get captivated by either money, sex, or power. I've heard all the explanations about the gurus not being "attached" to their money, sex, and power, but I'm not buying it. In my view, gurus need to act responsibly if they want their disciples to gain enlightenment. If disciples can't trust their gurus <u>absolutely</u>, they'll never let go of their attachments and jump into the unknown, which is what it takes to gain self-realization.

Martin: So, you consider your perceptions about enlightenment and fraudulent gurus to be caused by your 9th house and Jupiter afflictions?

James: Yes. Many disciples aren't bothered by these problems, but I am. My worst suffering, however, came from having a guru who was more concerned with saving the world than enlightening his disciples. This caused massive dilemmas for me that I won't go into here.

Now, let me give you another example of a stationary planet in a person's birthchart. I recently had an interesting experience analyzing a horoscope of an old friend who I hadn't seen since my college days, whose chart contains a stationary Mars. Although she had gotten her birth data from her mother (who was certain about the data) and was confirmed by a baby book, the 1st house of the chart didn't make sense to me. (See Deborah's rasi and navamsa charts in Class Seven, page 259.)

Notice stationary Mars in the first house with Ketu, close to the ascendant. Well, Deborah is one of the sweetest people I have ever known in my life and I have never heard her argue or fight or even get terribly assertive. In fact, before I did her birthchart reading she had read the analysis of Mars in the 1st house in my textbook, and said something must be wrong because the description did not fit at all. I considered the fact that because Mars was perfectly stationary, it may have worked in a more positive way than usual. I also considered that Mars may have been weakened by being so close to Ketu (Mars in this chart is also conjunct Neptune!). But the truth was I wasn't sure that a person could have <u>any</u> kind of Mars in the 1st house without being aggressive at least once in a while. As I said, Deborah is one of the sweetest, most gentle persons I have ever known.

Since it didn't make much sense that her mother and her baby book were wrong about the time, I decided to see if the rest of the birthchart fit. Whenever I try to rectify an ascendant, the first thing I do is look at the most obvious features and see if the results tally with my expectations. Since I consider a stationary planet to be the most powerful influence in all of astrology, of course I started my analysis with Mars. In this case, Mars rules the 3rd and the 8th houses. Since the 3rd house holds a fallen planet (Moon in Scorpio), I knew that 3rd house matters would be mixed rather than simply good.

Martin: And that wouldn't be much help in rectifying the chart?

James: Exactly. So, I looked at the 8th house, the other house Mars rules. The 8th house signifies inheritances, longevity, sexual attractiveness, and metaphysical subjects. It also rules money from the spouse. Well, I've known several people with powerful 8th houses who are incredibly lucky in terms of their mates giving them money. So, my first question to her was about her luck with joint finances. Oddly, the words that came out of my mouth were, "Does your husband turn over his money to you?"

Martin: What did she say?

James: She burst out laughing and said, "Yes, and he's an accountant!"

Martin: I guess stationary Mars rules her 8th house.

James: I think so. I told her that in all my years I had never asked anyone the question I asked her. I know that some men do turn over their paychecks to their wives, but the notion has always seemed so foreign to me. When I asked her why her husband would let her manage the money, since he was an accountant, she said he knew immediately that she would be great at it. Actually, the reason he gave her the money is irrelevant.

Martin: Because it's so obviously indicated in her horoscope?

James: Yes. As astrologers, we see this strong 8th house and we know generally what's going to happen.

Martin: So, did the rest of the chart work?

James: Mostly, yes. I still can't find anything in her behavior that matches a 1st house Mars. To me, this is one of those occasions where astrology simply misses the mark. It doesn't work.

Martin: What about the fact that Mars is two degrees away from Ketu? Also, you mentioned that Mars is conjunct Neptune in the Western chart.

James: Yes, that's all true. But Mars is perfectly stationary in this birthchart. Mars was not moving at all the day Deborah was born. In my experience, in the vast majority of cases, a stationary planet will not be overwhelmed by other birthchart factors. To me, this is simply a case of natal astrology being imperfect. Which reminds me — I've met some very learned astrologers who consider natal astrology to be the hardest and weakest branches of astrology.

Martin: What do you mean?

James: Before natal astrology was developed, astrologers practiced mundane astrology and *prasna* (known as horary in the West). Mundane astrology involves predicting wars and the weather and effects of kings, and so on. *Prasna* involves answering questions based on the time, place, and date that a client contacts an astrologer. Then there's also *muhurta*, or electional astrology, which we used to pick a good starting time to begin this teaching and book project. So, every time you get frustrated at some feature in a natal horoscope that doesn't work, give yourself a break and remember that this is probably the hardest branch of astrology!

Martin: Why so?

James: Well, I've had some experience with the other branches, *prasna* and *Muhurta*, but I'm not an expert. I'm telling you what I've heard from people who specialize in those fields. The reason I respect what I've heard is because when I do *a prasna* myself, and the chart is clear, the results are awesome and the process is simple. Since I only dabble in *prasna*, I don't give a prediction if the chart is very mixed.

Martin: What do you tell the person?

James: I refer them to Lee Lehman, who specializes in those fields. (Lee lives in Malabar, Florida and her phone number is listed in this book in the chapter titled "Services.") She is, by the way, the person I go to when I want to have a question answered professionally. She uses 17th century William Lilly techniques.

Martin: So that's Western astrology?

James: Yes. And Lee has been extraordinarily accurate for me. Not one hundred percent accurate, but pretty close.

Martin: Do you analyze *prasnas* for others often?

James: Once in a while. I include them in my practice mainly when I look at a chart that is so confusing, so mixed, and so difficult to interpret that I have no sense of confidence about the person's life or why they are coming to me for a reading. In those cases, I draw a chart for the time, date, and place of the person's appointment. (Note: In terms of chart data, if a person calls me with a question, I use the place that the client calls me from. If I am doing a natal chart reading by phone, I generally use my location.) This gives me a good idea of what the session will focus on, and what's on the person's mind.

Martin: What if that chart is unclear?

James: I don't think it's ever happened that a person's natal chart and the *prasna* for the person's appointment were both confusing. I've been doing astrology for a long time and have seen lots of unclear horoscopes, but it takes a lot for me to throw up my hands and go draw a *prasna* about an astrology session.

The idea of drawing a chart for the time of a person's astrology session is important, so please don't forget it. This is going to help immensely in your beginning days, when you see a horoscope that is so unclear it makes your eyes go crossed. But, be careful when you draw the chart. Remember that if you draw a *prasna* for the appointment time, and the person shows up late, the chart you have drawn may not be accurate (depending on how late the person is). When I was in India during my first visit, I went to see a well-known astrologer named Manik Chand Jain. I had an 11:00 A.M. appointment, but was about an hour late. Jain evidently drew a *prasna* for the appointment time of all his clients and had drawn one for me using 11:00 A.M.

Martin: What happened?

James: He thought I was consulting him about some sort of emotional problem. I wasn't. I wanted to get a good natal reading and I wanted to find a teacher to study with.

Martin: So, even if the natal chart is very confusing, knowing what's on the client's mind will help me?

James: You bet it will. You'll know what features of the chart to address and what current transits are important once you understand why the person has decided to consult you. You'll see how this works when you get some experience with *prasnas*. By the way, it's possible that the reason the person is consulting you will correspond to an area of the chart that is not very confusing. Astrology is quite a cosmic science. If the person's intention to find an answer, or to get help with a problem, is strong, he or she will find the right astrologer to provide what is needed. When you get a chart that's hard to read, you have to have faith that somewhere in the session (maybe in the middle, maybe in the end) things will work out for you and the client.

Martin: And they usually do?

James: If your intention to help a client is strong, the proper information will almost always show up, not matter how confusing the chart is. This depends on you of course. There have actually been times when I've had such a rough day that I've postponed a reading. It hasn't happened often, but it has happened. I need to feel clear and strong to serve a client.

I will also, by the way, occasionally do a *prasna* at the end of a chart reading. Sometimes during a session, a client will ask a question that just begs to be answered by a *prasna*, if you know what I mean.

Martin: I don't.

James: For example, a few weeks ago in the middle of a reading, the client suddenly said "I just put in a bid on a house. Do you think I'll get it?" Even if the natal chart indicated moving, I would have no way to know whether the house she just bid on would be the one she would get. So I noted the time she asked the question and told her I would draw a *prasna* after the session. I also told her that since *prasna* is not my specialty I would only answer the question if the chart was clear and definitive.

Martin: Was the chart clear?

James: Not clear enough for me to give a professional prediction. What I saw was the 1st house ruler aspected tightly (within one degree) by the benefic planet Venus, which happened to rule the 4th house.

Martin: That sounds great.

James:. Yes. That indicated that she would definitely get the house. But, there were complications.

Martin: Oh, oh. Another mixed chart?

James: Yes. First, the ascendant ruler was retrograde, which I assumed meant a delay. Second, the ascendant was Aquarius. This means that the tight Venus-Saturn opposition, which was good in the sense that the 1st and 4th house rulers were aspecting each other, appeared to indicate a seriously afflicted 4th house.

Martin: Why?

James: Because for an Aquarius ascendant horoscope, Venus rules the 4th house.

Martin: And Venus was aspected tightly by malefic Saturn?

James: Exactly. So, I found the chart confusing. I told her that I thought she would get the house after a delay, but she should call Lee Lehman, who makes her living doing horary.

Martin: Did she?

James: Yes. In this case, Lee (using her horary system) repeated what I had said.

Martin: Was she right?

James: Yes. The woman got the house after a slight delay.

I'll give you another example of when I would rather use a *prasna* chart instead of the natal. Sometimes I see an upcoming marriage in a chart that I mention to a client, maybe one that is scheduled to occur in a year or two. And sometimes the person asks (either right then or later in the session) whether the marriage will be to the person he or she is currently dating. So, I draw a *prasna*.

Now, I will only draw a *prasna* for a question like that if the person <u>needs</u> to know the answer. Most people don't have a true need or strong urge to know information like that, and *prasnas* only work if the question is genuine and compelling.

Martin: I see. So, do you agree that natal astrology is harder than the other branches?

James: I can't answer that authoritatively since I haven't mastered the other branches. But is makes sense to me that it might be easier to determine whether, say, a court case will work out favorably for someone based on a question that is posed a month before the trial rather than from a horoscope that was born thirty or forty years ago (i.e. the natal chart). People do grow and evolve, and there is free will. I think it is very possible that other branches have an edge over natal astrology, depending on what the astrologer is trying to predict.

Now, let's get back to the stationary planets we were discussing. I'm going to talk about Deborah's horoscope again later when I discuss *vargas* (divisional charts), because hers is an excellent example of what happens when a birthchart has a terrible natal 7th house while having a very good *navamsa* (marriage chart) 7th house.

Martin: What happens?

James: Essentially, the person experiences some very bad karma in love matters, but eventually has a happy marriage. I'll show you this later (see Class Seven).

Now, let me show you one final chart with a stationary planet. Look at Hank Aaron's horoscope, which has a stationary Jupiter.

Martin: James, can we go back to the marriage problems in Tipper Gore's chart? I want to know more about *Kujadoshsa* (also known as *Mangaldosha* and *Manglik*). I'm asking because Tipper met her husband at the age of sixteen and has never divorced. Doesn't *Kujadosha* consistently cause divorce, or does that only happen if the rest of the marriage indications are bad?

James: *Kujadosha*, in my experience, is an extremely reliable indicator of divorce, or at least <u>serious</u> marriage problems. Astrologically, the reason the Gores never got divorced, even though they are reported to have gone for marriage counseling, is that Al Gore also has *Kujadosha*. The best way for a person to deal with Mars Affliction is to marry someone else who has the condition. Indian astrologers always advise parents who have a child with *Kujadosha* to arrange a marriage with another person who also has it.

Let me give you some more details, because Mars Affliction occurs in about one-third of all charts. If a person has *Kujadosha*, he or she has caused harm to others in married life during past lifetimes, and now the time has come to reap the bad karma of those actions. This means that the person attracts partners in this life who will be bad love partners.

Martin: How so?

James: Usually, people with *Kujadosha* will have a least one major horror story about a spouse or lover who treated them very poorly or unfairly.

Martin: Doesn't everyone have a story like that?

James: In America, yes. Most people do. But there are a few telling distinctions about *Kujadosha*. First, a person with the condition always reports that he or she did absolutely nothing to cause the partner to act so offensively. Second, a person with *Kujadosha* usually continues to be attracted to lousy partners throughout the entire life.

Martin: So, that person is damaged for an entire life?

James: No. And here is where your help as an astrologer comes in. You must advise people who have *Kujadosha* not to marry until the late twenties or early thirties because that is when they will have more discrimination and experience in love matters. This advice is important because it allows the person to feel he or she is not doomed forever. But, you must be extremely clear in explaining that a person with *Kujadosha* will, most likely, always make poor love choices if he or she simply follows impulses and attractions. The key is to use intelligence and reasoning, rather than emotions and passions in choosing a spouse.

Martin: And you're saying people do that naturally after the late twenties?

James: Yes. If a person has the least bit of intelligence and common sense, and assuming that marriage indications in the rest of the natal chart or *navamsa* are not horribly afflicted, he or she will eventually develop better ways to choose a spouse. Usually, after experiencing three or four major bruises in love caused by completely following one's heart, the person begins to use his or her intellect. Or, the person ask friends and parents for advice in love matters. This usually happens after the age of twenty-seven, twenty-eight, or twenty-nine.

Martin: What if a person who has *Kujadosha* is very mature at the age of twenty? Does that person also have to wait to get married?

James: Yes. Maturity is one thing. But dealing with *Kujadosha* takes wisdom and experience. And that takes time. A person with Mars Affliction shouldn't get married early, in my view.

Now, there are some things other you need to know about *Kujadosha*, which so many of your clients are going to have. First off, you should only consider *Kujadosha* to occur if Mars occupies the 1st, 4th, 7th, 8th, or 12th house <u>in the natal chart</u>. If you <u>also</u> use the *navamsa* (marriage chart) to determine *Kujadosha*, the percentage of people that have it will jump to probably ninety percent. The same thing will happen if you <u>also</u> consider *Kujadosha* from the position of the Moon (i.e. if Mars is in the 1st, 4th, 7th, 8th, or 12th house from the Moon).

Martin: So, I only use *Kujadosha* from the natal chart?

James: Unless you want to find it in every chart you see!

Martin: In the case of the Gores, they both have *Kujadosha*, and they obviously didn't have an astrologer arrange the marriage. Does that happen a lot?

James: Very rarely. I'd say one out of thirty or forty people with Mars Affliction are lucky enough to naturally choose a partner who also has it. I do see a certain number of cases where two people with *Kujadosha* have found each other <u>after the late twenties and after one or two divorces</u>, but by then the person has suffered plenty.

Martin: What if I see a client who is thirty-five or forty and that person's spouse doesn't have *Kujadosha*? Does that mean the person is headed for divorce, or that he or she will be treated badly?

James: Maybe, but not definitely. Most people with *Kujadosha* figure out how to choose a partner more wisely when they are older, unless the rest of the chart is really bad for marriage. In any case, you don't want to scare a person who is married and has the condition.

Martin: It's too late for them to do anything anyway, right?

James: That's right. So, I wouldn't make a big deal about it in cases like those. I do tell the person that he or she has *Kujadosha*, so they can understand their karma and their past and future love experiences. But I try not to scare them about it.

Also, if a person with Mars Affliction got married in their early years and has stayed married until their early or mid-thirties, they have probably beaten the odds.

Martin: Basically then, I should advise people who have *Kujadosha* to choose partners based on reasoning, rather than passion.

James: Yes. That's the deal.

By the way, since most Westerners aren't able to check every prospective partner to see if *Kujadosha* exists in their birthcharts, I often advise such a person to try and find a partner who has also suffered in love matters. Even if that partner doesn't have Mars Affliction, he or she will be much more aware of how to treat a spouse than someone who has never experienced pain in that realm. You see?

Martin: Yes. But what about passion? A person with *Kujadosha* isn't usually attracted to another person with *Kujadosha*.

James: That's not exactly accurate. There can be some passion and some attraction between two *Kujadosha* people. It's just that the attraction and passion is not scorching. In our culture, a person needs to have some attraction to his or her mate. And that's not impossible between two *Kujadosha* people.

By the way — if Mars affliction occurs in a person's chart by way of Mars occupying the 1st house or the 7th house, even though that person will get victimized by a partner, he or she may also initiate a lot of fights. So don't think that a person with these Mars placements is only a victim of their past life actions.

Martin: People with Mars in the 1st house can be very aggressive.

James: And blunt and offensive. And <u>people</u> with Mars in the 7th house typically like to fight in their relationships.

Finally, I want to mention something about *Kujadosha* that contradicts textbook teachings. The texts give one exception for each *Kujadosha* placement. They say that *Kujadosha* is cancelled if Mars occupies the 1st house in the sign of Aries, the 4th house if in Scorpio, the 7th house if in Capricorn or Pisces, the 8th house if in Cancer, and the 12th house if in Sagittarius. Well, in my experience these exceptions are nonsense. They don't work. Maybe they work in India, but not in the West. Don't forget that, or your predictions about people's married lives will be wrong.

Martin: Okay. Now what about Hank Aaron? You said you wanted to talk about his chart.

James: Yes. There are lots of famous people who have stationary planets, but I'm trying to find charts that are very mixed or confusing, like Kennedy's. The more of those charts we analyze, the easier it'll be when you see clients with mixed conditions.

Martin: Great.

James: I wanted to use Hillary Clinton's chart, but her birthtime is considered "dirty data" by Lois Rodden (the professional birth data collector). That means, the time of her birth is questionable.

Martin: Does she have a stationary planet?

James: She has a near-stationary planet. She was born about a day-and-a-half after Mercury turned retrograde.

Martin: So, she must be very intelligent.

James: Yes. She is reported to have been a high-powered trial lawyer. Mercury usually moves about two degrees (or 120 minutes) per day. It was only moving about six minutes when she was born. Until her birthtime is known with certainty, we'll leave her chart alone.

Donald Trump is another person with a stationary planet in his chart. In his case, it's Jupiter, the planet of luck and abundance.

Martin: He certainly has a lot of abundance. He always does things in a huge way.

James: Yes, that's Jupiter. Just like Marlon Brando, who also has stationary Jupiter in the 1st house. He does everything excessively.

Martin: Even his body is excessive.

James: I read somewhere that when he eats ice cream, he eats a whole gallon! Anyway, Hank Aaron was born just <u>hours</u> before Jupiter stopped and turned retrograde. It was barely moving. His Jupiter rules the 4th and 7th houses. I don't actually know much about those areas of Aaron's life, other than the fact that Aaron acknowledges his mother (4th house) as having been a huge influence in his life. Also, he was married (7th house) twice, and his second wife was successful as a local television personality in Atlanta.

What I do know that relates to his stationary Jupiter is that he was the highest paid ballplayer for some years in the early 70's.

Martin: Because stationary Jupiter is in his 2nd house?

James: Yes. And speaking of money, notice that the ruler of his 11th house occupies the 2nd house. Whenever there is a connection between the money houses, 2 and 11, the person usually becomes a millionaire, unless the planets involved are afflicted, or the rest of the chart is very weak. I've seen this over and over.

Another thing I want to point out is that Aaron was in a Jupiter *dasa* from the age of seventeen until thirty-three (Dec. 1950-Dec. 1966). These were the bulk of his playing years.

Martin: So the periods and subperiods of a stationary planet are strong?

James: They definitely can be. I'm not certain that they are always dramatically powerful. I'd have to research that. But in Aaron's case the *dasa* was great.

Martin: James, what I don't get is why Hank Aaron is so modest and humble. He doesn't match what I would expect from a person with such a phenomenal Jupiter. He almost seems like the opposite of Brando and Trump. Are you sure his Jupiter is powerful?

James: Yes. I believe that the reason Aaron isn't a typical Jupitarian is because of other features of the horoscope that indicate the very opposite of a Jupitarian person.

Martin: There's the mixed influence you mentioned.

James: Exactly. This is the kind of chart that would drive any astrologer crazy. First, you notice this wonderful stationary Jupiter, and then you see a tight Sun-Saturn conjunction.

Martin: Which is what makes Aaron shy and modest.

James: Yes. It's also why he got very little press or notice when he was playing tremendously good baseball for so many years. Serious baseball fans knew about him, but not the general public. They only knew about players like Mickey Mantle and Willie Mays. Meanwhile, Aaron was stacking up home runs like crazy and achieving a tremendous batting average, while making very little noise and fanfare.

I know you've gotten the point now about stationary, or near-stationary, planets being incredibly powerful, so I'm not going to say anything about Aaron's Jupiter beyond what I've already said. It obviously made him extraordinarily lucky (he was one of the first blacks to make it in into pro baseball), and gave him great wealth, a very special spouse, and an unusually adoring mother. Enough said. I want to talk more about his chart because of how mixed it is and therefore how difficult it is to read.

Martin: Good.

James: By now, I've shown you enough mixed charts, or mixed influences in charts, for you to realize that I don't have any magical answer that will give you the ability to make spectacularly precise predictions about mixed influences or mixed charts. Mixed influences produced mixed results, and mixed charts produce mixed lives. The intensity of the planetary effects coincides with the intensity of the positive and negative effects. One good planetary effect does not, generally, cancel out one bad planetary effect. Simple?

Martin: Simple.

James: Okay. The distinction that I want you to get now is that it is easier to find your way with a mixed chart that you interpret for an adult than for a mixed chart of a baby.

Martin: Because I can get some feedback from that person?

James: Exactly. Let's use Aaron's chart as an example. If I were analyzing that chart around the time of his birth, I would definitely consider the possibility of a sports career, but I would have no way to know whether it would fit or not. I'll explain why. On the positive side of a sports career, the ascendant ruler (Mercury) is tightly conjunct with Mars (planet of sports). This almost always makes a person assertive, aggressive, physical, and a lover of sports. Also on the positive side are four planets (Venus, Sun, Saturn, and Rahu) occupying the 5th house, thereby tremendously energizing the house of sports. Better still, the ruler of the 5th house (Saturn) is in it's own sign, Capricorn.

Martin: What could be better?

James: I'll tell you what could be a lot better. How about if the 5th house ruler (Saturn), the planet ruling the house of sports, was not combust the malefic-natured Sun within two degrees, while the Sun is ruling the *dusthana* 12th house!

Martin: And, what about malefic Rahu also conjunct Saturn within one degree? Is that terrible for Saturn?

James: I'm not so concerned about Rahu's conjunction with Saturn. I would be far more concerned if Saturn were closely conjunct Ketu.

Martin: Why?

James: I've told you before that Rahu has a more intense and more malefic effect than Ketu in terms of the house it occupies, but a much more mild or benign effect regarding a planet it conjuncts.

Martin: How can that be?

James: I can't answer that with a *Jyotish* explanation, except to say that I am telling you what I have noticed over and over and over after almost twenty years of experience. I do have an explanation that comes from Western astrology, and if you want to hear it I'll tell you.

Martin: Of course I do.

James: Okay. Remember when I told you about how the North and South Nodes (Rahu and Ketu) operate in Western astrology?

Martin: The South Node reveals what a person has learned in past lives, and the North Node indicates what the person has to perform in this life.

James: Yes. Well, in Western astrology, any planet conjunct the North Node becomes a powerful and positive influence because its energy is operating <u>near the realm the person is consciously trying to activate anyway</u>. So if a person has, say, Venus conjunct the North Node, Venusian energy becomes fruitful and beneficial for the person.

Martin: So, the person could become an artist?

James: Right. Now, when a Hindu astrologer sees Venus conjunct Rahu, the last thing on his or her mind to predict is an artistic career. But many times you'll find exactly that. Likewise, if Mercury is conjunct the North Node, the person may go toward writing. If Jupiter is conjunct the North Node, the person may be driven toward religion and philosophy. This is purely a Western astrological teaching, but it works in either chart, for obvious reasons. This is not a one-hundred percent influence, but it works in lots of cases. <u>But please remember not to read Rahu in the person's Hindu chart as an indicator of the person's purpose and destiny, just because that's how it works in Western astrology</u>. That would be disastrous.

Now, back to what I was saying about Hank Aaron's mixed chart. I would not be able to predict a career in sports with certainty if I saw his chart when he was a baby, because the ruler of the 5th house is badly burned by being <u>closely</u> combust the malefic 12th lord Sun. If, however, Aaron was sixteen years old and said he loved sports, I would definitely encourage him to go for it.

Martin: So, this is a case where sports becomes a "wild card," something that is extremely strong in the chart and also extremely weak in the chart.

James: Yes. And once you know how that wild card is actually functioning, you'll get an idea of how it will continue to function in the future. Just like a mixed planet that gives good effects in most subperiods is likely to give good effects in an upcoming *dasa* period.

Martin: Then you wouldn't have been surprised if you were talking to Hank Aaron at the age of sixteen and he said he hated sports?

James: If he said he hated sports, I would have said: "That makes sense. Saturn, the ruler of the house of sports is in big trouble in this chart because it's tightly combust the 12th house ruler Sun." If he said he loved sports, I would have said: "That makes sense; the ascendant ruler is tightly conjunct Mars, and there are four planets in the 5th house." That's the nature of a wild card influence. It can go either way, and there's no way to know in advance, unless you're extremely psychic.

Martin: If, as a child, Hank Aaron had said he loved sports, couldn't you have said that it makes sense because even though Saturn is burned by the Sun, the negative effect is cancelled out by Saturn is occupying its own sign?

James: That's the last thing I would say, because positive astrological influences don't cancel out negative astrological influences, and vice versa. It just doesn't work that way.

Sure, it may work that way in a <u>few</u> charts, maybe ten or fifteen percent of the time. But <u>anything</u> in astrology works ten or fifteen percent of the time. We're looking for what works about seventy or seventy-five percent of the time.

Actually, I would be willing to bet that Saturn's affliction in Aaron's chart has caused some serious damage to other features of the 5th house.

Martin: Like children or speculations?

James: Yes. Or peace of mind. There has to be some significant damage caused by that afflicted Saturn. His 5th house is <u>not</u> simply well-disposed. It's definitely mixed, and if we knew enough about Hank Aaron, we would know exactly what the damage is.

Another glaring mixed influence in Aaron's chart is his personality. Can you imagine trying to predict this man's essential nature from the chart? Most people with close Mercury-Mars conjunctions (Aaron's is within two-and-a-half degrees) are constantly angry and agitated and annoyed. The fact that Mercury rules the 1st house and is conjunct Mars indicates the likelihood of a very aggressive and pushy personality.

Martin: Aaron is anything but that.

James: That's why I am using his chart. You're always complaining about how hard it is to read charts with contradictory features. This is an excellent example.

Martin: So how do you predict his personality?

James: His makeup is a bit of a wild card, <u>a mixture of extremes</u>. On one hand, he is very shy and humble and self-negating, due to the extremely strong Sun-Saturn conjunction. On the other, he could be aggressive, domineering and pushy due to the strong Mercury.

Martin: Is he both?

James: Yes. He is both. Fortunately, however, Aaron's Mars-like nature came out mainly in sports. Aaron is known as a great gentleman, but that never helped his opponents in baseball. He was extraordinarily aggressive on the field. Ask the pitchers who had to pitch to him.

Also, fortunately for Aaron, he has many more aspects indicating a fine personality than he does indicating an offensive one.

Martin: Because of the Moon-Jupiter conjunction?

James: Yes. That makes for a kind, religious person with high morals. Also, having a tight Sun-Venus conjunction makes him charming, soft, and gentle. And it certainly doesn't hurt that Jupiter, the planet of faith and religion, is stationary.

Martin: So, he has three or four kind-hearted influences and only one aggressive influence. The percentage is in his favor.

James: Exactly. Aaron is nice, considerate, and happy most of the time, and angry and pushy only once in a while. Astrology is a percentage game.

Martin: Well, my only wish is that astrology would work <u>one-hundred</u> percent of the time.

James: Think about how baseball players feel. The best and highest paid hitters hit an average of 320-350. Know what that means?

Martin: Out of every ten at bats, they only get a little over three hits.

James: That's right. And those are the best players! So consider yourself a genius if you get a seventy percent accuracy rate in astrology.

There's one other point I want to make about Aaron's chart. It has to do with the 5th house. You won't find this in many textbooks, but the 5th house has a lot to do with a person's character.

Martin: Some texts mention the 5th house indicates ethics and morals.

James: Yes. Well, I find that the 5th house has a lot to do with a person's character because the 5th house is the mind, and everything a person does springs from the mind. So, if Mars is in the 5th house, the person may not have the highest morals or ethics, because Mars signifies <u>personal</u> desires. On the other hand, if Venus or Moon occupy the 5th house, the person's character will be better, kinder and gentler.

If you look at Aaron's 5th house, it looks quite confusing because there are so many different influences there (Venus, Sun, Saturn, and Rahu). But try to get a feel for the art of interpretation — if you see that the Sun-Saturn conjunction, which indicates humility and a strong sense of responsibility, is in the house of ethics and morals, then you begin to think this is someone of extraordinarily high character. Of course, it doesn't hurt that the Moon is conjunct Jupiter. That's a very nice aspect in terms of making a person religious or spiritual.

I want to say one more thing about stationary planets before we move on to *Sade Sati*. Sometimes a person has a very average, or even weak, horoscope that happens to contain a stationary planet. If the person doesn't have the confidence to use his or her intense abilities signified by the stationary planet, it can almost be a curse.

Martin: How so?

James: In some cases, the person has a tremendous ability that he or she can't or won't use because of self-esteem problems, or emotional baggage from a dysfunctional childhood, or God-knows-what. There's nothing terrible about having an ability and not using it, but when a planet is stationary it usually signifies <u>extreme</u> talent, and if a person has extreme talent and doesn't use it, the end result is depression.

Martin: That's true.

James: That's how a stationary planet can become a kind of curse. It's hard when a person has a sense of destiny in some realm that he or she can't seem to manifest. Did you know that Winston Churchill used to have intense fits of depression that he called "the black dog?" His depression, in my view, was a result of having such great potential and such a strong sense of destiny that couldn't be fulfilled because he was politically out of favor for so long. Then, when the war broke out, everyone knew he was the perfect man for the job and he was able to fulfill his destiny.

Martin: Wow. So what do I do when I see a client with a very weak or afflicted chart and one stationary planet?

James: Well, you have to understand that when you start mentioning the great abilities this kind of person has because of the stationary planet, he or she will probably deny everything. The person will act like you are completely wrong.

Martin: What then?

James: Stick to your guns, and don't buy into the person's meekness. If the person has a stationary or very near-stationary planet, he or she is going to have some enormous talent. Of course, you have to mention <u>all</u> the potential realms that could be strong. Don't think that if the person has stationary Mercury that he or she has to be a writer. One of my brothers has a stationary Mercury and you wouldn't particularly know it from any Mercurial abilities of his. The houses that Mercury <u>rules</u> in his chart, however, are <u>intensely</u> strong.

Martin: That means I have to be able to locate my client's ability?

James: Well, you have to mention the different significations of the planet and the significations of the houses that the planet rules and occupies. This all sounds a lot harder than it is. Believe me, the person with the stationary planet knows deep inside what his or her intense talents are. But the person is going to act dumbfounded unless he or she knows that you know!

Martin: And then?

James: After a few minutes of prodding and sticking to your guns, the person will say something like, "Yes, well, I did score the highest in math in the last seventy years in the state of Ohio." Or, "Oh, well, my acting teacher in college said I could easily be one of the best actors in the world if I decided to stay with drama."

Martin: So, the person is basically dysfunctional?

James: I guess that's one way to say it. If a person has some enormous special talent and lets it go to waste <u>while living a powerless, ineffective life</u>, that is pretty dysfunctional.

Martin: And depressing.

James: That's right. Anyway, when it comes to stationary planets, you sometimes have to trust your astrological knowledge beyond your client's words.

Martin: That doesn't sound easy.

James: That's true. But if you maintain your confidence along with a strong sense of humility, you can usually sort out when astrology is accurate and the person's words are false, and vice versa. I know it's a hard task, but you need to develop that kind of discrimination for everything in life.

Martin: Otherwise, you're too either too gullible or too skeptical.

James: Exactly. Now, any questions?

Martin: James, can we go back to John Kennedy's horoscope (see page 135) for a minute? You said that Mercury in Kennedy's chart was weak because it was in the 8th house and closely conjunct malefic Mars. What I want to know is, does Mercury gain any benefit by the fact that Mercury is conjunct Mars <u>in Mars' own sign</u> (Aries)? In other words, could it be that Mars did not harm Mercury so badly because it was functioning well by being in Aries?

James: That's a good question. The answer is no. I would make no distinction regarding the negative energy Mars in its own sign throws onto Mercury. In theory, it may seem as though a planet conjunct Mars in Aries or Scorpio, or Mars in Capricorn (Mars' exaltation placement) would not be too harmed. But in practice the aspected planet is devastated.

Martin: Is there a condition, other than Mercury's stationary status, that could have eased Mercury's affliction? Is there something else that could have significantly strengthened Mercury despite all its intense afflictions?

James: Yes, but keep in mind that the Mercury-Mars conjunction in Kennedy's chart is an extremely delicate situation <u>because of the closeness of the aspect</u> (and because it occupies the "evil" 8th house, as the Hindus call it). I've said over and over that the orb of influence of an aspect is absolutely critical. There's almost nothing worse than a planet being conjunct a malefic <u>within one or two degrees</u>, and there's almost nothing better than a planet being conjunct a benefic <u>within one or two degrees</u>.

Martin: So, it couldn't have been saved?

James: Well, there are a few things that could have helped Mercury in Kennedy's chart, but they are not related to Mars — they are related to Mercury. If this Mercury, which occupies the 8th house and is so closely conjunct Mars, were also closely conjunct Venus or Jupiter or a bright Moon, then Mercury could start to have some power again. But the orb of the aspect that Mercury received from the benefic would be critical. In Kennedy's chart, Mars occupies 25° 45' (twenty-five degrees and forty-five minutes), while Mercury is at 27° 53'. So, the aspect occurs within about two degrees. Now, if either Jupiter, Moon, or Venus (the great benefics) were positioned at 26°, 27°, or 28° of Aries, that beneficial aspect would take precedence over the malefic aspect from Mars.

Martin: Because of the orb of influence?

James: Exactly. The best situation, in terms of saving Mercury, would be if a benefic occupied the space in between Mars and Mercury.

Martin: You mean 26 or 27 degrees of Aries?

James: Yes. Because then the benefic planet would act as a "buffer." It would take the heat from Mars, so to speak, and Mercury would be shielded.

Martin: What about the planet that acts as a buffer? Would it be hurt by being so close to Mars?

James: You bet it would. But it would also have some saving grace by being close to Mercury, which is essentially a benefic, even though not quite as wonderful as Jupiter and Venus. Let me give you an example, because I've seen situations like this plenty of times.

Let's say that the person has Venus in between Mars and Mercury, and the entire stellium occurs within three or four degrees.

Martin: Venus is the buffer, and Mercury is saved?

James: Yes. Now, the likelihood in such a case is that when you mention, say, throat, thyroid, skin, kidneys, or reproductive problems, which may occur because Venus is afflicted by its close conjunction to malefic Mars, the person usually says something like, "I have a sensitive thyroid, but somehow it never creates big problems." Or, "I do have a sensitive reproductive system, but no major illness with it."

Martin: And that's because Venus is helped out by the energy of benefic Mercury?

James: Yes. Now if Mercury, or some other benefic, wasn't aspecting Venus, the Venus afflictions would definitely be intense.

Martin: James, the conjunction you just described sounds kind of like yet another "wild card" influence.

James: That's true. In fact, I'd say it's one of the rare times when one beneficial aspect can <u>somewhat</u> balance out or neutralize a negative aspect. I say "somewhat" because Venus may still produce some very mixed results in its periods and subperiods, and even in certain of its natal implications.

Martin: This sounds important. Is this how to analyze a chart when there are four or five planets in one house?

James: Yes. Remember that in terms of the beneficial or harmful disposition of a planet, the <u>closest</u> aspect that a planet receives will take precedence every time. When a planet is aspected by more than one planet, you have to carefully contemplate the <u>degrees of the aspects</u> involved. I did a chart the other day for a man who had both Jupiter and Saturn aspecting the ascendant.

Martin: Sounds pretty spiritual.

James: Yes, but the aspect from Jupiter was wide, about 15 degrees. The aspect from Saturn was exact! The ascendant was twenty-six degrees of Scorpio and Saturn was sitting in 26 degrees of Aquarius. This poor man had such confidence problems because Saturn's aspect onto the ascendant was so tight. So, yes, this issue is incredibly important. And the funny thing is that many of the Hindu astrologers I've met don't bother looking at orbs.

Martin: That's terrible.

James: I know. Then again, I'd probably trade what I know about astrological technique for a good Indian astrologer's psychic ability.

Martin: In terms of saving Kennedy's Mercury, you said that a strong conjunction with a benefic planet would do the job. My question is this: Would the aspect from the benefic have to be a conjunction?

James: Excellent question. The answer is "no." An opposition would also work; or in the case of Jupiter, the 5th and 9th house aspects would work.

Martin: So, in Kennedy's case, with his Mars Mercury conjunction in Aries, an opposition from either Jupiter, Venus, or the bright Moon occupying Libra would have saved Mercury?

James: Yes, if the benefic planet occupied, say, 27, 28, or 29 degrees of Libra, in which case the benefic aspect is as tight or tighter than the malefic Mars aspect onto Mercury in Aries, then Mercury would be able to give good effects. By the way, out of these three possible aspects — Venus, Jupiter, and bright Moon — the <u>least</u> beneficial would be the Venus aspect. This is because Venus would be throwing its beneficial energy onto Aries, which cannot do as much good with Venus energy because Aries is the sign opposite Venus' rulership sign — Libra.

Martin: In other words, Aries doesn't like Venus' energy so much?

James: Right.

Martin: Regarding the three possible aspects you've mentioned, would you consider the good or bad energies each aspecting planet throws by virtue of their rulerships?

James: Definitely. But I would first ascertain whether the house receiving the aspect can possibly appreciate the aspecting energy. In the Kennedy chart, most houses would be thrilled to receive a Venus aspect because Venus rules such good houses that it becomes the *yogakaraka*, the union-maker for Virgo ascendant. But neither Aries nor Scorpio can benefit completely because Aries and Scorpio don't particularly appreciate Venus energy.

Martin: Because those are the signs opposite Venus' own sign?

James: Exactly.

Martin: What if Kennedy's Mars-Mercury conjunction occurred in the sign of Virgo, which is Mercury's exaltation sign. Would Mercury still be so harmed?

James: In that case, Mercury would have some degree of power, but if the conjunction occurred within two or three degrees of orb as Kennedy's did, Mercury would still be tremendously hurt. This is where that list of priorities that I gave you in an earlier class comes in. Planets in their own or exaltation signs are simply not the end all and be all.

Now, if Mercury tightly conjunct Mars occupied, say, the fourteenth or fifteenth degree of Virgo (the fifteenth degree of Virgo is Mercury's highest point of exaltation), then it would be in a lot better shape. In that case, I would consider Mercury a wild card. It would probably give some great and wonderful results as well as some terrible results.

Let's now discuss "*Sade Sati*" I told you earlier that *Sade Sati* has to do with the approximately seven-and-a-half year transit that occurs when Saturn transits the house preceding the Moon, the house that the Moon occupies, and the house following the Moon. Astrologers generally talk about *Sade Sati* as a very bad seven-and-a-half year period, and the more amateur the astrologer, the more he or she scares the client about it.

Martin: I've heard people worry about Sade Sati.

James: Well, if you simply use common sense and think about it, you'll realize that people's lives are unique. It's ridiculous to think that every single person on earth goes through a horrendous seven-and-a-half years every time they experience *Sade Sati*. It's ridiculous because *Sade Sati* comprises one-fourth of everyone's life. When I was in India, my mentor P.M. Padia taught me a technique called *Panoti Yoga* that will tell you if your *Sade Sati* transit is going to be difficult or not.

Panoti Yoga has to do with the exact placement of the Moon's position at the precise time that Saturn begins its *Sade Sati* transit. Actually, there are

Class Four

three delineations to be made for *Panoti Yoga*. You have to determine the Moon's sign placement (in the heavens) during the moment when Saturn begins to transit the house preceding the natal Moon, the house of the natal Moon, and the house following the natal Moon. In other words, each two-and-a-half-year period within the seven-and-a-half *Sade Sati* will have its own positive or negative effects by virtue of *Panoti Yoga*.

Martin: How does it work?

James: The directions for ascertaining *Panoti Yoga* are as follows: First, find the precise moment when Saturn (by transit) enters the appropriate signs (the sign/house preceding the natal Moon, the sign/house of the natal Moon, and the sign/house following the natal Moon). The exact moment that a planet enters a zodiac sign is called an "ingress."

Martin: How do I do that?

James: The best way is to own a computer program that lists the exact moment of all ingresses. If your computer program doesn't show them, you can usually find them in any good ephemeris (the book listing the daily motion of the planets, Sun, and Moon).

Martin: Isn't it hard finding a sidereal (not tropical) ephemeris that lists fifty years of planetary positions?

James: Very. And even if you do manage to get a sidereal ephemeris, it needs to be one that uses the Lahiri *ayanamsa*. The *ayanamsa* is the figure subtracted from the tropical (Western) zodiac in order to determine the sidereal one. (Note: Some astrologers prefer the *ayanamsa* determined by Mr. Krishnamurti; not the guru Krishnamurti, but the astronomer. That *ayanamsa* is only about six minutes different from Lahiri's and also works fine. The other *ayanamsas,* those of B.V. Raman, Swami Sri. Yukteshwar, Fagan-Bradley, are in my view so inaccurate that they will render *Panoti Yoga* completely useless.) Finally, remember that you have to find the exact moment of the ingress, which can be confusing using an ephemeris. The reason is that the ephemeris lists the time of ingress according to Greenwich mean time.

Martin: Which is five hours different from East Coast time.

James: Right. And eight hours different from West Coast time. And so on. If your computer program doesn't list the ingress, you can sit at a computer and keep entering different times until you hit the moment when Saturn hits zero degrees of the appropriate sign. But, depending on your program, you may only determine the approximate time of ingress.

Martin: Will that work?

James: Most of the times, yes. But occasionally it will not. You'll understand why in a minute, as I explain how *Panoti Yoga* works. You see, once you find the moment of Saturn's ingress into the appropriate signs (the sign preceding the natal Moon, the sign of the natal Moon, and the sign following the Moon), you have to see which sign the Moon <u>in the heavens</u> occupies <u>at that moment</u>.

Martin: So, I draw a chart for the moment that Saturn ingresses into each particular sign?

James: Yes. But all we're going to use from that chart is the <u>sign</u> that the Moon occupies. Nothing else.

Now here are the rules: When the Moon in the sky at the moment of Saturn's current ingress into each of the three *Sade Sati* signs occupies:

1) the 1st, 6th, or 11th sign/house from the <u>natal</u> Moon, then *Panoti Yoga* occurs on the "basis of gold" and the results are bad.

2) the 2nd, 5th, or 9th sign/house from the <u>natal</u> Moon, then *Panoti Yoga* occurs on the "basis of silver" and the results are good.

3) the 3rd, 7th, or 10th sign/house from the <u>natal</u> Moon, then *Panoti Yoga* occurs on the "basis of copper" and the results are good.

4) the 4th, 8th, or 12th sign/house from the <u>natal</u> Moon, then *Panoti Yoga* occurs on the "basis of iron," and the results are <u>terrible</u>. *Panoti Yoga* on the basis of iron is the worst.

Martin: Is there some reason for these good and bad placements?

James: If there is, I wasn't told. I know that it seems unusual that the worst *Panoti Yoga* occurrence, *Panoti* on the basis of iron, would include the 4th house placement. But this is how the technique works. Since I am now in the midst of a *Sade Sati* transit, let's use my chart as an example.

Martin: Wait. Why did you say that sometimes finding the approximate time of Saturn's ingress would work and other times it wouldn't?

James: Because the Moon moves about one degree every two hours. If at the moment of Saturn's ingress the Moon is near the very first or very last degree of a sign, and your ingress time is approximate, you may not have the accurate sign that the Moon occupies.

Martin: So it's good to have a program that lists the exact moment of planetary ingresses.

James: Yes. Now, look at my first *Sade Sati* of the present cycle. (See following page for my natal chart and page166 for my first *Panoti Yoga* chart.)

Notice in my *Panoti Yoga* chart that on Feb. 16, 1996 at 11:16 A.M. E.S.T., Saturn entered zero degrees of Pisces (the sign/house preceding my <u>natal</u> Moon position), and the Moon in the sky <u>at that moment</u> occupied one degree of Capricorn. Since my <u>natal</u> Moon occupies Aries, the Moon in the heavens during Saturn's ingress occupies the 10th sign/house <u>from my natal</u>

Moon (Capricorn is the 10th sign from Aries). This means that the first two-and-a-half years of my *Sade Sati* occurs on the basis of copper. So, those years are excellent, assuming that I'm not running a terrible *dasa-bhukti* or other terrible transits.

Martin: Have they been good?

James: Yes. The first part of my *Sade Sati* period began in February, 1996. We moved to Longboat Key in late 1995, and I've been very happy since we got here. We moved because my wife Vashti returned to college in 1993 and wanted to finish her last two years at New College in Sarasota. I wasn't looking forward to moving to a new city. But when we settled in Longboat Key (a wildlife sanctuary two blocks from the ocean and one block from the bay), with peacocks roaming the neighborhood, I knew I'd be happy. And I have been.

James Braha Natal Chart

James Braha
Male Chart
Oct 16 1951
7:36 pm EST +5:00
Fort Lauderdale, FL
26°N07'19" 080°W08'37"

South Indian Style

For North Indian, see Appendix B.

Pt	Name	Hs	Rules
☽	Moon	12	3
☉	Sun	5	4
☿	Mercury	6	2, 5
♀	Venus	4	1, 6
♂	Mars	4	7, 12
♃	Jupiter	11	8, 11
♄	Saturn	5	9, 10
☊	North Node	10	–
☋	South Node	4	–
As	Ascendant	1	–

Sg	Name
♈	Aries
♉	Taurus
♊	Gemini
♋	Cancer
♌	Leo
♍	Virgo
♎	Libra
♏	Scorpio
♐	Sagittarius
♑	Capricorn
♒	Aquarius
♓	Pisces

Martin: So, *Sade Sati* has been good for you?

James: Actually, it's been excellent. I'm finally out of the rat race of living in a big city, and I love it.

Martin: What about the rest of your life?

James: Marriage, career, finances, and daily work have all been fine. The only major difficulty has been making new friends. That's been very hard, but guess what? That's due to Saturn's transit of the 11th house, the house of friends. That problem will end as soon as Saturn leaves my 11th house, in April, 1998.

Martin: What about the second portion of *Sade Sati*?

James: The second two-and-a-half years of *Sade Sati* begins on April 17, 1998, at 3:37 A.M. E.S.T., when Saturn enters Aries, the sign/house holding my natal Moon. As you can see from the chart on the next page, the Moon at that moment will occupy 3 degrees of Sagittarius.

Martin: That puts the Moon in the 9th sign from your natal Moon in Aries. That's good.

James: That's right. The second portion of my *Sade Sati* occurs on the basis of silver. That means I have another good two-and-a-half-year period coming. (In fact, the period was excellent until the fall of 1999, when I entered Jupiter *dasa* Saturn *bhukti*, one of the most treacherous periods of my life.)

Martin: That's lucky.

James: Yes, it is. The final two-and-a-half years of my current *Sade Sati*, however, are not good. Look at the chart below for June 6th, 2000, when Saturn enters Taurus (the sign/house following my natal Moon).

Notice that the Moon at that moment will occupy 22 degrees of Cancer. Cancer is the 4th sign/house from Aries (the sign/house of my natal Moon). The *Panoti* instructions state that if, at the start of any of the three portions of *Sade Sati* (first two-and-a-half years, second two-and-a-half years, or third two-and-a-half years), the transiting Moon occupies the 4th, 8th, or 12th sign/house from the natal Moon, then *Panoti Yoga* occurs on the basis of iron. *Panoti* on the basis of iron is, as I already said, the worst.

Martin: What do you think the effects will be?

James: Well, when *Panoti* is bad it can cause money problems, setbacks, misery, burden, hardship, unhappiness, and so on. But it's particularly bad for loved ones, especially one's mother.

Martin: Because *Sade Sati* is mainly about Saturn's influence on the Moon, and the Moon is the *karaka* (indicator) of mother?

James: Yes. But, there's another reason, which astrologer Hart DeFouw explains very well in his book *Light on Life*. He says that during *Sade Sati* a person may lose his or her "protectors." In a person's first *Sade Sati* (during childhood), one may lose one of his or her grandparents. In the second *Sade Sati* (during mid-life), one may lose a parent, and in the third *Sade Sati* the person is in danger of losing his or her own life.

Martin: But don't you have to look at every case individually? Doesn't Hart DeFouw say not to expect the death of a loved one unless there are other corroborating astrological influences?

James: Of course. That's common sense. You should never forget the most important astrological saying of all: see an astrological indication once, the predictable outcome is possible. See an indication twice, the predictable outcome is likely. See the indication three times and you can bet on the outcome. In any case, I am now quite concerned about losing my mother, who is approaching the age of eighty.

So, now that you know about *Panoti Yoga*, you don't have to go running around predicting that one-fourth of everyone's life is going to be burdensome and terrible.

Martin: Have you used *Panoti* for a long time?

James: I've only used it in the last few years, mainly in the charts of friends and relatives.

Martin: If you learned it in 1982, why have you only used it recently?

James: Because there were discrepancies about the technique that I was too inexperienced to confront many years ago. After that, I just ignored it. The reason I teach it now is simply to dispel the superstition of *Sade Sati*. Too many astrologers haven't been able to reason out on their own that *Sade Sati* comprises one-fourth of a person's life, and therefore cannot be totally bad. I'm also, by the way, trying hard to stop amateur astrologers from misusing *marakas*. A *maraka* is a planet that rules or occupies either the 2nd or 7th house, and is said to be instrumental in causing death.

Martin: How do amateurs misuse them?

James: By thinking that death is just around the corner every time the period or subperiod of a *maraka* planet occurs. If you think about it for about a half a second, you will realize that the average person encounters a period or subperiod of a *maraka* about every three or four years! There are only nine planets running their periods and subperiods. So every three or four years one of those planets is bound to rule either the 2nd or 7th house. And if a person has one or two planets occupying the 2nd or 7th house, then the person will have a *maraka* period or subperiod even more often!

Martin: Then what good are *marakas*?

James: A *maraka* planet can kill you when it is your time to go. So, if you are looking at the chart of a seventy-five or eighty-year old person who is sick and in poor health, then you start to worry about the *maraka* period. When an amateur astrologer sees a *maraka* planet run its period in the life of a ten, twenty, or thirty year old, he or she often thinks the person is about to die. It's a lack of common sense. I've gotten so many phone calls from people scared about *marakas* that I wish I'd never mentioned them in my first book.

Regarding *Sade Sati* and why I didn't use *Panoti Yoga* for so long, remember that when you study *Jyotish* in India you are taught technique upon technique upon technique, and you eventually have to pick and choose the ones you feel are useful. In the early eighties, I couldn't possibly begin to confront the *ayanamsa* discrepancy involved with *Panoti*.

Martin: You mean regarding the different figures used to find the sidereal zodiac?

James: Right. The *ayanamsa* discrepancy is serious and at that point I was accepting on faith that the Lahiri *ayanamsa* was better than the others.

Martin: So, if you use the other *ayanamsas* you get different results for *Panoti*?

James: Take a look. When we use Lahiri's *ayanamsa*, my first *Sade Sati* began on the morning of February 16, 1996. On that day, Saturn entered Pisces and the Moon occupied one degree of Capricorn. If we look to find Saturn's entrance into Pisces using <u>Swami Sri Yukteshwar's</u> *ayanamsa*, then Saturn entered Pisces on February 4th, 1996 — a full fourteen days earlier, during which time the Moon occupied Cancer, instead of Capricorn. This means that the *Sade Sati* would have occurred on the basis of iron because the Moon in Cancer is <u>four</u> signs away from my <u>natal</u> Moon in Aries.

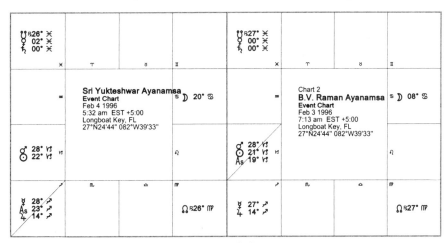

Martin: So according to Lahiri's *ayanamsa,* your first two-and-a-half years of *Sade Sati* were wonderful; and according to Yukteshwar's *ayanamsa,* those two-and-a-half years are terrible.

James: That's right. And if I use the B.V. Raman *ayanamsa*, then Saturn would have entered Pisces on February 3rd, 1996 — a day before the ingress according to Sri Yukteshwar. At that time, the Moon was also in Cancer, although the <u>degree</u> of the Moon position would have varied from the one according to Sri Yukteshwar. But the *Sade Sati* would also have been on the basis of iron.

Martin: So the *ayanamsa* is critical.

James: Yes. Incidentally, I don't know that Lahiri's *ayanamsa* is perfect. I know it's definitely close. It's in the ballpark of accuracy, and the starting times of my *dasas* and *bhuktis* according to Lahiri work better than the others. But I want to mention that there is widespread opinion that Mr. Lahiri's *ayanamsa* was somewhat of a compromise.

Martin: A compromise?

James: You see, the government of India was upset about astrologers using many different *ayanamsas*, so they commissioned a group of astrologers and astronomers to determine the correct mathematical figure, which they were going to call the Lahiri *ayanamsa*.

Martin: Because Lahiri was the head of the group?

James: Yes. In any case, some years ago, the famous Indian astrologer B.V. Raman (now deceased) told a friend of mine that Mr. Lahiri actually came up with a figure <u>slightly</u> different from the figure bearing his name. So it seems that there was some slight compromise involved.

Martin: But you basically get good results from the *Lahiri ayanamsa*?

James: I do. I've tried all the different ones, and I find most of them patently absurd. The only one that also works well is the Krishnamurti *ayanamsa*, which is about six <u>minutes</u> different. If you try the Krishnamurti *ayanamsa*, what you'll find is that anyone **born** into a <u>long</u> *dasa* (Saturn, Mercury, Venus, or Rahu) will have <u>all</u> their *dasas* and *bhuktis* begin <u>approximately</u> forty-five days earlier than the Lahiri system indicates. Anyone **born** into a <u>short</u> *dasa* (Sun, Moon, Mars, Ketu) will have all their *dasas* and *bhuktis* begin <u>approximately</u> twenty days earlier.

Martin: Then it shouldn't be too hard to figure out which *ayanamsa* works.

James: Not true. You shouldn't even begin to try to figure out which *ayanamsa* works until you've been practicing *Jyotish* for many years. First of all, you have to be grounded and accurate in the art of astrological analysis. Second, there are so many other factors that could cause the effects of a person's *dasa* to start earlier.

Martin: Like what?

James: First, a wrong birthtime. Second, some astrologers use what's called a parallax Moon, which sounds great but causes such erroneous results I'm not even going to explain it. Third, the *dasas* can be calculated using either a 360-day year or a 365-day year (the most popular system is the 365 day). And on and on and on.

Martin: Sounds like Shiva's curse that caused astrologers to disagree is still in effect.

James: You're learning fast. Do you have any more questions, or shall we quit for today?

Martin: James, two weeks ago we spoke about my chart (on page 50) and you mentioned Ketu in my 11th house. Could you say something more about it?

James: You remember the story of *Rahu* and *Ketu*? Lord Vishnu cut the *rakshasa*, or demon, in half, but the demon didn't die because it had swallowed the nectar of immortality. Well, Ketu is the bottom half of the serpent and it is the planet of psychic phenomenon, metaphysics, and astral experiences. It represents everything non-physical, and it represents introspection and introversion. If you know Western astrology, Ketu is just like Neptune — it represents gas, oil, magic, film, photography, and so forth. The 11th house governs friends and groups, so your friends are going to be of a Ketu-like nature. And you will belong to groups of a spiritual or metaphysical nature.

Martin: My friends are mostly spiritual or metaphysical. But they can also be pretty strange.

James: Yes, well Ketu does represent everything weird and strange. By the way, there are people who consider the 4th house to represent friends. I believe that the 11th house is the more dominant ruler of friends, but the 4th house has some say over friends because the 4th house rules comforts. Friends are a great comfort in life.

When you have a Saturn transit of the 11th house, you're likely to lose a few friends and you may have some hardship with groups you belong to. If you encounter an afflicted *dasa* or *bhukti* of an 11th house planet or 11th house ruler, you will also have difficulties with friends and groups, there's no question about it. But, I have also noticed that when a person has a rough dasa or bhukti of a 4th house planet or ruler of the 4th house, there may be similar problems. When my brother Charles entered his *dasa* of fallen Mars (See page 317), he lost nearly all his friends. Mars is the ruler of his 4th house, and he lost nearly all his comforts during those seven years.

Martin: So the 11th house reveals the kind of friends a person will have?

James: Correct. I have Jupiter in the 11th house. For me to allow someone into my life as a friend, the person has to be religious-minded or spiritual. I just don't feel completely comfortable with friends who don't have a strong interest in God and enlightenment, and so forth.

Because my 11th house ruler Jupiter is aspected within one degree by Saturn, my friends are almost all extremely Saturnian. So my closest friends have been very religious and spiritual, and all but one have been self-restricted, self-disciplined, thin, and very non-attached to the world. They've been a dramatic mix of Jupiter and Saturn.

The one really close friend of mine who is not Saturnian is an interesting case. He is purely Jupitarian (his Jupiter is stationary direct), without a hint of Saturn. We haven't lived in the same state since high school, and in the first several years after school he was better than me in keeping in touch. The reason for this is probably because I fit into his friendship scheme in a <u>major</u> way.

In Kerry's chart (see following page), Jupiter occupies the 11th house and Jupiter is stationary, so he gets famous or special friends. But look at the ruler of his 11th house. The ruler is Saturn, and Saturn is <u>tightly</u> conjunct Ketu. Saturn is very harmed by being next to Ketu; but on the positive side, Ketu is the metaphysical, spiritual planet. So my friend will be attracted to companions of a Ketu nature. In case you haven't guessed, I consider myself "Mr. Ketu" because my ascendant ruler, Venus, is conjunct within one degree of Ketu. As a child, I was so introverted and shy it was ridiculous. When I was single, I was always being chased by women who had Ketu in the 7th house (marriage). They were looking for Mr. Ketu as a husband!

By the way — because the ruler of Kerry's 11th house is closely conjunct Ketu, he lost his best friend from high school and college after that friend got married. Their friendship fell apart and it was quite painful for him. He was sure to suffer some heartache with friends due to that Ketu affliction. But on the other hand he has a Ketu-like friend (myself) who is very close. We have been good friends for thirty years.

Martin: James, how can we know whether Kerry would have good luck with friends or bad luck with them? He has an enormously favorable stationary Jupiter in the 11th house as well as an 11th house ruler closely conjunct malefic Ketu.

James: You have to predict mixed results. Some <u>extremely</u> good karma and some <u>extremely</u> bad karma. The results are extreme because the conjunction to malefic Ketu is so tight by degree, and his Jupiter in the 11th is stationary. These are both extreme conditions.

Martin: Then Kerry could also be wealthy. Isn't the 11th house the house of money?

James: It's not <u>the</u> house of money. The 2nd rules money. The 11th is the house of money from <u>side ventures</u> and money that comes in <u>large sums</u>. So yes Martin, you are learning astrology well. Kerry <u>is</u> a millionaire. He has the most amazing opportunities all the time, he almost always gets his major desires fulfilled, and he has special and famous friends. Kerry has actually met George Harrison more than once and turned down an opportunity to meet Bob Dylan. All these effects are caused by stationary

Jupiter in the 11th house.

At any rate, this 11th house ruler conjunct Ketu business brings us to a very important point. How to turn malefic influences in a horoscope into something positive. Kerry used the horrendously damaging Ketu influence in a positive way by getting a Ketu-like friend. What I'm saying is fairly obvious, yes?

Martin: Completely.

James: Okay, so this affects how you advise your clients. You tell this person with the 11th house ruler conjunct Ketu, along with Jupiter in the 11th house, that he may look for Jupitarian friends, but the person must also have some major characteristics of Ketu as well. He may choose friends who are wealthy, large or fat, religious, spiritual, famous, but they must also have a side of themselves that is seriously introspective, shy, metaphysical, strange or weird. <u>If the friend does not exhibit some major Ketu characteristics, the person is likely to lose that friend or have a major unresolvable conflict at some point.</u>

As another example, if a person has Ketu in the 7th house, he or she should be advised to find a spouse who embodies the positive nature of Ketu (spiritual, metaphysical, introspective, and so on). If the person chooses a mate who does not embody Ketu in the spiritual or metaphysical sense, or in some other <u>positive and obvious way</u> (perhaps relating to magic, oil, or gas), then you can bet there will eventually be divorce or some incident of illusion, deception, drugs, or alcohol that impacts married life. The person with the 7th house Ketu should look for a partner who is psychic or metaphysical, or interested in astrology or some other occult discipline.

Let's take a few more examples. If someone has the ruler of the 10th house (career) occupying the 12th house, he or she should look for a career that involves consciousness-raising. If the 10th house ruler occupies the 8th house, then a metaphysical, psychic, or research career should be practiced. Or, the person should use psychic energies within the career. If someone has the ruler of the 7th house occupying the 12th house, the person should be advised to look for a partner <u>who is pursuing enlightenment or final liberation</u>. Otherwise, divorce is certain because the 12th house is such a bad house. The way to deal with this situation is to choose a 12th house person in the <u>positive</u> sense, someone who embodies 12th house energy in a <u>positive</u> way. And when I say the spouse should be pursuing enlightenment, I mean just that. I don't mean that the person should be psychic or metaphysical; those are 8th house energies, not 12th house energies. This same advice, incidentally, should also be given to a person with a similar house placement that occurs in the *navamsa*, the marriage chart. But don't forget that the house placements in the divisional charts cannot be used unless you are <u>positive</u> the birthtime is exact. We'll discuss how to handle the *varga* charts later on (see Class Seven).

Martin: James, in one of your lectures, you mentioned something about the effects of season changes. Can you tell me about that?

James: Yes. In some Eastern cultures, people pay attention to solstices and equinoxes by performing rituals and ceremonies. This is a good idea because the change of seasons has a powerful influence on your health and well-being. I discovered how important this is a few years ago when I used to visit an acupuncturist regularly. It seems that every time there was a change of seasons, my acupuncturist would be inundated with agitated patients calling to schedule appointments. You don't have to make big changes during the solstices and equinoxes, but you should do your best to avoid stressful situations, get plenty of rest, and be aware of the changes around you. It's important for your health.

Martin: Do I concern myself only with the day of the solstice or equinox?

James: Actually, I would try to take it easy and be gentle with yourself for one day before the season changes and then for two or three days afterwards. You'll know when seasons change by noting the moment when the Sun enters the first degree of the cardinal signs (Aries, Cancer, Libra, Capricorn) in the <u>tropical</u> zodiac (the zodiac <u>most</u> Western astrologers use). Many yearly calendars also give the precise dates of solstices and equinoxes. Also, by noticing the effects that occur, you'll get some feeling for why Western astrologers use a season-based zodiac (as opposed to the sidereal zodiac, which is based on actual positions of constellations).

Before we quit, I want to explain an astrological technique that will help you delineate where a person gets his or her primary spiritual evolution. There may be other methods, but this is the one I was taught.

Martin: You mentioned this before, didn't you?

James: Yes, very briefly in our first session. And you may have read about it in my transit book (*How to Predict Your Future*). The importance of this matter depends on whether you are practicing astrology for spiritual seekers or the rest of the world. But you should certainly commit the material to memory.

There are three different evolutionary paths, so to speak, that relate to three different planets. Jupiter signifies Lord Krishna, Saturn represents Lord Shiva, and Mercury represents Lord Vishnu. Evolution through Lord Krishna means evolution through prayer and devotion. People who have Jupiter occupying or aspecting the 1st house or the 1st house ruler in their chart will gain evolutionary growth or spiritual development through devotion and prayer. The same is true if Jupiter aspects a person's Sun, because the Sun represents the soul, and the same is true if Jupiter aspects the Moon because the Moon represents the person. So the devotional types, like the Hare Krishna disciples, will almost always have Jupiter making these specific aspects in their horoscopes.

Saturn represents Lord Shiva. Shiva is the god of austerity, meditation, fasting, detachment of the senses, and non-attachment to the world. So people who are on an austere path and who are gaining their spiritual growth through meditation, introspection, or monkhood will have Saturn occupying or aspecting the 1st house, or Saturn aspecting the 1st house ruler, or the Sun, or the Moon.

Mercury represents Lord Vishnu. Lord Vishnu is the god of the mind, truth, astrology, seminars, Zen, intellectual functions, and dispelling the mistake of the intellect. People who gain their spiritual growth from Zen, seminars, astrology, the Bible, and any mental path will have Mercury occupying or aspecting the 1st house, or Mercury will be aspecting the 1st house ruler, or the Sun or Moon.

Martin: What if a person has aspects from both Jupiter and Saturn, or Mercury and Jupiter?

James: Then both spiritual paths will be open to the person. I've seen plenty or people in spiritual movements who gain evolution through all three different paths. Still, the strongest aspect in the chart is the one that will usually have the biggest influence.

Martin: What do you mean by "strongest" aspect?

James: If you have a chart where Jupiter aspects the Moon within one degree, and Saturn aspects the Sun within twenty degrees or Saturn aspects the ascendant *degree* within twenty degrees, obviously the Jupiter aspect is stronger than the Saturn aspect. The person can gain evolution through prayer and devotion (Jupiter), or through austerity and meditation (Saturn); but if he or she chooses a spiritual path or a spiritual movement to follow, it is most likely going to be a Jupitarian, rather than Saturnian, path.

When I did chart readings in Fairfield, Iowa, where the Transcendental Meditation organization is located, the strongest aspect influencing people's features (1st house, Sun, and Moon) was always Saturn. The most interesting thing occurred when I would do a reading for someone in Fairfield who had no Saturn personal aspect at all in their charts. I would ask, "What are you doing here?" After explaining that their chart revealed little energy for austerity, fasting, or avoidance of the senses, they would say very shyly and sheepishly, "Well, please don't spread it around, but I don't enjoy the austere part of the movement at all. I just love being here and being around the people."

The artwork and typesetting for my first book, *Ancient Hindu Astrology for the Modern Western Astrologer*, was done by the local Hare Krishna Center in Miami. During that time I was analyzing horoscopes of many of the devotees there. Sure enough, Jupiter was making the most powerful personal aspects in all the charts. Of course, you'll find Mercury prominent in the charts of people who spend lots of time in Zen centers or who are involved in Werner Erhard-type seminars. Mercury almost always makes strong personal aspects in the charts of astrologers.

Martin: I have one more question that I'd like to ask. What's the difference between astrological readings given by Indians using *Jyotish* and Westerners practicing *Jyotish*? I know you've said that Indians are generally more psychic, but are the readings otherwise very similar?

James: No. I'd say there is a significant difference. Because our culture is so different from the East, we are definitely going to practice astrology in our own particular way. It doesn't mean that we can't know everything Indians know, it just means that we will utilize the information differently. Our sessions with clients will be quite different. I'll explain.

Generally, a Hindu astrology reading given by an Indian (an Indian living in India — not an Indian who has resided in the West for 5 or 10 years) will be rather short and to the point. The reading may consist of five or six extremely specific predictions, some of which will be dramatically accurate, and some of which fail completely. A certain amount of information is given about a person's past, maybe about the parents and the upbringing, and some statements that relate to how to achieve happiness. The astrologer usually describes some events and circumstances of your previous years . But there is very little about who you are.

Martin: So, there's not much about a person's psychology, behavior, and feelings?

James: Not in the readings I've had. Of course, I'm sure there are exceptions, but I've spent time with several astrologers and that's how it's been.

Martin: Are the readings satisfying?

James: It depends on what you're looking for; what you're trying to find out. In a lot of cases, even though the readings are short, they're quite powerful. Never underestimate the impact that certain predictions can make. Indian astrologers can influence your existence in the blink of an eye, and if you visit a good one, there's a chance you'll hear some things that you won't forget until your dying day.

Martin: Like the prediction the astrologer made about you writing four or five books?

James: Exactly. That certainly opened my eyes. I was 32 years old and had never even thought of writing books. But, because the reading is sometimes short and abrupt, you can get quite frustrated.

Martin: Is there some reason why their readings are so short and predictive?

James: It amounts to the Indians' approach to astrology, as well as their experience of life. For an Indian, the point of astrology is to find out what is <u>fated</u>, what has been "determined" by one's past karma. Indians are very aware of the fact that there is little upward mobility in their culture. A person can work eighteen hours a day and never save money or get anywhere. (This is changing rapidly, however, as economic growth in the past ten years has been accelerating.) Therefore, Indians approach astrologers to ascertain what may happen to them in their material, worldly existence.

You also have to remember that Indians absolutely <u>expect</u> the astrologer to be accurate in making specific predictions. So the astrologer's consciousness is entirely focused on that task.

Martin: That's a narrow focus.

James: You bet. Focusing completely on predictions makes it very hard for a Hindu astrologer to talk about a horoscope for any length of time, to flesh out the chart, so to speak.

Martin: Which Westerners are good at.

James: That's right, we are. Generally though, if you talk to five or ten Indians who have visited local astrologers, they'll tell story after story about important astrological predictions that came about exactly as the astrologer promised.

Martin: You mean <u>all</u> of their predictions were accurate?

James: No, definitely not. But a lot of them are. Certainly enough to give *Jyotish* a special reputation.

In my experience, the greatest difficulty of working in the field of prediction, aside from the fact that predicting with absolute certainty is difficult enough, is the issue of <u>how much or how little</u> predictable material shows up in the horoscope at any particular time. In some horoscopes, a lot of accurate predictions can be made because the indications show up. But in a great many cases, the horoscopes are extremely mediocre, with very little happening when the person comes for the reading.

Martin: That seems odd. Shouldn't something be happening when a client shows up for a reading?

James: When you work for the general public, there is usually something happening; the stars are "popping" so to speak. But so many people come to astrologers out of boredom and curiosity, and in those cases there is often very little (of any great significance) happening. People who come to astrologers out of curiosity often hope to hear that they're going to get rich or married or have some stroke of luck. Indian astrologers are lucky in this regard because their clients don't have much discretionary money to waste. If an Indian visits an astrologer, it's usually because there's some current action in the person's life that appears in the horoscope and requires attention.

Martin: In the West, lots of people come to astrologers out of curiosity.

James: That's right. If the horoscope is dull and inactive, I can't just make something up. You would be amazed at how often I see charts that are relatively inactive for several years at a time. By relatively inactive, I mean there's little intensity, either positive or negative, in the upcoming periods or subperiods, or transits and progressions. What I want to say is, "Well, your love life, career, and financial situation will barely change in the next few years. Life will go on pretty much as before." But that's not good bedside manner for an astrologer.

Martin: What do you do?

James: I tell the truth, but I try to make the information sound a little more exciting, a little more inspiring. I may say something like, "The next subperiod is indicating a focus on money matters, and if you work hard you may do well." I don't say, "There is a big financial windfall coming to you."

Martin: Which is what the person is hoping to hear.

James: That's right. But if it's not there, it's not there.

Martin: Because the period is mediocre?

James: Yes. The period may be about money, career, or relationship, but if the *dasa* or *bhukti* planet is in a mediocre condition, there's no stunning prediction to make, either positive or negative. Then, the person walks away wondering, "Why didn't I have a dramatic experience? I've heard so much about how great Hindu astrology is for predictions."

Martin: When you read my horoscope about a year ago, you spent over an hour with me. I take it that Hindu astrologers don't do that.

James: Usually not. If you want a more thorough *Jyotish* reading, you're generally better off getting it from a Westerner. You'll likely receive more information, and as I said before, the material will be more fleshed out. You will almost certainly, however, not be told that on the second Thursday in October, your mother is going to break her leg. You will probably not be told, "You are positively going to write some books."

Martin: Predictions are not so set in concrete.

James: Right. They're not as flashy. I've had many clients say that when they listen to the cassette tape of their reading with me two or three years after the session, they are very impressed with the accuracy. But the initial experience is not necessarily dramatic, because I don't make extreme statements like the Indians.

Martin: But you do make extreme statements sometimes, right?

James: Of course, but only when the indications are blatant and when there aren't lots of mitigating factors. If I make five or six extremely specific predictions, in a reading, they can get lost quite easily within a sixty or ninety minute session. Indian astrologers often make five or six specific predictions in fifteen or twenty minutes and then the reading is over. In fact, I often get calls from Indians who want a reading from me because they're tired of the short readings they get from Indians! When that happens, I'm scared they have very particular expectations regarding predictions.

Martin: What do you do?

James: I tell them right away that I don't read charts like Indians. Then they almost always say, "I don't want a reading from an Indian. The readings are too short."

Martin: Do you consider a *Jyotish* reading by a Westerner better than one by a Indian.

James: Not at all. Neither experience, Western or Eastern, is necessarily better than the other. To a large extent, the client's fulfillment depends on his or her expectations going into the session. I've heard scores of Westerners complain that Hindu astrology readings by Westerners are not so powerfully dramatic and predictive. And I've heard lots of Indians complain about the sparsity of information given by Indian astrologers.

I must say, though, that some of the predictions made by fine Indian astrologers are mind-boggling. There is nothing like having a reading from an intuitive Indian astrologer when he or she make some dramatic prediction that seems to come comes straight from the ethers.

Martin: Is this intuition or astrological ability?

James: It's hard to pin down the answer to that because the dramatic predictions are clearly intuitive, but if you challenge the astrologer he or she will tell you the astrological basis for the answer. In my heart of hearts, I believe intuition is the key to the Indian astrologers' success. I also believe that Indians are exponentially more intuitive than Westerners because of their genetics, because of their culture. In the same way that the British are eons ahead of Americans in performing Shakespeare, Easterners are way ahead of us in terms of intuitive, mystical, and metaphysical ability.

Anyway, these are my opinions. I'm sure there are astrologers with different findings. For every personal conviction about how something works, there is some very experienced astrologer somewhere who feels differently.

Martin: Shiva's curse.

James: Yes. I suppose the best we can do is to pray to Lord Ganesh to help us. Lord Ganesh is the Hindu deity who presides over astrology.

Martin: That's why you have Ganesh pictures around your house?

James: Yes. It's a tradition I learned from my mentors in India. According to Indian Lore, the story of Lord Ganesh, the elephant God, goes something like this: Way back in time, Lord Shiva had gone away from his home for a long duration, while unaware that his wife Parvati was pregnant. When he returned home, he encountered a young man acting as a guard of the home who would not let him in. The young man was actually his son, but neither son nor father recognized each other. After some arguing, Lord Shiva became impatient and simply lopped off his son's head, which then rolled away somewhere into oblivion. Then Shiva went inside.

When the Goddess Parvati found out, she became very upset and told her husband he had just killed their son. Lord Shiva, being a God and all, told her not worry as he could easily fix the matter. He then ordered his servants to go scout the countryside and bring him the head of the first live being they encountered so he could have it to replace his son's headless body and bring him back to life. The first live being was an elephant and so you have Ganesh, the elephant God with the body of a man and the head of an elephant.

Ganesh is considered the remover of obstacles. Just as an elephant can clear a path in the jungle, Ganesh is said to eliminate a person's barriers and problems. Because Ganesh is the deity of astrology, you will almost always find a statement in Hindu astrology texts such as, "All glories to Lord

Ganesh for helping us bring out this knowledge."

Now, any other questions?

Martin: None that can't wait.

James: Bas. See you next week.

CLASS FIVE

James: We're going to spend the next two classes talking about the twelve houses. There is plenty of good material about the meanings of the houses in my basic text and in the Hindu astrology texts by other Western authors. But I want to say a few things about each house that may add a little something here and there.

Before I start, I want to explain why I am spending two full classes on something as basic as the twelve houses. The reason is because I meet too many astrology students who've never learned the basics well. Let me repeat that so I know you hear me. Most astrology students that I've met haven't learned the basics well. And it is only through learning the basics well and with precision that you will ever become a good astrologer. There's no other way. There are no flashy secretive techniques, no astrological yogas (astrological planetary unions), nothing that will make anyone a good astrologer other than knowing and memorizing the fundamental significations and principles. Astrology students always want some kind of magical technique. The real magic lies in the fundamentals. The best astrologers are the ones who are meticulous with fundamentals and don't "fudge" them. The reason I enjoy writing astrology books more than teaching classes is because whenever I teach I find that my students want to play "mix and match."

Martin: What's "mix and match"?

James: That's when you mix and match the meanings of houses or other astrological techniques. I see students and professionals do it, and it truly upsets me.

Martin: Can you give me some examples?

James: Sure. Mix and match is when you consider the 8th house to be sexual enjoyment, rather than the 12th house, because that's how it works in Western astrology. Mix and match is when you consider the food a person eats from the 6th house (instead of the 2nd house), because the 6th house rules the appetite. Mix and match is when you consider that the 3rd house represents teaching (instead of the 2nd house), because the 3rd house represents magazines and journals. Mix and match is when you consider the 9th house to represent spiritual growth, rather than the 12th house, because higher knowledge seems similar to spiritual evolution. And on and on and on it goes!

Martin: So "mix and match" is when your work becomes fuzzy.

James: Seemingly fuzzy, but in reality downright inaccurate. If you predict that a person is going to be a teacher or writer because of a strong 3rd house in the Hindu system, you're going to be wrong more often than right. If you predict that a person gets good spiritual evolution and enlightenment because of a strong 9th house, you're going to be wrong more often than right. Whether you like it or not, astrology is a very precise, detail-oriented art. It's only in the twentieth century, with the advent of Western "humanistic" (behavioral) astrology that astrologers have begun to get so sloppy with their craft.

Martin: But you like Western astrology.

James: I do like Western astrology. I have nothing against humanistic astrology. The point I am making is that because humanistic astrology is not event-oriented, astrologers can easily get away with sloppy work. Do you think that two or three hundred years ago an astrologer could study astrology for only four or five months and then begin analyzing horoscopes for money? It happens all the time now. Before the twentieth century, the job of Western astrologers was to make predictions about events and circumstances. British astrologer Alan Leo changed all of that because he was hounded by the law. The Church of England was upset that astrology seemed to contradict the doctrine of free will, so they made laws against astrology. Leo tried to circumvent the problem by changing astrology to a humanistic, psychological discipline. He succeeded in changing astrology, but got arrested anyway!

Martin: So Alan Leo is responsible for the way modern astrology is practiced?

James: Modern Western astrology, yes. It's interesting to note that although many astrologers today blame scientists for astrology's lowly status, it was the Church of England that did the greatest damage to our field. Western astrologers were forced to go underground, and consequently most of the knowledge that took thousands of years to develop got lost. But that's a long story.

Martin: Isn't that old knowledge resurfacing now?

James: Yes. Fortunately, some of the old material is being rediscovered. In the last five or ten years many older Greek and Latin transcripts have been translated into English. Also, there is a core of people working quite successfully with William Lilly's 17th century texts.

At any rate, people often think that because astrology is a highly psychic, intuitive art we don't have to be precise with the techniques. Actually, the opposite is the case! Because astrology is such a vast and infinite subject, we have to be as exact as we can with the meanings and significations involved. The 8th and 9th houses do not represent spiritual enlightenment just because they are spiritual houses. The 9th house does not reveal whether a person will live in a foreign country (a 7th house influence) just because it represents travel to foreign countries.

Martin: Basically you're saying that we have to memorize all the significations.

James: Yes, you have to memorize, and you have to memorize accurately!

Another issue that many beginning astrologers don't seem to realize is that to be a good astrologer you have to be able to think for yourself. You have to study the textbooks and then find out for yourself what works and what doesn't. Certain techniques may seem to work for every other astrologer in the world, but if they don't work for you, what good are they?

If you're not willing to first learn the precise teachings and then think about them and test them to see their level of accuracy, you're going to be quite poor at making accurate predictions. As an astrologer, you should be constantly thinking and reasoning about planetary meanings and house significations.

For example, in South India, the 9th house signifies the father while in North India the 10th house governs the father. Why? Because in South India, the father acts as spiritual mentor to his child and therefore he is seen through the 9th house. Not so in North india. So you see, astrology involves reasoning. If you're not willing to think and question and contemplate, you'll remain a mediocre astrologer at best.

Now, let's discuss the twelve houses. Remember, I'm not going to go over all the significations of the houses because that would be redundant. There are plenty of good texts that describe the houses. What I'm going to do is warn you about the typical mistakes people often make with house significations and point out subtleties that texts don't always mention.

First, since I will occasionally be mentioning examples of planets occupying houses, I need to make a few important distinctions about the Sun and the Moon. The Sun is somewhat misunderstood in its house positions because although it is a malefic, destructive planet, it is also one of the most personal, intimate influences. The Moon's house placement is sometimes misunderstood because it so dramatically supersedes other planetary influences that even when it is afflicted, its house position may still somehow flourish. Let's start with the Sun.

The Sun is an extremely personal influence because it is the *atmakaraka* or indicator of the soul. (There are two *atmakarakas* in every horoscope. One is the Sun and the other is the planet in the latest degree.) Whatever house the Sun occupies in a Hindu chart will be an extremely energized realm. And usually, the house that the Sun occupies will become strong and powerful. Take note of what I'm telling you because it takes experience to find this out. Nearly all basic astrology texts (mine included) emphasize problems and hardship to every house placement of the Sun (e.g. Sun in 1st house, Sun in 2nd house, and so on.). The reason for this is that basic texts are trying to isolate every astrological meaning for the reader. The isolated meaning of the Sun in a house is that the Sun is hot and therefore bad. But when you begin including subtleties and details, suddenly the positive potential of the Sun come into play.

The most fundamental meaning of the Sun, as a malefic, in any house is that there will be problems and hardship. There is no doubt about that. But because the Sun is also the indicator of the soul, the person will positively enjoy and be soulfully connected to the significations of the house. The benefits of this soul connection take time, of course. In my case, the Sun in the 5th house creates a hot mind, lack of mental peace, and so on. This was certainly not fun as a child. But as I matured, I learned to take advantage of the crispness and sharpness of that hot mind. I began to enjoy using my mind even though the mind was simultaneously a source of pain. The Sun is very interesting in the sense that it causes trouble but also reveals your soul connection or soul affinity.

Martin: So, my Sun occupies the 3rd house. What does that say about my soul connection.

James: The 3rd house represents siblings, desires, adventures, and so forth. Therefore, you would have a strong connection to any younger siblings, your soul would delight from being very active and adventurous, and you would be thrilled to be alive.

Martin: One of my greatest values in life is to always be willing to be adventurous and try new things.

James: Yes, I've certainly noticed that about you. So this is a perfect example. The 3rd house rules adventures and courage, and the indicator of your soul occupies the 3rd house, and therefore you value adventurousness tremendously and are always open to new experiences. Many people are scared of anything new or different.

Martin: James, it sounds like you're saying that when I read textbooks that describe the planets in the houses and they talk about all the negative effects that the Sun in each house creates, I'm supposed to allow for some good effects as well, yes?

James: Yes. But you have to use your head about this. Certain Sun placements will definitely improve more than others. Some Sun placements are so rough to begin with that the improvement is less dramatic.

Martin: Such as?

James: Well, I'm not much of a fan of the Sun in the 7th house. The Sun represents you, your very soul, and when it occupies the 7th house it occupies the house of another person — your spouse! This means your soul comfort and soul happiness depend on someone else's behavior. If that spouse does everything you ask of them, you're in luck. But if they don't, you suffer pretty significantly. Well, how likely is it that your spouse does everything you want them to? On top of that, if the person with Sun in the 7th is suffering in marriage, he or she has a very hard time leaving the spouse. If the person does leave, it generally takes years and years because the person feels such a soul connection to the spouse. So there are certain problems associated with the Sun in the 7th house, not to mention that the person's spouse is likely to be bossy, manipulative, or too willful.

Martin: Why is that?

James: Because the Sun rules willpower and it occupies the house of the spouse. Planets in the 7th house usually describe the marriage partner (I say usually because a house placement like Saturn in the 7th house can mean a Saturnian partner, but more often it simply means a bad or unhappy marriage.). In any case, the significations of the Sun's house position in the houses generally improve quite a lot because when a person is intimately and intrinsically connected to a realm of life, he or she is going to focus a great deal of attention in that area. The constant focus of human consciousness onto any realm will always have a positive effect. That is related to the free will factor.

Martin: The Sun rules the will, the willpower.

James: Exactly. The house containing the Sun, the ruler of the soul, eventually becomes a very important house, a house that is extremely energized and activated. When I wrote my first book, <u>Ancient Hindu Astrology for the Modern Western Astrologer</u>, I tried to give very traditional meanings to the planets in the houses. A lot has changed for me after many years of practical experience. I now view the effects of the Sun in the houses in a somewhat different light. I also find that if a fallen planet happens to be either the Sun, Moon, or ascendant ruler, there will of course be bad effects, but there will also be a huge interest in the realm of life signified by that house.

For example, in my text I said that if the fallen Moon occupies the 3rd house, the person would have no ability or interest in the fine arts. This is not always true. The Moon is so essential and all-important, that the person may be quite involved in 3rd house activities, even though the Moon is afflicted. The same kind of effect happens regarding a fallen or heavily afflicted ascendant ruler. If, for example, the ascendant ruler is Mars, and Mars is fallen (e.g. Mars in Cancer) in the 9th house, the person will certainly have some suffering in religious or spiritual matters, but he or she may be very interested and active in higher knowledge, religion, and philosophy.

Let me tell you, this is a very important matter. In my early days, if I saw a fallen Moon in the 5th house, I assumed that investments and speculations (a 5th house matter) were entirely off-limits to the person. Eventually, however, I kept seeing people with that placement becoming stock brokers.

Martin: Were there other indications in the horoscope for that?

James: Well, probably. Jupiter, the planet of investing, might be prominently placed or well-disposed. But don't think for a minute that the fallen Moon in the 5th house didn't play a part. The Moon is simply so important, it represents the person him- or herself, and therefore the person will be active in the realms signified by the Moon's house placement, unless perhaps the Moon is phenomenally afflicted. Incidentally, in the case of the fallen Moon (Moon in Scorpio) in the 5th house, we have a "double whammy" effect, because if the Moon is in Scorpio in the 5th house, it means that the Moon rules the ascendant, the 1st house. So now we have not only the all-important Moon in the 5th house, but also the all-important ascendant ruler in the 5th. Even though the Moon is fallen, it rules the person on two accounts.

Incidentally, I'm not saying that a person with a fallen Moon in the 5th house will be a successful investor or speculator. That's highly unlikely, if not impossible. I'm saying the person may become involved in the investment field, if there are other positive astrological influences pointing in that direction.

Martin: Could the Moon be so extremely afflicted that the person gets nothing good out of the Moon's house placement?

James: Certainly. It happens often enough. If the Moon is in the 3rd degree of Scorpio, its worst degree of fall, and is simultaneously tightly aspected by one or two malefics (like Mars, Saturn, Sun, or Ketu), the person may suffer horrendously on account of the Moon his or her entire life. The person experiences nothing but agony in the realms signified by the Moon's house placement. But, as I already said, the Moon in that house has to be extraordinarily afflicted, with no good mitigating factors involved. Otherwise, the person's continual attention, focus, and interest in the area involved will eventually produce some good effects. You'll see what I mean when you start analyzing horoscopes professionally. You simply cannot underestimate the significance of the Sun, Moon, and the ascendant ruler and the free will factor that comes into play with these planets due to the person's attention in the areas involved. Please don't forget what I'm telling you. I've just given you a second reliable way of observing how the human factor, free will, comes into play in horoscope analysis.

Martin: What was the first?

James: Retrograde planets. I told you earlier that if the ruler of a particular house is retrograde, then the significations of that house can be activated or not, entirely dependent on the person's wishes. Retrograde planets, in terms of the houses they rule (BUT NOT THEIR HOUSE PLACEMENTS — NOT THE HOUSES THEY OCCUPY) give almost complete free will.

In the case of the Sun, the significations of its house position are likely to improve as the years go by because of a person's constant focus and attention within that area.

Martin: Couldn't that be said of all the planets?

James: No, because a person never focuses as much constant attention on the significations of the other planets as he or she does on the Sun, Moon, and ascendant ruler. You can generally rely on the Sun's house position to become a more positive influence than is astrologically indicated, as the person matures.

Actually, there are two other circumstances where a person will focus constant attention on the significations of a planet, other than the Sun, Moon, or ascendant ruler. But they are rare. Remember when I taught you about how retrograde planets work? A retrograde planet is an influence that may have been out of balance in past lives. Therefore, a retrograde planet becomes a constant point of focus for an entire lifetime. The second influence is that of a stationary planet. A stationary planet is such an enormously powerful influence that it will cause a person to constantly focus on the realm of life signified by that planet. But as I said, these are rarities. Not everyone has a retrograde planet in their horoscope, and very few people have a stationary planet.

Regarding the Sun's house placement, and its ability to energize and invigorate the significations of its house placement, please be careful not to misconstrue what I'm saying. The Sun is a malefic, pure and simple. Just because a person gets a lot of vitality by activating the realm of life signified by the Sun's house position does not mean the Sun itself becomes good. The Sun is a hot star that burns the house it occupies and the planets it conjuncts or aspects. Any planet conjunct the Sun, within about six or eight degrees, becomes "combust" or burned by the Sun's hot rays and that planet is quite devastated (Note: Mercury, in its orbit, is never very far away from the Sun and therefore Mercury is not considered as badly burned unless the combustion is very close — within about two or three degrees). So please don't run around saying James Braha believes the Sun is a benefic planet. Essentially what I'm teaching you is that you must never forget that the Sun is the *atmakaraka*, the indicator of the soul, and there are very positive consequences to that equation. When you read textbook explanations of the Sun in the houses, they nearly always ignore that positive feature. Make absolutely sure you don't do that yourself.

Martin: It's a promise. But I have a few questions to ask. First, you said that the Sun and Moon are such personal influences that the houses they occupy become energized or invigorated, right?

James: Right.

Martin: Well, what about the houses they aspect? Do they get energized as well?

James: No. Not in the same way as what I'm trying to convey. Of course a Moon aspect thrown onto a house is excellent for the aspected house. But that is simply because the Moon is a benefic by nature. And although a waxing Moon is better than a waning Moon, I consider any Moon aspect to be benefic. But the distinction I am making is strictly about the Sun or Moon occupying a house. Because the luminaries represent the soul (Sun) and the person (Moon), the houses they occupy become extraordinary areas of interest. An aspect that a house receives from the luminary representing the soul, however, simply receives the hot energy of the Sun. You get it?

Martin: Yes, I get that. My second question concerns the hierarchy of the significations. You've said before that the Moon and the planet ruling the ascendant are the most important influences. This means that the Moon is definitely more important than the Sun, even though the Sun represents a person's soul. Is that right?

James: Absolutely. This is a lunar based-system, and the Moon takes precedence. Vashti had an interesting observation recently regarding the Sun and Moon. She noted that the Sun is only visible during the daytime (excluding eclipses), whereas the moon can actually be seen during the night and the day. It's an interesting point in such an observational art/science as astrology. The Moon's visibility changes depending on the seasons and the monthly cycle, but just the other day I looked for the Moon at around noontime, and saw it clear as ever.

So, let's talk about the houses. Remember, I'm not going to mention every feature of each house because that would be redundant. I simply want to make points that I think are lacking or under-emphasized in most basic texts.

THE FIRST HOUSE

The 1st house represents your personality and how people respond to you. It reveals whether you can gain fame and recognition on account of your presence, as opposed to recognition due to your actual work and performance. My second mentor taught me that in terms of ego, presence, and the ability to command some attention in the world, it's far better to have a planet in the 1st house or aspecting the 1st house than to have none at all. He was saying that even if the planet involved is a malefic, it's better to have some energizing of the 1st house than none.

I would qualify that by saying that I, personally, would certainly not want to have Saturn or Ketu in (or aspecting) the 1st house because those planets cause all kinds of personality problems, especially as they get closer to the ascendant.

Martin: You mean if a planet is closer to the ascendant degree, it's a more powerful influence?

James: Oh, yes. If Saturn occupies the 1st house, about ten degrees away from the ascendant degree, the person's birth will probably have been difficult. But if Saturn is one or two degrees away from the ascendant (and the birthtime is correct of course), the person's birth will have likely been <u>extraordinarily</u> difficult. If Mars is very close to the ascendant, the birth could be quick, but there would likely be blood all over the place. The same is true of planets aspecting the ascendant. If Jupiter aspects the 1st house, the person is spiritual, devotional, and generally lucky or fortunate. But if Jupiter aspects the ascendant degree <u>within a few degrees</u>, the results are dramatically increased.

By the way, if the ascendant degree is very early or very late, either the first two or three degrees or the last two or three degrees, then the ascendant is weak and the person's confidence will be seriously harmed. In terms of the person's sense of self, there will be a significant "void" beneath his or her appearance. And if the person also has good aspects to the 1st house, or if benefics occupy the 1st house, then there will be two features to the personality. The benefic planet will give great confidence and self-esteem (assuming the benefic planet is not fallen, badly aspected, or weak by virtue of rulership or some other way), but the person will simultaneously have a part of him- or herself that is entirely lacking in a sense of self. Of course, this effect is more intense if the ascendant degree is 29 degrees or 0 degrees than say, 27 or 3 degrees. Remember, however, that when you're looking at the ascendant <u>degree</u> of a horoscope you must consider that if the birthtime is wrong by four or five minutes then the ascendant degree will be wrong by one degree. (This is true in "normal" longitudes like America and Europe. In areas like Iceland, five minutes sometimes changes an ascendant by many degrees.)

There is a dreaded condition in Hindu astrology called *Gandanta Yoga* where the ascendant occupies the first three or last three degrees of a water sign (Cancer, Pisces, Scorpio). In those cases, there is a danger that the person may not live very long. In India, when this occurs many astrologers tell the parents they will not analyze the horoscope until the child reaches the age of three. I wouldn't worry much about *Gandanta Yoga* in the West because with all our medical advancement, it's extremely rare for a child to die. But *Gandanta Yoga* underscores the problem of a weak degree ascendant.

Incidentally, I've mentioned in my other books that oftentimes (but certainly not always) when a person has an extremely early or late degree ascendant, he or she may be adopted. If the ascendant is very weak, the person cannot hold his or her parents' attention. He or she may be ignored and sometimes actually given away. I remember a client of mine many years ago who was one of three brothers. His mother was so distraught with having to raise three children alone that she gave one of them away. Because my client had the zero degree ascendant, of course he was the one she chose to give up.

In any case, the 1st house is the most significant house of the chart and it is extremely important for that house have some strength; otherwise confidence and making one's way in the world are perpetually difficult.

Martin: What makes a house strong?

James: Benefic planets occupying the house, so long as they are not horribly aspected. As I said, even malefics like the Sun, Mars, and Rahu can energize the ascendant, but Saturn and Ketu powerfully weaken your confidence and make you shy and introverted. Of course, if Saturn is in its own or exaltation signs, the problems may not be quite so severe.

Planets other than Saturn aspecting the ascendant also make the ascendant strong. And the 1st house is particularly strong when the ascendant ruler is angular, or occupying its own sign, or aspected by benefics. If the ascendant ruler is closely conjunct Venus or Jupiter or Moon, the person's confidence is enormous and the person gains plenty of fame and recognition just for being him- or herself.

By the way, the 1st house is an angular house. Planets in angular houses are prominent and strengthened. So if Venus is in the 1st house (and therefore angular), the person's artistic sensibilities are increased. If Saturn is in the 1st house (and therefore angular), the person's depressive tendencies are increased. If Mars is angular, the person's aggressiveness and anger are strong. And so forth. Further, because planets in the 1st house are strengthened, this means that the houses ruled by those 1st house occupants are strengthened. For instance, if Mars is in the 1st house, while ruling the 2nd house (money), it means the person will make good money. If Jupiter occupies the 1st house and it rules the 10th house (career), then the career energy is strengthened. The 1st house, as an angular house, strengthens planets and the houses they rule.

THE SECOND HOUSE

The 2nd house represents money — the money that you make from your daily job as opposed from money that comes from side ventures, which is an 11th house matter. In order to be a millionaire, it generally takes a good 2nd house (so you make good money daily) and a good 11th house (so you can parlay that wealth into large sums).

Martin: The 11th house rules large sums of money?

James: Yes. Now, another 2nd house signification is the face. Therefore, a person can be good looking if the 2nd house is occupied or aspected by benefic planets. (A person can also be beautiful if the 1st house contains or is aspected by benefics because the 1st house rules the head.)

The 2nd house governs the food that you eat as well as speaking, writing, teaching, the memory, and the imagination. So the 2nd house indicates teachers and writers. It also reveals whether a person will use good speech or foul language, and whether the person tells the truth. Watch out for people with fallen planets in the 2nd house or two malefics in the 2nd house, because they can lie or cheat you in business without a second thought. Not all people with these placements do this, but a lot of them will.

Martin: James, I've heard some people say that the 3rd house rules writing and teaching. What's the story?

James: There are some astrologers practicing Jyotish who see the 3rd house as writing and teaching. But that's not how I was taught by either of my mentors and that's definitely not my experience. My first suggestion to you is to find five or six charts with Mercury in the 2nd house (planet of writing and communication in the house of writing and communication) and then observe those individuals. They are by far the wittiest, most literary and communicative people you will ever meet.

Martin: Because that planetary placement is the quintessential placement of writers?

James: Yes. Or, find some charts of people who are writers, counselors, educators, lecturers, and so on and look at how prominent and/or well disposed the 2nd house is, rather than the 3rd house.

Martin: Are you implying that astrologers who believe the 3rd house is writing and teaching aren't experience-oriented enough?

James: I can't speak for everyone, but I believe that the reason many Hindu astrologers see the 3rd house as writing is because they or their teachers have been influenced by Western astrology. In Western astrology, writing, teaching, speaking, and education are seen from the 3rd house. Remember that much of modern day *Jyotish* has been influenced by Westerners invading India. As I already mentioned, some of the most basic terms in *Jyotish* are Greek (*Kendra, trikona,* apoklima, *hora*) and have no meaning at all in Sanskrit — the language of the Vedas. There's also a method called *Varshopal*, which is a solar return (or yearly) chart that I'm told originates in Persia, but is often mistakenly thought to be Indian.

It's also quite possible that some Hindu astrologers get mixed up because the ancient texts never mention authors and writers but they give rulership of publications and written materials to the 3rd house. I agree that letters, magazines, and written materials are seen from the 3rd house, but definitely not the authors of those materials. If you look in almost any ancient *Jyotish* text for the meaning of the houses, you'll notice that the significations of speech and education are attributed to the 2nd house. If you have a text that doesn't list the meanings of the houses separately, look at the descriptions of planets in the 2nd house in that book. You'll find almost every single description of a planet in the 2nd house as either being good or bad for speech or education. Then, go to the descriptions of all the planets in the 3rd house and you'll see explanations about courage, siblings, hands and own efforts, and so on, with no mention at all about speech or education. Remember though, I'm speaking about ancient texts. I see no reason whatsoever why writing and teaching should be given to a different house than that of education and speech.

Anyhow, that's how I see it and I'm unlikely to change because I happen to be quite accurate when predicting that a person is a writer, counselor, or teacher in my astrology practice. In these classes with you, I've mentioned many instances where I'm unable to obtain excellent results (predicting eyesight, determining whether aspects from malefic planets cause harm to *upachaya* houses, use of the *saptamsa* chart (in Class Seven), determining whether conjunctions should be used in *varga* charts [in Class Seven), and on and on. I have as many vulnerabilities as any other astrologer, but predicting teachers and writers just isn't one of them. Even in my earliest days of practice I never had a problem predicting teachers and educators accurately from the 2nd house. As my mentor, Padia, used to say "You take it from me. I have marked this!"

Now on to the next point, which is something you must be very careful not to forget, because it's never emphasized thoroughly enough in basic texts. The 2nd house rules family life. It therefore has a strong bearing on a person's happiness in the first family (during childhood) as well as the second family (during marriage). Regarding marriage, there are an awful lot of features to analyze and so many students go wrong in their judgement because they ignore the 2nd house. Therefore, you should commit it to memory, here and now, that you must also consider a person's 2nd house if you want to know about his or her happiness in married life. The 2nd house tells whether or not a person is going to argue and bicker a lot and whether his or her domestic scene is smooth.

If Jupiter, Venus, Moon, or Mercury occupy the 2nd house, the person's family life is smooth and harmonious. The same happens if benefics occupy the 8th house, because planets in the 8th aspect the 2nd house. If malefics (Rahu, Ketu, Sun, Mars, and Saturn) occupy the 2nd or 8th house, then there is likely to be a lot of arguing and friction and discord on a daily level.

Martin: Are you saying that it's possible for a person to have a well-disposed Venus (love) and a good 7th house (marriage) and a good 7th in the *navamsa* (marriage chart) and still have a lot of friction in their marriage if malefic Mars occupies the 2nd house? Or if Saturn and Sun occupy the 8th house and throw malefic aspects onto the 2nd?

James: Yes. I can't tell you how many times I've seen a client with two malefics in the 2nd house argue and bicker with loved ones for the most insignificant reasons you can imagine. People with an afflicted 2nd house are often offensive in speech in general anyway. At any rate, remember that constant daily discords and conflicts can eventually ruin a marriage and it is your job to warn the person! People with an afflicted 2nd house often have no idea that their constant disagreeing and arguing is harmful. For them, it seems natural.

If a person with an afflicted 2nd house is smart and well-meaning, he or she can make a concerted effort to stop the bickering. Whenever I see a person with Rahu or Ketu in either the 2nd house or the 8th house (which generate roughness in family life) entering the *dasa* of either of these placements, I advise him or her not to make a big deal about the little annoyances that are going to be bothersome for the next seven or eighteen years (Ketu *dasa* lasts seven years, Rahu *dasa* lasts eighteen years). I tell the person that he or she can either make a big deal about the petty daily annoyances that are about to occur or take a more relaxed, easy going attitude.

Martin: Then it's up to the person?

James: Yes. This is where free will comes in. Another important point not emphasized enough in basic texts is that the 2nd house rules counselors and (partially) therapists (because counselors and therapists constantly speak and teach). So if you see a horoscope that indicates healing or medicine, and the 2nd house is prominent, then the person is likely to become either a psychologist or psychiatrist.

Martin: How do you tell whether the person is going to be a doctor? And how do you know the person is not just going to be a doctor who makes a lot of money (2nd house)?

James: Good questions. To determine that a horoscope indicates a doctor or healer, you just use basic astrological logic. If the ruler of the 10th house (career) occupies the 6th house (health matters), or vice versa, healing is obviously indicated. If there is a connection between the 3rd house (one's hands and efforts) and the 6th house (health matters), the person has healing talent.

Martin: What kind of connection?

James: The ruler of the 3rd house occupying the 6th house, or vice versa. Or if the rulers of the 3rd and 6th houses are conjunct, then healing ability is indicated.

Other clues to the horoscope of a healer occur when the 6th house is loaded with planets (especially personal planets) or when the 6th house is extremely well-disposed (an exalted planet or planet in its own sign occupying the 6th house, or the ruler of the 6th tightly aspected by a great benefic planet.

On top of this, if you know positively that the birthtime is accurate, then you can use the *dasamsa* or career chart. If the ruler of the 6th house occupies the 10th (or vice versa) in the *dasamsa*, then again you are pointed in the direction of medicine. Or if the ruler of the 1st house in the natal or *dasamsa* chart occupies the 6th house, especially in its own or exaltation sign, again you have strong indications. All of this is simple astrological logic, nothing fancy, nothing complicated. This is why I keep emphasizing that you learn the fundamental meanings of the planets and the meanings of the houses as perfectly as you can. Don't worry so much about complicated techniques and exotic systems.

Regarding your other question, about distinguishing the difference between a healer with counseling ability or a healer who makes a lot of money, you need to look at the quality, rather than quantity, of the 2nd house. If you see very personal planets occupying the 2nd house, planets like Sun, Moon, or ascendant ruler, then there is more likelihood that the person loves 2nd house matters and is therefore very enlivened by knowledge. Of course, the person could just as well love money, but they will also be thrilled by knowledge, education, writing, and counseling if the personal planets influence the 2nd house.

If, however, you simply see a very benefic 2nd house without a very personal feel to it, say a 2nd house that merely contains a strong or well-disposed Venus or Jupiter, then you should think money. Remember, however, that if the 2nd house Venus or Jupiter rules the 1st house, the most important and personal influence in a horoscope, then you must consider that the person probably loves writing, teaching, and counseling, and so forth. Because if Venus or Jupiter, or any planet for that matter, rules the ascendant, that planet immediately becomes a personal influence. Never forget that the Moon and the ascendant ruler (also called ascendant lord) are the most important and personal planets in a birthchart.

Now if Mercury (planet of knowledge) occupies the 2nd house, the person is extremely skilled in his or her speaking skills and you have to assume that he or she is going to do some sort of teaching, writing, or lecturing in whatever career is chosen.

Martin: James, is the 2nd house a relatively good house?

James: Actually, I consider it a slightly bad house. Although the rule is that the 2nd house is generally neutral, in terms of how it affects occupying planets, it doesn't really do much good. Although it's not a *dusthana*, a grief-producing house, in my experience the 2nd house seems to slightly harm planets or the houses those planets rule. I say it seems to harm planets because I don't want to make a big issue about this or make up some new rule.

I began to suspect that the 2nd house was harmful when I noticed that many people who had the ruler of the 7th house in the 2nd were divorced. Then I noticed that many people with the ruler of the 10th house in the 2nd were either not having any great career success or they were having minor career problems.

As a neutral house, the 2nd house sometimes brings up the issue of experiencing a glass of water as half-full or half-empty. In America, a person who has the ruler of the 7th occupying the 2nd house may view his or her marriage as "not very good," and therefore want out. A person in Europe with the same planetary position may feel that his or her marriage "isn't terrible, so why rock the boat?" But in fact, there is nothing particularly good about 2nd house energy, and planets affected by the 2nd house are usually slightly harmed by it.

Martin: But the 2nd house gives money, education, writing and counseling talent, right?

James: Yes. If you're 2nd house is strong and well-aspected, it means you will get lots of money and all, but that doesn't mean the house itself is a good house. For example, lets say a man has a Scorpio ascendant and he has Venus in the 2nd house (in Sagittarius). He will make good money because Venus, a great benefic, occupies the house of money. But he will also very likely have some significant marriage difficulties — possibly even divorce — because Venus as ruler of the 7th house occupies the 2nd house. The 2nd house just doesn't help its occupying planets.

Martin: But what about the fact that the 2nd house rules family life? Isn't that good for marriage?

James: Sure, that's good. If a benefic planet occupies the 2nd house, without affliction, the person is unlikely to argue and bicker within his or her marriage. But the person may eventually have marriage problems on account of the slightly negative influence that the 2nd house causes on the 7th house ruler. The good part about the ruler of the 7th house occupying the 2nd house is that the person gets a spouse who makes (or will eventually make) a lot of money, but marriage itself is not strengthened by the 2nd house energy.

To give you some more examples, if the ruler of the 3rd house occupies the 2nd, don't expect the person to have lots of younger siblings or great happiness with them. If the ruler of the 4th house occupies the 2nd house, the person will not have great happiness from his or her mother (even though this placement could make the mother wealthy). The 2nd house is nowhere near as devastating as the 6th, 8th, or 12th houses, but it isn't good either. You see the point?

Martin: Yes.

THE THIRD HOUSE

The 3rd house has to do with a person's ability to fulfill desires, to get needs and desires met. It also rules courage, adventures, siblings, fine arts, and so on. It is the 3rd house that makes artists, and it has a lot to do with publishing, BUT NOT WRITING. As I've already said, there are astrologers who take the 3rd house to be the house of writing, but I was taught that writing is ruled by the 2nd house, and that has been validated by my experience. A case in point is my Moon *dasa* that started around the age of ten or eleven. The Moon rules my 3rd house. Well, during the entire Moon *dasa*, I was useless when it came to writing anything in school. I barely passed English class and I never even did the required reading. On the other hand, the entire period was spent doing drama. I was an actor.

Martin: Third house.

James: That's right. I was completely fascinated by 3rd house significations, but not at all interested in reading and writing, which is a 2nd house matter.

There are astrologers who consider the 3rd house to be connected to one's personality, and I can see their point. Because the 3rd house has to do with a person's willpower and ability to concentrate and focus, it does affect one's personality. But I wouldn't go overboard with that signification since so much about the personality is seen through the 1st house. Two examples of 3rd house personality influences are: Ketu in the 3rd house gives an unusual, weird, strange, or spiritual personality. Saturn in the 3rd house gives a serious or stern personality. But these are minor influences compared to 1st house indications, which are obviously much more revealing.

When I say the 3rd house may have something to do with personality, I mean personality, not character. The personality, as I'm using the term, simply means a person's general temperament, manner, and disposition. I make the distinction because the 5th house will tell you a lot about a person's character. By this I mean a person's morals, integrity, humility, tendency to brag, selfishness versus selflessness, and so on. So if you see a chart with a well disposed 5th house, the person usually has excellent morals and excellent character. If the 5th house is maligned and afflicted, the person may be petty, selfish, domineering, narrow-minded, or egocentric.

Martin: Can you give me some examples?

James: Sure, but remember that in my examples I am isolating planets in houses. If I say Jupiter in the 5th house gives great character and morals, I mean Jupiter in the 5th house alone, not Jupiter in the 5th aspected by Mars, and not Jupiter in the 5th with the ruler of the 5th occupying its fallen sign and aspected tightly by some malefic planet.

If Moon, Jupiter, or Venus (the benefic planets) occupy the 5th house, the person usually has had a good upbringing, where proper values, ethics, and concern for others has been taught. Again, this assumes that the benefic planets in the 5th don't occupy their fallen signs or their detriments (signs opposite their ownership signs). And that these planets are not badly aspected and the 5th house ruler is not badly placed or afflicted.

If Mars occupies the 5th house, the person's character is not usually so fine, unless Mars is exalted or in one of its own signs (Aries or Scorpio). The person may be less than honorable or not particularly principled. There is too much concern with getting one's own way and not enough care about how others are affected in the process. In case it's not obvious, the reason the 5th house has to do with character is because it is the house of the mind. All our actions are predicated on our thoughts.

Please be careful to use discretion with these delineations and to think things through. If you think Saturn in the 5th house gives lousy character because Saturn is a malefic, you're dead wrong. Saturn is the planet of responsibility, humility, integrity, and so on. If anything, a person with Saturn in the 5th is too hard on him- or herself and too concerned with not harming others, if that's possible. Hank Aaron, whose chart we looked at in the last class, has Saturn in the 5th house in its own sign, and when he was playing he kept the lowest profile you can imagine. He was breaking lots of records and saying nothing about it. He let his actions speak for themselves. That's character.

Regarding the 3rd house, the most important point I can tell you is that many astrologers underestimate its importance. A person may have an excellent birthchart, but if there is a fallen planet in the 3rd, or if the ruler of the 3rd is tightly combust the Sun, or very close to Ketu, or greatly afflicted in any other way, then the person encounters constant obstacles and delays in their daily activities. The person may get money and success and love if the rest of the chart indicates such benefits, but he or she has to work two or three times as hard as others because there are always obstacles and barriers to fulfilling one's daily desires.

Also, don't forget that a person with a weak and afflicted 3rd house is very fearful because the 3rd house rules courage. Interpreting charts for people with afflicted 3rd houses is often difficult because the person is scared. Therefore, you find yourself having to baby the person when you're telling them any bad news about their horoscope. Because they're fearful, they take what you say and create psychological problems with the information, instead of using what you say to protect themselves and plan for the future.

The 3rd house is also connected to short journeys and experiences with neighbors and the local community. These significations are sometimes ignored in basic Hindu texts. And don't forget that even though the 2nd house rules speech, it is the 3rd that governs the voice. So, if you want to know why singers like Bob Dylan and Bruce Springsteen have peculiar, rather than melodious, voices, you should analyze the 3rd house of their charts.

THE FOURTH HOUSE

Regarding the 4th house, most of what is written in basic texts is fairly complete. I would simply add that it's extremely important to delineate happiness from the 4th house. As I've said many times in my lectures, the rarest features I find in the charts of Westerners are happiness in general, and a happy married life (married life is seen from the 7th house).

Whenever you see malefics in the 4th house, not in their own signs and not well aspected by Venus, Jupiter, or any benefic, the person will definitely be unhappy, somber, or depressed. It doesn't matter if the rest of the chart is wonderful, they're still unhappy. Money, fame, and all kinds of benefits won't change the feeling in the person's heart.

Martin: What if the person has a malefic in the 4th house that rules good houses? Say the ascendant is Cancer, and Mars, which rules the 5th and 10th houses, occupies the 4th house.

James: No good for happiness. In my experience, a malefic is a malefic is a malefic! Yes, a malefic that rules good houses (a "functional benefic") definitely brings some good with it, but if you examine people who have malefics in the 4th, whether the planets rule good houses or not, you'll find happiness and the sweetness of life are significantly missing.

If, however, Mars or some other malefic occupies the 4th house and that planet is very well-aspected, then happiness is not necessarily harmed. By well-aspected, I mean a malefic planet that is conjunct a benefic (Venus, Moon, Jupiter, or Mercury), with a tight or even medium orb — say within five or seven degrees. Or, if the malefic receives an aspect from a benefic from its opposing sign (the 7th house aspect), that will seriously mitigate the problem.

As always, some astrologers may disagree with my assessment. I am, beyond any doubt, a "planets first" astrologer. Not all astrologers are. Some consider rulerships more essential. I am simply relating my experience. To me, planets come first, rulerships second. It's up to you to test this it out. You'll see just how serious I am about the "planets first" concept when we talk about gemstones. I always recommend wearing the stones of benefics if a benefic planet is afflicted, regardless of the houses that benefic planet rules.

Martin: If a person has an afflicted or fallen Moon and the Moon rules the 8th or 12th house, you would tell them to wear a pearl?

James: Yes. But let's talk about gems later (Class Nine).

You're going to find that even if someone has a Libra ascendant where Saturn becomes a *rajayoga-karaka*, and Saturn occupies the 4th house in its own sign, Capricorn, happiness will be disturbed. Saturn is simply too "heavy" a planet to be in the 4th house.

Martin: Well, there must be some good effect caused by a *rajayoga* planet sitting in the 4th house, and especially sitting its own sign. What is it?

James: What do you think?

Martin: Wouldn't it be great for real estate?

James: Of course. It would be wonderful in that realm. The person would also have leadership ability by virtue of wisdom. The leadership would occur more after the thirty-sixth year, when Saturn matures, but it would be predictable. Leadership skills given by Saturn relate to wisdom and experience, whereas leadership coming from Mars is more of an assertive, bossy kind of leadership. Mars is the planet of commanders and gives an intense desire to boss others, to put one's own desires above everyone else. Saturn, on the other hand, makes the person wiser and more experienced than his or her peers. Most presidents have a phenomenally powerful Mars in their chart (e.g. Mars tightly conjunct Venus, Jupiter, or Mercury), whereas someone like Jimmy Carter is more Saturnian. In his chart, Saturn, which is the *rajayoga-karaka* planet, occupies the 1st house in Libra, its exaltation sign.

Regarding real estate, remember that in Hindu astrology Mars, not Saturn, is considered the planet of "landed property." My mentors always looked at the condition and prominence of Mars to delineate one's luck with property. But they also looked at Saturn because Saturn is the planet of construction.

Martin: Which is more important?

James: I treat them pretty equally. I find that when either Mars or Saturn occupies the 4th, the person has successful activity in real estate. Unless, of course, Saturn or Mars are seriously afflicted (fallen or combust, and so on).

If the 4th house is well-disposed, containing benefics, or if the ruler of the 4th house is aspected tightly by a benefic, then I expect the person to live in beautiful homes and to do well when they buy or sell their homes. But if Mars or Saturn, the planets of real estate, occupy the 4th, then I expect the person to actually become involved in buying or selling property. You see the difference?

In any case, you could say the 4th house is the most important house of a horoscope because if it is housing great benefics, the person is happy no matter what. Even if the person's 7th house is terrible and love relationships are ruined, or if the tenth house is harmed and career is unsuccessful, the person is still happy and lighthearted if the 4th house is housing unafflicted benefics. It's quite something to watch. Please test what I'm saying.

This brings us to the next important feature that is sometimes missed by Western astrologers practicing *Jyotish*. The 4th house represents the heart. This differs from Western astrology where the 5th house is the significator. If you see malefics in the 4th house, particularly if two malefics are there, you can predict with very high certainty that the person has a heart vulnerability. In many cases the person has a heart murmur or some defect that is known in childhood. But, sometimes the client isn't yet aware of the sensitivity, even though it's there. If you ask clients with a seriously afflicted 4th house whether heart problems run in their family, they almost always say yes.

Martin: When would the problems appear?

James: When the *dasa* of a malefic planet occupying the 4th house occurs, problems are likely. Also, if the Sun, which is the planetary significator (*karaka*) of the heart, is afflicted and it runs its *dasa*, problems may arise. Or, when Saturn transits the 4th house.

When you see a malefic in the 4th house, however, you have to note whether the malefic is in its own or exaltation sign because either of those would give a strong heart. In other words, if Mars is in Aries or Scorpio in the 4th the heart is very strong. Or if Saturn is in Capricorn or Aquarius, the heart is likely to be quite hardy.

Martin: This is confusing. You're saying that Mars or Saturn in the 4th house in good signs are beneficial for the heart, but not for happiness?

James: That's right. Marilyn Monroe was a typical example of a person with Saturn exalted in the 4th house who was quite unhappy. So, in case you haven't guessed, there's a lot of knowledge in *Jyotish* that comes with experience, with interpreting charts and watching the results. That's why it's important to have a teacher. You have practice and <u>keep your eyes open</u>. And be careful not to accept textbook teachings blindly, no matter who the author is.

Remember what I said some time ago about how textbooks say malefics in *upachaya* houses (the growing houses — 3rd, 6th, 10th, and 11th) are excellent? Well, try telling someone who has Rahu and Saturn in the 3rd house that they have luck and fortune with younger siblings (particularly the next-born sibling). Try telling a person with Mars and Ketu in the 11th house that he or she has excellent experiences with friends and groups. You'll be completely wrong. If you swallow textbook teachings without testing them, you'll never be much of an astrologer. You must go by your experience.

Another important point about the 4th house is that it governs endings of matters. I know most people don't care much to hear about the last two or three years of their life, but the term "endings" means much more than just the end of one's life. It means all endings. If a person has an afflicted 4th house, then ending a love affair or marriage, ending a job, a friendship, and so on will be painful or difficult.

If you take the time to look, you'll rarely find that person with a fallen planet in the 4th house or one or two malefics in the 4th house will have an amicable divorce. On the other hand, watch the endings of a person with Venus or Jupiter in the 4th. If there is a divorce, the person walks away feeling little or no animosity and bitterness.

A person with malefics in the 4th house may have a lot of grief or troubles at the very end of their college education.

Martin: Are all endings affected?

James: Yes, all endings. Finally, let me mention that even though education is seen from the 2nd house, the educational degree is seen from the 4th. If you see a client who has a really harmonious 4th house, say Venus and Moon, or Mercury and Venus, or a few unafflicted benefics in the 4th house, ask them how many educational degrees they have. Often you'll find they have several bachelors degrees or they have a masters or Ph.D. Don't forget this. Clients who have very afflicted 4th houses will be grateful when you explain to them how this works. It actually makes their lives a bit easier, just knowing why such a pattern exists in their lives.

THE FIFTH HOUSE

On to the 5th house. One of the biggest mistakes I make in this area is failing to notice mental illness or weakness of mind when the ruler of the 5th house is very afflicted. There have been many times when I've read a chart for someone and noticed, say, the 5th house ruler one or two degrees away from Ketu, or tightly conjunct a fallen malefic and simply thought that the person will have suffering on account of children (another 5th house matter). When I begin interacting with the client, however, I quickly realize the person is not mentally healthy, to put it mildly.

Martin: So mental illness is seen from the 5th house?

James: Yes, but if I begin to suspect mental illness, then I also look at both Mercury and the Moon.

Martin: Why the Moon?

James: Because the Moon is the mind. Whereas Mercury is the intellect, the Moon rules common sense and memory. A person with an afflicted Moon often cannot reason well because he or she is overwhelmed by unconscious forces, by moods and feelings. The person is always losing perspective. On the other hand, a person with an afflicted Mercury simply doesn't process information well. It's as if he or she is using an imperfect or defective tool when trying to study or analyze. In terms of delineating mental health, the distinction between Moon and Mercury is subtle because if either planet is afflicted, the mind is harmed.

Martin: What if both are afflicted?

James: Then you're looking at a person who experiences a lot of mental suffering. Which is a good way to express it. You never say to a person, "I see insanity or mental illness in your birthchart." But you could say, "Your chart indicates a lot of worrying and mental anguish, and you should wear the gemstones for Moon and Mercury, and chant mantras or have *yagyas* performed for these planets."

If both the Moon and Mercury are afflicted, I ask the person if he or she has headaches. The answer is almost always "yes." On the physical level, the brain is vulnerable. I therefore warn the person that if they some day encounter a strange or undiagnosable ailment that doctors are struggling with, the first area to check is the brain. You have to do your best to give the person this information without upsetting them. This is obviously a delicate task, since the person is, by definition, a worrier or anxious type.

Martin: But if you tell a person who has both mental planets afflicted, won't they obsess over it?

James: Maybe so, but I would rather the person be aware of the vulnerability so that if a problem occurs, it can be handled quickly. Brain tumors are nothing to play around with.

Martin: James, I have a question regarding children. Can you explain how you tell the nature or personality of the kids.

James: I generally find that the most obvious manifestation of the 5th house signifies the first child. Let's say for example, that Jupiter occupies the 5th house, while the 5th house ruler closely conjuncts Mercury (assuming that the conjunction occurs in an average house, not a *dusthana*, or grief-producing house). I would predict that the first child is likely to be Jupitarian — lucky, blessed, happy, and religious. I would expect the next child to be Mercurial — intellectual, talkative, psychologically-oriented, like that.

As a second example, if Venus occupies the 5th house, unafflicted, and the ruler of the 5th house is conjunct or strongly aspected by Mars, I would say that the first child is going to be artistic, happy, and beautiful, while the second child will be aggressive, hot-tempered, physically-oriented, and interested in sports.

The biggest mistake I make when analyzing children in a person's chart is not paying enough attention to Jupiter, the *karaka*, or indicator, of children. I have seen charts where the 5th house looks good enough to produce children without obstacles or delays, but because Jupiter is severely afflicted, the person has had miscarriages or difficulty conceiving.

Martin: How bad does Jupiter have to be to cause this? I see a lot of afflicted Jupiters.

James: It has to be <u>extremely</u> afflicted. If it's simply a matter of Jupiter being aspected by Mars, Sun, or Ketu, the person may not have any <u>major</u> problem with children. But if Jupiter is in Capricorn (fallen) and/or it is aspected by Saturn or Mars or Sun (malefics) within one or two degrees, look out! The person may have major suffering with kids. Or if Jupiter is tightly conjunct fallen Mars (Mars in Cancer) or conjunct fallen Saturn (Saturn in Aries), then the problems are serious.

There are some other points to remember about the 5th house. I've already mentioned how the 5th house has a lot to do with character (when I spoke about the 3rd house). That's because ethics and morals have so much to do with the person's thinking process, and the 5th house rules the mind. You also shouldn't forget that the 5th house signifies spiritual techniques. This is important because if see a very afflicted chart I want to know whether the person will enjoy, and have talent for, chanting mantras. If the 5th house is very rough, then I generally advise *yagyas* rather than mantras.

Also, don't forget that the 5th house rules *poorvapunya*, or past life credit. Of course the whole chart is a result of a person's karma from past lives, but whatever pertains to the 5th house, whatever is indicated there – good or bad effects relating to any particular events – <u>must occur in this life because the karma has been building for too many lifetimes</u>. So if, for example, the ruler of the 5th house occupies the 9th house and is well-disposed, the person <u>must</u> get good higher knowledge and good effects with gurus in the this life. If the ruler of the 5th house occupies the 9th house and is afflicted, then the person <u>must</u> suffer on account of gurus because of past life actions. That's how it works.

THE SIXTH HOUSE

Regarding the 6th house, there are some subtleties that make analysis of health and analysis of enemies and competitors quite difficult for beginners. This problem occurs because the 6th house is an *upachaya*, or growing house, where both benefic and malefic planets do well. First, let's consider the signification of enemies and competitors.

Malefics in the 6th house are incredibly good in terms of giving a person the ability to defeat enemies, jealous people, competitors, and so on. If a person has two malefics in the 6th house, and someone gets in his or her way, or someone decides to secretly usurp or overthrow the person, in the end the perpetrator will not only lose, the perpetrator will be destroyed! I've seen this occur many times. It's fascinating to watch. A friend of mine whose birthchart has Saturn and Ketu in the 6th house found out that her standing at work was being secretly undermined by one of her partners (she had three or four partners). In the end, the partner trying to overthrow her was thrown out of the company. This is not an isolated instance; I've seen this happen over and over again.

Martin: Do those with malefic planets in the 6th go out of their way to harm competitors or enemies?

James: No, absolutely not. But in my experience, a person with malefics in the 6th is extremely aware of enemies and knows exactly how to defeat them. The next point is something you will not find in textbooks. I find that people with malefics in the 6th house are very competitive. Their ability and knowledge of how to overcome competitors and jealous people has been developed over time. This means the person has been aware of competition from early childhood and has developed a strategy to handle the issue. Certainly, it is good to be able to defeat one's enemies and competitors. But I have noticed that people with malefics in the 6th house tend to feel threatened by anyone who might have greater success than themselves. It's not very pretty and it's not very gracious.

Martin: You're not just talking about defeating competitors. You're talking about being defensive or overly competitive.

James: Sometimes the competitiveness actually looks like a character flaw. Like the person can't allow someone else to have more success than him- or herself. But you can test this out for yourself. This is something I've begun to notice in the last five years. Also, the more malefics that occupy the house, the more competitive the person seems to be.

If you want to see how well malefic planets in the 6th operate in defeating enemies, look at Fidel Castro's horoscope. You'll see why he could never be overtaken. Do you have any idea how many Cuban exile groups (not to mention the entire U.S. government) have tried and failed to overthrow Castro? Not only does he have malefic Mars in the 6th house, Mars is in its own sign, Aries.

Now, let's talk about benefic planets in the 6th house. Benefics in the 6th

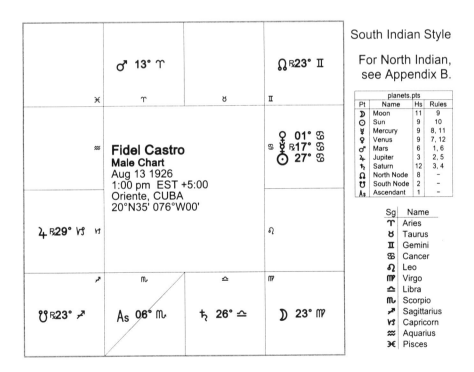

are tremendously good for defeating enemies and competitors, but in these cases the person is so well liked that he or she doesn't encounter enemies and jealous people. A person with, say, Jupiter and a bright Moon unafflicted in the 6th house is never going to be charged in a court case. There are very few enemies and competitors, and the person is liked by all. On the other hand, the person with malefics in the 6th could be hauled into court, but the person who charged him or her will wind up fairly ruined in the end.

Martin: Which do you consider better in the 6th house, benefics or malefics?

James: Regarding enemies and competitors (as opposed to health matters), I prefer benefics in the 6th house, but that's a matter of personal opinion, I think. If you like the concept of revenge, malefics in the 6th are better. Your enemy will wind up destroyed and running away with his or her tail between the legs. If you're a more forgiving person, benefics in the 6th house are definitely the way to go. You simply never have enemies!

A good example of someone with benefics in the 6th house is Al Gore. He has the Moon and Jupiter in Sagittarius (Jupiter's own sign). Do you remember his first debate with Dan Quayle when they were both running for Vice President? Dan Quayle was incredibly sharp and incisive in his attacks. Gore, with his enormously beneficial 6th house, didn't even react to the ruthless attacks and yet he won the election. He seemed not to even notice Quayle's nastiness, and in the end he won. And he won without getting

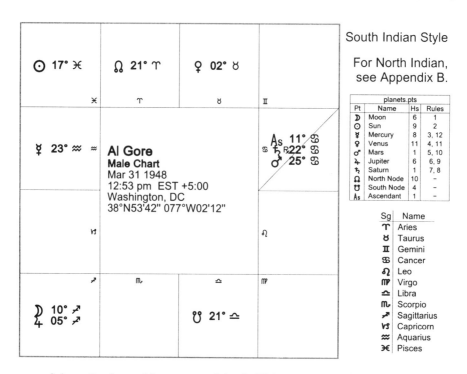

vengeful or the least bit mean-spirited. This is typical for a person with benefics in the 6th.

If Gore had malefics in his 6th house, he would have gone for Quayle's jugular! He would have reminded Quayle of his inability to spell "potato," or he would have found some way to humiliate Quayle so that Quayle would have regretted attacking so ruthlessly.

Regarding benefics in the 6th house, please remember that the whole equation is altered if the benefics are afflicted. If Venus or Jupiter occupies the 6th house, say in a fallen sign, or if they are aspected by malefic planets, then whenever those benefic planets run their dasas or bhuktis, the person may encounter nothing but enemies, competitors, and jealous people. In my chart, Venus rules my 6th house and it happens to be massively afflicted (it is tightly conjunct malefics Mars and Ketu). During my last Venus subperiod, enemies and jealous people came out of the woodwork. The whole period was painful in that respect.

Werner Erhard (founder of EST seminars) lost his empire when he ran his Venus *bhukti* (see page 315 for his birthchart). Venus rules his 6th house and is very afflicted (combust the Sun and aspected by Saturn). According to Erhard, what brought him down was an orchestrated attack by long-time enemies. The enemies had been against him for years and years, but in the vulnerable period of the afflicted 6th house ruler, they got him.

Martin: It sounds like generals and politicians could really benefit from knowing about a person's 6th house.

James: That's for sure. Did you know that when Napoleon was considering making a person a general, one of his top priorities was whether the person was lucky. It's damn good thinking.

In terms of health matters, benefics or malefics in the 6th house are good for warding off health problems (as long as the planets are not in bad signs or otherwise afflicted). A person with one or two malefics in the 6th house will be incredibly healthy. The person will hardly ever get sick and will heal quickly if there is an ailment.

Having a benefic in the 6th strengthens the house so the person's health is strong and healing is quick. For health purposes, however, I would rather have a malefic in the 6th. The reason is that benefic planets are more sensitive and therefore they are harmed by the *dusthana*, or grief-producing, energy of the 6th. Also, if you have a benefic planet in the 6th house and it is in the slightest way afflicted, you are likely to have health problems related to that planet. Afflicted Mercury in the 6th house gives lung, intestinal, or nervous ailments. Afflicted Moon in the 6th gives breast, brain, menstrual, or stomach problems. Afflicted Jupiter in the 6th gives allergies or ailments involving the liver, gall bladder, or spleen. Afflicted Venus in the 6th indicates problems with throat, thyroid, kidneys, reproductive system, and the skin. But the skin can also be indicated by Saturn. So if a client has acne or skin rashes, check both Saturn and Venus to see which planet must be strengthened to cure the problem.

Martin: I'm confused about one thing. If Venus occupies the 6th house, does it mean that the house of health is strengthened, or does it mean the person has health problems with the throat, thyroid, or reproductive system?

James: It depends entirely on whether that particular Venus is afflicted or not. To be honest, you would need a good amount of intuition in this matter because on one hand the benefic planet in the 6th house strengthens the house, while at the same time any benefic in the 6th house undoubtedly becomes vulnerable. I've seen it work both ways. Some people with a relatively unafflicted Venus in the 6th house have Venusian health problems, while others have excellent health. But if you see Venus in the 6th, you have to mention health sensitivities, because when health problems eventually arise (in old age or whenever), they are going to be Venus ailments. No matter how good a person's health is, almost everyone experiences some form of failing health eventually. People have to die of something!

When I am reading a chart, I always analyze the person's health and where their physical vulnerabilities lie. But this is not simply a matter of looking at the 1st house (the body) and the 6th house (health). If there is an extremely afflicted planet, anywhere in the chart, right away I expect some physical vulnerability signified by the planet involved. If Saturn is fallen and tightly combust the Sun, I expect arthritis, teeth, or bone problems. And since the Sun in this case is afflicted by its conjunction to fallen Saturn, I predict heart and spine sensitivities. If Mercury is hemmed in by malefics or is fallen and badly-aspected, I begin to think of illnesses involving lungs, intestines, and nervous system. These problems are likely to be there even if the planets have nothing at all to do with the person's health houses (1st and 6th).

Martin: But what if the 6th house is incredibly strong? What if one or two malefic planets are in the 6th indicating great health?

James: Then the person has incredibly strong health along with great ability to overcome illnesses. However, the person also has vulnerabilities with the health areas connected to the heavily afflicted planet. The difficulty is knowing when such health problems will arise, because if the health is extremely strong, the person may not experience any problems until old age, when the body naturally becomes weak. I've seen many clients with both an intensely strong 6th house as well as an extraordinarily afflicted planet. In many of these cases, the person doesn't have any health problems. But I still mention the vulnerability because it may eventually occur.

Something that will help immensely in your ability to predict health is to remember that nearly every health issue is governed by a planet and a house. Just the other day, I did a chart reading for a woman who had an afflicted Venus and an afflicted 8th house. Venus was in Virgo (its fallen sign) while the 8th house held fallen Mars without any beneficial mitigating factors. This means reproductive problems for sure, because Venus and the 8th house are the indicators of the reproductive system. As it turned out, the woman once had uterine cancer. So always look at the house and planet of an area of health. For a man, illnesses of the reproductive system mean prostate problems. If this had been a man's chart, I would have mentioned the prostate gland and told the person to have medical checkups every year after the age of thirty-five. I would also mention that health food stores carry herbal supplements to heal, or shrink, the prostate (products like zinc and saw palmetto).

Another health example is that of the Sun and the 4th house ruling a person's heart. If you find a person with the ruler of the 4th house seriously afflicted, or malefic planets in the 4th house, and you notice an afflicted Sun (fallen Sun in Libra, Sun tightly aspected by Mars, Saturn, or Ketu, and so on), then you must predict heart problems.

Martin: This is just like analyzing the 5th house and Jupiter for children.

James: Exactly. Other examples would be: For the throat, look at Venus and the 2nd house. For the lungs, look at Mercury and the 3rd house. For the stomach, look at the Moon and the 5th house (this is unlike Western astrology, where the 4th house rules the stomach).

Anyway, that's about all I wanted to say about the 6th house. Next week, we'll talk about the last six houses. See you then. Bas.

CLASS SIX

James: Today, we'll cover some subtleties of the last six houses. Do you have any questions about what we covered last week?

Martin: No, but I have to tell you that after our session I went back to my other basic Hindu astrology texts and I found that I was guilty of mixing and matching certain house significations.

James: Actually, most astrologers should probably go back to the basic texts once or twice a year as a refresher. I think astrology is such a complicated subject that it's easy to get house significations blurred over time.

Martin: I do have one question. Last week you said that the best astrologers are the most precise ones, the ones who know the fundamentals through and through. But in an earlier class, you implied that the best Hindu astrologers were using intuition and psychic talents. What's the deal?

James: Great question. The answer is that in order to be the best astrologer, you have to excel in both areas equally. This is obviously somewhat paradoxical.

I told you earlier that whenever I heard one of my Indian mentors make some incredibly accurate and specific prediction, I would question them because the prediction seemed so obviously psychic.

Martin: You said your mentors sometimes seemed to be getting information directly from the ethers.

James: Sure seemed that way. Every time I would question either of my mentors, they would immediately give me the astrological explanation for their predictions. This drove me a little crazy, because sometimes their predictions seemed so blatantly psychic and yet they always had an astrological answer at their disposal.

What I have finally reasoned after so many years is that the really fine Indian astrologers memorize every piece of technical information they can and then let their intuition tell them which techniques to use for each birthchart. The astrological information is at their fingertips and they let their intuition guide them to the applicable information.

Martin: That sounds like an impossible task.

James: Well, Easterners typically rely on instinct and abstractions far more than Westerners. They are not so linear and rational as us.

If you read the Indian texts or if you study in India for any length of time, you find that there are simply thousands upon thousands of astrological techniques and yogas (planetary unions). At first, the techniques seem impractical to the point of uselessness because there are simply too many of them. Let me give you one simple example. I heard one astrologer make a specific and accurate prediction gleaned from a technique called *karakamsa*.

[Rasi and Karakamsa charts for James Braha, Male Chart, Oct 16 1951, 7:36 pm EST +5:00, Fort Lauderdale, FL, 26°N07'19" 080°W08'37"]

Karakamsa is yet another method of ascendant. You've heard about *Chandra lagna* (literally, Moon ascendant), where you use the Moon as the ascendant and consider the house placements from the position of the Moon (e.g. if Mars is in the house opposite the Moon, it is like having Mars in the 7th house because the Moon becomes the first house, and so on). Well, in the *karakamsa* method you first determine the house placement of the natal ascendant ruler. In my horoscope the ascendant is Taurus, so the ascendant ruler is Venus, which occupies the 4th house. Since the ascendant ruler is in the 4th house, I count the same number of houses (four) <u>from the house position of the ascendant ruler</u> (i.e. the fourth house from the 4th house) in order to find the *karakamsa* ascendant.

Martin: Since your ascendant ruler is in Leo in the 4th house, you count four houses from Leo and arrive at Scorpio?

James: That's right. My *karakamsa* ascendant is Scorpio, and I can use that chart to analyze my life. Can you imagine that? Can you imagine using yet <u>another</u> ascendant on top of the natal ascendant and *Chandra lagna*?

Martin: In my case, my natal ascendant is Cancer; so I first look for the house number of the Moon (the ascendant ruler)?

James: Yes. Your Moon is in the 9th house in Pisces, and therefore you count <u>nine houses from Pisces</u> and you arrive at Scorpio.

[Chart: Martin Timmons Event Chart, Sep 21 1956, 2:20 am PDT +7:00, Los Angeles, CA, 34°N03'08" 118°W14'34" — Rasi and Karakamsa charts]

Martin: So you and I have the same *karakamsa* ascendant.

James: That's right. Now, I don't mean to be difficult, but I have to mention that you are also going to see Indian texts that tell you to use the <u>Sun</u> as yet another ascendant!

Martin: This would create more confusion than I can imagine. What if my natal ascendant has Jupiter in the 1st house, while the Moon ascendant has Mercury in the 1st house, and my *karakamsa* ascendant has Mars in the 1st house? Which one do I use?

James: First, let me remind you that you left out the ascendant from the Sun! You can now begin to see why the Indians are comfortable using their intuitive abilities. There is simply no way to take so many different factors into account. So they learn them all and let their feelings and intuitive abilities guide them.

Martin: Do Westerners practice *Jyotish* this way?

James: To a much lesser extent, perhaps. But I have to admit that there are plenty of times when I'm looking at a chart and I suddenly remember to check some technique that I haven't used in weeks, that is now clearly applicable. When that happens, I always have to laugh at how synergistic the practice of astrology can be.

Now let's talk about the last six houses.

THE SEVENTH HOUSE

The 7th house is where you see marriage and love relationships. The only thing I would add is to look for business tendencies from that house. As I mentioned before, people with active 7th houses love to interact with others and that promotes enjoyment of business and commerce.

Martin: Are there any particular planets that would indicate business more so than other planets?

James: Well, Mercury is definitely more inclined to commerce than other planets. But if the 7th house holds two or three planets, especially personal planets (Sun, Moon, Mercury, ascendant ruler), I usually mention business. Personal planets, in my opinion, make the person more inclined toward personal interaction than, say, Saturn, Rahu, or Ketu. Of course, if the ruler of the 10th house occupies the 7th house <u>in the natal or *dasamsa*</u> (career chart), you also have to mention business.

If you want to know about a person's spouse, make sure you look at the planets in the 7th house <u>as well as the ruler</u> of the 7th house. If the ruler of the 7th house occupies the 9th house, look for a mate that is from a foreign country. If the ruler of the 7th is in the 10th, look for the partner to be a career person. If the ruler of the 7th occupies the 4th, look for a landowner; in the 3rd, look for an artist or adventurous, highly active person; the 5th, look for a spouse who is connected to a person's past lives; the 11th or 2nd, look for a wealthy partner; the 6th, look for a doctor, nurse, or healing person, and also expect marriage problems because the 6th is a *dusthana*, or grief-producing house.

But make sure you notice whether the 7th house ruler is well-disposed or afflicted, because it makes all the difference in the world. For example, if a person's 7th house ruler occupies the 10th house in its <u>fallen sign</u>, the spouse has huge career problems. If the ruler of the 7th occupies the 9th but is heavily afflicted, then the spouse has big problems with religion. And these issues necessarily affect the person's marriage. I've seen many cases where a person has the ruler of the 7th house in the 9th, <u>in the planet's fallen sign</u>, and the marriage is very difficult because the couple can't get along in their religious beliefs.

Martin: Are you speaking only about the natal chart or also the *navamsa*?

James: Either one.

On top of this, you must notice any planets in the 7th house from the Moon in the natal chart. Some of the worst astrological features that can harm marriage are Mars, Saturn, or some fallen planet (benefic or malefic) occupying the 7th house from the Moon. Of course, the closer the opposition by degree, the worse the problems will be.

If the ruler of the 7th occupies the 8th house, then of course you expect divorce or major problems in married life. The key to healing the problems in this case, aside from gemstones, mantra chanting, and performance of *yagyas*, is to marry an 8th house person.

Martin: What is an 8th house person?

James: A person who exhibits <u>lots</u> of 8th house tendencies. Someone who is interested in astrology, psychic phenomenon, and so forth. It could also simply be a person who is remarkably psychic.

If the ruler of a person's 7th house occupies the 12th house, then the person should marry a 12th house person.

Martin: Someone pursuing spirituality?

James: Yes. But I don't simply mean a person who meditates. I mean someone who is seriously pursuing enlightenment. This would be a person who thinks about enlightenment all the time, practices a lot of meditation (or some other spiritual technique), and someone who is more introspective rather than involved in worldly goals. Then, the person with the ruler of the 7th house in the 12th will satisfy the 12th house karma of his or her marriage, without all the problems. Of course, because the 7th house ruler occupying the 12th house indicates divorce, the person is unlikely to choose a 12th house partner during his or her first thirty years or so. But, after one or two very rough relationships, the person can finally begin to use some intelligence in love matters.

Another important 7th house matter, that is sometimes neglected by textbooks and astrologers, is living in a foreign country. In India, during the time astrology was formulated, it was considered a terrible fate to leave the country to live elsewhere. When a person has a seriously maligned 7th house, there is a strong chance he or she may leave the birthplace. But you should not predict that every person with a bad 7th will leave his or her homeland. These days, there are simply too many people with damaged 7th houses.

If, however, you are doing the chart of a person who lives away from his or her homeland, take a look at the 7th house and you'll see that it is very afflicted (in most cases).

Martin: When I see a chart with a damaged 7th house, should I predict that the person will live in a foreign land?

James: Here is where your intuition comes into play. Sometimes you will see a chart with a rough 7th house and you'll suddenly get a very strong feeling that the person will leave their birth country at some point in their life. Other times, you won't get that feeling.

Sometimes a person asks whether he or she will leave his or her birth country. When I did a workshop in Iceland and was reading charts, nearly every person asked whether or not he or she would be able to live outside the country. When I was reading charts in South Florida, I had a fair amount of Cuban clients. Their 7th houses were a mess, which is why they left Cuba.

Martin: Were their love-lives harmed?

James: They were bad. I guess that brings up a question to be studied statistically — do all immigrants have difficult love lives?

Martin: James, this makes me wonder. Are the meanings of houses always linked? Do all people with an afflicted 5th house have problems with children and investments and sports, because the 5th house rules all these realms?

James: I think I talked about this before, but it's worth going over again. To an extent, the answer is yes, but in order to know for sure you have to look at the *karakas*, the indicators for each particular realm. In other words, if the 5th house is damaged (by malefics or malefic aspects), then you should consider all 5th house significations to be vulnerable. The next step is to look at Jupiter, the *karaka* for children and speculations. If Jupiter and the 5th house are rough, the person is most likely going to have problems in both realms. Then, you check out the Sun, the *karaka* for politics (another 5th house matter). If the Sun is exalted in the 10th house or some other important house, politics will not necessarily be ruined. It will not be out of the question for the person to be a leader even though the house of kingship (leadership and politics) is harmed. This is because the *karaka* of politics is strong.

But you will often see links. Why do you think so many politicians played varsity sports in high school? Because Mars and the 5th house, which both rule sports, have so much to do with politics (the 5th house rules kingship, while Mars signifies aggressiveness and the tendency to boss others).

Why do you think religious and philosophical people love to take trips to foreign countries? Because the 9th house rules religion and philosophy, as well as travel.

Now, remember that the 7th house reveals a person's sexual passions as well as the ability to fulfill daily desires. Of course, the 3rd house is the quintessential house of daily desires, but the 3rd, 7th, and 11th are all desire houses, and if the 7th house is powerful, that helps a lot in fulfilling one's daily wants and cravings. In terms of the 7th house ruling sexual passions, it simply shows how passionate the person is about sex. It does not tell whether the person can enjoy sex. That would be seen from the 12th house.

THE EIGHTH HOUSE

James: The 8th house is, of course, a *dusthana,* or grief-producing house. Therefore, any planet in the 8th house is harmed. And the houses that planet rules are also harmed. So, if Mercury occupies the 8th house in a birthchart with a Gemini ascendant, where Mercury rules the 1st and 4th houses, then Mercury is harmed as are the 1st and 4th houses. If the chart has an Aries ascendant and Venus occupies the 8th house, then Venus is damaged and so are the 2nd and 7th houses, the houses Venus rules in this chart.

Martin: How damaged are they?

James: Seriously damaged. In the case of the Aries ascendant, with Venus in the 8th house, you would have to predict divorce. This is because Venus rules the marriage house (7th) and "it is gone in the 8th," as my Indian mentor used to say. Also, love matters are harmed because Venus is the *karaka*, or indicator, of love and it is damaged by the 8th house. The exceptions to divorce would be if the person comes from a culture where divorce is not an option, places like India or many countries in Europe. The person would then simply have a lot of marital suffering. It's also possible (not probable, but possible) that the person's spouse could die — the 8th is the house of death.

Now even though Venus rules the 2nd house as well as the 7th in this case, 2nd house matters would not be nearly so afflicted as 7th house matters because Venus is aspecting the 2nd house (all planets throw aspects onto their opposite sign in Hindu astrology). And in this case, Venus is aspecting its own sign, Taurus. So there would be some good effects on 2nd house matters, as well as some bad.

Martin: Why both?

James: Because if the person runs a Venus period or subperiod, there would be some 2nd house affliction due to Venus being in the 8th house, and in a bad sign. Because it is opposite Venus' own sign, Scorpio is not a good sign for Venus. My assessment then would be that in Venus periods and subperiods, the person has problems with everything Venus rules in the chart. <u>Natally</u>, however, the 2nd house is powerful because it is aspected by its ruler (house of Taurus, aspected by Venus).

As bad as the 8th house is and as much damage as it can create, it is crucial not to lose your balance about it. Don't ever think that if a person has lots of planets in these houses, he or she is bad or evil. Nor is the person's life completely ruined. There will be problems for sure, but the person will also be extremely metaphysical and intuitive. There will be all kinds of 8th house benefits, unless the 8th house planets are afflicted by malefic planetary aspects or if one of the planets is in its fallen sign. Beginning Hindu astrologers never seem to understand that the 8th house is not all bad. No house is. Even the 12th house, as bad as it is, governs the greatest benefit of human life — enlightenment, final liberation!

Aside from ruling death, accidents, and intense problems, the 8th house governs some very good significations. It rules metaphysics, psychic ability, sexual attractiveness, longevity, wills, legacies, and money from partners. So if a person has a benefic planet in the 8th house, the planet itself is harmed while the 8th house benefits tremendously.

Martin: If a person has Jupiter in the 8th house and the ascendant happens to be Scorpio (in which case Jupiter rules the 2nd and 5th houses), the person would have problems with money, education, investments, children, and peace of mind, right?

James: Yes.

Martin: Wouldn't children and investments would be especially hurt since both Jupiter and the 5th house are burned by the 8th house?

James: Absolutely. If the 5th house and Jupiter are hurt, children and speculations are harmed. What you need to be clear about, however, is that in this case the 8th house benefits greatly from Jupiter's beneficial energy. Therefore, the person gains money from wills and legacies, has a long life, and is intuitive. He or she will love astrology and metaphysical subjects. These are great advantages, don't you think? In fact, the example you gave indicates that the person's *poorvapunya* (past life credit) is connected to 8th house matters.

Martin: If the 5th house ruler is in the *dusthana* 8th house, wouldn't it ruin the person's past life credit?

James: Only if Jupiter is badly aspected or in a bad sign. If it is simply occupying the 8th, or if it is well-aspected in the 8th, then the person's *poorvapunya* will be connected to metaphysics, longevity, and joint finances.

Let me give you another 8th house example that shows how a planet in the 8th is afflicted, while the 8th house benefits. Let's say a person has a bright Moon in the 8th house. He or she is going to experience a great deal of emotional suffering (poorly placed Moon) throughout life. There will also be problems with the person's mother (signification of Moon). However, the person is going to live long, be interested in psychic and metaphysical subjects, and is likely to gain money from the spouse and/or from wills and legacies. You have to try for balance when you analyze the *dusthana* houses (6th, 8th, and 12th). Don't be one-dimensional about them.

People who come for readings are likely to have planets in the 8th and 12th houses, because these houses govern metaphysical and spiritual realms. Many of your clients will have a planet in its own sign in the 8th house. That is why they pursue astrological readings. I hope you're not going to analyze a planet in its own sign in the 8th house as bad. If an 8th house planet (or 12th house planet) occupies its own sign, it's going to give good results.

Martin: If a planet occupies its own sign in the 8th house, would the houses that planet rules be destroyed by the 8th house energy?

James: Not in my opinion. The planet is functioning well. It's quite happy and harmonious in its own sign. Let's say, for example, that the ruler of the 7th house is in the 8th <u>in its own sign</u>. To me, that means that the person is going to get a metaphysical spouse and have good marital happiness. Actually, Vashti (my wife) has this placement. She has a Capricorn 7th house, with Saturn in Aquarius (Saturn's own sign) in the 8th. So, she gets an astrologer husband.

If the ruler of the 10th house occupies the 8th house <u>in its own sign</u>, then, the person is likely to have a successful metaphysical career. Or, the person could be successful in a career with the C.I.A. or some underground organization. Research endeavors would also be indicated.

Martin: So if the ruler of the 4th is in the 8th in <u>its own sign</u>, then the person's mother would live a long time and be metaphysical.

James: Yes. I would predict happiness with mother. Be careful, though, because there are two *karakas* (indicators) governing mother. You have to look at the condition of the Moon as well as Mercury. It's very easy to ignore Mercury and go wrong in your analysis. I have seen cases where I predicted happiness with the mother because the person's 4th house and Moon were in good condition, only to be dead wrong because Mercury was intensely afflicted. In a case like this, Mercury would have to be severely afflicted to offset the strong 4th house and Moon. I've had this occur plenty of times.

Incidentally, I don't tell a person with a powerful 8th house to play lotteries. The reason is that the odds are terrible. The person's 8th house has to be better than everyone else's in order to win. In America, it's probably easier to get murdered on the street than to win a million dollar lottery.

Martin: But a person with a powerful 8th house is likely to obtain money from unearned means, right?

James: Of course. All I'm saying is that if millions of people (or even hundreds of thousands) of people enter each single lottery, it is ridiculous for you to tell every person you see with a strong 8th house to go play one.

One of the best things about having a strong 8th house is that your spouse will make a lot of money. More importantly, if your 8th house is powerful and well-aspected, you will have access to your mate's money.

Martin: So if someone's 8th house is weak, the person has difficulty getting money from his or her spouse?

James: Yes. The person has problems with joint finances, alimony, the

I.R.S., and so on. Many years ago, I dated a woman who had a fallen planet in her 8th house. Whenever I bought her something or picked up a check in a restaurant, she would get quiet and strange about it. When I finally asked her what the problem was, she said she felt conflicted and guilty about my paying for her. She enjoyed presents and gifts, but getting them from a lover or spouse felt odd. Had I continued to go out with her, she probably would've convinced me not to share any wealth with her.

In terms of inheritances, the 8th house is critical. I've done lots of readings for people who have afflicted 8th houses and have been cheated out of inheritances.

Martin: So, an afflicted 8th house means a fallen planet in the 8th, or the ruler of the 8th is fallen, or the ruler of the 8th is tightly conjunct Saturn or Ketu or some other malefic, right?

James: That's right. And a well disposed 8th house occurs if benefics occupy the 8th house, or if the ruler of the 8th house is exalted or tightly conjunct benefics.

THE NINTH HOUSE

The 9th house is clear-cut in my opinion. There aren't any hidden or cryptic meanings to warn you about. The 9th represents religion, philosophy, and higher knowledge. It also represents gurus, spiritual teachers, and mentors. These are obvious. Sometimes, however, it's easy to forget that the 9th house rules *higher* education, meaning one's experience with universities and colleges. This is different from education in general, which is governed by the 2nd house. Imagine that a person has a strong 2nd house, but a seriously afflicted 9th house. The person is probably going to do well in the first twelve years of school and be favored by his or her teachers, but have significant problems in college. This, however, does not necessarily influence the person's ability to obtain a degree. Educational degrees are ruled by the 4th house. If the person has Venus, Moon, or Jupiter (benefics) in the 4th house, and that planet is not afflicted by aspects from malefic planets, he or she will have an easy time getting a degree and may even obtain more than one.

If a person has an afflicted 9th house, he or she could have troubles with mentors and college professors.

Martin: But that person could still graduate and get a degree?

James: Of course. But if the person has a <u>very</u> afflicted 4th house, then there may be obstacles and delays in getting a degree. Or, the person may not get one at all. Some people go to college for four years and leave without a degree because they lack five or ten credits. I've seen it happen. I've also seen people with weak 4th houses change their major three or four times, and that stops them from getting a degree.

Incidentally, in my experience most clients have "mixed" 9th houses. By this I mean that the 9th house is strong and well-aspected by benefics, but Jupiter, the *karaka* (indicator) of the 9th house is afflicted. Or, the 9th house holds a planet in its own or exaltation sign, but the ruler of the 9th house is tightly aspected by Mars, Ketu, or Saturn. A person with a "mixed" 9th house should generally not get attached to one guru or mentor. The person should get the higher knowledge he or she desires and then move on. Otherwise, there will eventually be some upsetting experiences in the area of religion.

Martin: What kind of upsetting experiences?

James: Every case is different, but some of the possibilities are: finding out that the guru or priest is deceptive, not what he or she seems; having trouble with the guru's politics or the organization the guru has created; being used or manipulated by the guru; becoming bitter about the guru, etc. Once in a while you see a chart with a completely positive 9th house and an unafflicted Jupiter, but it's rare in my experience.

Another important 9th house feature is luck. Everyone needs luck, especially in emergencies. Sometimes you find a chart that is overall quite rough but contains a strong and positive 9th house. Maybe Jupiter or Venus or Moon occupies its own sign in the 9th house, while the rest of the chart is afflicted. In this case, no matter how bad other features of the horoscope are, the person has luck that suddenly appears whenever it is truly needed. When I watch the news on television and hear stories about someone who got murdered simply because of being in the wrong place at the wrong time, I always assume that the 9th house of the person wasn't well fortified, wasn't strong.

As I see it, the luck that results from the 9th house occurs because the person's faith in God, or nature, is so strong that he or she doesn't react rashly to sudden problems. The person is optimistic that God will take care of things, and, generally, these expectations are rewarded.

If both the 9th house and the chart as a whole is strong, the person's luck may be startlingly good. The person always seems to be at the right place at the right time. Don't forget that the 9th house governs luck.

The 9th house also represents a person's second marriage. I know that some astrologers use a different house for the second marriage, but I was taught to use the 9th house, and it works pretty well. Let's take a few examples. First, let's look at my chart (see page 50) and my wife's, since Vashti is also in her second marriage (see the following page).

In my horoscope, there are no planets occupying the 9th house, and no aspects to the 9th. However, the 9th house ruler, Saturn, occupies the 5th house, the second best house in a birthchart (9th house is the best). It is in the sign of Virgo and is aspected <u>to the degree</u> by benefic Jupiter. Saturn is also widely conjunct the Sun (a fifteen degree aspect).

Martin: Looks pretty good.

James: Yes, it does. First, the strongest and most obvious feature about Saturn is that it is tightly aspected by Jupiter. Even if Saturn was somehow afflicted, the Jupiter aspect is so strong that the overall results would be good. This means the marriage is favored and the partner should be Jupitarian. The fact that Jupiter rules the 8th house and is tightly aspecting Saturn means that there will either be some problems in the marriage or that the partner is going to be metaphysical or psychic.

Martin: Vashti is metaphysical.

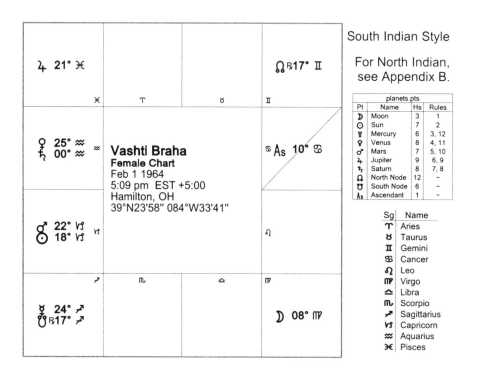

James: Yes, she is. At one time, she practiced astrology professionally. She's extremely intuitive, and psychic ability runs in her family. Her grandmother was constantly having prophetic dreams and her mother gives psychic readings. The fact that she embodies 8th house energy in a <u>positive</u> way means there is little chance that the second marriage will be characterized by negative 8th house energy. So, if you were analyzing my chart before my second marriage took place, it would have been your job to advise me that since the 8th house ruler Jupiter aspects Saturn (which, as the 9th house ruler, governs my second marriage), I should try to find a metaphysical or psychic spouse.

Martin: Is your second marriage very Jupitarian because of the intense aspect Jupiter throws onto your 9th house ruler?

James: Yes, I married a Jupitarian spouse. Look at Vashti's chart and you'll see her optimism and her philosophical, spiritual nature right away.

Notice that Jupiter aspects the most personal features of her horoscope — the Moon and the ascendant. Aspects like these will give a Jupitarian nature because the Moon and the ascendant are so personal. Also notice that the Jupiter aspect to her ascendant is being thrown onto Cancer, Jupiter's exaltation sign. This is excellent in terms of conferring Jupitarian qualities. As for Vashti's metaphysical interests and talents, you can see those indicated by Saturn in its own sign (Aquarius) in the 8th house (metaphysics) conjunct benefic Venus.

During my second journey to India, in 1984, when I asked astrologers about finding my second spouse, several of them said, "You will get a spiritual wife." In my first marriage, spiritual compatibility was weak. I wanted a spiritual life, while my ex-wife wanted a life in theatre.

In order to have a good marriage, a person has to be compatible on four levels: physical, mental, emotional, and spiritual. In my second marriage, spiritual compatibility is actually our best feature. I think you could say that in my chart the 9th house clearly indicates my second marriage.

Martin: James, the ruler of your 9th house (Saturn) occupies Virgo and that would indicate that your second marriage might be to a Virgonian person. Since Vashti has her Moon in Virgo, isn't that another corroborating factor?

James: Probably so. Especially since the Moon takes on double importance since it rules her ascendant.

Now, let's look at Vashti's second marriage. She has Jupiter in its own sign (Pisces) in the 9th house, aspected by the Moon. The fact that Jupiter occupies the house of the second marriage is a clear indication that her second partner is spiritual. Because Jupiter is in its own sign, it intensifies the religious or spiritual nature of the partner.

Because the 9th house ruler (Jupiter) is aspected by the Moon, her second partner should be either emotionally nurturing or special in some way. Although Venus, Jupiter, and Mercury are also benefics, I always reserve the term "special" for the Moon. For example, if Jupiter occupies the 5th house, a person will have excellent luck and happiness with children. And at least one child will be religious or spiritual, assuming Jupiter is not afflicted. If Venus occupies the 5th house, the person will have lots of happiness and good fortune with children and at least one of the person's children will be artistic. With the Moon in the 5th house, the person will also have excellent results with children, but you can definitely rely on one of the children (probably the first one) being <u>special</u> in some way. The child may be brilliant or famous.

Martin: Why does the Moon get the distinction of being special?

James: I can't say with certainty. I assume it has to do with the fact that the Moon is <u>the most important planet</u> in Hindu astrology. It's a lunar-based system.

Martin: So, Vashti's second husband is special. I guess that refers to your fame as an astrologer.

James: I think so. Her first husband was also metaphysical, but he wasn't well-known. You can see why she gets metaphysical husbands — by the 7th house ruler (Saturn) in its own sign in the 8th house (Aquarius), conjunct with benefic Venus.

Martin: When you analyze the second marriage, is all the information about married life from the 7th house and the *navamsa* completely ignored?

James: Not at all. Whatever is indicated by the 7th house of the natal chart and the 7th house of the *navamsa* indicates the person's <u>overall</u> inclinations and leanings. Those tendencies never completely go away. But you have to analyze each chart individually. There are cases, and Vashti's is one of them, where the 9th house is so dramatically different from the 7th and the *navamsa* 7th house, that the second marriage is dramatically different from the first. Vashti's first marriage ended in about a year. She and I have been together now for nine years (married for seven).

The Sun-Mars conjunction in Vashti's 7th house certainly still operates in our marriage. We fight occasionally, and sometimes I'm too bossy (Sun in the 7th indicates a bossy spouse). But on the whole, it's a Jupitarian marriage. Our spiritual compatibility tends to override the smaller stuff.

Martin: It must be <u>really</u> Jupitarian, James. Your second marriage is indicated to be predominantly Jupitarian and so is Vashti's!

James: That's true. Both of our 9th houses are influenced strongly by Jupiter.

Incidentally, one thing that you must realize about Vashti's chart is that <u>any</u> marriage of hers would have to be Jupitarian, because Jupiter is in the 7th house from her Moon, and occupies its own sign (Pisces).

Martin: *Chandra lagna.*

James: That's right, Moon ascendant. Similar to having Jupiter in Pisces in the 7th house from the natal ascendant.

Martin: Was Vashti's first husband spiritual?

James: Yes. From what I'm told, he used to meditate for several hours a day.

Now, I'd like to show you an intensely afflicted 9th house. It's the 9th house of John Lennon's birthchart. In order to do this, however, we have to take a major detour. I believe it's a detour worth taking. See, there is a discrepancy about Lennon's birthtime. In one of the books written about

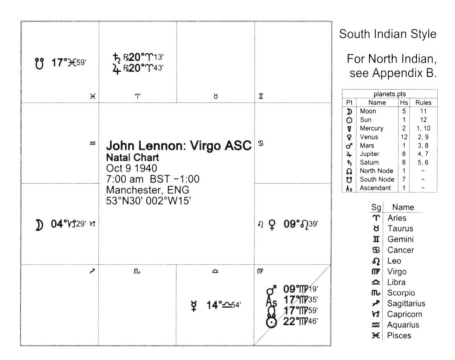

Lennon, a relative (either his sister or his aunt) said that he was born around 7:00 AM. She said she remembered the birth distinctly because family members were hiding under tables due to the air raids going on during 1940, and the birth was very close to dawn. I don't know if 7:00 AM was the exact minute Lennon was born, but the Virgo (early morning) ascendant fits perfectly in my opinion. And the Virgo ascendant chart was the one that was used by most astrologers for many years.

However, Lois Rodden, the astrologer who writes books with famous people's birth data, said that a relative of Lennon saw 6:30 <u>PM</u> on the birth certificate. So now there is a problem with Lennon's data, which astrologers strongly disagree about.

Martin: What ascendant does 6:30 PM give?

James: Pisces, which by my analysis does not fit. Pisces also doesn't tally with Richard Houck's (author of <u>The Astrology of Death</u> and <u>Digital Astrology</u>) analysis. I mention Richard Houck because he is extremely skilled at rectifying charts.

Martin: Is he the astrologer who rectifies the chart of every client he works with?

James: Yes, and he doesn't just rectify the ascendant, he rectifies the birthtime <u>to the minute</u>, using several kinds of progressions as well as transits. If you are rectifying charts, you must use progressions (tertiary, primary, and secondary progressions) because they are more specific than *dasas* and *bhuktis*. Anyway, Richard Houck uses 6:50 AM, which gives a Virgo ascendant.

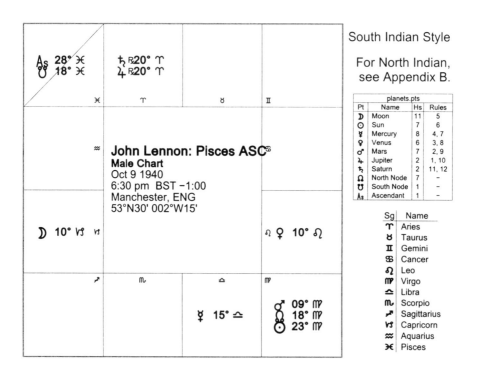

Now, I want to give you a few astrological reasons that I think Lennon's Virgo ascendant chart is accurate, but I'm not trying to prove the point. I'm convinced that astrologers are going to forever disagree about Lennon's accurate birthtime, and I have no interest in debating this issue. I simply want to show an excellent example of an extremely afflicted 9th house. And I want to demonstrate why as an astrologer you must think for yourself and follow your own experience. Many people accept the Pisces ascendant horoscope for Lennon because Lois Rodden learned that there were no air raids during morning hours in October, 1940 and because a relative saw his birth certificate with a 6:30 PM birth.

First of all, it is quite possible that there were <u>some</u> early morning air raids in England that never got recorded. Over the years I've had problems drawing some birthcharts because city authorities and local newspapers were actually wrong about the existence of daylight time during certain periods in their locale. Second, how odd would it have been for a secretary to record 6:30 PM instead of 6:30 AM if the birthtime was recorded several hours, or even days, after a home birth?!!! It's an incredibly easy mistake to have made.

In any case, even as I tell you why I think the chart should be a Virgo ascendant, you shouldn't necessarily accept my findings. You should look at both charts and determine which one is right.

Martin: But what if I don't have enough experience?

James: If I were you, I would put the matter on hold until you do. It may take you two years until you can realistically draw a conclusion or it may take you ten years. The worst thing you could do is say, "Well, James Braha says the ascendant is Virgo, so he must be right" or, "Lois Rodden is the expert on birthtimes, so she must be right." Neither Lois Rodden nor myself were present at Lennon's birth. Therefore, the data is questionable and you have to deal with that.

Now, I'll give you four reasons why the Virgo ascendant works and the Pisces one doesn't.

1) The Virgo ascendant chart shows a person with an <u>essentially</u> huge presence (indicated by *stationary, exalted* Rahu <u>extremely close to the ascendant</u>), and an aggressive personality (indicated by three malefics — Mars, Sun, and Rahu in the 1st house).

Pisces ascendant shows an <u>essentially</u> shy, introverted, invisible personality due to *stationary* Ketu <u>extremely close to the ascendant degree</u> (in an opposition aspect). It also shows a person who would have no confidence whatsoever and no ability to be recognized due to the <u>severely</u> afflicted ascendant ruler — Jupiter.

Martin: What about the fact that if the ascendant was Pisces, the Sun and Mars would throw an aspect onto the 1st house? Wouldn't that make Lennon aggressive?

James: The strongest feature using the Pisces ascendant is Ketu, because it is stationary and so close to the ascendant degree. The degrees of orb are extremely important. Also, the 1st house ruler (Jupiter) would be totally destroyed by the tight conjunction to fallen Saturn. There's no way such a 1st house would give Lennon such enormous presence and such enormous fame.

2) Aside from being a musician, Lennon was an artist. He went to art school for painting and then dropped out. There is even a large John Lennon collection that Yoko Ono now publicizes and sells. The Virgo ascendant

shows the all-important Moon in the 5th house, the house of painting, drawing, and crafts (the 3rd house governs music, dance, and drama).

The Pisces ascendant chart has the Moon in the 11th house, aspecting the Cancer 5th house. This indicates a good 5th house, but does not particularly indicate a painter.

3) The Virgo ascendant chart has Mercury in the 2nd house, the quintessential placement of writers and witty people. Lennon was the wittiest of the Beatles. He was known for his lyrics, not his melodies. He was also the only Beatle who wrote a book while the group was together (*In His Own Write*). All of this is because Mercury occupies the 2nd house and is aspected by Jupiter and Saturn.

4) In the Virgo ascendant chart, Ketu occupies the 7th house and the ruler of the 7th is Jupiter, which is tightly conjunct fallen Saturn. Lennon's first marriage was forced by a pregnancy and was never comfortable for him, according to biographies (7th house ruler Jupiter afflicted in the 8th). His marriage of choice was to Yoko Ono. Yoko was seven years older than John (ruler of 7th conjunct Saturn), and Yoko is a typical Ketu type (Ketu in the 7th house). If you remember, Yoko was considered "weird and strange" by the public the minute they saw her. She is also deeply interested in astrology, tarot, and metaphysics.

Martin: Typical Ketu.

James: Exactly. If anyone embodies Ketu, it is Yoko Ono. Now, if Pisces was the ascendant, Lennon would have had Sun, Mars, and Rahu — three malefics in the 7th house! That would have produced a nasty, shrewish wife. I just don't perceive Yoko that way. She could possibly be calculating or devious (significations of Ketu), but she doesn't appear to be particularly mean or shrewish. Also, Lennon's first wife, Cynthia, was extremely sweet. She was the antithesis of one who is signified by Mars, Sun, and Rahu.

Martin: Was Cynthia also a Ketu type?

James: From what I know, she has a shyness about her and she loved meditating in India. Those are certainly characteristics of Ketu. What I can say positively is that she is not the kind of wife characterized by three malefics. That's for sure.

Martin: But even with the Virgo ascendant chart, Lennon's wife would have to have some very intense traits because of Sun and Mars aspecting the 7th house, right?

James: Yes. But the wife's essential nature, her most dominant feature is Ketu — the planet occupying the 7th. Remember that on October 9th, 1940, Ketu was stationary direct. Ketu had stationed only hours before Lennon's birth. So even though the 7th house is aspected by the Sun, which would give a strong willed-wife, Ketu takes precedence because it is stationary. Ketu also has an enormously strong effect because it is so nearly opposite the ascendant degree. This means Ketu is exactly on the <u>descendant</u>, or 7th house cusp. (The four <u>angular points</u> of a chart are the ascendant, descendant, nadir, and midheaven. These points are extraordinarily powerful.) Even if Lennon was born at 6:30, rather than 7:00, stationary Ketu would still be close to the descendant (about five degrees away).

Martin: I see.

James: So those are some of the reasons I believe Lennon's birth was nearer to 7:00 AM than 7:00 PM. Now that our detour is over, let me make a few points about Lennon's 9th house.

Notice that the ruler of the 9th house (Venus) occupies the *dusthana* (grief-producing) 12th house in an enemy sign. Notice that there are no positive planetary aspects thrown onto the 9th house. And notice that Jupiter, the *karaka* (indicator) of religion, philosophy, and spiritual gurus, is the most afflicted planet in the chart. The only good aspect is the eleven degree aspect that the 9th house ruler (Venus) receives from Jupiter.

Martin: Lennon must have had problems with gurus and religious teachers. Or with religion in general.

James: You bet he did. I'll give you two instances, and the first one was a whopper. Remember when the Beatles were vilified because of Lennon's statement, "We're more popular than Jesus?" The Christians in the U.S. were in an uproar over that. Lennon made the statement quite offhandedly and had no idea it would even be printed! It was the first time the Beatles had <u>any</u> negative publicity. That mess was due to a very afflicted 9th house and 9th house *karaka,* Jupiter.

Martin: I remember that. In fact, the Beatles were nervous playing in the Deep South during that tour.

James: Trouble in foreign lands and trouble with religious people. Results of a heavily afflicted 9th house and Jupiter.

Secondly, remember when the Beatles went to India to practice meditation with Maharishi Mahesh Yogi?

Martin: Yes, in the late sixties.

James: That's right. Well, after a month or two there was a scandal when the Beatles reportedly suspected that Maharishi tried to have sex with Mia Farrow. Since Maharishi is a celibate monk and an enlightened being supposedly above earthly desires, this was bad news. According to Beatle biographies, the group discussed the problem. When George Harrison, the one who believed in Maharishi the most, began to have doubts, the Beatles abruptly decided to leave. (Harrison and McCartney have since said they believe the accusation was completely false.) Well, Lennon was the one who approached Maharishi and told him they were leaving. According to the reports, when Maharishi asked why, all Lennon said was, "You're so cosmic, you should know."

Martin: Sarcastic.

James: That's right. According to her book *A Twist of Lennon*, Cynthia Lennon, who was in India with The Beatles, felt that it was quite unfair not to at least tell Maharishi why they were leaving and allow him a chance to defend himself.

Martin: But Lennon was a spiritual man.

James: Correct. That is because Lennon's 12th house (*moksha* or enlightenment) is very strong. The 12th house contains Venus, which is a benefic and also is the *yogakaraka* or union indicator for Virgo ascendant. He also got good spiritual techniques (mantras and such) because of the Moon in the 5th house.

Another point I want to make about the 9th house is that when it is weak or afflicted the person will have difficulty gaining higher knowledge. Since astrology provides higher knowledge for people, a person with a very damaged 9th house is likely to have problems determining his or her birthtime. I see this over and over in my practice. This is yet another reason that Lennon's Virgo ascendant chart makes sense. His 9th house is in terrible shape and his birthtime is in question. Do you know that in one of Lois Rodden's earlier books (*The American Book of Charts*) she gives Lennon's birthtime as 8:30 AM and quotes her source: Sybil Leek's *Astrology January 1972*, "from him (Lennon) recently by telephone."

Martin: Lennon himself thought it was 8:30 AM?

James: Yes, according to astrologer Sybil Leek.

Martin: So a relative said she was at Lennon's early morning birth and Lennon himself believed he was born in the morning.

James: Right. So the birthtime problem is intense in Lennon's case. If you want to see something interesting, take a look at the 9th house in the charts of the next five people who call you for a reading and say that there is a discrepancy with their birthtime. If a person says he or she was born somewhere between, say, 9 and 10 PM, and those birthtimes give two different charts, the accurate chart is likely to be the one with the seriously afflicted 9th house. I'm not saying to rectify a horoscope just by the 9th house. But in most cases, that's how it works. Anyway, the afflicted 9th house had a major part in causing Lennon's inaccurate birthtime.

Martin: Does this mean that if a person has a very strong 9th house that his or her birthtime is likely to be accurate?

James: Generally, yes. But, remember that the 9th house should be in excellent shape and the planet of high knowledge, Jupiter, should also be well-disposed.

By the way, when I do chart readings for people, I always look at the condition of the 9th house to see if I'm going to have problems with the client. If the 9th house is badly afflicted, the person will either insult me in some way, put me on a speaker phone without asking, send in payment very late, or do something annoying. This is how people with damaged 9th houses create bad feelings with those who are trying to give them higher knowledge. Something else to notice is that when the 9th house is in terrible shape, it's hard to read the chart. It's like pulling teeth to get information from the chart because the person has poor karma getting higher knowledge.

Martin: That must mean that if the 9th house is strong it's a cinch to read the chart.

James: That's right. The easiest time I have reading charts is when I go to spiritual communities. The people have such good karma in gaining higher knowledge that the information jumps right off the chart into my head.

One last point. If the chart has a connection between the 7th house and the 9th house, the person will likely marry someone from a foreign country. If the ruler of the 7th house occupies the 9th, or vice versa, the spouse may come from a country other than the person's birthplace. Forget about the cultural background of the person though. This feature relates to the <u>birth country</u>. This means that if, say, Srinivas Mohan Gupta <u>was born in the U.S.</u> and has the ruler of the 7th house in the 9th, or vice versa, then his spouse will probably be born outside the U.S. The fact that Srinivas is Indian is irrelevant. His birth country is the United States.

Martin: Does this work with the *navamsa* (marriage chart) also?

James: Absolutely. As long as you know that the birthtime is accurate enough to be able to use the *navamsa*. We'll talk about how to determine the accuracy of the *varga* charts in another session (see Class Seven).

Martin: James, before you talk about the 10th house, I have one more question about John Lennon's chart. When you gave the four reasons that prove the Virgo chart is the accurate one, you never even mentioned the Jupiter-Saturn *dasa-bhukti* that killed him. Jupiter and Saturn are in the 8th house, and I know that in your lectures you always mention the *dasa-bhukti* that killed Lennon because it shows so well how *Jyotish* works.

James: First off, let me repeat that my four reasons don't <u>prove</u> anything. They are some of the critical reasons that I believe the Virgo chart works. If I took the other side of the issue, like professional debaters do, I could find four reasons that the Pisces ascendant chart works. It's just that I would have a much harder time defending the reasons. I would also be "reaching and stretching," and most importantly, I would be ignoring the fact that the Virgo ascendant chart works much better.

Now to answer your question about why I don't use Lennon's *dasa-bhukti* as evidence of his Virgo ascendant, I'm about to say something that Westerners practicing *Jyotish* may find controversial. As much as I love the *Vimsottari dasa* system, as much I am indebted to the *Vimsottari dasa* system, I would never use *dasas* and *bhuktis* to rectify a chart. Never. I'm not going to discuss *dasas* in these sessions because I have nothing more to add of any great significance to what I already wrote in my book on transits and *dasas* (<u>How To Predict Your Future; Secrets Of Eastern And Western Astrology</u>). But I have to tell you that in all my years of experience with *Jyotish*, I find that *dasas* and *bhuktis* work very well in most charts and are completely ineffective in others. If you are rectifying someone's chart, you have no way to know whether or not *dasas* work in that particular person's chart.

Martin: That means that if you play with the birthtime until a *dasa* or *bhukti* fits, you may have just altered the person's real birthtime!

James: Exactly right. You can do a client an amazing disservice using *dasas and bhuktis* for rectification. To determine the ascendant or the exact degree of the ascendant, transits are much more precise. Or, if you know <u>for certain</u> a small time frame within which the person was born, say between 8 A.M. and 8:30 A.M., then the house positions of the *varga* charts can be used for rectification. (Note: There is a *dasa-bhukti* method of rectification that uses <u>house rulerships</u> of the *dasa* and *bhukti* planets only for their <u>positive</u> or <u>negative</u> value within the *navamsa*, or marriage, chart. This method is highly technical and mechanical, and does not rely on the specific symbolisms of the periods and subperiods in effect. I do not have extended experience with that method and therefore have no opinion about it.)

Martin: Are you saying *dasas* and *bhuktis* of the *Vimsottari* system don't work for everyone? That's pretty upsetting, James.

James: They work like clockwork for most people. In those cases, your clients will be amazed at their accuracy. But you will also have a significant number of clients that cannot relate to their *dasas* <u>if you bother to ask them</u>. I know one astrologer who talks to his clients about their *dasas* and if the person can't relate to them, he drops them. By the way, I'm not simply saying that *dasas* are imperfect because clients don't always relate to them. I rarely trust clients as much as my own research, anyway. But I have found several charts of friends and relatives <u>whose lives I know intimately</u> where the *dasas* and *bhuktis* just don't work. Sorry, but that's the truth of my experience. I know how upsetting this news is because I was extremely troubled when I finally had to face that fact.

Martin: How long did it take?

James: About two or three years of professional practice. Maybe more. *Dasas* work so incredibly well in my chart, and in so many other charts, that I tried to find every possible reason other than the fact that the *dasa* system is fallible. I thought, maybe some people are giving me wrong birthtimes, maybe Lahiri's *ayanamsa* is wrong, maybe we should be using a 360 day year instead of 365, maybe we should calculate the position of the parallax Moon, maybe we should calculate *dasas* based on the ascendant degree (rather than the Moon) in the charts where *dasas* don't work (as the ancient texts suggest). In the end, after careful study, I had to ask myself one very significant question: why are there forty — that's right forty — *dasa* systems in existence in India? If the *Vimsottari dasa* system worked so well — and by the way the *Vimsottari* system is considered by far the best — there would have been no need for so many others.

Martin: This isn't such good news, James.

James: Well, I've told you about five or ten times already that astrology is probably about seventy or seventy-five percent accurate, and that's for the best astrologers. I've also told you that I've never seen any astrological feature that hasn't blatantly failed at one time or another (e.g. an exalted planet that doesn't produce good results, or a terribly afflicted planet that produces excellent results). Why should the *Vimsottari dasa* system be any different?

By the way, if you think *dasas* and *bhuktis* reveal all the significant effects of a person's life, try locating the astrological reasons for the sudden, violent deaths through the *dasas* and *bhuktis* for the following people: John Denver, James Dean, Ricky Nelson, John F. Kennedy, and John F. Kennedy Jr. (To find their birth data, contact astrologer Lois Rodden or buy her birth data books). You will definitely fail. Incidently, this doesn't mean that their *dasas* and *bhuktis* don't work. It just means that the *dasas* and *bhuktis* didn't reveal these people's deaths.

Martin: But you do know people whose periods and subperiods don't work at all?

James: Yes. And if you go by your experience, you'll see charts where the *Vimsottari dasa* system just doesn't work.

Now, some astrologers might say that a few of the people whose deaths I mentioned died because the person was in a *maraka*, or death-inflicting period. But *maraka* periods occur every time a planet ruling or occupying the 2nd or 7th house runs its *dasa* or *bhukti*, which is typically at least every four or five years. This makes predicting death through *marakas* utterly impossible unless the astrologer is massively psychic, in which case he or she doesn't need to use a horoscope! *Marakas*, actually, are best used to predict death during extreme old age or in situations when a person is obviously close to death.

Martin: What about the possibility that the *dasa-bhuktis* of these dead people were inaccurate because their birthtimes were wrong?

James: Anything is possible, of course, but the birthtimes of the people I just mentioned are not in question by the astrological community. More importantly, their *dasas* and *bhuktis* work fairly well, aside from revealing their deaths. In fact, John Denver's periods and subperiods work so well that I used his chart in my transit and *dasa* book. I certainly didn't see his upcoming death, and I never received any letters from readers (who often write to me about teachings in my books) saying they saw Denver's approaching death.

Do you know that there are lots of Indian books on rectification, and the ones I've seen never mention using *dasas* and *bhuktis*? Also, how can you possibly rectify charts using *dasas* and *bhuktis* when there are so many disagreements on the exact *ayanamsa*? *Dasas* and *bhuktis* are calculated according to the degree and minute of the Moon. If the *ayanamsa* is even slightly off, the periods and subperiods will be significantly altered.

Just so you remember this point, I'm going to say it three times to make sure you hear it. The *Vimsottari dasa* system is not consistently accurate enough to use for rectifying charts. The *Vimsottari dasa* system is not consistently accurate enough to use for rectifying charts. The *Vimsottari dasa* system is not consistently accurate enough to use for rectifying charts.

Martin: This sounds like a pet peeve of yours.

James: It is. Can you imagine if someone tried to rectify the horoscopes of the five dead people I mentioned (after they died) by using the periods and subperiods of their deaths to draw conclusions? Every rectification would be wrong.

Martin: The hard part is letting go of belief. I believe the *dasa* system should work all the time.

James: Me too. But it doesn't. As one of my college professors used to say: "It is what it is."

One final point about the 9th house. I've already mentioned that some astrologers consider the 9th house to represent the father and others give that signification to the 10th house. In my years of practice, I've seen it work both ways. In some charts the condition of the 9th house corresponds beautifully to the person's experience of the father, and in others the 10th house works best. I just wanted to tell you that according to Parasara, the originator of the system we're using, the 9th house represents the person's experience of father, while the 10th house governs "matters pertaining to the father." I guess this is how a person could have a lot of happiness from the father even while the person's father is suffering terribly. Or vice versa.

Martin: Does that teaching work, James?

James: I'm really not sure. I'm just telling you what he said.

Martin: Well, what do I do if a client asks me about his or her father?

James: The way I handle it is to analyze the condition of the Sun, the *karaka* (indicator) of the father. I tell the person whatever I can about the father from that viewpoint. Then, I explain that either the 9th house or the 10th house could also represent the father, and I tell the client the results of both houses.

Martin: And let the person decide which one fits?

James: Exactly. At this point, that's the best I can do.

THE TENTH HOUSE

I'm going to spend part of one whole class talking about the 10th house and focusing on career (see Class Seven), so right now I'll just mention a few general points to remember. The 10th house significations are pretty clear. Career, type of profession, and fame and status are all 10th house matters. I don't have anything significant to add to that. Just remember that it's extremely important to be able to analyze a person's profession, because when you practice professionally, you are going to get so many people coming to you specifically because they have trouble finding their proper career path. Ninety-nine percent of the clients I see want to know about career, love matters, health, and money. A few want to know about their spiritual life, and a few call because of some sort of emergency outside these areas.

Martin: Like what?

James: A kidnapping, a law suit, or a problem with an enemy. But these, for me, are very rare.

Martin: Do you ask the client why they're calling?

James: Actually, when I take phone calls to set appointments I try to be fairly quick about it. I don't like spending a lot of time talking to the client <u>before</u> the consultation. I prefer to know as little as possible beforehand so I can be objective in my analysis and not be influenced by the person's feelings and opinions. (Of course, I allow plenty of time for questions after my interpretation.) When clients ask if I want to know why they're coming for a reading, I usually joke with them. I say, "Wait, let me see how good my psychic energies are working today. You want to know about career, love, money, and health. How did I do?" Then they laugh and tell me I'm psychic.

Martin: So it's better not to know anything about the person?

James: No, no. That's not my point. I'm saying that my <u>personal</u>

preference is to work without prior input. Many astrologers like to talk to a client and maybe even interview them thoroughly before the reading. Each astrologer has to find his or her own way. My method works for me because most of my clients are astrology students who have bought one of my books and are calling to learn more.

Astrologers "out in the world" have a much more difficult practice than I do. They get plenty of clients who are stressed-out because of some emergency. I had that kind of practice before I wrote my books and I didn't like it. There were too many people who came for readings with no intention to work on their problems or their spiritual growth. There was no way to make a difference with these people. It wasn't much fun.

Martin: Can we talk about how to analyze a person's profession through the 10th house?

James: Actually, I'm going to spend a large part of our next class discussing horoscopes in terms of career, health, and marriage. Right now, I just want to give you some general information about career that may be helpful.

First off, it is very important to consider the 10th house in the context of the entire chart. If you think you're going to predict a person's profession just by 10th house indications, or even the 10th house and the *dasamsa* (career chart), you're mistaken. A person's career is so all-encompassing that you have to use all the information available. I think that as society evolves and the masses become wealthier, people have more and more available options. People today don't want to do what they are merely capable of or what simply feels natural. They want careers that make them happy and fulfilled, excited and enthusiastic.

Martin: Something that will make a difference in the world.

James: Absolutely. Therefore, you have to look at the entire chart. If you look only at the 10th house and the *dasamsa* (career chart), you may predict the kind of career the person chooses at the age of twenty-five or thirty. But that is not necessarily what the person will do his or her entire life, and it may even be a profession that is unfulfilling and unrewarding.

Most *Jyotish* texts don't tell you to look at the house placement of the Moon when trying to find a person's career. But how can you possibly ignore the Moon, the planet showing what makes a person comfortable, and still find a suitable career? It's pretty much the same with the ascendant ruler. The ascendant ruler and the Moon represent the person him- or herself. These are the most critical features of the horoscope. How can they not have huge impact on someone's career path?

I see lots of charts where career indications alone (10th house and *dasamsa* chart) definitively indicate a career in something that will make them less happy than would another profession.

Martin: Can you give me an example?

James: Sure. I have seen charts where construction or real estate is indicated, but the person would clearly be happier and more vitalized in music, dance, or drama.

Martin: How does that happen?

James: The person has the ruler of the 4th house (real estate) in the 10th (career), and that planet happens to be Saturn (planet of construction and real estate). Maybe Saturn is even aspected by Mars, which doesn't hurt when it comes to real estate. (Technically speaking, Mars rules "landed property" in *Jyotish*. In practice, both Saturn and Mars govern real estate.) On top of this, maybe the 10th house ruler occupies the 4th house.

Martin: That would be an exchange of signs. Ruler of 4th in the 10th, and ruler of 10th in the 4th.

James: Right. That's called *Parivartana Yoga*, or exchange of signs (known as mutual reception in Western astrology). And then in the *dasamsa* chart, maybe the 4th house ruler also occupies the 10th house. So you have a powerful confluence of indications supporting a career of real estate or construction. And these indications will likely lead the person in that direction. If, however, there are a few choice benefics like Venus and Moon, or Venus and Jupiter, in the 3rd house or possibly even in the 5th house, <u>that are clearly unafflicted</u>, the person will just adore the arts and be happiest functioning in that realm.

Martin: Could the person do real estate as a career, and art as a hobby?

James: That's possible. But it's much more likely that the person will be unhappy in the real estate career because he or she knows that art brings much greater fulfillment.

Martin: Does this happen a lot?

James: It happens often enough. In my experience, this problem occurs most with ex-lawyers. Do you know how many clients I've seen who have spent years and years getting a law degree only to find out they hate the practice? It's not that law is necessarily a bad profession. Many lawyers love their work. I believe it has to do with the horoscope.

Martin: How so?

James: Well, law is considered a "technical field." Therefore, it requires a very powerful Mars and a significantly placed Jupiter.

Martin: In my reading, you mentioned my possibly being a lawyer because Mars is opposite Jupiter.

James: That's a typical placement for lawyers, as is Mars conjunct Jupiter. Other common features are aspects between Venus and Mars, as well as aspects between Mercury and Mars. I would say the Mercury-Mars conjunction is the most typical aspect of lawyers, because it makes the person skeptical, discriminating, argumentative, very down to earth, and able to manipulate situations and influence juries.

When you think about it, a person with a Mercury-Mars conjunction or opposition is going to be fairly nervous or mentally agitated throughout his or her entire life. If that person decides to spend a lifetime debating, arguing, fighting, and nitpicking with words, which is what lawyers do, it's going to intensify the mental agitation and nervousness.

Martin: That's true, but I can see how a Mercury-Mars person would be excellent at arguing cases.

James: Yes, but that kind of career could easily make the person unhappy. And happiness today is critical.

Martin: Don't people in other cultures also want a career to bring happiness?

James: Depends on the culture. Every society has its owns rules and quirks. Whenever I analyze a chart of a person born in India, even if he or she lived in the U.S. for ten or twenty years, I can only predict the person's career if it's a money maker. If the chart indicates art, religion, creative writing, or some "impractical" career, I always tell the person he or she is probably an engineer, doctor, or businessman, and is miserable because of being so far away from the career that would bring happiness.

Martin: Really?

James: Then the person thinks I'm a genius astrologer. It's just the way of the modern Indian culture. Indian parents have a really big influence on their children, and they almost never support a career that isn't practical and lucrative.

What fascinates me about this is that India has the biggest film industry in the world. So there must be plenty of actors in India.

Martin: What must their charts look like?

James: I don't know. I assume that they have typical artist horoscopes, and that somehow these people resisted their parents' influence. Recently, an Indian told me that being an actor is considered a "low" profession, so that may have something to do with the problem.

In all my years of practice, I can think of <u>one</u> Indian client with an artist's horoscope who actually became an artist. She said she upset her family and relatives tremendously by going against their wishes, but she eventually prevailed.

Martin: James, this means that if I want to practice astrology for people in other countries I need to know something about their cultures.

James: That's true. It can be a problem. I had a terrible time predicting divorce for Europeans. I've been to Switzerland several times and still have no idea how to predict divorce for anyone there. I've seen charts of married couples (lots of married couples) where one or both of the people had 7th houses and Venuses that would make your skin crawl.

Martin: And they stayed married?

James: Yes. I would ask the couples or the individuals if they were on their second marriage and they would say no, they've been married for ten, fifteen, or twenty years. It was upsetting. Years later, my Swiss friends told me that many of the people whose charts I analyzed did have terrible marital problems, but in that culture divorce isn't a realistic option. So I assume the charts were accurate.

Another interesting thing occurred with the Swiss charts. Many of them clearly appeared artistic, and yet so few of the people were artists, the Swiss friend who sponsored my trips asked me whether I might have been "projecting" art onto those people because I was once an artist. I found that really surprising, because if I ever do any accidental projecting, it's usually about spirituality or fame. So I asked my friend whether art was a viable profession for Swiss people, and he said, "not very." There was his answer.

When I was doing charts in Iceland, I had a terrible time predicting careers for people. I can't say why for sure, but it could be related to the fact that in Iceland there are only about five ascendants that ever come up in a chart (Cancer through Scorpio). The other ascendants last about ten minutes each.

I was told that when the famous Indian astrologer, K.N. Rao, came to America he complained that he couldn't predict Westerners' careers well. He has no problem predicting the professions of Indians.

There's another problem we should discuss that occurs when predicting careers. Many times, you'll see a horoscope that indicates a particular career plain as day, but the person acts like he or she doesn't know what you're talking about when you mention it. I'm talking about a horoscope that clearly indicates some powerful or very creative career (law, writing, counseling, fine arts, healing). In cases like these, where you are certain that the birthtime is accurate because all or most of the indications aside from career are correct, look for an extreme lack of confidence indicated in the chart. These are cases where the person actually knows deep inside his or her best choice of career but won't go near it because of fear, lack of confidence, or weak self image. This is a very important tip I'm giving you, so don't forget it. It happens in a good number of cases.

Martin: James, you mentioned in an earlier class that a person could have the genetics for a certain career, but not be interested in pursuing it. How do you tell the difference between that situation and a person who doesn't pursue a career due to low self-esteem?

James: The difference is that the person who appears to have the genetics to be a healer (which you determine by asking if his or her parents or grandparents were doctors), but has no interest in that field, has chosen some <u>other</u> viable, significant career. In the cases I'm referring to now, the person has a wonderful chart for fine arts, but instead takes a menial job. The confidence is so low that the person doesn't even think about practicing a career. Whenever you see cases where a person only pursues jobs, rather than a career, it's generally either because of low confidence or a severly dysfunctional childhood. A childhood where there was no support from the parents.

Martin: So how do you see this? The low confidence, I mean.

James: I look for a weak and afflicted 1st house. And I look to see if Saturn is <u>tightly</u> aspecting the Sun, Moon, ascendant ruler, or the ascendant <u>degree</u>. I've seen charts that indicate powerful careers but the lack of confidence is intense. Usually, the person is from a dysfunctional home.

Martin: And that shows up through tight Saturn aspects to personal planets?

James: Yes, or the ascendant. It can also show up through afflictions to personal planets or the ascendant that are <u>not</u> caused by Saturn. The ascendant ruler may be fallen and tightly combust the Sun. Or a personal planet may be too closely conjunct Ketu. There's a lot of ways that weak confidence can show up. That's why when you're analyzing horoscopes, you have to look at the whole chart before you make a judgement about <u>anything</u>. In my beginning days, I made far too many judgements without considering the entire chart. As my second mentor, P.M. Padia, used to say: "You must have a computer mind to do astrology."

This brings up the issue of the traditional 10th house *karakas*, or indicators, of career (Sun, Jupiter, Saturn, and Mercury). I'm not very enthusiastic about them. In my experience, Saturn alone is much more of a 10th house *karaka* than Jupiter, Mercury, or Sun. That doesn't mean the four traditional *karakas* didn't work fine in India thousands of years ago. It means that they don't work well for the charts I do for modern Westerners. In my view, it's best to look at the 10th house of the natal chart, the natal chart as a whole, Saturn in particular, and the 1st and 10th houses of the *dasamsa* (career chart). But I'm going to cover how to analyze a chart for career in our next class.

Class Six

THE ELEVENTH HOUSE

James: I find the 11th house to be pretty straight-forward. It represents friends, groups, major goals and desires, dancing (which most astrologers are unaware of), and money from side ventures. One note of caution is that many astrologers neglect the importance of the 11th house.

Martin: How so?

James: If the 11th house is strong, a person generally fulfills his or her most compelling long-term desires in life. The person is able to fulfill <u>major</u> desires easily.

Martin: As opposed to minor desires that are ruled by the 3rd house?

James: Exactly. It's really sad to watch how a person with a seriously afflicted 11th house may be able to get daily desires fulfilled (depending on the condition of the 3rd house), but if a desire becomes extremely important it becomes nearly impossible to get it realized.

Martin: How bad does the 11th house have to be for that to happen?

James: By now you know that there are many ways a planet or a house can be afflicted, but I'm talking about a situation where, as I sometimes remark during a reading, "There's nothing good about this house." That means the house is afflicted <u>and</u> there are no mitigating circumstances whatsoever.

Martin: No saving grace.

James: That's right. If the 11th house is badly afflicted, with no saving grace, then the more a person wants something, the harder it is to obtain.

Martin: Does this mean that if the person doesn't particularly want money, he or she can still get it, whereas the person who craves money finds it impossible to get?

James: Exactly. Remember, though, that we're talking about a <u>heavily</u> afflicted 11th house. An 11th house that contains, for example, a fallen planet, while the 11th house ruler is also damaged.

Martin: So, there's nothing good about the house.

James: Nothing. There is one 11th house influence that is somewhat of an oddity, and that is dancing.

Martin: Doesn't the 3rd house rule music, dance, and drama?

James: Yes. But, when it comes to dancing, you <u>also</u> have to look at the 11th house. For example, if I see a powerful or energized 3rd house, I begin to think of fine arts meaning (music, dance, and drama). I then look at certain other houses to try to determine what kind of artist the person may be. If the 5th house appears significant, I consider that the person may be a painter or craftsperson. If the 11th house is activated, I consider dance. If the person has a strong 1st house or very prominent Moon, I begin to think of drama.

Martin: Why the Moon and 1st house for drama?

James: Because if those influences are strong, the person wants a lot of attention. If the moon is in the 1st or 10th house, the person wants to be the center of attention. Music is indicated more by a Mercury-Venus conjunction, which is an extremely creative aspect, whereas actors usually have a great need to be recognized.

By the way, some students are startled when I say that the 11th house governs dancing, but that's what I was taught, and it definitely works in the vast majority of cases. If you find a chart with three or four unafflicted planets in the 11th house, that person is going to love to dance. Even if the person isn't a professional dancer, he or she will love to dance. And this doesn't occur because 11th house planets throw aspects onto the 5th house (one of the houses of art). It happens because the 11th house rules dance. So if a person aks about being a professional dancer, you must analyze the 11th house ruler and any planets occupying the 11th house, as well as the 3rd house (the house of fine arts).

The 11th house also rules money from side ventures and large sums of money that come in sporadically. The 11th house has a lot to do with money matters, and is almost always strong in the charts of millionaires. So, if you don't give the 11th house proper attention in your chart readings, you'll have trouble recognizing the chart of a millionaire.

Martin: Really?

James: Yes, really. A strong 2nd house indicates that the person makes great <u>wages</u>. The 11th house tells whether the person can take those earnings and go on to build a fortune.

Martin: I don't look to the 5th house for that?

James: No, you don't. You look to the 5th house to see if the person likes to gamble. Gambling includes certain investments of course, namely stocks and bonds and other speculations. But most millionaires don't make their millions through speculating. Speculators make their millions through speculating. Most millionaires make their millions by working hard, earning good wages, and putting their earnings to work. In other words, they find other outlets for earnings.

Martin: Side ventures.

James: Yes. But not speculations, unless the <u>5th house</u> is prominent. This is a typical "mix and match" problem, so be careful. When you tell a person with a tremendously strong 11th house that he or she can make lots of money through side ventures, that person will naturally assume you mean to include speculating. You must actually advise the person not to speculate or gamble unless the 5th house is in excellent shape.

I'll tell you an interesting story about the 11th house. I once saw a client who was obsessed with making money. His chart, unfortunately, was terrible for finances. Anyway, he sent me the charts of about seven or eight billionaires to show me how his chart was similar to theirs (which it wasn't). Do you know what was the common denominator of these billionaire charts? The ruler of the 2nd house occupied the 11th house, or vice versa. And in several cases, the rulers of the 2nd and 11th houses exchanged signs.

Martin: *Parivartana Yoga.*

James: Yes. Mutual reception. Whenever you see a connection between the 2nd and 11th houses (assuming one of the planets isn't fallen or badly aspected), there's a likelihood that the person will, over time, build a fortune.

Regarding friends, some astrologers consider friends to be a 4th house signification because the 4th house governs comforts, and friends are a great comfort in life. But the quintessential significator for friends (and groups) is the 11th house. The nature of a person's friends are seen from the 11th house. For example, I have Jupiter in the 11th house, so my friends are religious and spiritual. Most of them are also very Saturnian because Saturn aspects Jupiter, the 11th house ruler, in my chart within one degree.

Martin: So your friends are both Jupitarian and Saturnian?

James: Yes. They are religious and spiritual, but they are also austere, highly responsible, and they love to meditate. If Jupiter was in my 11th house without the aspect from Saturn, my friends would be more devotional and expansive and concerned with pleasures and comforts. Instead, they are interested in enlightenment, which means final liberation from everything, comforts and all.

Martin: Do you look at both the 4th and 11th houses for friends?

James: I do, but I give the 11th house much more weight. If I want to know the <u>nature</u> of someone's friends, I look to the 11th house. If I want to know if the person has many friends, then I look to the 11th and the 4th houses. Ultimately, the 11th house is more essential regarding friends and groups.

Regarding the 11th house as significator of the eldest sibling, remember that we're talking about the <u>eldest</u> sibling only, not all elder siblings. And if you see a horrendously afflicted 11th house, it often means that the person has no older sibling, rather than trouble with the eldest sibling. (An extremely afflicted 3rd house can mean either no younger siblings or trouble with younger siblings.) Sometimes, the 11th house is so incredibly damaged that it indicates that the person's parents had a miscarriage or abortion before the person's birth (i.e. the person's eldest sibling died before birth).

THE TWELFTH HOUSE

It's important to understand the 12th house well because so many of your clients will have prominent 12th house influences. This is because most people who consult astrologers, or even "believe" in astrology, are spiritually or metaphysically oriented. If your practice is anything like mine, probably half of the clients you see will have the ruler of the 1st house occupying either the 8th house (metaphysics) or the 12th house (*moksha* or final liberation). Or, they'll have the ruler of the 8th or 12th house in the 1st. Or, the 1st house ruler will be tightly aspected by the 8th or 12th house ruler. You have to know the full ramifications of these influences.

Martin: You've said before that aspects involving the 8th or 12th house and any personal influence (Sun, Moon, ascendant, or ascendant ruler) can make a person metaphysical or spiritual but lacking in confidence.

James: That's right. If you always remember that, you'll be in excellent shape. Remember that the closer the aspect, the more intense the result. If the 12th house ruler is within three or four degrees of the ascendant degree, the person is going to be extremely introspective and spiritually oriented, but his or her confidence is going to be <u>very</u> damaged. If the ascendant ruler is aspected by the 12th house ruler with a wide orb, say within fifteen or twenty degrees, the person will be <u>somewhat</u> spiritual and <u>somewhat</u> lacking in confidence, but the effects will not be nearly so glaring.

Martin: Can you say why the 12th house influence is so bad for most significations?

James: Because it represents "otherworldly" matters. If the 2nd house is influenced by an otherworldly influence, how can financial affairs benefit? If the 10th house is influenced by an otherworldly influence, how can career benefit?

Essentially, a person with a very prominent or influential 12th house is functioning more on the spiritual (rather than earthly) plane. This means that for a 12th house type person, the world and all its affairs are stressful and unnatural.

Martin: So a strong or prominent 12th house makes enlightenment and introspection natural for the person, while anything worldly or material becomes unnatural or unfamiliar?

James: Yes, exactly. That's why so many spiritual disciples have a terrible time making money and succeeding in a career. The typical 12th house person is great at exploring spiritual realities, abstract concepts, and infinite awareness, but has a hard time with practical matters. When it comes to worldly matters, 12th house people are usually like fish out of water.

Martin: Can you tell from the 12th house whether a person will actually get enlightened in this lifetime?

James: No. I don't think that is something that can be seen from modern *Jyotish*. You can tell from the horoscope who is going to spend a lifetime trying for enlightenment and who might become a monk, although for monkhood you also have to check the 7th house to see if marriage or love relationships are indicated. I've analyzed hundreds, if not thousands, of horoscopes of people actively pursuing *moksha* and the only difference between their horoscopes and the charts of widely accepted enlightened gurus is that the gurus' charts also indicate worldly fame and power. Of course, these are the charts of "known" gurus.

Martin: You've looked at the charts of lots of famous gurus?

James: Of course. Most astrologers have. Now, you will see horoscopes that are extremely strong for enlightenment both in the natal implications and the *dasas* and *bhuktis*. But there is no way to know for sure who will actually get enlightened. Reaching enlightenment is so rare anyway. I doubt I've ever seen an enlightened client, but I've certainly had hundreds of people ask if their birthchart indicated final liberation.

In terms of debts and expenses, remember that if the 12th house is strong and well-disposed the person gets bargains.

Martin: Really? I thought it just mean that the person isn't bothered by unexpected debts and expenses and that the person is good at holding onto money.

James: No. It also means that the person buys things at good prices. And when a person has a positive 12th house transit, like Jupiter transits through the 12th house, you have to predict bargains, good sexual experiences, luck with travel to remote foreign countries, and good meditation practice. These are all 12th house matters. The most difficult thing for beginners to understand about the *dusthana* houses (6th, 8th, and 12th) is that when a *dusthana* house is strong or well-disposed, the person gets many specific benefits. If Venus or Jupiter or a very bright Moon occupies the 12th house, the person gets bargains, good sexual experiences, lots of spiritual evolution, and great experiences in remote foreign countries throughout life.

Martin: But the benefic planet occupying the 12th house would suffer because the 12th house is a destructive house?

James: Correct. Unless the planet in the 12th house is in its own or exaltation sign, or unless that planet is aspected very tightly by another benefic planet. You see?

Martin: Then if Venus occupies the 12th house and is tightly aspected by a full Moon or by Jupiter, it won't feel the pinch of the 12th house energy?

James: That's right. But the aspect has to be <u>tight</u>, within two or three or four degrees. Then, that well-aspected Venus would simply give great spiritual results. If the person in this case enters a Venus period or subperiod, he or she would gain lots of spiritual evolution, and <u>the houses that Venus rules would not suffer</u>. Or they would suffer only slightly. So be careful not to go overboard with the negativity of the 12th house.

On the other hand, if a planet occupies the 12th house and is <u>not</u> well-aspected or occupying its own sign, that planet is going to be seriously afflicted, pure and simple. For example, if the ruler of the 7th house occupies the 12th without any positive mitigating effect, then you have to predict at least one divorce.

Martin: What if that 7th house ruler occupies the 12th and is tightly aspected by Jupiter? Would that simply indicate getting a spiritual husband? Or, would the person get a spiritual spouse and have a bad marriage?

James: If the 7th house ruler is in the 12th <u>and</u> very well aspected or occupying its own sign, there should not be any problems <u>as long as the person has obtained a spiritual spouse</u>. There are cases where a person with this kind of placement chooses a worldly mate for some reason, and the results are disastrous. But eventually, the person realizes the mistake and chooses a spiritual partner and lives happily ever after. Many times, though, in a case like this the person simply gets a good spiritual spouse from the start.

Likewise, if the ruler of the 10th house (Career) occupies the 12th house, and is either in its own sign or very well-aspected, then you should predict a successful spiritual career.

Martin: Or a successful career involving sex.

James: That's right. The 12th house governs sexual pleasure and I expect that if you analyzed the charts of sex therapists you would find a very active 12th house. The 12th house is not just spiritual, and you have to remember that when you're analyzing horoscopes.

Let me show you a chart with a very interesting 12th house. This is David Stockman's horoscope (see following page).

Martin: The famous budget director for Ronald Reagan?

James: Yes. Stockman has four planets in the 12th house (debts and expenses) and he was one of the few persons in government who was ever serious about balancing the U.S. budget. He couldn't succeed because no one wanted to accept the cuts he knew were necessary. But Stockman was brilliant not only at holding onto money (12th house), but he was also great with numbers (math) because all of his 12th house planets aspect his 6th

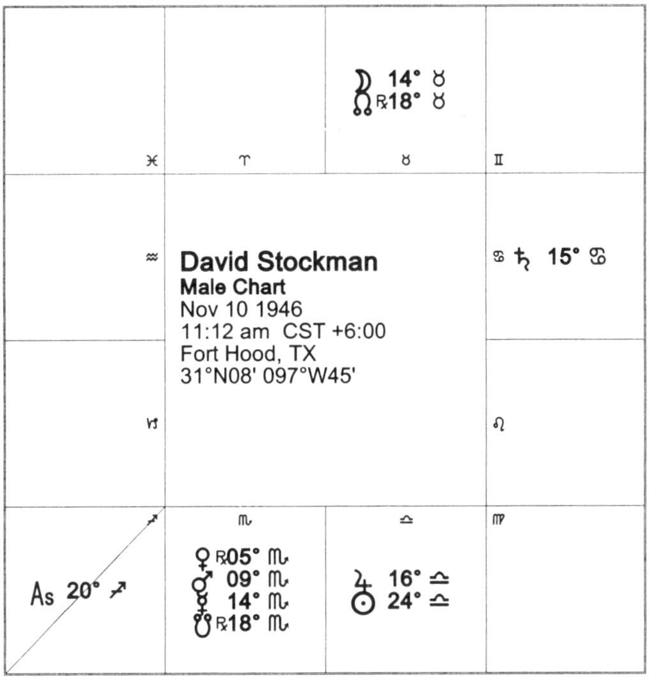
☽ 14° ♉
☊ ℞18° ♉
♓
♈
♉
♊
♒
David Stockman
Male Chart
Nov 10 1946
11:12 am CST +6:00
Fort Hood, TX
31°N08' 097°W45'
♋ ♄ 15° ♋
♑
♌
♐
♏
♎
♍
As 20° ♐
♀ ℞05° ♏
♂ 09° ♏
☿ 14° ♏
☋ ℞18° ♏
♃ 16° ♎
☉ 24° ♎

South Indian Style

For North Indian, see Appendix B.

planets.pts

Pt	Name	Hs	Rules
☽	Moon	6	8
☉	Sun	11	9
☿	Mercury	12	7, 10
♀	Venus	12	6, 11
♂	Mars	12	5, 12
♃	Jupiter	11	1, 4
♄	Saturn	8	2, 3
☊	North Node	6	-
☋	South Node	12	-
As	Ascendant	1	-

Sg	Name
♈	Aries
♉	Taurus
♊	Gemini
♋	Cancer
♌	Leo
♍	Virgo
♎	Libra
♏	Scorpio
♐	Sagittarius
♑	Capricorn
♒	Aquarius
♓	Pisces

house, and the 6th house governs details. I've mentioned before that many accountants have Venus in the 6th house. Benefics in the 6th house are wonderful for detail work.

Martin: Are benefics in the 6th better for detail work than malefics in the 6th?

James: I believe benefics are better when it comes to detail work. Malefics in the 6th are excellent in the sense that they help a person defeat health problems and competitors. But as for detail work, I think that Mars, Rahu, and Sun are helpful, while Ketu and Saturn are not.

Martin: James, I understand that if the ruler of any house occupies the 12th, it gets harmed because the 12th house hurts worldly matters. But what if the ruler of another otherworldly or spiritual house occupies the 12th?

James: That occurs when the 8th house ruler occupies the 12th, and I would say that's an excellent position for the metaphysical significations of the 8th house, but that's all. That placement would make the person excel with astrology, intuition, and psychic ability. But the person would not get good results with longevity, inheritances, and the reproductive system. Only the metaphysical or otherworldly affairs would benefit. I know there is a *yoga* that states that bad planets in bad houses are good, but I've not been particularly impressed with that *yoga*. It probably only works in some cases, and we're supposed to intuitively know which cases those are.

Any questions before we quit?

Martin: No.

James: See you next week. Bas.

CLASS SEVEN

James: Today we're going to cover several important topics. We'll focus on analyzing career, health, and marriage, using several example horoscopes. We'll also look at the *varga* (divisional) charts which are used for marriage and career, and I'll show you how to determine whether or not a *varga* chart can be trusted, since the marriage *varga* ascendant changes approximately every seventeen minutes and the career *varga* ascendant changes about every fifteen minutes. Always remember that the birthtimes on birth certificates are usually off by several minutes because nurses are in delivery rooms to help deliver babies, not to record *exact* birthtimes. I mentioned earlier that on the day my baby was born, the hospital clock was off by four minutes. Remember that when a client says, "I'm sure my birthtime is exact," what he or she means is that the time he or she gives you is exactly what's on the certificate. You need to explain to most of your clients that the time written on the birth certificate is usually several minutes off.

I've made some lists of key points to remember when analyzing career, health, and marriage. But first I want to show you how I use *varga* charts, and how to know whether one is *likely* to be accurate, in terms of a person's recorded birthtime.

Martin: Do all Hindu astrologers rectify *varga* charts before using them?

James: In India there's little need to do so because people take note of exact birthtimes so they can have their babies' horoscopes done immediately. In the West, we *know* that most birthtimes are inaccurate. Therefore, if a Westerner practicing *Jyotish* uses *vargas* without first determining the likelihood of their accuracy, it's usually due to uncritical thinking or just plain laziness. In my view, there's no excuse for that.

I'm not going to go into how the *varga* charts are drawn because I've already done so in my textbook, <u>Ancient Hindu Astrology for the Modern Western Astrologer</u>. The main points to grasp, in terms of understanding birthtimes and *varga* charts, are how many *natal* horoscope *degrees* it takes to alter each particular *varga* ascendant and how many minutes of birth make up one horoscope degree. Here are the significant points:

1) The *dasamsa* (career) chart changes by virtue of every three degrees *of the natal ascendant* in a person's horoscope. Each *dasamsa* ascendant falls

somewhere in between 0°- 3°, 3°- 6°, 6°- 9°, 9°- 12°, 12°- 15°, 15°-18°, 18°- 21°, 21°- 24°, 24°- 27°, 27°- 30°. So, you must memorize the degrees of change as follows: 3°, 6°, 9°, 12°, 15°, 18°, 21°, 24°, 27°, 30°.

If a person has a horoscope ascendant of four degrees and happens to have a Capricorn ascendant in the *dasamsa* chart, then you make a mental note that the person has entered the Capricorn ascendant by one degree. This is because the four degree Capricorn ascendant has passed the three degree cutoff point (0°-3°, 3°-6°, 6°-9°, and so on).

In this case, if the birthtime was off by enough *time* to make a one degree error in the *natal* chart on the *earlier* side (i.e. if the accurate ascendant was slightly less than three degrees rather than four degrees), then the *varga* chart is going to be wrong. It will have an earlier ascendant (Sagittarius instead of Capricorn).

Martin: How much time makes up one degree of ascendant?

James: Assuming the person is born in a longitude of Europe or the United States, each ascendant degree equals *approximately* four or five minutes of birthtime. If the person is born in an out-of-place latitude and longitude, like Iceland's, then the ascendant changes quite erratically, and you should use a computer to figure when each one begins.

One note of caution, however. In common longitudes of the U.S. and Europe, one degree of ascendant equals about four or five minutes with *most* ascendants. There are actually four ascendants that move faster, about three or four minutes per degree.

Martin: Which ones?

James: Aquarius, Pisces, Aries, and Taurus. I learned this recently from an article written by Hank Friedman in *The Mountain Astrologer* magazine. So in the case I just mentioned with the Capricorn *dasamsa* ascendant, if the person's *natal* ascendant was four degrees of Aquarius or Pisces or Aries or Taurus, it would only have taken about a three or four minute birthtime error, rather than four or five minutes, to give the earlier ascendant (Sagittarius).

Now let's see how well you understand this. Using the example I just gave you with a four degree natal ascendant (assuming a zodiac sign other than the slightly faster moving ones) and a *dasamsa* chart with Capricorn ascendant, and knowing that the *dasamsa* ascendants change every three degrees (0°, 3°, 6°, 9°, 12°, and so on), and that each natal ascendant degree equals four or five minutes, how many degrees of ascendant and how many minutes of birthtime error would it take to create an Aquarius rather than Capricorn ascendant (i.e. a *later* birthtime error) in the *dasamsa*?

Martin: Easy. About two natal ascendant degrees, or an eight to ten minute later birthtime than was recorded.

James: Yes. Because in our example the natal ascendant is four degrees, and the next *dasamsa* ascendant begins at six degrees. That's a difference of two degrees, or about ten minutes. Very good.

Now, how likely is it that the real birthtime was actually eight or ten minutes later than was recorded?

Martin: Not very.

James: That's right. If the birth was in a hospital, chances are that first the baby is born and then about three or four minutes later the nurse looks at the clock (which, you must never forget, may or may not have been accurate).

Regarding *navamsas*, marriage chart ascendants change every three degrees, twenty minutes. Each *navamsa* ascendant falls somewhere between 0°- 3° 20'; 3° 20' - 6° 40'; 6° 40' - 10°; 10° - 13° 20'; 13° 20' - 16° 40'; 16° 40' - 20°; 20°- 23° 20'; 23° 20' - 26° 40'; 26° 40' - 30°. So, you have to memorize 0°, 3° 20', 6° 40', 10°, 13° 20', 16° 40', 20°, 23° 20', 26° 40, 30°. This means each *navamsa* ascendant changes approximately every seventeen minutes (assuming each degree equals five minutes). Let's use my horoscope as an example (See page 50). My natal ascendant degree is 2° 33' of Taurus. My *navamsa* ascendant is Scorpio. How many degrees and minutes would it take to throw my *navamsa* ascendant off? (Note: Because my ascendant is in such an early degree of a sign, an earlier birthtime would change the *natal* ascendant. This is important to note because with a different ascendant, the *navamsa* chart would change so dramatically that one should not assume my *navamsa* ascendant would only go backwards one sign, to Libra. In fact, if my natal ascendant fell backwards to a late Aries ascendant, my *navamsa* ascendant would be Sagittarius.)

Martin: Since 2° 33' is in between 0° and 3° 20', it would have to go back exactly two degrees and thirty three minutes. You said that the ascendants of Aquarius through Taurus move about three or four minutes per degree (about one minute faster than most), so it means about eight or nine minutes.

James: Right. Just remember that these are <u>approximations</u>. You'd have to get on a computer to determine exact figures. Now, what's the likelihood that my *navamsa* is accurate?

Martin: Better than average. It's unlikely you were born eight or nine minutes earlier than what was recorded. I can see that it's *possible* you could have been born two or three minutes later than the time you were told, but not very likely. Birthtimes are usually earlier than what is recorded.

James: That's right. Most birth certificate birthtimes are recorded a few minutes after the birth. Not always, but most of the time. If my birthtime had come from my mother or a baby book, then I would be somewhat wary because there would be more possibility of a two or three minute discrepancy on either side. But nurses in hospitals usually record birthtimes a few minutes <u>after</u> a baby is born.

There's something that also makes it more likely that my birthtime was earlier rather than later.

Martin: What's that?

James: My birthtime was recorded as 7:36 PM. That means someone at least took the time to try to be precise. That doesn't mean the time is exact. I still could easily have been born a few minutes earlier. But the fact that the time was not estimated (e.g. 7:30 or 8:00) is helpful. If I was actually born later than 7:36, it would most likely have to have been because of an inaccurate clock. Most birthtimes are wrong due to human error.

Martin: So I should always check the birthtime to see if it looks like an approximation?

James: Absolutely. I see so many approximate birthtimes from Latin countries that I almost never bother with their *varga* charts. It seems that everyone born in Brazil, Cuba, Argentina, or Colombia tells me they were born at 8:30 or 9 or 12 or 12:30. Everyone says they were born on the half hour! Nobody's born at 8:32 or 12:47. I rarely bother trying to rectify *varga* charts for these people because I haven't a clue as to how erroneous their birthtimes are — and a detailed rectification takes hours.

Martin: Okay, so what do you do if a person was born a few minutes after a *varga* ascendant change? In the example we just used with the *dasamsa* Capricorn ascendant, what do you do? Do you read the *dasamsa* chart as is, or what?

James: I explain that there is a chance that the *varga* chart may be wrong because a five minute earlier birth would create a different *dasamsa* chart. Then I explain that because of the way birthtimes are recorded, a five-minute discrepancy is extremely possible. This is important. Most of my clients think their birthtime is exact because they got it from a birth certificate. When I question my clients about their birth data (which I suggest you always do), most of them say, "I got it from my birth certificate, so I know it's exact." That's a common mistake on their part.

In cases where a particular *varga* chart falls within four or five minutes of an ascendant changeover, I tell the person the results that <u>both</u> charts indicate. I say to the person, "If you were born within these particular fifteen minutes, the results will be thus and so. If you were born within these other fifteen minutes, the results are as follows."

Martin: In the example we're looking at, would you read the Capricorn ascendant chart as well as the Sagittarius ascendant chart for the person?

James: Yes. It's not very hard since I'm mainly looking at only one house. For the *dasamsa* (career) chart, I'm mainly analyzing the 10th house. For a *navamsa* (marriage) chart, I'm mainly looking at the 7th house.

Martin: You're not analyzing the entire chart?

James: No. I know that lots of astrologers analyze divisional charts the same way they do the natal chart. But I have not found that to work with even a small degree of consistency. And while we're on the subject, let me state bluntly that I'm not terribly impressed with all fifteen *varga* charts. I generally get useful results from the career and marriage charts — information that I wouldn't get from the natal chart. Not always, but often enough. I certainly can't say that about the *saptamsa*, the chart that delineates children. I've tried using *saptamsas* of people that I have known intimately for years and years, and have found very little accuracy.

Martin: That's not very good news.

James: I know. All I can suggest is that you do your own research on *vargas* and talk with other astrologers who say they get good results from them. But before you take their advice, let me remind you that many of the astrologers I've met who practice *Jyotish* in the West are not experience-oriented enough. Because they so greatly respect Indian tradition, they simply accept what they've read or heard. And that's definitely not good enough in this field. In fact, it causes all kinds of problems — problems that many Indian astrologers don't have to deal with because they are more skeptical and discriminating. The good Indian astrologers I've met give full lip-service to traditional astrological techniques, but they only use what works in their practice.

Martin: So I should do as the good Indian astrologers do, not as they say.

James: That's right. Trust me on this because I've seen it over and over.

Martin: And you're saying that you've worked with *vargas,* and you're not impressed with all of them?

James: That's right. Sometimes *navamsa* charts and *dasamsa* charts in people's horoscopes work wonderfully. What I'm not impressed with is the consistency factor. When I say that I find astrology to be about about seventy percent accurate, I mean that <u>all</u> natal horoscopes work with about seventy percent accuracy. When it comes to *varga* charts, sometimes they work and sometimes they don't, <u>even when I know for sure the birthtime is accurate</u>. It's not like a natal chart where the bulk of the chart fits the person and only part of it doesn't. This is a serious problem.

Martin: That's not so good, James.

James: I know. In any case, the best results I get are from the marriage chart and the career chart, and that's only if I restrict my analysis to the 7th house of the *navamsa* chart and the 10th house of the *dasamsa* chart. If I try to analyze those charts as a whole, the results are inaccurate more often than not.

Analyzing *varga* charts the same way as natal charts reminds me of Solar Return charts. Lots of astrologers swear by them, but I've tried them in my own life for about ten years, and they have never worked. I've tried using Solar Returns in all kinds of different ways because every time I tell some astrologer they don't work, I hear about another method that works best (using the precession, not using the precession, using only the angles, using the chart like a transit chart, and on and on). Solar Returns don't work for me, and they didn't work for my Indian mentors. (Note: Indians know Solar Return charts as *Varshopal*.)

Martin: But the *navamsa* and *dasamsa* charts work fairly well when you use them in the way you've mentioned?

James: That's right. They work fairly well, and I get useful information from them. Bear in mind, by the way, that there are teachers of Hindu astrology who will show you many *dasamsa* examples where the chart <u>as a whole</u> works very well in describing people's careers. My guess is that for every chart that teacher shows you that works well, there are about eight or nine that don't. In my experience, it is mainly the house connected to the particular *varga* (7th for *navamsa*, 10th for *dasamsa*, and so on) that is critical.

Martin: If a career chart contradicts the natal chart 10th house, which information should be used?

James: That's a hard question to answer. The fact is that after all these years, I still haven't put any patterns together. To do that, I'd have to sit down with fifty different charts just analyzing 10th house matters along with each corresponding *dasamsa* chart to give an empirical answer.

Martin: Do you see contradictions like these often?

James: I do. I see instances where the 10th house of the natal chart and the natal chart as a whole indicate a career in the arts, for example, but the career chart indicates, say, medicine. And I see charts where the 10th house is in excellent condition, indicating great career success, while the 10th house of the career chart holds a fallen planet and the 10th house ruler in that chart is badly placed by sign. These are cases where the career chart obviously contradicts the professional indications in the natal chart.

I would advise you to make your own study using about fifty charts, or as many as you can find with accurate birth data (or charts where the birthtime would have to have been about ten minutes earlier than the recorded time to throw off the *dasamsa* ascendant), and see what you can find.

You're also going to have some confusion when the *navamsa* chart contradicts the natal marriage conditions, but it's not quite as tricky as with the *dasamsa*. I'll show you an example chart in a minute to explain why.

Martin: You said in an earlier class that you also look at the 1st house of *varga* charts. Is that right?

James: Yes, but I only give the 1st house of *varga* charts about ten percent significance. The other ninety percent goes to other birthchart features. Some astrologers consider the 1st house of the *varga* charts to be the most important of all.

Martin: Really?

James: Yes. And their *reasoning* makes sense. But in practice, this doesn't work very well.

Martin: Then why do you say the reasoning makes sense?

James: Because in a *rasi* (natal) chart, the 1st house is the essence, or nucleus, of the horoscope. The same is true of *prasna* (horary) charts. The 1st house is all-important. But I've tried assigning the 1st house tremendous significance in *varga* charts and it just doesn't work. The 1st house and the placement of the 1st house ruler give me some useful information, but nowhere near as much as the house that is connected to the significations of the particular *varga* in use.

Martin: In the *varga* charts, when you say that you look at certain houses and certain rulers, do you do this in the same way as with the natal chart? I mean, do you use aspects and all traditional natal methods?

James: Mostly, yes. The main thing I do NOT use, however, are the planetary aspects. I just don't find that aspects work in the *varga* charts (with the possible exception of conjunctions). Many astrologers use the aspects in divisional charts and many don't. My first Indian mentor did not find them to work. I don't remember if my second mentor did or not, but I seriously doubt he did, or he would have argued with me about it. He was intense about teaching me which techniques work and which ones don't, and I had already determined that they didn't work before I met him.

In my experiences with aspects in *varga* charts over the years, I have noticed that conjunctions to the 7th house ruler in the *navamsa* and conjunctions to the 10th house ruler in the *dasamsa* work just enough to make me take note of them in the charts I'm analyzing, but not enough to rely on them. This means that after almost twenty years of practice, I will occasionally say to a client *who studies astrology*, "The ruler of the 7th house in your *navamsa* chart is conjunct with Jupiter. Conjunctions are the only aspects that might work. If they do, then there is a chance you may marry someone spiritual and have a lot of happiness. I'm still not positive that any aspects should be used in divisional charts, but I have noticed that conjunctions work some of the time." But I don't make such statements to non-astrologers.

I told you when we started these lessons that I would teach you what I have found to work in my practice and that's just what I'm doing. I definitely don't recommend analyzing *varga* charts in the same way you do natal charts.

Martin: Aside from the *varga* 1st house and the house that is most related to the signification of the *varga* chart, do you look at anything else?

James: For the *navamsa* chart, the answer is no. The 1st and 7th are all I concern myself with. I must say, though, that if I see a *navamsa* chart with three or more planets in their own or exaltation signs, I will take some note of that and try to determine what it means. But that's about all.

Martin: How do you determine what it means?

James: I ask the client questions. Usually I find that if a person has a lot of well- placed planets (well-placed by sign, not houses), the person's spouse is special. The spouse may be wealthy, brilliant, of high character, and so on.

Regarding the *dasamsa* chart, I look at the 1st and 10th houses, and then I look at the house placement of the Moon, and any house containing three or more planets. But in terms of percentages, I weight the 10th house at about eighty or ninety percent, and everything else a total of about ten or twenty percent. Don't forget what I saying about percentages here. In any *varga* that I'm using, I consider the house relating to the significations of the *varga* chart to be by far the most important. In my experience, that works best for predictive accuracy.

Martin: Are you going to put this information in your book, James? I bet other astrologers are going to be surprised to hear your views on this.

James: Some will and some won't. Do you think I'm the only one who has had trouble with *varga* charts? Don't you think I ask other astrologers how well *vargas* work for them?

Martin: What do they say?

James: Some say they get good results, and some don't use them because they can't get them to work. Just the other day, one of my peers asked me again (he forgot that he has asked me more than once over the last five years) whether *varga* charts work or not. He doesn't do well with them. My advice is that you not assume that *varga* charts work until you actually see them consistently produce accurate results. Now I want to give you an example of what happens when the *navamsa* chart indications contradict the marriage results indicated in the natal chart. Remember Deborah from Class Four? Her natal chart reveals a very rough 7th house, while the *navamsa*, chart indicates happy married life.

Notice the severe afflictions to the 7th house of the natal chart.

Martin: They're obvious. Malefic Rahu occupies the 7th house, Mars aspects the 7th house, and the aspect is <u>really</u> strong since Mars occupies the same degree as the ascendant (i.e. Mars aspects the exact point of the *descendant*), and the 7th house ruler, Jupiter, is fallen in Capricorn and closely (within six-and-a-half degrees) conjunct the 12th house ruler, the Sun.

James: That's right. Regarding marriage, this is a very afflicted chart. The only good 7th house feature is the fact that the 7th house ruler, Jupiter, is conjunct Venus and Mercury. But these aspects are much wider than the negative aspect Jupiter receives from the 12th house ruler Sun. The Venus aspect occurs within about twelve degrees, and the Mercury aspect is within about twenty degrees. These can't possibly mollify all the other afflictions.

	Rasi				Navamsa		
☊ ℞15° ♓				☽	♀ ♈	☋ ♉	As ♂
≈	**Deborah** **Female Chart** Feb 11 1950 9:46 pm EST +5:00 Pittsburgh, PA 40°N26'26" 079°W59'46"	♋	☿ ≈		♑		♋ ♃
☉ 29° ♑ ♀ 23° ♑ ♃ ℞11° ♑ ☿ 03° ♑		☊ ♄ ℞24° ♌				♌
☽ 29° ♏	♎	☋ ℞15° ♍ As 17° ♍ ♂ 17° ♍	♐	♏	☋	♎	☉ ♍

Now look at the *navamsa* chart. The ruler of the 7th house is exalted Jupiter (Jupiter in Cancer) in the 2nd house, the house of wealth.

Martin: I know the 2nd house isn't a terrible house, but it's not good either, right?

James: Right, but because the 7th house lord is very content in its exaltation sign, it will produce excellent 2nd house results. This means lots of wealth, happy family life, and nice foods to eat. It could also mean marriage to a spouse who is a successful writer or teacher (2nd house significations). However, I wouldn't go overboard in predicting 2nd house effects. I would simply tell Deborah that her marriage chart indicates happy married life to someone who either has great wealth or who will earn great wealth.

Martin: What happened?

James: In her teens and twenties, she had an extraordinarily painful relationship that had huge ups and downs and caused more suffering than

I can describe. The relationship was nightmarish for her. When that relationship finally ended, she quickly found a wonderful man who treats her very well, and this couple has been happily married for longer than almost anyone I know.

Martin: Is he rich?

James: I don't know exactly how rich he is, but he's definitely well-off. He's quite successful and makes enough money that Deborah doesn't have to work. And Deborah and her husband travel a lot.

Whenever you see a chart where the married karma is a mixture of extremes, whether the extremes occur between two different charts (natal and *navamsa*), or simply in the natal chart, you should expect some really bad relationships (or marriages) and an excellent, happy marriage. And you should expect the bad relationships to come first. The good marriage always comes after the bad karma is paid back.

Martin: So it's rare to find a person who has a great marriage whose spouse leaves or dies, followed by a marriage which is painful or full of suffering?

James: Almost never happens. Sometimes I see people whose charts indicate a mixture of good marriage karma and bad relationship karma, but the person never actually finds the good marriage. In these cases, I believe it's due to the person's misuse of free will. In other words, the person is standing in his or her own way.

Martin: You mean the person hasn't processed what went wrong in the first marriage?

James: Yes. The person was psychologically damaged by the divorce, or has decided not to take a risk again or something like that. Regarding the *navamsa* chart, I find that it usually gets activated after a person is married. This means that if a person has a happy married life indicated in the natal chart, but has a very afflicted marriage chart, then he or she may have a wonderful time with a prospective spouse until the marriage occurs. Then the *navamsa* gets activated and marriage is terrible, leaving the person extremely confused.

Martin: Because everything was fine when they were dating?

James: Exactly. A soon as they tie the knot, things start going very wrong. But this doesn't work in the reverse. If the *marriage chart* is good and the *natal chart* is bad, the person has to go through a bad marriage first.

Martin: Even though the *navamsa* is in good shape?

James: Yes. Deborah is one of the rare few I've seen where her severely painful relationship occurred entirely before marriage. But if you see a chart where a person has a good *navamsa* and you know the birthtime is accurate enough to use that *navamsa*, you must predict that the person will have a good marriage eventually.

Martin: Assuming the person hasn't been so damaged that they stop their good karma from coming back by standing in their own way?

James: Yes. But that's the exception, not the rule. Most people with a good 7th house in the *navamsa* chart <u>with accurate birth data</u> will eventually have a good marriage.

Martin: Some astrologers say that the *navamsa* chart indicates where a person is headed in the future, is that true?

James: That's a fairly traditional perspective about the *navamsa*, but I'm not sure it works. I tried using the *navamsa* that way for a while. I considered that it was much more relevant to a person's life after the age of thirty-five or forty. And here I'm talking about using the <u>whole</u> chart, not just the 1st and 7th houses.

Martin: And?

James: I'm just not sure. My teachers didn't teach me that technique. After experimenting with it for a year or two with the charts of friends and clients, I wasn't impressed with the results enough to use it in my practice. You may want to do your own research and see what you find.

In a few minutes we're going to analyze some charts for the effects of career, health, and marriage. But first I have some lists to show you.

Martin: What kind of lists?

James: Key points to look for. But take these with a grain of salt. They're not the end all and be all. They're just pointers, helpful hints.

Martin: Okay.

KEYS TO CAREER

<u>Above all else, look at the chart as a whole.</u> — (Note points 1-5.)

1) House placement of the Moon. And the aspects thrown onto the Moon.

2) House placement of ascendant ruler. And the aspects onto the ascendant ruler.

3) Any stationary direct planet (or within one day on either side).

4) Any <u>phenomenally</u> strong planet that stands out (e.g. a planet <u>tightly</u> aspected by a benefic, a planet <u>highly</u> exalted, or a planet in its own sign that is <u>also</u> well aspected).

5) Any house that contains <u>several</u> planets, and its opposite house (because that house is aspected by all the planets opposite it).

6) Planets in 10th house.

7) House placement and condition of 10th house ruler.

8) Planetary aspects to 10th house.

9) House placement of Saturn (which I consider the main *karaka*, or indicator, of career).

10) *Dasamsa* (Career) chart (Note: I don't use planetary aspects in *vargas*).

10A) Planets in 10th house.

10B) House placement of 10th house ruler.

10C) Planets in 1st house. (Only give this about ten percent significance.)

10D) House placement of 1st house ruler. (Only give this about ten percent significance).

10E) House placement of the Moon. (Only give this about ten percent significance.)

Let me explain a few of these points. It's obvious that to find career, you have to pay close attention to the 10th house. But the 10th house is not everything, not by a long shot. When I say to look at the chart as a whole, this means that if the chart as a whole is extremely artistic, and the 10th house ruler occupies, say, the 4th house, I would not expect the person to become involved in real estate for a significant part of his or her life.

Martin: Because the artistic indications outweigh the 4th house indications?

James: That's right. The person might, at some point, get involved in the real estate business, but either it wouldn't last long, or it would happen after the person got bored with the arts.

Do you know what I mean when I say the chart as a whole is artistic?

Martin: That would occur if there are lots of planets in the 3rd house, or maybe a few planets in the 3rd house and a few in the 5th house.

James: Right. But it could also occur if the ruler of the ascendant is a few degrees away from Venus. Or, if the Moon is a few degrees away from Venus. Any indications that tell you about the person him- or herself are <u>extremely</u> important. A person with the Moon or ascendant ruler conjunct Rahu may be very interested in science. If the Moon or ascendant ruler is tightly aspected by Mercury, the person will love writing or teaching.

Intense personal aspects with Jupiter lead to law or religion; personal aspects involving Saturn may lead to carpentry; and personal aspects with Mars may lead to sports, and so on.

Art (particularly music) is also strongly indicated by a tight Venus-Mercury conjunction <u>anywhere</u> in the chart.

Martin: Even if it occupies a bad house, like the 8th or 12th?

James: Absolutely. If Venus-Mercury occupies the 12th house, look at the aspects those artistic planets throw onto the 6th house.

Martin: The house of daily work.

James: Right. And if the conjunction occupies the 8th house, it aspects the 2nd house, the house of writing and poetry. That can mean writing music.

In looking at the chart as a whole, if there is one planet that is extraordinarily powerful, the person may choose a career in the significations of that planet. If one planet is phenomenally strong, the person is extremely gifted in the realms signified by that planet. These are common sense statements I'm making. You'll figure all this out on your own with experience.

Martin: I'd rather learn now and save myself the time! I want to understand this properly. Are you saying that the house placement of the Moon and ascendant ruler and the aspects to those planets are as important as the 10th house and the 10th house ruler when you're delineating a person's career?

James: Yes. The Moon and the ascendant ruler represent the person. How can you not look at the disposition of the person in the chart? If the 10th house has one indication of medicine or healing, but there are <u>several</u> other indications powerfully suggesting one particular love, which career do you think the person will choose?

Martin: The one the person loves.

James: That's right. Most often, that's how it works. It may have been different in ancient Indian times, and it may be different in other cultures, but that's how it works in this country in this day and age.

Let's use my chart as an example of how to use the ascendant ruler and the Moon in terms of my natural interests. In my chart, the Moon occupies the 12th house.

Martin: *Moksha* (final liberation).

James: Right. The first thing an astrologer should realize is that I am interested in consciousness, spiritual matters, and remote foreign countries.

Martin: You taught meditation.

James: Yes. I spent the 1970's pursuing enlightenment, and I taught meditation. Now notice the aspect that Mercury throws onto the Moon. That indicates my love for knowledge and teaching. Do you get the point? Anything connected to the Moon is a natural and comfortable ability.

Martin: I see.

James: Now look at my ascendant ruler, Venus. It occupies the 4th house.

Martin: Real estate.

James: Yes. So there should be some interest in real estate. But here's where you have to look at the whole chart. Do you really think I'm going to be terribly interested in real estate as a career? Aside from the fact that my 4th house ruler (Sun) is the in the last degree of a sign (which greatly weakens 4th house matters), my chart as a whole is overwhelmingly spiritual and metaphysical (Moon in the 12th house, ascendant ruler conjunct Ketu and conjunct the 12th house ruler Mars). On top of that, the 10th house ruler is aspected to the degree by Jupiter, a spiritual planet that happens to rule the 8th house (metaphysics). Would I really be that interested in selling houses?

Martin: Probably not.

James: That's right. Now look at the aspects to Venus, the ascendant ruler. Aside from the spiritual aspects it receives (by being close to Ketu and the 12th house ruler), Venus is indicating a possible interest in sports because it is tightly conjunct Mars, the planet of sports. I love sports and have since I was a child. So you see how critical are the dispositions of the Moon and the ascendant ruler. You must never forget to consider their conditions when analyzing career.

Martin: So the Mars conjunction to Venus is why you wanted to become a baseball player when you were young.

James: Yes, and that interest is greatly intensified by the fact that the 10th house ruler occupies the 5th house, the house of sports. The problem there, or should I say one problem there, is that the 10th house ruler is aspected within one degree by the spiritual planet Jupiter, and sports is not a spiritual profession. Sports is not about consciousness-raising.

Martin: Are you saying that the tight Jupiter aspect onto Saturn demands that you have a spiritual career?

James: Yes, I am. If the aspect was seven or eight degrees away, it would just be one influence to consider among many others. But because the aspect is so tight, there's no way it can be ignored. It has to have a major impact on my career. Remember that you may see a chart with an intense aspect like mine where the person doesn't do the kind of profession that's indicated. But guess what? That person's going to be contacting you because he or she is suffering as a result of being in a wrong career.

Martin: I don't understand. If the aspect is so incredibly strong, why isn't the person in that career?

James: That's for you to find out. The likely reasons are that the person is scared, has no confidence, had a dysfunctional childhood with no support from parents, or something along those lines. Your job is to direct the person to his or her strongest *dharma*.

I've made you a list of house meanings in terms of career (see following page). <u>You have to know the meanings of these houses inside and out.</u> They have to be at your fingertips whenever you analyze a chart.

Look at these placements in terms of: the 10th house ruler occupying one of these houses, the ruler of these houses occupying the 10th house, or many planets occupying the house. By the way, I've underlined certain points and in a minute I'll tell you why.

Martin: So, why did you underline certain points?

James: Either because they need explaining or because they need to be remembered. I underlined "money career" because I never advise a person to pursue a career simply to make money, except under very particular circumstances. When a person says he or she is going to spend some years making money in order to pursue a real dream later on, I advise against it because the vast majority of people who try that get lost and never find their way back to their proper *dharma*. If a person is doing a career only for money reasons and there is no significant connection between the 2nd house (money) and the 10th house (career), that person will never be happy in the career.

Martin: But if the 2nd house is heavily emphasized, or connected to the 10th house, then the person can just choose <u>any</u> money making-career?

HOUSES AS THEY RELATE TO CAREER

1st) own career, physical body.

2nd) counselor, writer, teacher, analyst, psychologist, <u>money career</u>, translators, <u>consultants</u>, bankers.

3rd) arts, public relations, advertising, <u>publishing</u>, mechanical work, massage, <u>computer work.</u>

4th) real estate, farming, nurseries, cars, boats, planes.

5th) politics, sports, speculations, stock broker, giving out mantras, working with children.

6th) health, healing, hairdressers, waiters, servants.

7th) business, merchant, works with spouse.

8th) astrology, metaphysics, psychic work, CIA, research.

9th) religion, travel, higher knowledge, import/export, law.

10th) government, leadership.

11th) works with groups, money career, dancing.

12th) consciousness-raising, remote foreign countries.

James: Pretty much. If a 2nd house career is indicated, and does not have an emphasis on knowledge, communications, counseling, or writing (other 2nd house matters), I will actually tell the person, "Look for where the money is and go after it." The person's *dharma* is connected to money, and there's nothing wrong with that. But, you should do your best to get a "feel" for whether an emphasized 2nd house is indicating money matters or more literary, teaching functions. Also, be careful, because most people who go after money are chasing a dead end that will never bring fulfillment. I don't see a lot of charts where making money will be *dharmic* and bring happiness, fulfillment, and evolution.

Martin: Which is what a proper *dharma* should do?

James: Correct. I underlined "consultants" because that is becoming a bigger and bigger profession today, and it is a 2nd house signification. It's essentially a form of teaching. Many people won't become teachers because there's not enough money, or there's too much restrictiveness. But certain clients will go for becoming a consultant, if you mention that option to them.

I underlined "computer work" because it's not a typical Hindu astrology feature (because *Jyotish* is so ancient). But in my experience, computer work is seen by the planet Mars (technical work) and the 3rd house (the hands).

I underlined "publishing" because some see it through the 9th house, and some through the 3rd. I was taught that it is the 3rd house. In Western astrology, the 9th house is publishing. In Hindu astrology, I believe it's the 3rd house, because the 3rd house rules written materials, like journals, magazines, and so forth. Also, publishing is *such* an active, errand-running profession. It's easy to confuse this one because if you have a bunch of planets in the 9th house, they of course aspect the 3rd.

Martin: Which causes the 3rd house to become strong.

James: Yes. And don't forget that the 9th house signifies law and import/export. If there is a connection between the 9th and 10th houses, then the person should do something with other countries. It may be higher knowledge that comes from other countries, or it may be selling items from other countries, but it should be something with foreigners and foreign countries. And don't forget that the 8th house represents <u>any</u> kind of research, not just the metaphysical kind.

Let's look at the list I made concerning health.

Keys To Health

I. To determine strong or weak constitution, look at:

1) Planets in 1st house
2) Ruler of 1st house
3) Planets in 6th house
4) Ruler of 6th house
5) *Karakas* of 6th house — Mars and Saturn
6) *Karaka* of 1st house — Sun

II. In order to determine health vulnerabilities:

1) Any planet that is very weak or afflicted:

Sun: heart, spine, lower back, <u>eyesight</u>

Moon: stomach, breast, <u>brain</u>, menstrual cycle, <u>eyesight</u>, mental health

Mars: blood, muscles, bone marrow

Mercury: lungs, intestines, nervous system, <u>mental health</u>

Jupiter: liver, gall bladder, spleen, thighs, <u>allergies</u>

Venus: <u>skin</u>, throat, thyroid, reproductive system, ovaries, prostate, semen, glands, kidneys, venereal disease

Saturn: skin (along with Venus), arthritis, paralysis

Ketu: ulcers, cancer

2) How the houses determine parts of the body:

Note any house containing malefics, <u>especially</u> two malefics

(malefics are okay in *upachaya* houses — 3, 6, 10, 11 <u>if they are not in bad signs or badly aspected.</u>)

1st: head, face, appearance, (<u>health in general</u>)

2nd: face, mouth, tongue, eyesight (right eye), neck, throat, speech problems, imagination

3rd: lungs, nervous system (fears), hands, arms, shoulders, hearing (right ear)

4th: heart, chest

5th: stomach

6th: intestines, <u>health in general</u>

7th: veins, loins

8th: reproductive system, prostate, ovaries, uterus, venereal diseases, chronic illnesses

9th: thighs

10th: knees

11th: legs, ankles

12th: rectum, hemorrhoids, hearing (left ear), eyesight (left eye), feet.

In number one, I underlined "eyesight" for the Sun and Moon because even though the Sun and Moon rule eyesight, I haven't had great luck with these significations.

Martin: You mean they don't work?

James: I've seen very many cases where someone's Sun or Moon is heavily afflicted and they don't need glasses. It may be that for the eyes to be weak a person needs an afflicted luminary (or two afflicted luminaries) as well as a weak house governing eyesight.

Martin: What houses are those?

James: The 2nd house rules the right eye, and the 12th house rules the left eye. Anyway, I have to be honest and say I'm pretty useless at predicting eyesight problems just using the Sun and Moon, and that's why those are underlined.

Under the heading of the Moon, I underlined "brain" and "mental health" because it's easy to forget that a person with a heavily afflicted Moon could have mental instability or brain tumors. I'm not saying that you should tell every client with an afflicted Moon that he or she will have such problems. But you have to consider the possibility.

Martin: And then look at the 5th house, the house of the mind?

James: Exactly. And then look at Mercury (planet of intellect) as well. I've done too many chart readings where I've talked to someone for fifteen or twenty minutes before the person started talking and revealed some obvious level of insanity.

Martin: Insanity?

James: I don't mean clinical schizophrenia or manic depression. I mean the person doesn't have much of a grip on reality. When this happens, I feel stupid for not having realized it while analyzing the chart beforehand. It may just be my own failings, but I'm not usually looking for someone's mental condition when I analyze a chart. I'm looking to analyze money, career, love life, health, and the obvious concerns everyone has. So unless the chart jumps out at me and says "crazy," I find a person's mental condition a little to easy to miss.

I underlined "blood" (for Mars) because a lot of astrologers don't tell clients with a heavily afflicted Mars to watch out for weak blood or a lack of iron. I underlined "skin" because there are two planets ruling the skin.

Martin: Venus and Saturn.

James: That's right. I underlined "allergies" (for Jupiter) because lots of people have allergies and it's important for them to learn that the cause may be a weak liver, gall bladder, or spleen. Those are the significations of Jupiter. I underlined "health in general" for the 1st house and the 6th house because those are the most important houses in delineating a person's health. That's kind of obvious, but sometimes you can forget to scrutinize BOTH houses.

Now, let me give you a list of key points I look for when I'm analyzing a person's marriage, and then we can start looking at some birthcharts.

KEY POINTS TO LOOK FOR REGARDING MARRIAGE

1) 7th house of natal chart (planets in the 7th and planetary aspects to the 7th).

2) 7th house ruler (its house and sign placement and planetary aspects that it receives).

3) *Kujadosha* (Mars affliction harming married life). Mars occupying

the 1st, 4th, 7th, 8th, or 12th house.

4) Condition of 2nd house (happiness in family life and the tendency to argue and bicker).

5) Condition of Venus (*karaka*, or indicator, of marriage).

6) *Chandra lagna* (Moon ascendant) — Any planets opposite the Moon function exactly like planets in the 7th house.

7) *Navamsa* chart 7th house.

8) *Navamsa* chart 7th house ruler.

9) *Navamsa* chart 1st house. (Only give ten percent weight to this signification.)

Martin: I have some more questions. In numbers one and two, you mention planetary aspects to the 7th house as well as aspects to the 7th house ruler. Is one more important than the other?

James: Not really. But you have to consider the intensity of the aspects. Say, for example that Saturn aspects the 7th house. In our culture, there's almost no doubt that the person will have a divorce. If, however, the ruler of the 7th house is <u>tightly</u> aspected by a great benefic, like Venus, Jupiter, or a bright Moon <u>within one or two degrees</u>, then that positive aspect is going to be a stronger influence than the damaging one.

Martin: But that doesn't cancel out the divorce that Saturn indicates, right?

James: Right. One negative astrological feature *usually* doesn't cancel out one good one. In this case, the person would probably have a divorce or very painful relationship and then go on to have an extremely happy married life due to the tight benefic aspect onto the 7th house ruler (assuming, of course, that the benefic planet isn't throwing its aspect onto its fallen sign, and assuming it doesn't rule a terrible house like the 8th or 12th).

If the Saturn aspect onto the 7th house is being thrown onto Aries, which hates Saturnian energy (Saturn is fallen in Aries), then Saturn's negative aspect becomes much worse and isn't outweighed by the tight benefic aspect. In this case, the person might not only have a divorce, but the 2nd marriage would also have some problems as well. In other words, the marriage would be very mixed. It would be good because of the tight benefic aspect, but it wouldn't be problem-free. In *Jyotish*, you have to take <u>all</u> factors into consideration.

Martin: Okay. Now, regarding number three about *Kujadosha* (also known as *Manglik* or *Mangaldosha*), you once said that you don't find the exceptions to apply, is that right?

James: Right. The textbooks state that Mars doesn't cause marriage problems in the following houses and signs: 1st house in Aries, 4th house in Scorpio, 7th house in Capricorn or Pisces, 8th house in Cancer, and 12th house in Sagittarius. But these exceptions don't work for the overwhelming majority of cases I've seen. And, I've seen a lot! They probably work fine in cultures where divorce is a major taboo, but they certainly don't work for Americans.

Any other questions?

Martin: Regarding number six, *Chandra lagna*, do you really mean to say that a planet in the 7th house from the Moon functions *exactly* like a planet in the 7th house?

James: Yes, and you can take that technique to the bank. It works nearly one-hundred percent of the time. Of course, you should note the degrees involved in the same way you note the degrees involved in a planet in the natal 7th house.

Martin: What do you mean?

James: If a person has an early ascendant, say around three degrees of Virgo, and Saturn occupies the 7th house in a very late degree, say twenty-seven degrees, there will certainly be marriage problems. But if Saturn in this person's chart occupies two or three degrees of Pisces, or seven or eight degrees of Pisces, the problems will be far more intense and painful.

Martin: So, in the case of *Chandra lagna,* if the Moon is twenty-four degrees Libra and Jupiter is twenty-six degrees Aries, the benefits are extremely strong?

James: That's right. In that case, you have to predict some very good marital effects and a Jupitarian type of spouse.

Let's look at several charts in terms of career, health, and marriage. We'll begin with the chart of a friend named Henry (see following page).

He's an actor.

Martin: Moon in the 3rd house.

James: Yes, the all-important Moon occupies the house of music, dance, and drama, and is well-aspected by benefic Jupiter. Also, the 3rd house ruler (Mercury) is exalted.

Martin: But it's combust the Sun and aspected by Saturn. Isn't that bad?

James: It is bad. I would prefer that Mercury not be aspected by malefics. But look at the Sun combusting Mercury. Notice that the Sun rules the 5th house, the other house of art (5th house rules painting and crafts and art in general).

Martin: You're saying that the 5th house is strong because its ruler is conjunct Mercury, which is a benefic?

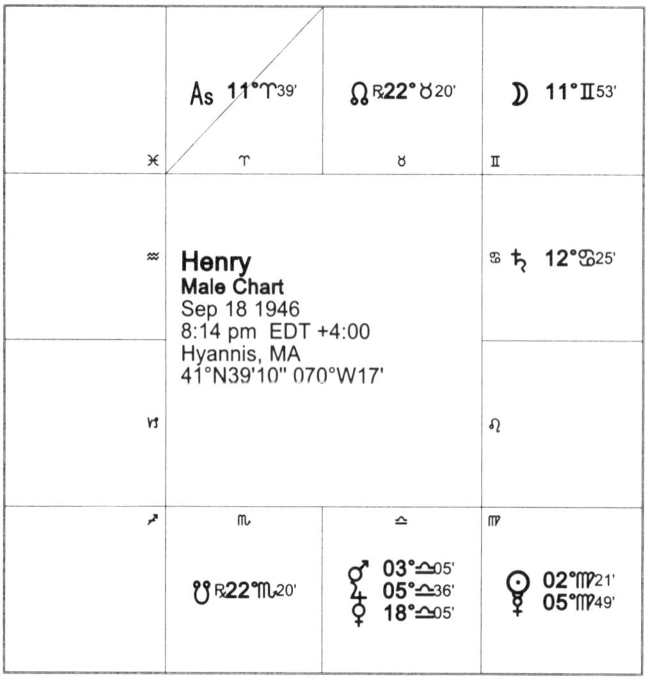

```
┌─────────────┬─────────────┬─────────────┬─────────────┐
│             │ As 11°♈39'  │ ☊ ℞22°♉20'  │ ☽ 11°♊53'   │
│         ╲   │             │             │             │
│    ♓    ╲  │      ♈      │      ♉      │      ♊      │
├─────────────┼─────────────┴─────────────┼─────────────┤
│             │                           │             │
│     ♒       │   Henry                   │ ♋ ♄ 12°♋25' │
│             │   Male Chart              │             │
│             │   Sep 18 1946             │             │
│             │   8:14 pm EDT +4:00       │             │
│             │   Hyannis, MA             │             │
│             │   41°N39'10" 070°W17'     │             │
├─────────────┤                           ├─────────────┤
│     ♑       │                           │     ♌       │
├─────────────┼─────────────┬─────────────┼─────────────┤
│     ♐       │             │             │             │
│             │             │     ♎       │     ♍       │
│             │     ♏       │ ♂ 03°♎05'   │ ☉ 02°♍21'   │
│ ☋ ℞22°♏20'  │             │ ♃ 05°♎36'   │ ☿ 05°♍49'   │
│             │             │ 18°♎05'     │             │
└─────────────┴─────────────┴─────────────┴─────────────┘
```

South Indian Style

For North Indian, see Appendix B.

planets.pts			
Pt	Name	Hs	Rules
☽	Moon	3	4
☉	Sun	6	5
☿	Mercury	6	3, 6
♀	Venus	7	2, 7
♂	Mars	7	1, 8
♃	Jupiter	7	9, 12
♄	Saturn	4	10, 11
☊	North Node	2	-
☋	South Node	8	-
As	Ascendant	1	-

Sg	Name
♈	Aries
♉	Taurus
♊	Gemini
♋	Cancer
♌	Leo
♍	Virgo
♎	Libra
♏	Scorpio
♐	Sagittarius
♑	Capricorn
♒	Aquarius
♓	Pisces

James: Yes, but it's not just conjunct a benefic. It's <u>tightly</u> conjunct <u>exalted</u> Mercury. So now the 3rd house and the 5th house are both prominent. Also notice that Venus, the planet of art, is in its own sign, Libra, and is angular. On top of that, Venus is in a house with a *rajayoga* (for Aries ascendant the Jupiter-Mars conjunction forms a royal union). Being aspected by such good house rulers (Jupiter rules the 9th house, Mars rules the 1st house) strengthens Venus. There are a lot of features for art, and they're going to get even stronger when we analyze his *dasamsa* chart in a few minutes.

Remember when I said you have to look at the chart as whole whenever you are analyzing career? Look at Henry's 1st house. Can you see how strong it is? A 1st house like this gives a very big ego and strong tendency to be recognized. This translates into the fact that he craves recognition. What profession in our culture gets the most recognition?

Martin: Celebrity actors.

James: That's right. What makes Henry's ascendant so strong is the fact that Mars aspects its own sign, Aries. On top of that, the *rajayoga* planets Mars and Jupiter aspect the 1st house. That's similar to having a *rajayoga* in the 1st house. On top of that, the ascendant ruler Mars is *tightly* conjunct with the great benefic planet Jupiter, which happens to be the *yogakaraka*, the best planet for Aries ascendant. So there is a great need for, and likelihood of, recognition in this horoscope. That often points to acting, when the chart as a whole is artistic.

Martin: Then this is a classic chart for an actor?

James: Yes. Remember what I said about career in Class Six, when I was going over the different meanings of houses? I said that in this day and age, you have to look for many different careers for people to see which is the best, most natural fit. Also, you have to find more than one career because so many people get bored with their careers after ten or twenty years. Let's look at what else Henry might do.

Martin: How about real estate? The ruler of the 10th house occupies the 4TH house.

James: Excellent observation. He has sold real estate. But based on his horoscope, would he be happy doing that?

Martin: Maybe not, because Saturn is in Cancer, the sign opposite its own sign.

James: That's right. Saturn is not well-placed.

Martin: Was he successful selling real estate?

James: Yes. Notice that Saturn, the planet of real estate aspects the 10th house and the aspect is being thrown onto Saturn's own sign, Capricorn. That's good for a Saturnian type career. And Mars, the other planet of real estate (sometimes called "landed property" by the Hindus), is involved in a tight *rajayoga* with Jupiter.

Martin: James, this brings up a point that's been bothering me a lot. The ruler of the 10th house (Saturn) is afflicted by being in a bad sign, so that means career problems. But then the 10th house benefits because it's aspected by its own ruler. What's the deal? Is this good or bad?

I saw a chart the other day that had the ruler of the 2nd house occupying the 8th house and the same kind of problem came up. When I looked up the meaning of 2nd house ruler occupying the 8th house in your textbook, you gave all these terrible results. But then I realized that every time the ruler of the 2nd house occupies the 8th house, which is obviously bad (because the 8th house is a *dusthana*, or grief-producing house), that planet will be aspecting its own sign in the 2nd house (Note: this occurs because in Hindu astrology all planets aspect their opposite signs). How the heck does this work?

James: You know, Martin, there comes a point when you have to think for yourself. When you have to start taking responsibility for what I'm teaching you. The whole point of these lessons is for me to teach you the reasoning process of *Jyotish*. I don't mind answering any question you ask me, if I can possibly help. But your question bothers me because of the way you're asking it. You're asking as if I have a final proclamation that I can reveal to you, and I keep telling you astrology doesn't work that way. It never has, and it never will. There will always be many different opinions, many different methods, and many different viewpoints.

By the way that you asked the question, you revealed that you have everything you need to answer it yourself. You said that the if the ruler of the 2nd house was in the 8th, it was bad, and you said that if the ruler of the 2nd house is in the 8th, it aspects the 2nd house, which is good. So, what must the answer to your question be?

Martin: The 2nd house is "mixed"?

James: Exactly. The point here is that you've already demonstrated that you're capable of analyzing horoscopes. I've seen you look at people's charts and be quite accurate. Now you've got to start thinking on your own. It startles me that you are confused because of what you read in a book. I think my books are wonderful, but they are just books! You have to get this point and you have to get it now: astrology books can only take you so far. Astrology isn't math or engineering. And because it's not a hard science, books can only function as a GUIDE. Nothing more. I'm harping on this because you're doing exactly what almost every astrology student I've ever met does. At some point, you have to realize the limitations of books and teachers, and let go of them.

Martin: And that time is now?

James: Yes. I know it's hard for you to be objective about when your time comes. But you should try to be mindful about asking questions that you have all the resources to answer yourself.

Martin: Got it.

James: When you look at this horoscope as a whole, what else strikes you as a possible career? I'll give you a hint. What house in the chart is obviously incredibly strong?

Martin: Well, the 7th house holds a *rajayoga* as well as a planet in its own sign (Venus). The 7th house is the marriage partner. It's also the house of business. Could he be a merchant?

James: Yes. Because it's so hard to make a living in the theatre, he has opened up a business where he sells yard goods to theatre companies. He makes a lot of money at it.

Now let's look at Henry's *dasamsa* chart for career (see following page). First of all, let's get in the habit of noting everything we need to check when using *varga* charts. First, let's look at his birthtime (which came from a birth certificate) to see whether we think anybody cared about writing down an accurate time.

Martin: He was born at 8:14 P.M.

James: Right. That means the time wasn't approximated. It doesn't necessarily mean the time that's written down is accurate, but it helps to know someone cared a little.

As I taught you earlier, the *dasamsa* changes by virtue of every three degrees (3°, 6°, 9°, 12°, etc.) in the <u>natal</u> ascendant, and Henry's natal ascendant was eleven degrees, thirty-nine minutes. So, how many minutes does it take to go back all the way to a nine degree ascendant?

Martin: About two degrees and thirty-nine minutes of arc (actually, two degrees and <u>forty</u> minutes of arc are needed in order to effect the changeover) or about seven or nine minutes of birthtime. (Note: Aries is one of the faster moving ascendants.)

James: That's right. And that kind of birthtime error is not very likely in this case, where the birthtime was obviously not approximated. So we don't have to worry much that his *dasamsa* Cancer ascendant will be thrown back to Gemini. Now, what would it take for the ascendant to move *forward* to Leo?

Martin: About half a degree. Therefore, the birthtime would have to have been about two minutes later than what was recorded.

James: Good. And how likely is that?

Martin: Not very. Because most people are born earlier than what is recorded. And we know almost for sure the time is not an approximation, since it doesn't say 8:15 or 8:30 or 9.

James: That's right. It's possible that the clocks were off, but it's also quite likely that he was born a bit <u>before</u> the clock said 8:14, because the nurse probably didn't look at the clock the instant he was born. She probably looked at the baby for a few minutes first to see how he was doing, if he was breathing or had any problems.

In looking at the 10th house of the *dasamsa*, we see Venus in the 10th house and the ruler of the 10th house in the 5th. What does that tell you?

Martin: The arts are indicated.

James: That's exactly right. He already has an artistic natal horoscope.

Once you see Venus in the career house (10th) in the *dasamsa*, you have more corroboration for an artistic career. Aside from art *in general* (as opposed to the 3rd house, which specifically governs music, dance, and drama), the 5th house indicates children, investments, spiritual techniques, and so on. But we're not going to go in that direction because everywhere we look we keep seeing art. That's how it works. The only thing Henry ever passionately wanted to be was an actor.

Martin: Because so many features indicate art?

James: Yes. His horoscope is rare in terms of what I usually see. It may be that a disproportionate amount of people come to astrologers for career counseling, which is why I see so many charts with lots of career choices. Henry's life is like an arrow to the target, in terms of an artistic career.

Martin: What about his 1st house in the *dasamsa*?

James: Before we even look at that, let me repeat that I only weight the 1st house at about ten percent of all the astrological factors. And at this point, whatever the 1st house tells me won't make much difference, because both charts already strongly reveal an artistic career.

The 1st house holds Saturn. Saturn rules the 7th house, so this is another indication of the likelihood of a business, or merchant-related, career.

Saturn rules real estate, which is also indicated as a possible career in the natal chart. Real estate is therefore indicated fairly strongly. This is because on top of the real estate indications we've already noted, the 10th house Venus in this *dasamsa* is ruling the 4th house (house of real estate). So even if he was involved in theatre his entire life, he would still have an interest in real estate.

By the way, I also give the Moon in the *dasamsa* some weight (not too much, but some) on two accounts. First, the Moon is always important; and second, it happens to rule the ascendant.

Martin: The Moon in the *dasamsa* is in the 3rd house.

James: That's another indication for an artistic career.

Martin: James, what about a career in healing? Aren't there strong indications for healing in Henry's natal chart (see page 272)?

James: At first glance, it looks that way. First, you see that exalted Mercury occupies the 6th house; then you see the Sun, which is the *atmakaraka*, or indicator of the soul, in the house of healing. But you also have to notice that the 6th house ruler (Mercury), is aspected pretty tightly by two malefics — Sun and Saturn. If, and this a big "if," the chart wasn't so well disposed for art, then Henry probably would have thought about healing.

Martin: Or writing.

James: Yes, Mercury in the 6th house is a great placement for a writer or teacher. But the contrast between the all-important Moon in the 3rd house (art) <u>aspected within about six degrees by benefic Jupiter</u>, as well as Venus in the 10th house of the *dasamsa*, versus a very mixed Mercury in the 6th house, makes it pretty obvious that the arts would take precedence over a healing career.

If this chart didn't have the well aspected Moon in the 3rd house, and if this chart didn't have a wonderfully strong 7th house (strong for business, mixed for marriage), then you would be correct in advising Henry to think about healing. You see?

Now let's look at this chart for physical health. Notice that the ascendant ruler, Mars, is tightly conjunct benefic Jupiter and involved in a *rajayoga*. Also notice that Mars aspects its own sign, Aries. Then notice that the *rajayoga* planets, Mars and Jupiter, aspect the 1st house, as does benefic Venus. This is one tremendous 1st house, which means Henry has a spectacular constitution.

Martin: And because Mars is so well-aspected, it gives strong blood.

James: That's right. It's a tremendous health benefit to have strong blood.

Martin: James, you said in another class that Venus aspecting Aries isn't so good because Venus is aspecting the sign opposite its ownership sign. Is the Venus aspect bad?

James: No. It's just not as good as it would have been if it were aspecting some other sign. A Venus aspect may sometimes cause trouble if it aspects Virgo, the sign that hates Venusian energy (Venus' fallen sign). But that aspect can go either way. Sometimes it's an okay aspect and sometimes it's harmful. All other Venus aspects I consider good, unless Venus rules the 8th or 12th house and the aspect is incredibly tight by degree (two, three, or four degrees).

Regarding the 6th house, that house definitely has some problems. It's good that the malefic Sun occupies the 6th house, because malefics are good in the 6th. But the 6th house ruler, Mercury, being combust and aspected by Saturn, poses serious problems to Mercury.

Martin: Does he have problems with the lungs, intestines, or nervous system?

James: Actually, his health is quite strong, but many years ago he contracted Bell's palsey, which caused paralysis of one side of his face. The disease was related to the nervous system, since many of the nerves in his face atrophied.

Martin: Would you have predicted such a serious problem with the nervous system in this case, where Mercury is damaged, but also exalted?

James: No. I would have mentioned the possibility of minor problems with lungs, intestines, and the nervous system, but that's all. I believe the Bell's Palsey illness is largely related to *Kala Sarpa Yoga* in this chart (all the planets sitting on one side of the Moon's nodes). But, before I discuss *Kala Sarpa Yoga*, I want to mention the other natal weakness, health-wise. Notice that Jupiter is extremely close to malefic Mars. This means that Jupiter has some affliction, and that can harm the liver, gall bladder, or spleen.

Martin: Even though Jupiter and Mars form a *rajayoga*, Jupiter can be harmed by Mars?

James: Definitely. I know that some astrologers have contrary opinions about this matter, but I've seen planets involved in a royal union become extremely damaged when the conjunction is tight, and one of the planets is a malefic. I've seen it happen time and time again.

Martin: Does he have liver problems or allergies?

James: No, he doesn't. But I still consider the liver, gall bladder, and spleen area to be afflicted. This means that when he's old and he has to die of something, these organs are prime candidates. His father, by the way, died of pancreatic cancer, which spread to the liver. So the genetics indicate a likelihood of weakness in the same area. Also, now that I think of it, Henry had Yellow Jaundice as a baby. That's a liver affliction.

Martin: Tell me about *Kala Sarpa Yoga*.

James: *Kala Sarpa Yoga* exists whenever all the planets are on one side of Rahu and Ketu. In Henry's case, the nodes occupy the 2nd and 8th house axis, and all the other planets are in houses three through seven.

I don't consider the placements of Uranus, Neptune, or Pluto, when checking for *Kala Sarpa*. I mention this because even though I don't use the outer planets in Hindu horoscopes, I couldn't just ignore them every time I saw a *Kala Sarpa* chart. Whether the ancients used the outer planets or not, they exist in the sky today, so I had to look at them in my beginning days to see if they had an impact on *Jyotish* charts in terms of this yoga.

Martin: Do they?

James: No. *Kala Sarpa Yoga* will still be in effect and still cause problems even if one or more of the outer planets escapes the bundle of planets on one side of Rahu and Ketu. That's been my experience.

The technical explanation for *Kala Sarpa Yoga* is that a person who has the condition may have killed a pregnant snake in a past life. This can be taken literally or symbolically. I always take it symbolically. A snake represents coiled up energy. A *pregnant* snake indicates even greater potential energy. To me, this condition means that the person wasted a tremendous amount of energy in a past life and now pays the price for that abuse. When I say "wasted energy," what I mean is having great talent and not using it, committing suicide, or something like that. When you explain *Kala Sarpa* to clients who have it in their charts, watch how many tell you they had a past life regression that revealed suicide in a past life. It's pretty uncanny.

Martin: So what are the effects of having it in the chart?

James: I find that a large proportion of these people (not all of course but a lot of them) have some physical problem or disability. Second, the person experiences tremendous ups and downs in life. The person can go way up to the top of success and way down to the bottom. I'll give you a list of some famous people with *Kala Sarpa:* Paul McCartney, Donald Trump, Margaret Thatcher, Indira Gandhi, and Johnny Carson.

Martin: So, it doesn't ruin a person's life. These people are extremely successful.

James: That's right. And when I explain the meaning of *Kala Sarpa* to clients with the condition, I always mention these famous people. This lets them know that they shouldn't be too scared of it, even though it is clearly an undesirable yoga.

The other intense effect of *Kala Sarpa* is that a person who has it usually experiences one area of life over which they have absolutely no control. Be very careful with this statement. Everyone has areas of life over which they have no control, right?

Martin: Of course.

James: What you're looking for with *Kala Sarpa* is an <u>extreme karmic condition</u> under which the person is helpless.

Martin: Is there any way to know where that area will be?

James: Sometimes. Not always, but sometimes it will be indicated by the house position of <u>either</u> Rahu or Ketu. For example, in Henry's case the *Kala Sarpa* occurs in the 2nd and 8th houses and his problem involves paralysis of the face.

Martin: 2nd House!

James: That's right. I've seen a lot of cases where the *Kala Sarpa* nodal placements occur in the 1st and 7th houses, and the person has an exceptionally weird or difficult history in love relationships.

Martin: 7th house.

James: Yes. I consider *Kala Sarpa Yoga* to be one of the most karmic of all astrological yogas. It always seems to render one or two areas of life uncontrollable. If you use this phrase "uncontrollable area of life" to your clients with *Kala Sarpa*, they'll fill you in on the details. And remember to check the significations of the houses that Rahu and Ketu occupy, because those are the likely realms to be affected.

Regarding Henry's health, the only other realm to be noticed is the peace of mind. Whenever he comes to a Mercury period or subperiod, his peace of mind can be disturbed. Generally speaking, however, if it weren't for his mixed 6th house ruler, Mercury, and his *Kala Sarpa Yoga*, which is kind of a "wild card" influence, we would have to say that his health is quite strong.

Now let's look at how love matters fare in Henry's natal chart and *navamsa*. First, look at the *navamsa* and tell me how likely is it that his *navamsa* is accurate (see following page).

Martin: Okay. The *navamsa* changes every three degrees, twenty minutes of the natal ascendant, so we memorize 3°20', 6°40', 10°, 13°20', 16°40', and so on. His natal ascendant is eleven degrees, thirty nine minutes, which is in the middle of ten degrees and thirteen degrees, twenty minutes.

James: Which is good.

Martin: Yes, because the ascendant would have to have backed up about a degree and a half to throw his *navamsa* Cancer ascendant back to Gemini. And that would have taken about five or six minutes, since his natal ascendant is Aries, which is one of the four fast moving ascendants (it moves about one degree every three or four minutes).

James: That's correct. And the birthtime would have to have been about six or seven minutes later than what was recorded in order to throw the *navamsa* ascendant forward to Leo. That's because his ascendant degree is nearly two degrees away from the next changeover (thirteen degrees, twenty minutes). Two degrees, for a fast moving ascendant, takes six or eight minutes. We have to be somewhat careful in using his *navamsa* chart, but we feel more confident than usual because his birthtime is obviously not an approximation.

In case you haven't noticed, analyzing Henry's marriage karma from his natal chart is rather complex.

Martin: The 7th house is very mixed.

James: Yes. It's a mixture of extremes. There are some excellent features and some terrible features. Always remember what I told you about mixed karma regarding marriage in a horoscope. The person must have some major bad karma in his or her love life first, and then some very strong happiness in marriage later. That's how it works.

The negative aspects of marriage relate to the fact that *Kujadoshsa* exists in this chart and to the fact that Mars in the 7th house is simply a rough placement for married life. I don't care about the fact that Mars is well aspected or involved in a *rajayoga*. Mars or any other malefic planets in the 7th house will always create a significant amount of suffering in relationships.

Martin: But he would eventually have to have a happy married life because of Venus in its own sign (Libra) in the 7th house and because of the *rajayoga* in the 7th, wouldn't he?

James: Absolutely. And that's exactly what happened. He has been happily married for over twenty years. But he had some very rough relationships before he got married in his late twenties.

Now let's look at his *navamsa*, and see what that indicates. One thing to

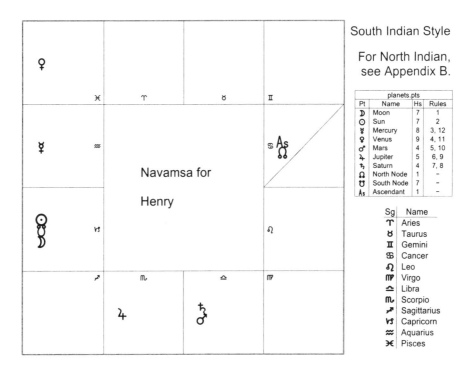

realize is that his natal chart is giving so much specific information about marriage, that the *navamsa* would have to be very unique to have a big impact.

Martin: How so?

James: If, for example, Saturn or Mars occupied the 7th house of the *navamsa*, then I would give it a lot of weight.

Martin: Why?

James: Because in my experience, those are is the most negative planetary placements for a 7th house in the natal or *navamsa* chart. And they would cause serious trouble. Another *navamsa* condition I would be concerned about with anyone who has a fairly good natal chart for marriage would be a fallen planet in the *navamsa* 7th, or a fallen 7th house ruler in the *navamsa*. These would wreak havoc.

Martin: If Mercury was in Pisces in the 7th house of the *navamsa*, that would be really serious?

James: Darn right. Or if Venus was in Virgo, Mars in Cancer, or Sun in Libra, in the *navamsa* 7th house, there would be very big problems.

In Henry's *navamsa* 7th house, he has Sun, Moon, and Ketu. The fact that the lights (Sun and Moon), the most personal influences in a chart, are in the 7th means that Henry will be extremely <u>close</u> to the marriage partner. The bond of his union will be extraordinary. This is intensified by the fact that the Moon also happens to be the *navamsa* ascendant ruler.

Martin: Would the Sun in the 7th make the spouse bossy or very strong-willed?

James: Sure. And Ketu in the 7th means a certain amount of ups and downs will occur in married life. But I wouldn't give too much weight to any of these features because the natal chart already has so many specific indications that have to be realized. As I said, I would only make a big deal out of Henry's *navamsa* if it revealed some really <u>intense</u> conditions.

Martin: What about the ruler of the 7th in Henry's *navamsa*?

James: Saturn rules the 7th and is exalted in the 4th, which means the spouse may own some land or have some interest in real estate (in fact she does). Saturn is also in the same house with Mars. As I said earlier, I definitely don't use most aspects in the *varga* charts but I do take notice of conjunctions. Sometimes I find that conjunctions in divisional charts work quite well, and sometimes they don't.

Martin: How would you judge the Mars conjunction to Saturn?

James: In this case, I'm not so interested in the *navamsa* for reasons already mentioned. However, if Henry's natal chart indicated lots of marriage problems, then I might ask him questions to determine whether the Mars conjunction to Saturn is causing problems. I would ask whether there is a lot of friction, tension, fighting, and so on. That's how I would find out if the Mars conjunction to his 7th house ruler, Saturn, was active.

Any more questions before we move on?

Martin: Well, I just want to say that if I was looking at Henry's *natal* chart without you, I would really be impressed with the 7th house. It's possible that I would have favored a business career for him, rather than the arts. I mean, look at the *rajayoga* in the 7th, and the 7th house ruler (Venus) in its own sign in the 7th, and the fact that the ascendant ruler is in the 7th. Also, the 7th house jumped out at me when I saw this chart because there are three planets in the house.

James: Well, I would have thought the same thing at first glance. But remember that to find a person's career, the most important thing is to look at the <u>whole chart</u>. Henry has an immensely powerful 1st house. This is someone who wants recognition, who is destined to get recognition! Always look at the chart to see where a person's happiness comes from. Notice that the Moon is in the house of the arts, <u>and receives a fairly strong aspect from Jupiter</u>. Aside from the fact that this indication points to art, you have to ask yourself, "How would this man get fame and recognition and happiness from business?" All he would get from business is money and that definitely wouldn't fulfill the indications of this monster ascendant. The people who actually <u>love</u> business, who love interacting with people are the ones with the Sun, Moon, and/or ascendant ruler in the 7th house. I know that Henry has the ascendant ruler (Mars) in the 7th, and the *rajayoga,* and he is an excellent businessman; but look at the happiness that comes through the arts. In this culture, people want to be happy.

Martin: If he was from India, he would have been a businessman.

James: That's right. And in many other cultures, he would have favored business over the arts. But he is American.

Actually, I'm glad we used this chart because it shows you how significant the *dasamsa* chart can be. The *dasamsa* has art written all over it. The ascendant ruler Moon occupies the 3rd house, Venus occupies the 10th house, and the 10th house ruler (Mars) occupies the 5th house (art in general). This is a case where the *dasamsa* chart puts you over the top in predicting art as a more essential profession than business. At least that's how I see it.

Martin: Maybe he would have been an artist even if he was from another culture.

James: If he was from one of those cultures that is overly concerned with money or where the arts is frowned upon, he would probably do business and become wealthy, but he would be somewhat unhappy about never pursuing art. I say "somewhat" unhappy because his 7th house is so strong and well-disposed that it does bring a certain amount of happiness. But if he did pursue business, it would likely involve the arts or beautiful objects.

Martin: Because of the artistic indications of the *dasamsa*?

James: Yes. And in fact, after Henry left acting due to his paralysis, he opened up a business selling cloth goods to <u>theatre</u> companies. So his business is in the arts. Personally, I was surprised that he didn't become a director or writer. When I asked him about that, he said the only thing he ever wanted to do was act.

Martin: The well-aspected Moon in the 3rd house.

James: Yes, but also the incredibly strong 1st house. I know that directors can get lots of recognition, but it's a different kind of recognition. I was an actor for some years and I've also directed a few times. I know the ego thrill that only acting can bring.

Let's take another person and look at career, health, and marriage (see next page). This is a friend named John who died a few years ago. This is a great example because it forces us to look at the entire chart and not rely so heavily on 10th house indications. This is because the horoscope reveals intense career problems. Whenever there are serious career difficulties, analyzing the chart as a whole is critical.

Martin: The 10th house ruler (Venus) is fallen.

James: That's right. On top of that, notice that the 10th house ruler (Moon) in the *dasamsa* (see page 286) is fallen. Clearly, John must have generated very negative career energy in past lives to have such 10th house afflictions in this life.

In order to use this *dasamsa*, his chart would have to be accurate within about four minutes on the earlier side and about eleven minutes on the later side. The birthtime is not *terribly* specific. 5:35 could be an approximation, but at least it's not 5:30. Whenever birthtimes are exactly on the half hour, I become extremely wary. Having known John for so many years, I am convinced his *dasamsa* is accurate. When I tell you the weird, extremely karmic problems he has had in his career during his entire life, you'll see why I'm convinced.

But, for the sake of learning about divisional charts, let's say that I didn't know John and that he came to me as a client.

Martin: Yes, what do you do when the chart has a margin of error of four minutes?

James: First, let me say that I only concern myself with a four minute error if it means the person might have been born four minutes earlier. As I've said over and over, most people are born a few minutes earlier than the birth certificate says (Note: if the birthtime comes from a person's mother or a baby book, the time is often an approximation and could be easily be wrong on the earlier *or* later side.)

In John's case, if the birthtime is correct, he's going to have very serious career problems and karmic losses in career because the *dasamsa* chart simply echoes the natal chart's fallen 10th house ruler effects. Therefore, I would first ask him just how bad his career problems have been. If he says they have been upsetting, but not extremely significant, then I would begin to doubt the *dasamsa*. If, however, he tells me all kinds of career horror stories that are neverending, then I know both the natal chart and the *dasamsa* chart have fallen 10th house rulers.

But if a divisional chart is sensitive to birthtime error by four minutes

2nd house. The 2nd house is writing. As soon as I think of writing as a possibility, I look at the condition of Mercury — the planet of writing. Mercury is prominent and well-disposed because it is in the 1st house and <u>tightly</u> conjunct benefic Jupiter. So John is naturally gifted in writing and teaching.

Martin: What about Venus as the 10th house ruler being conjunct with Mars? What does that mean?

James: This is a tight conjunction, so it is <u>very</u> important. Mars rules the military and it rules technical or mechanical work. John spent some years in the army, but I don't know if he enlisted. He was sent overseas and was lucky enough to be the only person in his group that was spared battle. (Note Jupiter in the 1st house, which is an extremely lucky and protective influence.) Anyway, he had no desire to make a career of the military.

Regarding technical fields, Mars relates to law, drafting, and engineering. So those careers have to be considered and they have to be considered *in light of the fact that the chart reveals intense career problems*. I say this because one of the results of having a fallen 10th house ruler, not to mention the same condition in the career chart, is career confusion. People who have *serious* career confusion do not usually spend four or five years learning a difficult, highly demanding trade. If they do, it's very likely they will have trouble succeeding because of such intense career afflictions. For that reason, I would not predict law or engineering as one of John's choices.

Martin: Is he capable of doing technical or mechanical careers?

James: If you mean, "does he have the talent for such careers?" the answer is yes. If you mean, "will he ever do those careers successfully for any length of time," the answer is no, not very likely. The chart is simply too afflicted for him to have a successful career like the ones I've mentioned. They confer too much status for a person with such 10th house damage.

If he was willing to chant astrological mantras for his fallen Venus, the 10th house ruler in the natal chart, or if he was willing to have *yagyas* performed for some years for Venus, then he would have had a chance of enjoying career success in any number of fields. Aside from the 10th house problems, his natal chart reveals tremendous talent. But without God's grace, this chart most likely indicates career problems for a whole lifetime. Remember, I'm saying this because <u>both</u> the natal and career charts indicate career problems. I wouldn't tell every client who has a fallen 10th house ruler in the natal chart that they will suffer in the career for an entire life.

Martin: But such a person would suffer?

James: Of course. That person would certainly experience career problems, but the problems *might* not be *so* intense that career success was always out of reach. Assuming that the fallen planet wasn't placed very close to the worst <u>degree</u> of fall and assuming that rest of the horoscope was decent and the person was willing to work hard, he or she would probably have some career happiness along with some career problems. You always have to look at the whole horoscope to get an accurate picture.

In John's case, the natal chart indicates extreme talent and the chart is powerful and lucky in many ways. But having <u>both</u> charts indicate career problems is just too intense to overcome without some very serious intervention (mantras and *yagyas*).

Look at the extreme creativity indicated in John's natal chart and look at how well disposed the ascendant is. The ascendant is the most important house in the chart. It's the essence or nucleus of the chart. This is a wonderful horoscope that is seriously damaged by the many 10th house problems already mentioned.

John had a great appearance and was very well-respected. Notice the Sun in its own sign (Leo) in the 1st house. Notice the two benefics, Jupiter and Mercury, in the 1st house, and remember that Jupiter rules the 5th house, the house of *poorvapunya* (past life credit). I don't see many ascendants as good as John's, even though Saturn aspects his ascendant.

Martin: What about his creativity?

James: My favorite choice of career with a chart like this is writing. Aside from the fact that the 10th house (career) ruler occupies the 2nd house (educating and writing) in <u>both</u> the natal and career charts, there are several other literary aspects going on. Mercury in the 1st house makes a person extremely communicative.

Martin: Wait, James. Are you saying that even though the 10th house rulers in both charts are fallen in the 2nd house, a literary or educational career is indicated? Doesn't the fact that these planets are fallen hurt the 2nd house significations?

James: Here's where astrology requires a computer mind and years of experience. Here's where you have to ignore textbook descriptions of fallen planets in houses. Having a fallen 10th house ruler in the 2nd house will certainly damage both the 10th and 2nd house. But there is still a connection between the 2nd house and the 10th and that connection is significantly intensified because it happens <u>twice</u> — in the natal chart and the *dasamsa*.

On top of that, Mercury occupies the 1st house, which is a great placement for communicators, and Mercury happens to rule the 2nd house — the house of writing.

Martin: The ruler of the 2nd house in the 1st. That's a typical placement of writers and teachers.

James: Exactly. As if all that weren't enough, there's the <u>tight</u> Mercury-Jupiter conjunction, which expands the Mercurial nature tremendously. So writing is a very obvious choice for John.

Martin: You keep mentioning writing. But if the 2nd house is education as well as writing, why not predict that he would be a teacher?

James: Teaching is a definite possibility in John's case, but it would never be my first choice. This chart is simply too creative and artistic for teaching to outweigh writing.

Martin: You're saying that writing is a more creative endeavor than teaching.

James: It's more artistic and creative. If a chart is highly artistic and indicates communications, then I expect the person to be a writer. I'm not talking about writing technical books or science manuals! I'm talking about writing novels or plays or movies.

Martin: Why is John so artistic when Venus is fallen and it rules the 3rd house? Both the 3rd house and Venus rule art!

James: Again, this is where experience comes in. In the first few years of my practice, I probably would not have predicted art for a person with a chart like this. But after so many years of practice it would take all of about ten seconds to realize that John would have talent and interest in art.

Martin: First of all, why? Second, what kind of art?

James: You have to look at everything in a chart before you draw any conclusions. You have to be able to isolate every single astrological signification and you also have to look at the chart as a whole. It's true that Venus and the 3rd house are afflicted, but this chart *screams* creativity. Look at the 5th house, the house of art *in general*. The 5th house ruler occupies the 1st house, making him artistic. The 5th house ruler Jupiter is conjunct Mercury, which is a benefic by nature and is the planet of intelligence and self-expression. On top of this, Jupiter aspects the 5th house, which it happens to rule (i.e. Jupiter aspecting its own sign, Sagittarius). These are all positive indications for an artist. Even the Venus-Mars conjunction involving fallen Venus is good for art.

Martin: Why?

James: People with Venus-Mars conjunctions are passionate. They are expressive about beauty, romance, and art. Remember that when you analyze charts, a very intense planetary aspect can be just as important as the disposition of a horoscope house. As soon as I see a tight Mercury-Jupiter conjunction, I know the person is going to have intense creative abilities. The Venus-Mars conjunction is yet another artistic indication.

Aside from art and literary functions, the only feature in John's entire horoscope that is prominent is spiritual interest.

Martin: Because of the Moon in Cancer (the Moon's own sign) in the 12th house.

James: That's right. The all-important Moon in the house of *moksha* (enlightenment). Now, want to hear about John's career? He was an actor, a writer, and he painted. Most of his career years were spent in Hollywood, and most of the money he made came from writing. He was definitely talented, but he was never extremely successful.

Once, after submitting a few chapters of a novel to a publishing company, he was given a hefty advance to finish the project. He spent a year on it and when he was on the very last chapter, the manuscript was stolen by thieves who broke into the wrong hotel room (they were looking for drugs or something) and took his briefcase.

Martin: He was on the last chapter?

James: Yes, and this was before the age of computers. I'm not sure how common copying machines were at the time, but he hadn't made an extra copy of his work. He was so demoralized that he quit and went to Hollywood.

Before he went to Hollywood, he sent a screenplay to a friend who was working temporarily at a movie studio to show to the executives. They were interested, but this so-called friend never relayed the message, and John found out many years later (after the executives were long gone) that they liked his work and wanted to see him.

Martin: That's terrible.

James: For John, it was typical. These things happened all the time to him. In his younger years, he was an actor who studied at the Neighborhood Playhouse, a famous acting studio in New York run by Sandy Meisner. According to John, Meisner loved his work, which is saying a lot. High-powered acting teachers are *extremely* picky in terms of whose work they respect.

Martin: What happened?

James: John did some work in the theatre and appeared in small roles in a few movies and then gave up acting saying that the vast majority of actors he knew were depressed and unhappy ninety percent of the time. He complained that he didn't like being around actors and said the profession was awful, so he quit.

Later, when he was writing in Hollywood, he hooked up with a group of film makers and just about the time they were supposed to produce some films, they ran into a spell of bad luck, lost their financial backing, and shut down. With John's career, it was just one problem after another. It may sound like he just didn't apply himself, but the truth is his career luck was awful. And the more bad experiences he had, the less able he was to follow through and become successful. But he was a talented man.

Now, let's look at John's chart for health. What do you see?

Martin: The 1st house is strong because the Sun is in its own sign (Leo) in the 1st house. So his constitution is strong. And his 6th house is strong because Ketu occupies the 6th and malefics are great for overcoming health problems and creating strong health.

James: That's exactly right. The 6th house ruler is in the 11th house in a friendly sign, which is okay. Generally we have to predict strong health all around. Now, what kind of health sensitivities would he have?

Martin: Venus is the most afflicted planet in the chart. That means potential problems with the throat, thyroid, kidneys, and reproductive system.

James: Yes. And possibly the skin. Both Venus and Saturn govern the skin. (Note: Some astrologers say Venus rules the skin, while others say Saturn. I have noticed both planets have some influence.)

As far as afflicted houses, the 3rd house is extremely damaged because it is ruled by Venus, which is fallen and tightly conjunct Mars. The 3rd house rules the lungs and John died of lung cancer.

Martin: Really?

James: He was a smoker who tried to quit many times but couldn't. I never would have predicted lung cancer because Mercury is so strong in this chart, but in retrospect I believe the weakness of the 3rd house got him. He was quite healthy most of his life though.

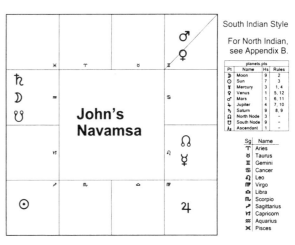

Now let's look at married life in John's natal chart (see page 285) and *navamsa*.

First of all, let me tell you that I don't know a heck of a lot about John's love life, and since he has passed away, I can't ask him. I do know that he never married.

Martin: Really? With all those planets aspecting the 7th house?

James: Yes. And I would not in a million years have predicted that. I would have certainly predicted troubles in his relationships (Venus in John's natal chart is terribly afflicted) and I would have predicted many relationships, but I don't know the exact reason that he didn't marry. I asked him once and he said something about feeling that he would never make a good husband or something; like he was too much of a free spirit. Which he definitely appeared to be.

I would say his unaspected 7th house ruler in the natal chart is an indication of a person who wouldn't marry, but the three planets in the 1st house that aspect the 7th would usually confer lots of relationships and *at least* one marriage.

As for the *navamsa* chart, I have grave doubts about its accuracy. The *navamsa* chart changes every three degrees, twenty minutes. If we count 3°20', 6°40', 10°, (*navamsa* ascendant changeovers) and so on, you'll notice that John's natal ascendant, which is 6°53', just barely made it to the Gemini *navamsa* ascendant. Six degrees, fifty-three minutes is only thirteen minutes *of arc* past the six-forty cut-off point. If he had been born only *about* a minute earlier, the *navamsa* ascendant backs up to Taurus. I can't know for sure, of course, but the Taurus ascendant makes better sense than the Gemini ascendant for a person who never married.

Martin: Why?

James: Because with the Gemini ascendant the Sun occupies the 7th house. Even though that's not a good placement for happy married life, the Sun is the *atmakaraka*, the indicator of the soul. A person with Sun in the 7th in either the natal or marriage chart usually has a very strong need to be married.

Martin: What about the fact that Gemini is....

James: Please don't. Please, please, please don't ask whether the *navamsa* Gemini ascendant has something to do with not getting married because it's such a fickle sign. Or a barren sign. Use common sense and remember that approximately one twelfth of the world will have a Gemini *navamsa* ascendant. All people with Gemini ascendants don't stay unmarried their whole life.

Martin: Okay.

James: That kind of logic reminds me of an astrology student who insisted that John Lennon must have a Pisces ascendant (rather than Virgo) because so many people with Pisces ascendants are musicians. Can you imagine if every person with a Pisces ascendant was a musician or every person with a Gemini *navamsa* ascendant stayed unmarried? That would make astrology incredibly simple.

Martin: James, when you talked about the 2nd house (in Class Five), you said it showed whether a person had happy family life and that it would have an effect on marriage. But you didn't mention Henry's 2nd house, and you haven't mentioned John's. Why?

James: I definitely look at that house when I analyze a chart for domestic happiness, but neither of the 2nd houses of the two charts we've seen tells me much. The reason is that they are both mixed. In Henry's chart (see page 272), Rahu occupies the 2nd house, and the 2nd house is aspected by malefic Mars. So, there has to be a fair amount of arguing and bickering. There has to be some suffering in family life. But the 2nd house ruler (Venus), is very well-placed in it's own sign (Taurus) in the 7th house. So along with the arguing, there has to be some smoothness and sweet talk. I can't make a very definitive statement about Henry's family life, because it's mixed.

Martin: And you don't look at the 2nd house of the *navamsa*, right?

James: That's right. I mainly look at the 7th house and 7th house ruler of the *navamsa*.

In John's chart, the 2nd house is also mixed. The 2nd house ruler, Mercury, is very well-placed because it's tightly aspected by benefic Jupiter. On the other hand, he has fallen Venus and malefic Mars in the 2nd house. It's the same result. Some suffering in family life and some smoothness.

Martin: I guess that in Venus or Mars periods he could have roughness in the domestic scene.

James: That's an excellent point. And Henry would have family problems in Rahu periods. John would have good family experiences in his Mercury periods, and Henry would have good Venus periods.

One thing to notice about John's relationships is that he would be likely to have love partners who are friends. He could marry a friend because the 7th house ruler in the natal chart occupies the 11th house.

Martin: The house of friends.

James: Yes. The fact that three planets aspect his 7th house tells me he would have lots of relationships. Most Americans with a chart like his would have two or three marriages these days. It is quite likely that because the 7th house ruler is totally unaspected and not prominently placed, he never met anyone who really knocked his socks off. But most people with a chart like his would have married in spite of that fact.

Let's look at another chart (see following page). This is the chart of a young woman who is rather talented in a lot of ways.

Martin: This is a confusing chart, James. It's very mixed.

James: True. So, we have to predict some very mixed results. Much of what happens in a chart like this depends on the *dasas* and *bhuktis*.

Martin: The Sun is incredibly mixed. It's strong because it's exalted and aspected tightly by a full Moon. But it's also afflicted because it receives a bad aspect from Saturn. The Saturn aspect is within three degrees and it's being thrown onto the Sun in Saturn's fallen sign — Aries.

Annie
Female Chart
May 3 1977
12:15 pm EDT +4:00
Louisville, KY
38°N15'15" 085°W45'34"

South Indian Style

For North Indian, see Appendix B.

Chart positions:
- Pisces: ♀ 15° ♓, ♂ 11° ♓
- Aries: ☊ ℞ 00° ♈, ☿ ℞ 14° ♈, ☉ 19° ♈
- Taurus: ♃ 12° ♉
- Cancer: As 09° ♋, ♄ 16° ♋
- Libra: ☋ ℞ 00° ♎, ☽ 21° ♎

Pt	Name	Hs	Rules
☽	Moon	4	1
☉	Sun	10	2
☿	Mercury	10	3, 12
♀	Venus	9	4, 11
♂	Mars	9	5, 10
♃	Jupiter	11	6, 9
♄	Saturn	1	7, 8
☊	North Node	4	–
☋	South Node	10	–
As	Ascendant	1	–

Sg	Name
♈	Aries
♉	Taurus
♊	Gemini
♋	Cancer
♌	Leo
♍	Virgo
♎	Libra
♏	Scorpio
♐	Sagittarius
♑	Capricorn
♒	Aquarius
♓	Pisces

James: That's right. Aries hates Saturnian energy. The Sun in this chart is kind of a wild card. It could give some phenomenal results or it could give some terrible results.

Martin: Or both.

James: Or both, for sure. I wouldn't make predictions relating to the Sun or the house that it rules (the 2nd house) until I asked Annie some questions about how 2nd house and Sun significations have functioned so far.

Now look at Mars, which I consider the strongest planet in the chart. It's in the 9th house, the best house of a chart, and is tightly conjunct with an *exalted* benefic (Venus in Pisces).

Martin: It's also the *rajayoga-karaka*.

James: Yes. But that doesn't make Mars well-disposed *for itself*. That simply means that because it rules good houses it will confer some good energy onto any house it occupies or any planet it aspects (along with the malefic energy it brings as a first class malefic). I know that many people talk about a planet that is a *yogakaraka* (union indicator) or a *rajayoga-karaka* (royal union indicator) as if it is well-disposed just because it rules good houses. I don't see it that way.

Martin: I'm confused by that.

James: Well, if you see a chart with a Cancer ascendant, and Mars (the *rajayoga-karaka*) happens to be in the 3rd house, it means that the 3rd house benefits tremendously because it is holding a planet ruling great houses (the 5th and 10th), right? But Mars is not particularly well-disposed just because it rules good houses. In this case, Mars is actually somewhat poorly disposed because the 3rd house is a mildly bad house.

Martin: So, the 5th and 10th houses would be slightly harmed by Mars' 3rd house occupancy?

James: Yes. You can't assume that the 5th and 10th houses become strong just because Mars rules those houses.

Martin: I see. But Mars will have some extra strength and give some powerful results in its periods and subperiods?

James: It will have *some* extra strength because it rules good houses, but it only becomes well-disposed if it is well-aspected (aspected by benefic planets) or occupying a very good sign like its own or exaltation sign. In my beginning years, I used to predict excellent results for any *dasa* or *bhukti* of a *rajayoga* planet. Anytime I saw someone with a Libra or Taurus ascendant, I predicted great things for Saturn periods and subperiods because Saturn rules such good houses for those ascendants. Now, I only predict good periods for *rajayoga-karakas* if the planet involved is well-aspected or in a very good house, and my accuracy is much higher.

Martin: But I've heard you say that when a *rajayoga-karaka* planet "matures" the person may experience a rise in his or her life.

James: That's true, and I still agree with that assessment. The person experiences a rise because certain very important houses suddenly come of age. (Note: For information about the maturity of planets, also known as "the great years of the planets," see my book, <u>Ancient Hindu Astrology for the Modern Western Astrologer</u>.)

At any rate, because Mars is so phenomenally strong in Annie's chart, it's going to have a huge impact on her life. And just to give you an idea of how well Mars functions, do you know that Annie hits baseballs in my batting cage at ninety miles an hour? Her physical coordination is incredible.

Martin: Mars is the planet of sports and in her chart it rules the 5th house (the house of sports). Could she become a professional athlete?

James: The ability is there, but I think her chart is indicating activities that are much more social and educational. I'll explain that in a minute. First, I want to make sure that you notice that this is a full Moon birth.

Martin: That's very important information.

James: You bet. I said in an earlier class that a person born on a full Moon or very bright Moon (three or four days before full or two or three days after full) gives a person extra power in life. Aside from obtaining more abundance and luxury in life and possessing more "emotional or visceral confidence," the person has a very strong presence. Full Moon people tend to be great achievers, unless the rest of the chart is massively afflicted, which Annie's is not. She has some real rough spots in the chart, no doubt, but she also has some very powerful influences. So I consider this chart a *mixture of extremes*. She has extreme afflictions and she has extreme benefits. Extreme difficulties and extreme talents.

I want to make sure you understand how to determine the brightness of the Moon and whether it is waxing or waning, because you need to know this for every chart you analyze. You can always spot a full Moon birth because the Moon will be in the sign opposite the Sun. Each degree of the Moon represents about two hours of time. Since the Moon is past the Sun's opposition by about two degrees in Annie's chart (Sun is nineteen degrees, Moon is twenty-one degrees), it means that she was born about four hours after the exact full Moon.

If the Moon is conjunct the Sun, the Moon is new or completely dim.

Martin: Which is bad.

James: Right. A dim Moon is very weak.

Now, if the Moon is in a sign that is moving *toward* the opposition of the Sun, the moon is waxing — it's getting bigger. If the Moon has reached the opposition sign of the Sun and is moving *away* from that opposition (and toward the conjunction) of the Sun, then the Moon is waning, or getting smaller. Every zodiac sign that the Moon moves toward or past the Sun represents about two-and-a-half days. That means that if Annie's Moon had been in Virgo (one zodiac sign preceding the opposition to the Sun) she would have been born two-and-a-half days before the full Moon. If her Moon had been in Sagittarius (one zodiac sign past the opposition to the Sun), she would have been born two-and-a-half days after the full Moon. The most important thing about the brightness of the moon is NOT whether it's waxing or waning, by the way. The most important thing is whether the Moon is bright or not. This contradicts what the ancient textbooks say, but believe me — a Moon that is two days after full (waning, but very bright) is going to give far better results than a waxing Moon that occurs only two or three days after a new (completely dim) Moon. In fact, there's no comparison between these two Moons, despite the incredibly misleading fact that the waxing Moon is labeled a benefic and the waning Moon a malefic by the ancient *Jyotish* texts.

Let's look again at Annie's chart. I'm going to focus on Mars for a minute because it is so much more powerful and well-disposed than any other planet in the horoscope. What should you think about when you see a Mars that stands out tremendously?

Martin: Technical skills.

James: Which means?

Martin: Law, architecture, engineering, mechanical ability. Also sports.

James: Good. Which house is the house of Law?

Martin: The 9th.

James: Bingo. Annie's father is a lawyer and she could easily be one herself. Notice that her well-disposed 9th house Mars is ruling the 10th house (career).

Martin: What about Jupiter? Doesn't it rule lawyers?

James: It does. Jupiter is a *karaka,* or natural indicator, of the 9th house. So if you see a chart with a strong Mars and Jupiter, or a strong Mars and 9th house, you should think law.

Martin: What about a strong Jupiter and 9th house?

James: That's probably going to be too spiritual for law, unless Mars is extremely prominent. A person with a powerful Jupiter and 9th house and an ordinary Mars is most likely going to want to do a lot of travel, or philosophical/spiritual study.

Martin: What about the three planets in Annie's 10th house? I'm always confused when I see a stellium of planets in one house.

James: First, you should notice which planet is in the *earliest* degree in a house with a stellium, and give that some extra weight. That planet often has an unusually big impact, unless the ruler of the house is in its own sign within the stellium, or unless there is an extremely well-disposed planet (e.g. a planet that is aspected extremely tightly by a benefic) or an extremely poorly disposed planet in the house.

Martin: So, if the ruler of a house is in its own sign in a stellium of planets, it will usually take precedence?

James: Yes. Or if one planet within the stellium stands out as being extraordinarily strong or weak, it may take precedence. Remember, however, that even if a planet is in its own sign within a stellium, it won't function well if it also happens to be very afflicted. I've already showed you several examples of charts where Venus was in Libra, but very damaged by being tightly conjunct Saturn. I've also showed you charts where Jupiter was exalted in Cancer, but terribly damaged by being closely conjunct fallen Mars.

Martin: If those conditions existed within a stellium of three or four planets in that house, you would basically consider the house afflicted?

James: Usually — yes. At the very best, that house would be mixed. The house ruler is such an important part of a house that even if there are benefics in the house, there has to be major damage. I think I told you earlier that the ruler of a house has *slightly* more impact than a planet (or planets) in a house. I can't tell you what to expect from every single chart that has an afflicted house ruler along with a good planet in that house (or vice versa), because in practice you're going to see every possible result. But you have to assume mixed results, not results that are simply positive or negative. That's for sure. And the results depend, of course, on just how afflicted or well-disposed the house ruler is and just how good or bad the planets occupying the house are. That is key.

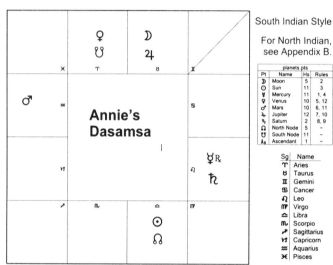

Now in Annie's chart, the Sun is very well-aspected (by the *extremely* bright Moon) and it is in its exaltation sign (somewhat past the Sun's highest degree of exaltation — the 10th degree — but still exalted). It is, however, also terribly aspected by the very tight Saturn aspect occurring in Saturn's fallen sign (Aries). And since the ruler of the 10th house is not involved in that stellium, I would give most weight to Ketu, the planet in the earliest degree of the stellium. Ketu is also aspected by Saturn, but the aspect is not too strong, because it occurs within sixteen degrees.

Martin: Ketu represents spiritual and metaphysical activities.

James: And consciousness-raising. Annie is heavily involved in Feminism, which isn't related to enlightenment but is a form of consciousness-raising. Annie is young of course, but based on her chart I think she will always be an activist of some sort.

Martin: Look at the ruler of the 10th house in the *dasamsa* chart occupying the 12th house. That makes me think that she might want a spiritual career, a career involving enlightenment. How do you discern between her getting involved in spiritual consciousness-raising versus Feminism or social consciousness-raising?

James: First, remember that Annie has a natal ascendant of nine degrees and forty-four minutes (about three quarters of one degree past the *dasamsa* cut-off point of nine degrees). That means that if her birthtime was really three or four minutes earlier, her *dasasmsa* ascendant will back up from

Gemini to Taurus. (Note: If the *dasamsa* chart changes to Taurus, then the 10th house ruler — Saturn — would occupy the 4th house and real estate would be a possible career.) I don't know for certain which *dasamsa* is correct, but for teaching purposes we'll assume her birthtime is accurate and she has a Gemini *dasamsa* ascendant.

By the way, I know I've told you this already, but I want to remind again you that this business of using four or five minutes of birthtime per one degree *of arc* only works in places like America and Europe. It doesn't work in out of the way places like Iceland. Don't forget that or you'll be inaccurate when rectifying *varga* charts for certain foreigners. You have to get on a computer to figure out how the degrees work in out of the way places.

Martin: How do you discern between Annie getting involved in religion and philosophy versus something like Feminism?

James: Well, it wouldn't be surprising if she eventually does get involved in religion and spirituality. That's certainly an option for her, isn't it? But every chart has a certain "feel" to it, and Annie's has the feel of one that is much more worldly. She has no planets in the 8th or 12th houses, no personal planets *tightly* conjunct Ketu. On the other hand, she has a highly activated career house and the typical features of a lawyer. On that basis alone, I would predict that she would have more of a "worldly" life than a spiritual one, at least during the first thirty or forty years. After that, she might decide to use her talents towards spiritual matters. But even then, she would almost certainly wind up teaching spirituality to others (as opposed to working exclusively on her own evolution) or helping a spiritual organization promote its message. This is not the chart of a renunciate or a mystic. It's the chart of a very public, community-oriented person.

Look at the educational and social aspects of this chart. Mercury is in the 10th house and so is the 2nd house ruler (Sun). These are both very literary, teaching features.

Martin: And the ruler of the 2nd is exalted and aspected by the full Moon.

James: Right. And then there's Jupiter in the 11th house. She's got to love groups and friends. Jupiter in the 11th house indicates strong social tendencies, not to mention three planets occupying the career house.

Annie's chart is also very strong for leadership. This is because of the prominent Sun in the 10th house and the incredibly powerful Mars. Mars is the planet of commanders and bosses.

Martin: But she has Saturn in a bad sign (Cancer is the sign opposite Saturn's own sign, Capricorn) in the 1st house. Wouldn't that ruin her confidence?

James: It would hurt her confidence, no doubt. But it's not going to cancel out the power of the rest of chart. I mean, it could. I've occasionally seen a badly placed Saturn practically ruin an entire chart (this can occur if Saturn *tightly* aspects the Sun, Moon, ascendant ruler, or ascendant degree). But the masculine planets, Sun and Mars, are very prominent in Annie's chart, and Saturn is not *that* close to the ascendant degree. She's definitely going to be a mover and shaker. That's obvious.

Remember that Saturn in the 1st house can also make a person a leader and give tremendous organizational skills. I wouldn't normally think leadership for a person with Saturn in a *bad* sign in the 1st house. But when the rest of the chart screams leadership, as Annie's does, then I fully expect her to take Saturn's restrictiveness and "turn lemons into lemonade" as they say.

Another thing you need to realize about Annie's chart is that on top of being born on a full Moon and having an incredible career house, her 5th house is phenomenally well-disposed. The 5th house is so important because it rules the mind, and the mind is the basis for everything. Everything we do springs from our minds.

The 5th house also rules *poorvapunya* (past life credit) and politics (kingship). Look at the ruler of the 5th house, Mars. Mars is so strong and well-disposed because it receives the vibrations of an exalted benefic (Venus) and it occupies the best house in a chart (the 9th). Also notice that benefic Jupiter aspects the 5th house, and the aspect is better than a usual Jupiter aspect because Jupiter in her chart rules the 9th house. Jupiter is a good planet for a Cancer ascendant chart.

Martin: And there are no malefic aspects thrown onto her 5th house.

James: That's right. So she's extremely bright, if not a genius; she has political or kingship ability, and her past life credit is strong. This is wonderful. It's true that she has a terribly afflicted Venus, a rough Saturn in the 1st house, and a very mixed Sun, but look at the upside of this chart.

Martin: You didn't mention her full Moon as being a great thing. Is that because it's also aspected so tightly by the malefic Sun?

James: Yes, I consider her Moon a wild card. I wouldn't be surprised if the Moon gives her great results, but neither would I be surprised if she suffers a lot of emotional pain in life due to the harsh Sun aspect thrown onto the Moon.

I'm glad you asked about the power of her full Moon. Perceptions like that allow you to be become very accurate with your clients. Make all the positive predictions you want about Annie's powerful Mars, 9th house, 5th house, and all the negative predictions you want about her afflicted Venus and her Saturn in the 1st house. But unless you're psychic, steer clear of making definitive predictions about the Sun and the Moon because those planets are both wild cards. They have extremely good features and extremely bad features.

Martin: Isn't Annie's past life credit connected to art because Mars as ruler of the 5th house (*poorvapunya*) is so close to exalted Venus? And isn't it also connected to religion because the 5th house ruler is well-disposed in the 9th house?

James: You're showing off now, aren't you Martin? Well, you're exactly right on both accounts, but don't forget that the 9th house is philosophy as well as religion. This is where Feminism comes in. It involves philosophy. People with Mars in the 9th house are great at promoting religion and philosophy, and that's all Annie cares about right now. As I said, I think she will always be an activist, a promoter of some religion or philosophy. She's also considering becoming a lawyer, and I'm sure she would be excellent at it. I think she would be happy with law, as opposed to so many who get a law degree and then quit because they hate the practice. Annie will also travel a lot because of her strong 9th house.

Martin: James, you said that Mars in Annie's 9th house is very strong, but Venus is afflicted. So, there's one good planet in the 9th and one that's afflicted. Does that cause the 9th house to give mixed results?

James: If there is any affliction to the 9th house, it certainly isn't because of Venus. Venus' exalted vibrations only help the 9th house. There could be some affliction caused by malefic Mars in the 9th, but very little.

Martin: Why very little?

James: Aside from the fact that Mars rules good houses and becomes a *rajayoga-karaka*, Mars is functioning very well because it receives wonderful vibrations from exalted Venus. You have to try and get a feel for planetary placements, and that takes experience. So trust me on this, Annie's 9th house is great.

Let's talk about Annie's health now.

Martin: Wait. I need to understand something about the *dasamsa* chart. How come you hardly mentioned it? Is it just that you don't pay much attention to the *dasamsa* chart in general, or does hers not tell you anything?

James: It's not that Annie's *dasamsa* chart is insignificant; it's that there is <u>so</u> much information about her career that arises from the natal chart. Therefore, I don't care as much as I normally would about her *dasamsa*. Her natal chart is so strongly <u>dictating her career karma</u> that the *dasamsa* probably isn't going to have too big an impact.

Martin: But it will have some impact?

James: You bet it will. Assuming that the birthtime is accurate and we can use her Gemini *dasamsa* ascendant, it becomes clear that Annie is either going to have some career problems and/or several career changes due to the 10th house ruler (Jupiter) occupying the 12th house. Or, she is going to be involved in consciousness-raising, maybe even spiritual consciousness-raising (i.e. helping people obtain enlightenment), *as a career* at some point in her life. I would definitely tell her that in a chart reading. But generally I would not expect her *dasamsa* indications to overwhelm or supercede the natal career indications.

Martin: Does it ever happen that the *dasamsa* chart indications supercede the natal career indications?

James: Sure that happens. I wish I could tell you what makes that happen, but I can't. I see plenty of cases where a person follows the career revealed from the 10th house of the *dasamsa* chart rather than the 10th house of the natal chart and the natal chart as a whole. It's extremely unlikely to happen to Annie, though, because the natal chart is giving such intense boundaries, such intense leanings. You follow?

Martin: Yes.

James: Annie will never lose her teaching and leadership tendencies. How can she? With the Sun as 2nd house (education) ruler in the 10th, along with the mental planet (Mercury) in the 10th house, she's a natural-born educator. That tendency can never waver or go away.

In looking at Annie's health, tell me which is the most afflicted planet in her chart, and which planets are mixed enough that they could give health problems?

Martin: Venus is in bad shape. It's too close to a malefic planet (Mars). Venus rules the throat, thyroid, kidneys, and reproductive system, and possibly the skin. Does she have these kinds of problems?

James: She already has thyroid problems. I don't know about any of the other areas, but you're right about those realms being vulnerabilities. What else?

Martin: Well, she might have bad menstrual cramps because the Moon is hit so hard by the Sun's aspect, but that's not a certainty because the Moon is also strong by being full, right?

James: So far, so good. And don't forget that the Moon rules the breast and brain.

Martin: Yes. She must get breast exams regularly as she gets older.

James: That's very important to tell anyone with an afflicted Moon.

Martin: The Sun is also very mixed because although it's angular and exalted, it's *tightly* aspected by Saturn (within three-and-a-half degrees) throwing an aspect onto Aries, which hates Saturnian energy. If the Sun, as a mixed planet, is more problematic than good, she'll have back or spine problems, or heart problems. The 4th house rules the heart, and it's in a mixed condition.

James: That's right. The ruler of the 4th house is afflicted Venus, but on the positive side, the 4th house holds a full Moon. These are mixed results which aren't going to help much in terms of predicting heart problems. You have to ask questions to find out how the 4th house is actually operating in her life.

Now pay close attention to what I'm about to tell you, because it can help immensely in your practice. When you see a client like Annie, who has a chart that is a mixture of extremes, you tell her everything about her life that you can using all the astrological indications that are clear enough to read with certainty. You talk about her sports and physical abilities (strong Mars and 5th house), you talk about her wanting to promote religion and philosophy (tight Venus-Mars conjunction in the 9th house), you talk about her low confidence or self-esteem problems (Saturn in the 1st house in a bad sign) which occurs simultaneously along with her powerful leadership and aggressive tendencies (prominent and strong masculine planets Sun and Mars), you talk about her big presence and ability to gain abundance (full Moon in her chart), her blatant career desires (three planets in the 10th house), and her activities with spiritual friends or spiritual groups (Jupiter as the 9th house ruler occupying the 11th house).

And then, <u>after</u> you've gained her respect as an accurate astrologer, you ask questions that tell you how her mixed planets are actually functioning. If she tells you she has terrible menstrual cramps, you know the Moon is having problems and will probably cause difficulties in <u>other</u> areas governed by the Moon and in her Moon *dasas* and *bhuktis*. Of course, when you're making predictions about future *dasas* and *bhuktis* <u>involving mixed planets</u> you should always ask your clients how the previous periods and subperiods of those planets have gone.

If Annie tells you that she's always had problems with money, her back, or her heart, then you know that the Sun is definitely taking a beating from the aspect it receives from Saturn, and that the Sun's exaltation status isn't helping much. You see what I mean?

Martin: I know the Sun rules the heart and back, but why money?

James: The Sun rules the 2nd house, the house of money.

Martin: What if parents want me to read the chart of their baby? I can't ask any questions then.

James: Then, when you see planets that are extremely mixed, you have no choice. You say the three magic words that allow you to maintain your integrity and to not give out inaccurate information. You say, "I don't know." If you're confident about much of the chart and accurate in many respects, not only will you be forgiven for admitting what you don't know, you'll be <u>respected</u> and <u>trusted</u>!

Let's look at Annie's tendency to get sick. What do you think about her 1st house and her 6th house?

Martin: The 6th house looks okay. The only planet aspecting the 6th is Ketu, and that doesn't seem like a major problem. Malefic planets occupying *upachayas* (the growing houses — 3, 6, 10, and 11) are good, so I doubt the aspect of one malefic thrown onto the 6th would be very bad.

James: That's right. After all my years in astrology, I'm still not sure whether malefic aspects <u>thrown</u> onto *upachaya* houses are good or bad. But they're certainly not terrible, or I would have noticed.

Martin: The ruler of the 6th house isn't particularly well-aspected, but it's not afflicted either. So her ability to heal is okay and there are no health problems indicated from the 6th house.

James: I agree. What about her constitution? What about the 1st house?

Martin: It looks mixed. Saturn in the 1st house is an affliction, but without asking Annie questions, I don't know whether the ascendant ruler (Moon) is causing problems or not. It looks like the 1st house could be a problem, but I can't be sure.

James: Good. That's what I think. I'm not sure about her constitution. I've seen people who have a full Moon that is afflicted have only good experiences and I've also seen the opposite. There's no way to know how her Moon is without asking her questions.

Martin: What do you tell her about her health?

James: I tell her that her ability to heal is pretty good, but her vulnerabilities are with the areas of the body that are ruled by afflicted planets. The throat, thyroid, kidneys, and reproductive system could all be vulnerable because of Venus. And there *might* be some heart sensitivity due to the negative aspect Saturn throws onto the Sun. And there might be some bad menstrual cramps, as well as brain or breast vulnerabilities due to the Sun's tight, harsh aspect thrown onto the Moon. Annie's old enough to be able to give some feedback as to how all these areas are doing. This wouldn't be a problematic case.

By the way, I would definitely be concerned about her reproductive system because not only is Venus afflicted, but so is the 8th house — the house governing reproductive ailments. The 8th house is not *terribly* afflicted, but it's not good that the 8th house ruler Saturn occupies Cancer — the sign opposite its own sign (Capricorn). All this doesn't mean she'll definitely have those ailments, but the odds are certainly higher. Therefore, she should be told to be careful with regard to her reproductive system.

Now let's briefly look at Annie's relationships.

Martin: There have to be some problems. In her natal chart, the poorly placed Saturn in Cancer rules the 7th house. Also, Saturn aspects the 7th house. On top of that, Venus is afflicted.

James: That's true, she must have some difficulties, and a divorce is likely if she marries before the late twenties or early thirties. She's obviously a passionate person in love matters as indicated by the tight Venus-Mars conjunction. Therefore, she's not going to want to hear that she shouldn't make a big commitment early in life. Nevertheless, she should be warned not to marry early.

She'll get a special partner, of course. The fact that the 7th house is aspected by its ruler (Saturn aspecting Capricorn) in the natal chart means that her partner will be an authority figure or special in some way.

Martin: But the aspect is also bad, isn't it? The 7th house has a very bad time with malefic planetary energy no matter what, right?

James: Absolutely. The aspect is definitely bad and is likely to cause a divorce or serious love problems in the first thirty years or so. But it also creates some good effect. Most importantly, Annie also has to avoid an early marriage because in the navamsa chart the ruler of the 7th house (Jupiter) occupies the 8th house, which is a bad house.

Martin: And this navamsa is probably accurate. She would have to have been born about thirteen or fourteen minutes earlier for the ascendant to back up from Virgo to Leo.

James: That's true, but the 12:15 birthtime could be an approximation. If her natal ascendant of nine degrees and forty-four minutes moves forward to ten degrees, her navamsa ascendant goes to Libra. She would only have to have been born approximately a minute and a half later to throw the navamsa off.

If the Virgo ascendant is accurate, and the 7th house ruler (Jupiter) occupies the 8th house, what would you tell her that could somewhat ameliorate the affliction so she could have a happy marriage?

Martin: Other than marrying after the late twenties, she should find a 8th house partner — someone phenomenally psychic or someone pursuing astrology and/or metaphysics.

James: Exactly. You're getting quite good at this Martin. I'll see you next week. Bas.

CLASS EIGHT

James: Today we're going to discuss planets that occupy their highest degree of exaltation as well as: planets in their worst degree of fall, planetary conjunctions with *Ketu*, and what happens to a natural benefic conjunct with a natural malefic. Mostly, though, I'm going to talk about some extremely overrated techniques, namely *neechabhanga rajayoga* and *vargottama* (also called *vargothamamsa*). *Neechabhanga* is known as the cancellation of a fallen planet. *Vargottama* is a condition where a planet occupies the same sign in the *rasi* (natal) chart as it does in the *navamsa* (marriage) chart. A *vargottama* planet is supposed to function with the strength and power of a planet in its own sign. And if you believe that it does, I have some have waterfront property in Arizona to sell you.

But before I start, let me warn you that I'm going to give a lot of examples of these two techniques that I believe work very poorly. It's not that I'm trying to beat a dead horse, it's that I don't want you to think I'm taking isolated instances to make my case. Whether or not you agree with my findings about overrated techniques is up to you. Either way, you'll see how Hindu astrology is supposed to work. You'll get a sense of the kinds of predictions that are made from this event-oriented system. I mention this because sometimes when I demonstrate how *neechabhanga* and *vargottama* don't work, students make all kinds of excuses and rationalizations for the techniques. By showing you lots of examples, you will at least understand what kind of results a *rajayoga* should give in an event-oriented system. This could only be an issue in the West, where astrology is geared toward psychology and behavior. In an event-oriented system like *Jyotish*, how well a technique works becomes quickly obvious when you are clear about what your looking for.

Martin: Okay.

James: Let's start with *neechabhanga rajayoga*, which I've already told you in my experience is almost completely worthless. Bear in mind, by the way, that *neechabhanga* is a *rajayoga* — a royal union, a kingly union. That means that a *neechabhanga* planet is not one which simply has its fallen status canceled. It is supposed to produce enormously good effects. Okay?

Neechabhanga occurs when any of the following conditions exist: 1) An exalted planet occupies the same house as a fallen planet; 2) The ruler of the house holding the fallen planet is exalted (e.g. if Mars is fallen in Cancer, and the Moon occupies its exaltation sign, Taurus, *neechabhanga* occurs); 3) The ruler of the house holding the fallen planet is in a *kendra* (angular house: 1, 4, 7, or 10) from either the ascendant or the Moon; 4) The planet which would be exalted in the sign holding the fallen planet is in a *kendra* from either the ascendant or the Moon.

The reason *neechabhanga* is worthless is because it only succeeds in reducing the damage of a fallen planet about ten or twenty percent of the time. Since astrology is generally only practiced with between sixty and eighty percent accuracy, a technique that works ten or twenty percent of the time is useless! Because astrology is not an absolute science, any technique you want to create from thin air can work ten or twenty percent of the time. The absolute best thing I can say about *neechabhanga* is to repeat what one astrologer told me he heard from astrologer/author Hart DeFeow. He said that DeFeow considers *neechabhanga* to be like a prosthetic for an amputated limb. In other words, if you lose a limb, it's gone and you can forget about ever getting back the full power of that limb. On the other hand, it is possible to obtain an artificial limb that may give partial help.

Martin: So *neechabhanga* does have some power?

James: Let me repeat, the statement given by Hart DeFeow is the best thing I can say in support of *neechabhanga*. The worst thing I can say is that it only works ten or twenty percent of the time, which makes it essentially useless since the practice of astrology is nowhere near an absolute science.

If you see ten clients with *neechabhanga* and you tell all ten people not to worry about the fallen planet in question because that planet has had its fallen status reversed by *neechabhanga rajayoga*, you are going to be dead wrong in at least seven or eight of those cases!

Martin: So if I see ten charts with *neechabhanga rajayoga* and I completely ignore the condition, and predict entirely bad results regarding the fallen planet, I'm going to be right seven or eight times?

James: That's right. And seventy or eighty percent accuracy is about the best you can hope for in astrology because of free will and several other factors.

As with everything in astrology, you have to analyze lots and lots of charts and do your own research in order to find out what works and what doesn't. But in today's class I'm going to present a number of charts where *neechabhanga* reveals itself to be a sham.

Martin: Before you start, what about astrologers who give examples of how good *neechabhanga* works?

James: That's an excellent point, because I can also give examples of charts where *neechabhanga* works. I could take the charts of Jodie Foster, Hugh Hefner, and many others where *neechabhanga rajayoga* works flawlessly. But those charts would simply come from the ten or twenty percent of charts where *neechabhanga* works! What I am telling you is that when you begin practicing astrology on your own and you see that *neechabhanga* only works in about one or two out of ten charts, you are completely correct in concluding that the technique is worthless. Most astrologers that I know who also found *neechabhanga* to be worthless waited a year or two before throwing it out of their practice. You needn't wait that long because the jig is up on that technique!

Martin: Why does everyone wait so long?

James: Because *Jyotish* is very ancient and has a tradition worth respecting. But *Jyotish* is definitely not infallible, as you'll find out when you start practicing professionally. It's amazing how you begin to trust what actually works and what doesn't when people are paying you good money to be accurate.

Let's look at some example horoscopes where *neechabhanga* occurs. Please bear in mind, however, that most of my examples are from horoscopes of famous people.

Martin: Is there some problem with that?

James: Well, you have to be careful when you are using famous horoscopes because such charts are very powerful as a whole, which is why these people are famous to begin with. If you do a lot of astrological research using only famous people, your results may be somewhat flawed. This reminds me of how wrong I went many years ago when Werner Erhard (founder of Est seminars) entered his Moon *dasa* and I expected the entire ten years to be dreadful because his Moon was fallen and badly aspected.

I had seen many ordinary people experience *dasas* of a fallen planet where the entire period was devastated. Because so many of the other planets in Erhard's chart are extremely well-disposed, however, many of his subperiods were very successful. In other words, even though his Moon was severely afflicted, his Saturn *bhukti* was good because Saturn occupies its own sign — Aquarius. His Mercury *bhukti* was good because Mercury is exalted in Virgo. And his Mars *bhukti* was good because Mars occupies its own sign, Scorpio.

Martin: Then if an ordinary person goes into the *dasa* of a fallen planet, the whole ten years could be bad.

James: Yes. If most of the other planets in a chart are weak, then the *dasa* of a highly afflicted planet can be rough during the entire period. On top of that, the problems of a bad *dasa* can affect everything in the person's life to some extent.

Martin: You mean as opposed to only the significations governed by the afflicted planet?

James: That's right. In any case, let's now look at some typical cases where *neechabhanga* didn't do much to help the person. First, let's look at Al Pacino's horoscope, where there are not one, but three fallen planets that achieve *neechabhanga rajayoga*. Pacino's chart is fascinating because although there are three fallen planets (Mercury, Moon, and Saturn), there are also three very well-placed planets: Venus in *swakshetra* (own sign), Sun exalted in Aries, and Rahu exalted in Virgo.

Martin: Some astrologers would disagree with Virgo as the exaltation sign for Rahu and Ketu, right?

James: Yes, because Parasara, the originator of the system we're using,

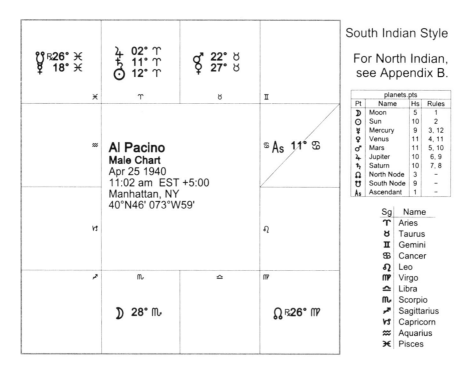

says that Rahu is exalted in Taurus. But most of the astrologers I met in India took Virgo as the best sign for both Rahu and Ketu. And that has been my experience. In fact, if you question Rahu's exaltation in Virgo, take a look at how great Pacino's work has become since entering Rahu *dasa* in 1992. Rahu occupies the 3rd house — the house of music, dance, and drama in Hindu astrology — and it was in 1993, just after Rahu *dasa* began, that he won his first Oscar. In case you haven't noticed, Pacino's performances have improved remarkably since his Rahu *dasa*. He wasn't doing many films during the eighties. From what I've heard, he was doing lots of acting workshops to hone his craft, but rarely performed publicly. When his Rahu *dasa* started, his career re-ignited. Other than his <u>Godfather</u> films, and a few other films in the seventies, his best work has definitely occurred in his current Rahu *dasa*.

Let's look at Pacino's three *neechabhanga* planets. In his chart, Mercury achieves *neechabhanga* because Mercury occupies Pisces, the ruler of which is Jupiter, and Jupiter is angular (occupying the 10th house). The Moon achieves *neechabhanga* because the Moon is in Scorpio, which is ruled by Mars, and Mars is angular from the Moon (Mars is in the 7th house from the Moon). Saturn achieves *neechabhanga* because Saturn occupies Aries, which is ruled by Mars, and Mars is angular from the Moon. Saturn also achieves *neechabhanga* because Saturn is conjunct with an exalted planet, the Sun in Aries.

Let's play a game. Imagine that you've just returned from India, having studied *Jyotish* for a year or so. You've learned well, accepted everything your teachers told you about all the traditional teachings, read lots and lots of *Jyotish* books, and you're excited to begin your astrology practice. One day, Mr. Pacino comes to you for a reading and you want to do your best. For our purposes, imagine that the year is 1960 or 1970 and Pacino is twenty or thirty years old, just beginning his adulthood.

You see Saturn fallen in his horoscope, as the ruler of the 7th house (marriage). But then you notice Saturn is *neechabhanga*, so you say, "Well Mr. Pacino, the ruler of your marriage house is fallen, but don't worry at all because Saturn achieves the famous *neechabhanga rajayoga*. You'll have a wonderful marriage." Oops! You just made a whopper of a wrong prediction. Pacino has never married and in his interviews indicates that he's a very unlikely candidate. He's now in his early 60's, having been born in 1940.

Then you look at Pacino's 5th house and you notice that the Moon is fallen in the fifth house, which is terrible for mental health and peace of mind (5th house rules the mind in *Jyotish*). So you say, "Well Mr. Pacino, there is a fallen planet in the house of the mind, but don't worry because the Moon achieves *neechabhanga*. You will have excellent mental health! Also, since the Moon rules the 1st house, your confidence will be tremendous." Oops, you did it again. You made a whopper of a wrong prediction. Take a good look at Pacino in the two or three television interviews he has given over the last twenty years. He is not your typical movie star. He appears incredibly shy and lacking in confidence.

As for his mental health, Pacino was reportedly plagued by mental anguish and alcoholism for many years, particularly from 1975 to 1985, during the ten years of his Moon *dasa* (the same Moon that achieves *neechabhanga*). Did you forget to tell Mr. Pacino that he would be seeing a therapist during his Moon *dasa*?

Martin: I have the feeling that all of Pacino's *neechabhanga* planets are going to cause trouble.

James: Next, you begin to predict that Mr. Pacino has wonderful karma with children. You notice that the ruler of the 5th house is Mars, which is clearly one of the strongest, most well-disposed planets in the chart. Although Mars is in a bad sign because it occupies Taurus, the sign opposite its own sign (Scorpio), it is <u>tightly</u> aspected (within five degrees) by benefic Venus, <u>in Venus' own sign</u>. Mars is also aspected by an extremely bright Moon (about three days after the full Moon), and the Moon's aspect is incredibly strong because it throws its light onto Taurus, <u>the Moon's exaltation sign</u>. This is one heck of a strong Mars.

Of course, you notice the fallen Moon in the 5th house, but you say to Mr. Pacino, "Don't give the fallen Moon in the 5th house a second thought, Mr. Pacino, because it achieves *neechabhanga rajayoga*. You're going to have <u>at least</u> two children and probably more!"

Martin: Why at least two, James?

James: Two children are indicated because the ruler of the 5th house (Mars) is aspected tightly by <u>two benefics</u>. More than two should occur if the Moon's fallen status is transformed into a *rajayoga*, as *neechabhanga* is <u>supposed</u> to do. Remember that *neechabhanga* <u>rajayoga</u> means that the fallen planet is supposed to form a *rajayoga*, a kingly union! The Moon is not merely supposed to lose its fallen status, it is supposed to function extraordinarily well! As you can guess, of course, the children prediction is wrong. As of his late 50's, Pacino has only one child, and if the 5th house ruler wasn't <u>incredibly</u> strong, I'm sure he wouldn't have any children, or he would have one child with <u>a lot of problems</u> due to the fallen Moon in the 5th house.

Let's continue and see just how much trouble *neechabhanga* can cause an astrologer trying to make accurate predictions. Now you notice that there is a fallen planet (Mercury) in Pacino's 9th house (the father) so you say, "Mr. Pacino, there is a fallen planet in the house of your father, but don't worry because that fallen planet has achieved *neechabhanga rajayoga*. You'll have excellent experiences with your dad."

Martin: Let me guess, James. Wrong again?

James: You got it. Pacino's father left the family when Al was just a baby. Pacino mentioned in one interview that his father had been married five times. This kind of instability is perfect symbolism for fallen Mercury in the house of the father. Mercury is a changeable, fickle planet. When it is fallen, it becomes so changeable that it often functions in a rather crazy way. If I see Mercury fallen in 7th house (marriage) either in the natal chart or *navamsa* (marriage chart), I always ask the person if he or she attracts very unstable or crazy love partners. Unless the fallen Mercury is tightly aspected by some great benefic, the answer is almost always yes.

Martin: James, what would you say about the fallen Saturn in Pacino's 10th house? He has had a spectacular career. I would guess Saturn hasn't caused too much damage in the 10th house.

James: I'd say that Pacino would have been better off without fallen Saturn in the 10th house. I know that some astrologers would say that Saturn achieves *neechabhanga rajayoga* and that is what caused Pacino's fame. I consider that ridiculous, because Pacino's fame is caused simply by a phenomenally strong 10th house. Look at Jupiter in the 10th house. Look at exalted Sun in the 10th house. Look at how energized the 10th house is with three occupants. Most importantly, look at the enormously powerful 10th house ruler, Mars, in this chart. I've already told you that Mars is aspected by Venus in its own sign (Taurus) within five degrees, and it is aspected by an almost full Moon within six degrees, in the Moon's exaltation sign. In other words, the Moon is throwing its aspect onto Mars in Moon's exaltation sign. Naturally, Pacino was likely to gain fame.

Martin: Isn't the Moon a malefic, though, because it is waning? Doesn't it throw a negative aspect because it's waning?

James: Absolutely not. The Indian textbooks greatly exaggerate (as usual) the benefic or malefic status of the Moon regarding waxing and waning. Of course, I always prefer a waxing Moon to a waning Moon, but the notion that the Moon becomes a malefic influence two or three days after its fullest point of brightness is absurd (Pacino was born about two-and-a-half days after the full Moon). If you go by your experience, you will find that it is the relative brightness of the Moon that is the most significant factor. Perhaps in *Prasna* (horary astrology), which is an extremely technical branch of astrology, a waning Moon might be malefic. I don't know. But in natal astrology, where you analyze the charts of people, waning Moons produce tremendously good effects if the Moon is very bright.

I was born two days after the full Moon, and in no way does my Moon function as a malefic. My Moon is afflicted, of course, by its position in the 12th house, and has certainly caused problems. But the incredibly bright Moon has been a tremendously positive influence on my 12th house. The 12th house rules meditation, spiritual growth, *moksha* (enlightenment), and experiences in "remote foreign spiritual countries" such as India, Nepal, and Israel. In all these realms, I have been blessed. If every waning Moon was truly a malefic influence, then I would have no happiness from spiritual, remote foreign countries. I would have no happiness from meditation and would gain little spiritual growth in this life.

Martin: I guess your Moon has to be benefic because you've been meditating for over twenty-five years now, and you're always talking about spiritual stuff.

James: I would say that meditation and other 12th house matters are the most consistent features of my life. I even taught meditation during most of the seventies. But let me give you another example that demonstrates my waning Moon as a benefic influence. Look at the Moon's aspect onto Mercury in the 6th house in my horoscope. It is clearly this aspect that is responsible for my writing books. If you tell every person who has Mercury in the 6th house that he or she is going to write books, you're going to be wrong very often. But if you see Mercury in the 6th house aspected by a very bright Moon as mine is, then you will not go wrong predicting that the person will be a teacher, writer, or author.

Regarding Pacino's chart, you can see his fame from common sense astrological analysis. You can also see his career as an artist pretty clearly. The ruler of the 10th house is conjunct with Venus, the planet of art. He has an exalted planet in the house of art (Rahu in Virgo in the 3rd house).

Martin: What about the ruler of the 3rd house (Mercury) being fallen?

James: Good question. Fallen Mercury in this case causes a lot of trouble to the 9th house, the house Mercury occupies, and to the 12th house, the other house that Mercury rules. It does not cause much trouble, however, to the 3rd house because Mercury occupying the 9th house throws an aspect onto the 3rd house. And in this case, Mercury is aspecting its exaltation sign, Virgo, which is great.

Martin: I see.

James: Planetary aspects always throw special energy if they aspect their own or exaltation signs.

Martin: James, since all planets aspect their opposite sign, this means that whenever a planet is exalted it throws a bad aspect onto its fallen sign.

James: That's right. And whenever a planet is fallen, it throws a wonderful aspect onto its exaltation sign. This happens because exaltation and fallen signs for each planet are always opposite each other.

Now let's consider another case of *neechabhanga rajayoga*. Look at Werner Erhard's horoscope (see following page). Notice the terribly afflicted Moon in his chart. It's fallen, aspected by Saturn, and conjunct with Mars. And please don't forget that a conjunction in Hindu astrology occurs if the two planets are simply within the same sign. This is different from Western astrology where conjunctions occur within eight or ten degrees, depending on the astrologer.

Martin: Wow, this is one afflicted Moon.

James: Exactly. And being that the fallen, afflicted Moon occupies the 7th house, do you want to guess what happened as soon as Moon *dasa* began? Oh, and don't forget, the Moon gains *neechabhanga* because the ruler of the house holding the fallen planet — in this case Mars — is angular (both from the ascendant and from the Moon).

Martin: Did he get divorced?

James: Yes. Once again the famous *neechabhanga rajayoga* failed to deliver. As soon as the Moon *dasa* began (April 1981), his marriage began to unravel. The divorce was reportedly messy and went on for some years. Allegedly, it took a long time to get Mrs. Erhard to sign the agreement that said she would not publicly discuss any details of the divorce or their marriage. The Moon *dasa* also brought an end to Erhard's empire. During the Moon-Venus *dasa-bhukti*, he was publicly disgraced by the news show "<u>60 Minutes</u>." The Moon and Venus are his most afflicted planets. Note that Venus is retrograde, combust <u>very closely</u> with the hot, malefic Sun, and is aspected by Saturn.

It often happens that if both the *dasa* and *bhukti* planet are weak, the

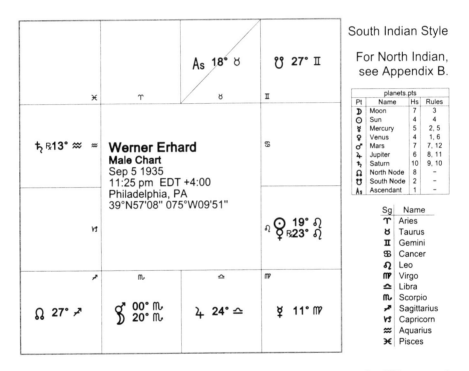

period-subperiod of those two planets will be very rough. When you're analyzing charts, it's easy to spot a rough period if the *dasa* and *bhukti* planets <u>aspect each other in a harmful way</u> and the *dasa-bhukti* of those two planets run their periods. For example, if Mercury and Saturn are within five or six degrees and the Mercury-Saturn *dasa-bhukti* comes along, you know there's about to be big trouble. But astrologers often miss a terrible period when both the *dasa* and *bhukti* planets are simply weak.

Martin: You mean weak and unrelated?

James: Yes. For example, in Erhard's chart, the Moon and Venus are not aspecting each other in any harmful way. Therefore, it's not so easy to predict that the *dasa-bhukti* is going to be horrendous. I have seen this type of situation occur in many horoscopes, so you need to be aware that two weak planets running their period-subperiod can often be extremely bad. The person simply has no power in such a period.

Can you imagine telling Mr. Erhard that the years from April 1981 to April 1991 would be excellent for him because he was running the *dasa* of a planet achieving the famous *neechabhanga rajayoga*?

The next chart we'll look at is that of my brother, Charles (see following page). Notice Mars in Cancer (fallen), in the 12th house. Mars rules the 9th house and the 4th house in this chart. Mars achieves *neechabhanga* because Jupiter is the planet that would be exalted in the house holding the fallen Mars, and Jupiter is angular <u>from the position of the Moon</u> (Jupiter is in the 1st house from the Moon).

Now, where shall I begin explaining the problems that this Mars has caused? As soon as the Mars *dasa* began, my brother lost his three stores and all his money. He got divorced and suffered unrelentingly for seven years, barely paying his bills. My brother was rich before Mars *dasa* came. He got rich in Moon *dasa* because the Moon occupies the 5th house, the second best house in a chart, and is tightly conjunct benefic Jupiter.

Martin: Wait a minute, I don't understand. I can see that the Moon *dasa* would be excellent, but why did your brother get rich during it? Neither the Moon or Jupiter rule the 2nd house (money).

James: Because his luck in that period was tremendous. Whatever he touched turned to gold. Strictly speaking, you wouldn't actually predict money from his Moon *dasa*. You would predict 5th and 12th house benefits because those are the houses that the Moon rules and occupies.

Martin: That's what I thought. As a 5th house planet, the Moon *dasa* should have brought luck with children, the stock market, speculations, and spiritual techniques. Or, as the 12th house lord, benefits with meditation, sexual enjoyment, foreign countries, and bargains (in the same way debts and expenses are a negative 12th house feature, bargains are a positive 12 house feature.)

James: Always remember that an extremely good *dasa* can have positive effects on everything in a person's life, and a really bad *dasa* can harm everything.

In any case, because of fallen Mars' rulership of the 12th house, my brother began to experience overwhelming debts and expenses.

Martin: A 12th house signification.

James: Exactly. Regarding *neechabhanga* Mars as the ruler of the 4th house (mother), our mother has had mental problems for about forty or fifty years now. Her life has been as difficult as you can imagine. It's only in the past two or three years, since I've been getting her three-day and seven-day *yagyas* regularly, that her schizophrenia has abated.

Regarding Mars' rulership of the 9th house (father), my father's life became extraordinarily difficult from the time he married my mother. My brother didn't have a bad relationship with my father, but he had to witness my father's suffering and very difficult life. My father's life was damaged in all kinds of ways due to my mother's health problems.

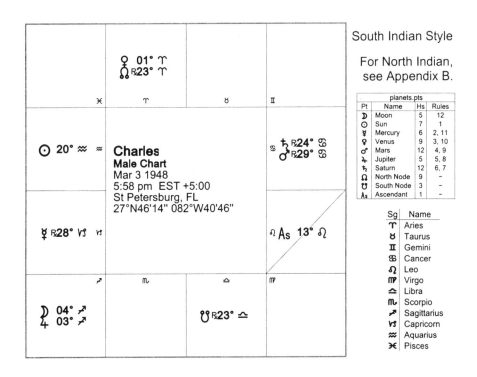

Martin: Is there some way to know, astrologically, whether an affliction involving a relative means that the relationship is bad versus that relative having a lot of problems?

James: Astrologically speaking, I would say there is not. Most of the time, however, your intuition will tell you where the problem is. I don't make that statement lightly, mind you. From my first days in astrology, I've been rather indifferent to using intuition and psychic ability. I know intuition is necessary and I know it's a large part of what makes so many Indian astrologers excellent. It's just that my interest has always been with astrological techniques alone. So when I say that your intuition will tell you where the problem lies, it's because that's how it works for me, and I don't even try to use intuition.

Many times when I'm reading a birthchart and I see a problem with the mother (4th house, Moon, and Mercury signify the mother), I simply say "I can see that there was little or no happiness from your mother." I use the same words given in the ancient texts ("The person gets little or no happiness from mother"). Usually, however, my intuition will tell me if the mother's life was difficult or if the relationship with the mother was damaged.

I'll give you one more example of *neechabhanga* failing and then we'll move on. The truth is I could show you hundreds of examples where *neechabhanga* is useless, but I think you must be getting the point by now. Look at the fallen Moon in the 12th house in Francis Ford Coppola's birthchart (see following page).

The Moon occupies Coppola's 12th house, the house of debts and expenses. The Moon achieves *neechabhanga rajayoga* because the ruler of the house holding the fallen Moon (also known as the <u>dispositor</u> of the house), Mars, is angular (Mars occupies the 1st house). It is common knowledge that Francis Coppola constantly goes way over budget when making a film. Although he has made huge amounts of money, Coppola has occasionally managed to spend it all and wind up in <u>serious</u> financial trouble. Some movie studios have gotten so tired of Coppola's overspending that they have actually put clauses in his contracts stipulating that as soon as his film goes over budget, Coppola pays for it from his pocket. This kind of contract was supposedly used for the filming of <u>Godfather Part III</u>. The first two <u>Godfather</u> movies made astronomical amounts of money, and still the studios didn't want to incur Coppola's overspending! Can you imagine saying, "Well, Mr. Coppola, there is a fallen planet in your 12th house, but don't worry. You won't have big debts and expenses because the Moon achieves *neechabhanga rajayoga?*"

Martin: I guess not.

James: By the way, if you alert certain astrologers about how poorly *neechabhanga* works, they may say that they use the condition as only <u>one factor</u> in helping to judge the fallen planet's strength or weakness. I would call that utter nonsense. For a technique to have any value, it has to stand on its own. It has to work powerfully and it has to work a significant percentage of the time. Actually, in the ten or twenty percent of cases where *neechabhanga* does work, the fallen planet gives tremendously good results. But since it works only ten or twenty percent of the time, it is practically useless!

Martin: Unless an astrologer is psychic enough to know those few cases in which it will work.

James: That's true. If you have <u>perfect</u> intuition, knock yourself out having fun with *neechabhanga*. Just don't tell every person with *neechabhanga* planet that his or her fallen planet is going to give good results.

Martin: James, what about the possibility that Al Pacino is the huge star that he is because of having three planets that have *rajayoga* status? You

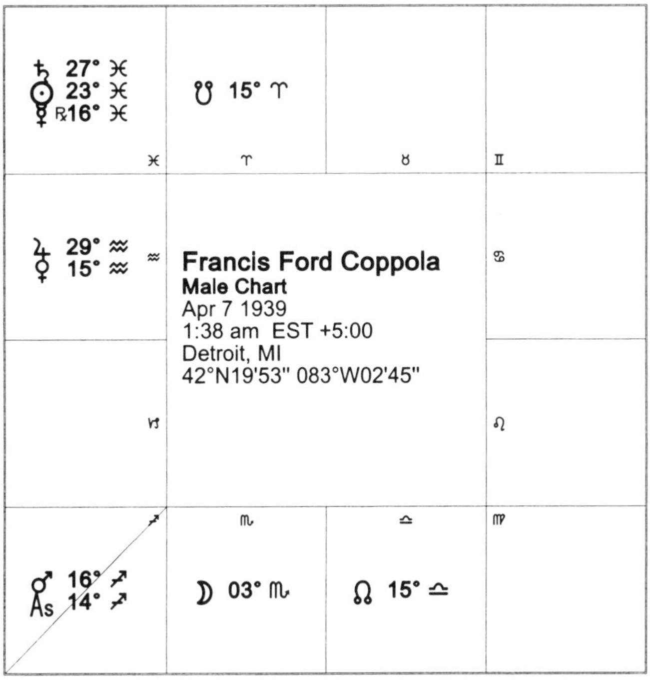
♄ 27° ♓
☉ 23° ♓
☿ ℞16° ♓
☋ 15° ♈
♃ 29° ♒
♀ 15° ♒
Francis Ford Coppola
Male Chart
Apr 7 1939
1:38 am EST +5:00
Detroit, MI
42°N19'53" 083°W02'45"
♂ 16° ♐
As 14° ♐
☽ 03° ♏
☊ 15° ♎
♓ ♈ ♉ ♊ ♒ ♋ ♑ ♌ ♐ ♏ ♎ ♍

South Indian Style

For North Indian, see Appendix B.

planets.pts

Pt	Name	Hs	Rules
☽	Moon	12	8
☉	Sun	4	9
☿	Mercury	4	7, 10
♀	Venus	3	6, 11
♂	Mars	1	5, 12
♃	Jupiter	3	1, 4
♄	Saturn	4	2, 3
☊	North Node	11	-
☋	South Node	5	-
As	Ascendant	1	-

Sg	Name
♈	Aries
♉	Taurus
♊	Gemini
♋	Cancer
♌	Leo
♍	Virgo
♎	Libra
♏	Scorpio
♐	Sagittarius
♑	Capricorn
♒	Aquarius
♓	Pisces

said that *neechabhanga rajayoga* is actually a Royal Union. Could that be one explanation of where the great effects occur?

James: That's a great question. I've thought about that myself, and I do consider it a possibility. I mean, I don't think the ancient seers and sages who cognized *Jyotish* were idiots. They must have had *something* on their mind about the good effects of *neechabhanga*. I don't know the answer to your question, but I can definitely tell you that if you expect *neechabhanga* planets to function well in the natal sense or in the *dasas* and *bhuktis*, you're going to be sorely disappointed.

Now, let's talk about planets that are *vargottama* (also known as *vargothamamsa*). A planet is called *vargottama* if it occupies the same sign in the *rasi* (natal) chart as it does in the *navamsa* (the marriage chart). A planet that is *vargottama* is said to be so favored by its special status that it functions as if it occupies its own sign. In other words, if Venus is *vargottama*, it is supposed to function in the same positive way as Venus in Taurus or Libra. If Jupiter is *vargottama*, it should operate like Jupiter in Pisces or Sagittarius.

Martin: You mean it's supposed to operate extremely well in the natal chart?

James: Yes, in the natal chart. Unfortunately, in my experience with thousands of clients, *vargottama* consistently fails to produce the promised benefit. The only times I have seen a *vargottama* planet function in an extraordinary way are when that planet was already well-disposed due to powerful benefic aspects that it received from other planets. Or due to the fact that the planet was stationary or exalted, or some other clearly positive condition. Take note of what I'm telling you because I'm not saying that *vargottama* works ten or twenty percent of the time, like *neechabhanga* planets. In my experience, *vargottama* is a totally worthless distinction.

Martin: Do other astrologers agree with you?

James: Pretty much the same astrologers who are willing to admit that *neechabhanga* is a sham agree that *vargottama* also doesn't work. If you simply go by your experience, rather than swallowing what the texts say, you'll find that the clients who have *vargottama* planets do not experience those planets as giving results similar to a planet in its own sign.

Martin: Maybe the ancient astrologers were exaggerating how great the benefits of *vargottama* are. Could it be that a *vargottama* planet is good but not great?

James: I don't think so. I have five *vargottama* planets in my birthchart and I don't experience any particular benefit from them. I'll give you the data and you tell me whether these planets function as if they're occupying their own signs.

In my case, the Sun is *vargottama*, because it occupies Virgo in both the *rasi* and *navamsa* charts. Mars and Ketu occupy Leo in both charts. Mercury occupies Libra in both charts. And Rahu occupies Aquarius in both charts. Let's start with the Sun, which occupies Virgo in both charts, and see if it functions as if it occupies its own sign (Sun in Leo).

The Sun in my natal chart is not terribly afflicted, but it is definitely weak. It has a very wide (fifteen degrees) positive aspect from Jupiter and an equally wide (fifteen degrees) negative aspect from Saturn. Neither of these aspects are intensely good nor intensely bad. The Sun is in a neutral sign in Virgo and it occupies the 5th house, which is a good house. The Sun is also conjunct within three degrees of Mercury, and this is a good aspect because Mercury is a benefic by nature and is considered a functional benefic because it rules good houses in a Taurus ascendant birthchart (see page 381 for chart of functional benefics and functional malefics). The significant problem with the Sun is that it occupies the last degree of a sign, which takes away its power and vitality. Also, if we use the *bhava* chart (a different house system from the *Sri Pati* method, where planets more than fifteen degrees past the ascendant degree are considered to occupy the following house, and planets more than fifteen degrees earlier than the ascendant degree are considered to occupy the preceding house), then the Sun occupies the 6th house, a *dusthana*, or grief-producing house. (Note: I was trained to take notice of both house systems — *Sri Pati* and the older system known as

| Rasi | Navamsa |

[Chart: James Braha, Male Chart, Oct 16 1951, 7:36 pm EST +5:00, Fort Lauderdale, FL, 26°N07'19" 080°W08'37"]

Rasi:
- ♃ R 14° ♓
- ☽ 23° ♈
- As 02° ♉
- ☊ R 15° ♒
- ☌ 14° ♌, ☿ R 15° ♌, ♀ 16° ♌ (Rahu, Mercury, Venus)
- ☿ 02° ♎
- ☉ 14° ♍, ♂ 29° ♍

Navamsa:
- ♄ in ♉
- ☊ in ♋
- ☋ and ♂ in ♌
- ☽ and ♃ in ♏ area
- ☿ in ♎
- ♀ and ☉ in ♍

"whole sign" houses — for each horoscope, but to give greater weight to the whole sign house system.) Ultimately, I would say that the Sun in my chart is not terribly afflicted, but it is definitely weak.

Martin: James, tell me again what the difference is between a weak planet and an afflicted one?

James: In terms of results, not much. An afflicted planet is one that is aspected by malefic planets (Mars, Saturn, Rahu, Ketu, Sun) or is occupying a fallen sign or a *dusthana* house (the 6th, 8th, and 12th houses). Afflicted planets give noticeably bad results both natally and in their periods and subperiods.

A weak planet is one that simply has no power, no energy. And although weak planets are difficult to notice sometimes, they give poor results. A weak planet may occupy the first or last few degrees of a sign, or have no aspects from other planets whatsoever. A weak planet may be isolated and occupying the 2nd or 3rd house rather than a *kendra* or *trikona* (angular or trinal house). In theory, a weak planet sounds a lot better than an afflicted planet, but a weak planet has no power to do good, so what benefit can it give? If a planet representing money is weak, it can't help you earn any wealth. A weak planet representing love can't help you find a mate. In the end, a weak planet doesn't help you reap the benefits of its significations any more than an afflicted planet. Oftentimes, a *dasa* or *bhukti* of a weak planet will cause serious problems and suffering.

Let's consider the Sun in my horoscope and see whether its *vargottama* condition made it function as if it occupied its own sign, as *vargottama* is supposed to do. I remember the entire six years of my Sun *dasa* (1956 to 1962) being awful. I felt powerless as I watched my father suffer as he struggled with my mother's worsening illness. The Sun, of course, rules the father. I was quite young during the Sun period, so I don't know too many details about what my father was experiencing. But I can tell you that he lost his business during my Sun *dasa,* and had to go work for others. This was very painful for a man who had always been self-employed, and was once very successful. I distinctly remember how my perceptions of my father as a powerful figure started to change, and I distinctly remember feeling powerless about the situation.

My feelings of powerlessness and the suffering of my father during the Sun period fit perfectly with the Sun's placement in the last degree of a sign in the 6th house of the *bhava* chart. Clearly, these results should not have occurred if the Sun occupied its own sign (Leo), which my *vargottama* Sun was supposed to simulate.

The Sun in my chart rules the 4th house (mother). My mother did not suddenly get well or begin acting powerful in the Sun *dasa*, which might have happened if the Sun's *vargottama* condition helped at all. Most importantly, the affliction of my Sun *dasa* was not an isolated occurrence. Throughout my life, whenever I encounter Sun subperiods, the results have been mediocre to poor. In my Sun *bhuktis*, I generally feel weak and ineffectual.

Aside from the *dasas* and *bhuktis*, if the *vargottama* status improved the strength of my Sun, it would not function as poorly as it does in its natal implications. The Sun rules my 4th house, the house of mother and real estate. I've already told you about my mother's life being so difficult. Let me tell you my experience with real estate. In forty-five years, I've never owned a house. Now that I'm married, Vashti and I are planning to buy (we bought in 1997). It's not that I never had the money to buy a house. I could have bought one in my late twenties or thirties. I just didn't have much interest then.

Martin: Even with Venus, Mars, and Ketu in your 4th house?

James: Those planets energize my 4th house a lot, but the weak 4th house ruler (the Sun) doesn't help matters. The Sun's placement in the 30th degree of a sign removes a lot of vitality from the 4th house. Remember that the ruler of a house (also known as house lord) is generally slightly more important than planets occupying a house.

Interestingly, I almost bought a house once, around 1978 or 1979. I put a down payment on a three story $20,000 home (yes, $20,000) just outside

Class Eight

of Boston. Due to a host of factors (mainly fear combined with a high-pressure, unethical real estate broker), I panicked, backed out, and decided to avoid real estate for a long time. Well, two or three years later, the value of Boston real estate went ballistic and the house tripled in value. My $20,000 house, which I would have bought with a $4,000 down payment, would have appreciated by about $40,000 in two years (over $125,000 in today's dollars). But I backed out. Does this sound like the story a person with the ruler of the 4th house in its own sign would tell?

Martin: I don't think so.

James: It's interesting that I actually have the quintessential favorable aspect for prospering in real estate; the ruler of my 12th house (Mars) occupies the 4th house. Any connection between the 4th and 12th houses is great for real estate. (Note: In ancient times, any connection between the 4th and 12th house meant an affliction indicating that a person would unfortunately have to rent out part of his or her home. In modern day, this same astrological placement is wonderful for success in real estate.) But the weak Sun has damaged my enjoyment of real estate, at least during my first forty-five years.

Now look at Mercury in my horoscope. Mercury is in the 6th house and is *vargottama* because it occupies Libra in the *rasi* and *navamsa* charts. The 6th house rules health, and Mercury rules the lungs, intestines, and nervous system. I have had chronic lung and intestinal sensitivities my entire life. As a child, I was always getting bronchitis. I was also extremely nervous. Although meditation has calmed my nerves dramatically, my lungs bother me constantly. I cough every morning like clockwork and neither practitioners of Chinese medicine or Ayurveda have been able to ease the problem. My lungs and intestines also bother me whenever I'm under stress.

Granted, Mercury is combust the Sun. But still, does this sound to you like a Mercury that occupies its own sign?

Martin: No.

James: Mercury never moves far away from the Sun. Therefore, Mercury combustions are quite common and somewhat less painful than other combustions. Also, in my case the combustion occurs within three degrees, which is strong but not extreme. If Mercury were truly acting as if it were in its own sign, as the *vargottama* Mercury is supposed to, my Mercurial health problems would not be strong. The *vargottama* condition should have taken the edge off of the affliction. It definitely has not. Every time I encounter a Mercury subperiod, I become jittery and develop nervous ailments. And I get rather argumentative. Does that sound to you like Mercury in the 6th house in its own sign? Don't make up excuses and don't go on a fishing expedition. Would Mercury in its own sign (Mercury in Gemini or Virgo) in the 6th house produce such results?

Martin: No.

James: Ketu and Mars are also *vargottama* in my chart, and if you think they function as if they occupy their own signs, think again. They occupy the 4th house, and my mother's life (4th house rules mother) has been rough beyond belief. Venus in the 4th has had some mitigating features so that I have definitely had some happiness with my mother, but her life has essentially been a nightmare. Schizophrenia is not a pretty disease. This can be seen in my chart from the weak Sun ruling the 4th house, along with the two first-class malefics in the 4th.

If you love *vargottama* so much, try imagining the ruler of my 4th house in its own sign producing my mother's nightmarish life. Try imagining Venus occupying the 4th house, along with Mars and Ketu in their own signs in the 4th house producing my mother's unrelenting suffering. Next, imagine the three *vargottama* planets connected to my 4th house (Sun, Mars, Ketu) producing a person who obtains no real estate in forty-five years, and who actually tells a story of tremendous missed opportunity in that realm!

Martin: So much for *vargottama*.

James: I'm not asking you to take my word about *vargottama*, or anything for that matter, as gospel. I'm simply advising you to test the technique with a critical method. If you analyze ten *vargottama* planets that are not already well-disposed before *vargottama*, and seven or eight of them function like they occupy their own sign, then by all means use the technique. But if the planets are entirely unaffected by *vargottama*, then don't use it. In order for a technique to work meaningfully, it has to stand on its own. This business of rationalizing techniques that don't work by saying, "I use this particular technique as one of many factors" is absurd. At some point a technique has to produce a noticeably positive or negative effect on its own.

Martin: Why do astrologers bother with useless techniques?

James: Two reasons. One, we trust textbooks too much. Two, we are not experience-oriented enough. If you want to be a good astrologer, you have to go by your experience.

In a minute, I'm going to show you some horoscopes to illustrate a very specific point about exaltations and falls. But first I want you to be familiar with a graph (see page 379) that gives the positions of "exaltations" (best sign placements for every planet) and the "fallen" placements (worst positions for each planet). In Hindu astrology, an exalted planet is called *uchcha* (pronounced "oocha") and a fallen planet is called *neecha*. Notice that the Hindus have listed the exact degree of exaltation and fall. Take, for example, Jupiter. Jupiter's exaltation, the point where Jupiter functions its absolute best, is the fifth degree of Cancer. Of course Jupiter will be excellent in the second degree of Cancer. It will be exalted in the second degree. But it will be better in the third degree, better still in the fourth degree, and the best in the fifth degree. After the fifth degree, Jupiter will function very well, but it quickly begins to lose its incredible strength the further it moves away from the fifth degree.

As for fallen placements, take, for example, Venus. Venus is most ruined in the twenty-seventh degree of Virgo. Now, Venus will function quite poorly, or fallen, in the tenth degree of Virgo. But it will be a lot worse in the twentieth or twenty-fifth degree of Virgo. When a planet gets to within two degrees of its worst point of fall, look out! It then becomes a wild card. You know the planet will cause a lot of harm, but when the client tells you the exact harm it has caused you'll be somewhat stunned. The person usually tells you a horror story about the realm of life governed by that planet, or the houses that planet rules or occupies. Similarly, when a planet gets to within about two degrees of exaltation, the luck and fortune the planet creates (related to the nature of the planet and the houses it rules and/or occupies) is thrilling. Jack Nicholson has the Sun in the highest degree of exaltation (tenth degree of Aries) in the 10th house (career), as ruler of the 2nd house (money). His career and financial success have been phenomenal.

♄ 06° ♓	♀ ℞01° ♈ ☉ 09° ♈ ☿ 28° ♈	☊ ℞23° ♉	
	Jack Nicholson Male Chart Apr 22 1937 11:00 am EST +5:00 Neptune, NJ 40°N13' 074°W02'		As 08° ♋
♃ 03° ♑			
	♂℞12° ♏ ☋ ℞23° ♏		☽ 06° ♍

By the way, the tenth degree means nine degrees and some minutes. Once the planet hits ten degrees and some minutes, it is already in the eleventh degree and has passed its highest point of *uchcha* (exaltation) and quickly begins to lose its wonderful strength. It doesn't become afflicted or weak, but it loses its incredible power. Don't forget that.

In Albert Einstein's chart, Venus occupies its exaltation sign in the twenty-fifth degree of Pisces, two degrees away from its point of greatest strength. It rules the 5th house (the mind) and the 12th house (*moksha* — enlightenment, higher consciousness, spiritual growth), and it occupies the 10th house (fame and career success). Einstein was blessed in all these areas.

Look at the Moon in Mick Jagger's chart (see following page). It is in the exact highest point of exaltation and it rules the 1st house. Fame and recognition are very favored by this feature alone, not to mention his extremely strong 10th house (Mars in its own sign in the 10th house) and all the planets energizing his 1st house. You get an idea of how this works. A planet near its highest degree of exaltation produces very dramatic results.

Martin: James, in Jagger's chart, the Moon is in exactly three degrees of Taurus. If it moves past three degrees it becomes weaker, right?

James: Yes. And very quickly. But that doesn't mean that it's in trouble. It just means that it's not extremely powerful. It's quite good, but not great.

Martin: In Einstein's horoscope, Venus is conjunct with two malefics, Saturn and the Sun. How does that affect exalted Venus?

James: Venus is not terribly harmed by these aspects because of a combination of two reasons. First, the aspects from malefics are not extremely close (Saturn is twelve degrees away from Venus and the Sun is twenty-three degrees). Second, Venus is <u>so highly</u> exalted, so close to its highest point of exaltation (the twenty-seventh degree of Pisces), that it must be strong. If, however, Venus was <u>tightly</u> conjunct a malefic, say within three or four degrees, it would have been badly harmed. Or, if Venus was conjunct these two malefics (<u>even with the wide orb</u>) in a sign that did not strengthen Venus dramatically, then Venus would have been badly damaged. That's for sure.

Now let me give you an example of what happens to a planet that occupies its fallen sign close to its most intense degree of fall. I know two people, both born on the same day, whose Sun occupies the ninth degree of Libra (8 degrees and 55 minutes), extremely close to its absolute worst position in the horoscope (tenth degree). Both of these people experienced intense suffering on account of their fathers.

Martin: Because the Sun is the *karaka* of father?

James: Exactly. In one case, at around two years old the person's father left home forever never to be seen again. The father was also a severe alcoholic. In the other case, the person's father became sterile a few years after his child was born. When the child was told his father was sterile, he thought sterility meant sexual impotence. He reported that this had an extremely negative impact on his own life and his manhood. His sexuality was damaged and he felt scarred for life. The person's father must also have suffered to a large extent since his sterility was caused by chemicals he encountered while fighting in the Vietnam war.

Martin: All of this because the Sun was so close to its worst position of fall?

James: Yes. I've seen over and over that when a planet gets within one or two degrees of its highest exaltation or most intense point of fall, it functions like a wild card. Very spectacular or incredibly damaging.

Martin: Is it kind of like a stationary planet?

James: Yes, in the sense that the person will have a special story to tell about the significations of the planet involved. You need to understand, however, that if a planet is exalted or fallen it can still be altered by the aspects it receives.

Now I want to look at a few horoscopes with you to make some points about what happens when a benefic planet conjuncts a malefic planet. I've already shown you how this works, but I want you to see several examples. Misunderstanding how these aspects and conjunctions work is one of the biggest problems I see in astrologers and students.

Many astrologers think that if a planet is exalted (or well-disposed by sign) it cannot have any problems, and if a planet is fallen (or poorly disposed by sign) it is completely ruined. Take a look at this chart that has a benefic planet in its own sign (Venus in Libra) tightly conjunct a malefic in its exaltation sign (Saturn in Libra).

Both planets are well-placed by sign. There's no way, however, for Venus to function well when it is so close to malefic Saturn. And Saturn, which is already powerful because it is exalted, becomes tremendously strengthened by being so close to Venus in its own sign. (Note: Saturn will also experience some damage by being so close to the *dusthana* 6th house ruler.)

```
                    As 09° ♉    ☊ 12° ♊
         ♓      ♈       ♉       ♊

♂ 12° ♒         Man with Thyroid Problem   ♃ ℞05° ♋
                Male Chart                 ☽ 05° ♋
                Dec 12 1954
                4:18 pm EST +5:00
                Miami, FL
         ♑      25°N46'26" 080°W11'38"        ♌

                    ♏       ♎       ♍
☋ 12° ♐    ☿ 20° ♏    ♀ 22° ♎
           ☉ 27° ♏    ♄ 23° ♎
```

This man has a successful career due to Saturn, the ruler of the 10th house, being so strong. At the same time, he has confidence problems.

Martin: Because the 1st house is harmed?

James: That's right. The ascendant ruler, Venus, is very damaged by being near Saturn. Many astrologers tell clients like this not to worry about Venus being hurt because Venus is in its own sign and because Venus' conjunction is to exalted Saturn, which is the *rajayoga-karaka*, the royal union maker (because Saturn rules the 9th and 10th houses). This, of course, is nonsense. If you advise clients that way, then call yourself "Dr. Feelgood." You make the client feel good, and then he or she goes home and suffers an entire life with this terrible affliction.

Martin: What do you do?

James: I tell the person that Venus is in bad shape and the way to strengthen it is though gemstones, mantras, and *yagyas*. And I tell the person that a gemstone is not enough to heal the problem. The gemstone, diamond (white sapphire is a "secondary" stone), will give some protection during Venus *dasas* and *bhuktis*, that's for sure. But it will not dramatically alter the natal problem. For extreme afflictions, mantras and *yagyas* are needed.

The whole point of *Jyotish* is to alter the problems that exist in a horoscope. So, there's nothing to be scared about when you see afflictions in a birthchart. Granted, some afflictions are incredibly rough, but the possibility of grace always exists. When you chant mantras or have *yagyas* performed, you are going directly to the Lord of Karma of the afflicted influence and asking for intervention. In my experience, both with clients and my own life, some relief is always given. How much depends on how afflicted the planet is and how many *yagyas* you do, or how much chanting you do.

Martin: In this man's case, do the planets aspecting the 1st house (Mercury and Sun aspect the ascendant) help or hurt, as far as confidence?

James: I think they help, actually. The aspects aren't terribly strong, however, by degree. The ascendant degree is nine and some minutes and Mercury and the Sun are twenty and twenty-seven respectively. So the aspects are far away from the ascendant degree. Still, these aspects energize the house and give the person some prominence. Let's put it this way. If these planets, along with Mars (Mars aspects the ascendant too), did not aspect the ascendant, this person would be not only shy, but rather invisible. Venus is simply very devastated. So the aspects thrown onto the 1st house are a benefit, in terms of gaining some presence in the world.

Martin: The person lives with a sense of insecurity and inferiority because the ascendant ruler is so afflicted, but at the same time he has some charisma, some personality prominence.

James: Exactly. When he entered his Venus *dasa* a few years back, he began having a lot of problems. Can you guess what they were?

Martin: I would say health problems, because Venus rules the 1st and 6th houses.

James: What kind of health problems?

Martin: Throat, thyroid, kidneys, or reproductive illnesses.

James: Yes. His thyroid was affected and he has to take medication for it. He also had some enemies (a 6th house signification) come after him. A few years into the Venus period, someone sued him. Enemies, jealous people, competitors, and court cases are ruled by the 6th house.

Venus also rules the skin, by the way. He probably had acne or skin problems as a child.

Martin: Did he have skin problems when Venus *dasa* began?

James: I don't know. This man was a client, not a personal friend. But the likelihood is strong that he had acne problems as a child and Venus subperiods during his entire life would have caused problems. Anyway, this man's Venus *dasa* has been rough from the start.

On the other hand, he had excellent career success because Saturn rules the 10th house and Saturn is so well aspected by Venus. And his religious life has been strong because Saturn rules the 9th house.

I don't know this for a fact, but I would bet that he has had some ups and downs with 9th and 10th house matters due to Saturn being so close to the 6th house ruler. But overall he's had very good results from career and religious endeavors.

Martin: So, if Saturn was not conjunct Venus, there would have only been excellent 9th and 10th house effects?

James: Absolutely. At any rate, I hope you get the point regarding aspects involving a benefic and a malefic. In the early 1980's when I began teaching *Jyotish*, this issue was probably the hardest for students to learn. One way I explain it is like this: imagine that a thief with low consciousness is in the same room with a guru or highly evolved person. The thief would gain some benefit by receiving the energy of the evolved person, while the evolved person would suffer on account of the vibrations of the thief.

Martin: That's pretty clear.

James: I know. But I see so many students get it wrong. I'll give you one more example, just because it's an easy one. Look at the chart of Orson Welles (see next page).

Notice exalted Venus in Pisces conjunct within four degrees of malefic Mars. Mars becomes extremely powerful because it is not simply conjunct with benefic Venus, it is conjunct with exalted Venus. The vibrations of exalted Venus help Mars far more than ordinary Venusian rays. In Welles' case, Mars rules the 6th house, the house of appetite as well as enemies and competitors. Orson Welles was physically huge, so clearly his 6th house was powerful. Regarding his ability to defeat enemies and competitors, he once told a story on television that demonstrates his great 6th house.

When Welles was a stage actor, some time before he was famous, he wanted to play some leading Shakespearean roles. Being that Welles had a very close Venus-Mars conjunction (about four degrees), he was not a patient person. Venus-Mars conjunctions in angular houses indicate a leader and passionate person who wants immediate results.

Martin: You have a Venus-Mars conjunction, James.

James: Don't remind me. At any rate, Welles evidently didn't want to put years in a theatre company "paying his dues." So he went to Ireland and lied. He told a theatre director that he was a famous American actor looking for a foreign repertory company in which to play leading Shakespearean roles without any publicity. The director believed him and the ploy worked. Because his 6th house was so strong, he defeated his actor "competitors" instantly!

Although Welles' Mars was incredibly powerful by being next to exalted Venus, Venus became extremely hurt by the harshness of Mars. Even though Venus is the *yoga-karaka* (union indicator because it rules the 5th

Orson Welles Chart

♂ 22° ♓ ☿ 18° ♓	♀ 22° ♈ ♄ 27° ♈		As 01° ♊ 06° ♊
♃ 28° ♒ ☊ 00° ♒	\multicolumn{2}{l|}{Orson Welles Male Chart May 6 1915 7:00 am CST +6:00 Kenosha, WI 42°N35'05" 087°W49'16"}	
☽ 26° ♑			☋ 00° ♌

South Indian Style

For North Indian, see Appendix B.

planets.pts

Pt	Name	Hs	Rules
☽	Moon	8	2
☉	Sun	11	3
☿	Mercury	11	1, 4
♀	Venus	10	5, 12
♂	Mars	10	6, 11
♃	Jupiter	9	7, 10
♄	Saturn	1	8, 9
☊	North Node	9	–
☋	South Node	3	–
As	Ascendant	1	–

Sg	Name
♈	Aries
♉	Taurus
♊	Gemini
♋	Cancer
♌	Leo
♍	Virgo
♎	Libra
♏	Scorpio
♐	Sagittarius
♑	Capricorn
♒	Aquarius
♓	Pisces

house), and even though it's exalted (in Pisces), Venus suffers by being so close to malefic-natured Mars. In Welles' chart, Venus rules the 12th house (debts and expenses). Do you know why producers avoided Welles like the plague after they got to know him? It was because he would perpetually go way over budget.

Martin: Like Francis Coppola?

James: Yes. But there is widespread dispute about whether Welles' expenses were due to artistic expenses or because he threw lavish, expensive parties for his film crew and fellow actors. Nevertheless, he couldn't stop the spending and eventually producers refused to work with him. He actually had to close down one of his theatre companies because he couldn't pay the bills. These are typical effects of an afflicted 12th house. There's no other affliction to Welles' 12th house, by the way. No planets in the chart aspect the 12th.

Martin: James, when you see a client like this with a one-degree ascendant, do you worry about the birthtime?

James: Yes. I never interpret a chart with a sensitive birthtime without first asking questions to make sure the chart fits. Before I taught you about Hank Aaron's horoscope, who also has a one-degree ascendant, I analyzed it to make sure that the Virgo, rather than Leo, ascendant fit. You can tell that Welles' chart is accurate by looking at the strongest planet in the chart

(Mars) and seeing whether the houses it <u>rules</u> are strong.

Mars rules Welles' 6th house and look at his enormous weight problem. Also, look at how he effortlessly defeated his enemies. If his birthtime was slightly earlier and the ascendant backed up to Taurus, then his 6th house would be afflicted because Venus, which is bombarded by a tight conjunction to Mars and receives a bad aspect from Saturn, would rule the 6th. Also, with a Taurus ascendant, Mars would rule the 7th house and he would have had a fantastic marriage. There would have to have been some problems of course because Venus (*karaka* of marriage) is afflicted, but ultimately he would have had incredible domestic happiness. So, I believe the Gemini ascendant is accurate. And to answer your question again, I certainly advise you to make sure that any chart with a twenty-nine degree ascendant or a one-degree ascendant actually tallies with the person's life.

Incidentally, Welles' afflicted Venus also gave him a lot of love problems. He was married more than once. As far as children (5th house), I don't know many details about his life, but problems are definitely indicated. I do know that he named his daughter Christopher, a boy's name!

Martin: That's bizarre.

James: I can't imagine what he was thinking. Maybe he wanted, or expected, a boy due to the fact the 5th house ruler is conjunct Mars.

As the ruler of *poorvapunya* (past life credit — 5th house), Venus caused intense career problems by being afflicted in the career house. For all his fame, Welles had one of the most checkered careers of any successful film maker. Some of his films that are now considered classics <u>and required viewing</u> in film schools were box office flops that got terrible reviews. He was constantly disappointed by the public's and critics' reactions to his films.

Martin: If he had past life career debt, then how did he gain fame in the first place?

James: Although Venus is afflicted by being near Mars, which gives rise to past life credit career problems, the Venus-Mars conjunction in the 10th house creates a leader and gives tremendous professional power.

Think of it this way: Mars alone in the 10th house is a wonderful placement for career success. What you're seeing in Welles' case is a <u>phenomenally strong</u> Mars in the 10th (because it is tightly conjunct <u>exalted</u> Venus. The strong Mars in the 10th house made him technically-oriented, which is why he wanted to make his own films and not just star in them. He was not merely an actor who turned to directing. He was an actor who made his own films! That's a rare distinction, particularly in his day. Without such a strong Mars, he would not have had such great technical skills. Remember, Mars is conjunct <u>exalted</u> Venus in the 10th.

Martin: Isn't it odd that he was an artist with an afflicted Venus?

James: It is somewhat odd, but a lot of artists have afflicted Venuses. The reason he was an actor and director is because of his strong 3rd house. Look at the 3rd house ruler (the Sun) exalted in Aries in the 11th house. Look at the ascendant ruler, Mercury, conjunct the 3rd house ruler Sun. Look at Jupiter aspecting the 3rd house. Ketu in the 3rd house is not generally an artistic position, but Ketu does rule film.

Martin: Ketu rules film?

James: Yes. Obviously there was no film or photography in the days that *Jyotish* was conceived. But Ketu is like Neptune. It rules things that are weird, strange, unseen, astral, and metaphysical. Therefore, Ketu represents gas, oil, magic, film, and photography.

If a person has Ketu in the 3rd house, don't predict the person will work with film or photography, <u>unless art is otherwise indicated</u>. In Welles' case, the 3rd house is very prominent; Venus (planet of art), even though in a very mixed condition, occupies the career house (10th).

Martin: I know you covered this earlier, but I want to ask anyway to be sure I understand properly. Does Venus throws better-than-ordinary energy in its aspects because it is exalted.

James: No, not in my opinion. There are astrologers who see it that way, but I do not. In fact, the energy that Venus throws onto Virgo is questionable because Virgo is Venus' fallen sign. Venus energy doesn't do well in Virgo to begin with.

Martin: That means that all exalted planets throw harmful aspects onto their opposite house, right?

James: Yes, because those exalted planets throw their energy onto their fallen signs. And all fallen planets throw good aspects onto their opposite signs, their exaltation signs. Whenever I teach this to a classroom of students, someone inevitably asks, "Then what's so bad about a fallen planet? It's half-bad and half-excellent." But there is a big difference between a planet in a house, and a planet *aspecting* a house. If Saturn aspects the 7th house, a divorce is almost certain (in non-divorce prone areas like Europe and India, marital problems, but not divorce are indicated). But that doesn't mean the person is going to suffer in relationships for an entire life. If Saturn <u>occupies</u> the 7th house, the person can easily suffer marital problems his or her entire life. There is a difference between a house holding a benefic or malefic versus receiving an aspect from one of those planets.

Some astrologers contend that the stronger a planet is, the better the aspect it throws. I have not found this to be true, other than in the case of the conjunction. For example, if Jupiter is in Pisces, conjunct the Moon, the Moon receives distinctly better Jupiterian energy than if the conjunction occurred in Aries or Leo, or some sign that does not dramatically favor

Jupiter. But I have not found that Jupiter throws better-than-normal Jupiter energy onto other houses just because it is in its own sign (Pisces or Sagittarius).

For example, when Jupiter occupies Pisces, it aspects the signs of Cancer, Virgo, and Scorpio. Of course the Cancer house benefits tremendously, because Jupiter is throwing its aspect onto its exaltation sign, but it hasn't been my experience that the other houses (Virgo and Scorpio) benefit more than usual due to Jupiter being in a good sign.

Martin: And that means that Mars in Scorpio doesn't throw any better aspects than Mars in any other sign.

James: That's my experience. You're completely welcome to do your own research on the issue. But my advice is that you not take someone's word that planets in their own signs throw better-than-usual aspects.

I'd like to give you an example regarding this issue, but it's difficult, maybe even impossible, and I'll explain why. A benefic, like Jupiter, always throws a good aspect (unless it is aspecting Capricorn, its fallen sign). So how do I prove that Jupiter in Pisces or Sagittarius in someone's horoscope is throwing a good but not great aspect onto some house?!

The best I can do is to take a subtle variation on the theme. I can give you an example of a malefic planet occupying a powerful state — a malefic planet in its own sign — and show you that when that malefic throws its aspect onto some house, the aspect hurts as much as ever. The malefic planet doesn't suddenly throw a benefic aspect just because it is functioning at its optimum.

For example, if Mars is in either of its own signs (Scorpio or Aries) in the 4th house, where it aspects the 7th house (due to its 4th house, or ninety degree, aspect) and you predict divorce, you will be correct seventy or eighty percent of the time (This is true, despite the fact that *kujadosha* — "Mars affliction harming married life" — is supposedly nullified). Mars does not suddenly throw a good aspect because it occupies its *swakshetra* (own sign).

Martin: This works the same way as *yogakarakas* (union indicators) and *rajayoga-karakas* (royal union indicators). When those planets happen to be malefics, they also throw harmful aspects.

James: That's exactly right. A malefic planet that is a *yogakaraka* or *rajayogakaraka* throws harmful energy because it is a malefic, while also throwing some good energy due to ruling excellent houses. Bear in mind, however, that the planet throws partial good energy due to ruling good houses, not because it is inherently powerful. A planet ruling the 9th house throws some 9th house energy with its aspects and the 9th house rules luck! A planet ruling the 5th house throws some 5th house energy and the 5th house rules romance, pleasures, parties, and favoritism from benefactors. It throws some very positive energy when it aspects other planets and houses strictly because of the dramatically positive significations it rules.

Now I want to discuss exalted planets or planets in their own signs that are conjunct with Ketu. I cannot tell you how many clients I have seen who were told by astrologers that their exalted planets conjunct Ketu, or *swakshetra* planets (planets in own sign) conjunct Ketu, would produce excellent results, when in fact those planets were devastated by Ketu's "otherworldly" influence. Let's look at an example.

This is the horoscope of a man who had been told by many astrologers that he would have wonderful career success. In fact, he has severe career problems, and in my opinion will continue to have them unless he does a lot of mantra chanting for Mercury, or a lot of yagyas for Mercury. Or unless he chooses a Ketu-ruled career (consciousness-raising, film, magic, oil, gas).

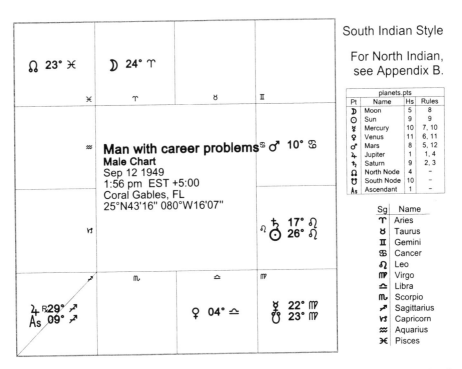

Martin: This is a case where Mercury looks excellent because it's exalted, but is harmed by being near Ketu?

James: Yes. And this dramatically harms his relationships, because the afflicted Mercury rules the 7th house.

Martin: What about the fact that Ketu is well disposed by being in Virgo, which you consider Ketu's best sign?

James: Ketu is phenomenally strong. In fact, I'd say Ketu is the strongest planet in this chart, beyond any doubt. Ketu is in Virgo, its best sign placement (because Ketu, as an animalistic or demon influence benefits tremendously by the intelligence of Mercury) and is conjunct with <u>exalted</u> Mercury. What a great Ketu!

Martin: This man must be very spiritual and psychic.

James: He is. And I advised him to enter a spiritual, metaphysical, consciousness-raising career. But so far he has floundered terribly in the professional realm. In my view, he'll continue to flounder unless he chooses a Ketu-type of career. What was so upsetting, however, is that other astrologers told him he would have a wonderful career due to exalted Mercury in the 10th house. He's also been told to expect wonderful Mercury periods and subperiods, which will in fact be very difficult periods for anything other than spiritual endeavors.

Martin: This is what you said about close aspects from malefics in the list of priorities you gave me earlier (in Class Three).

James: That's exactly right. Malefic aspects can hurt a planet that is well-disposed by a sign in an instant. Now, do you have any questions?

Martin: No.

James: See you next week. Bas.

CLASS NINE

James: Today we're going to talk about what I consider the most important aspect of *Jyotish* — the *upayes*.

Martin: Gemstones, mantras, and *yagyas* (also spelled *yajnas*).

James: That's right: the methods to ameliorate the problems that exist in people's lives and show up in the horoscope. I hate to say it, but I think that Shiva's curse (described in Class two) really has a big impact in this realm. There are disagreements amongst astrologers about *upayes* all over the place. It's easy for disagreements to arise because in the ancient *Jyotish* texts so little information about *upayes* was given. Almost no guidance was given about gems and how to wear them.

Martin: Are you serious? Gemstones are such a big part of Hindu astrology. That's hard to believe.

James: Well, look in the ancient texts yourself. There's almost nothing there. It's critical that you never forget this fact.

Martin: Why?

James: Because for every ten people whose charts you analyze professionally, two or three will come back to you (taking your valuable time) to ask you why your gem recommendations don't match those of some other Hindu astrologer. My advice is that when you prescribe gems for a person, you tell him or her that there are disagreements about gemstone prescriptions and explain why. Tell the person, "The only information given in ancient astrology texts about gems is that ruby is the stone of the Sun, diamond is the stone of Venus, emerald is the stone for Mercury, and so on. No other gemstone information is given in *Jyotish* scriptures." (Note: There may be some old texts that talk about gems, but I have never seen an ancient *Jyotish* text give any instruction other than which stone fits which planet.) Do you see how important this is?

Martin: You mean that when astrologers talk about secondary stones and the sizes that should be worn, they are speculating?

James: In a worst case scenario, we are speculating. In the best case scenario, we are going by our experience.

Martin: I've already noticed that many astrologers don't go by their experience. Many go by what someone told them.

James: That's a good observation. Before you advise your clients on which gemstones to wear, prepare them for the likelihood that after they buy a large, expensive yellow sapphire, some other astrologer is going to see it on their finger and exclaim, "What are you doing with that gemstone? You should never wear a yellow sapphire. Jupiter rules bad houses in your chart." Or some astrologer may say, "You can't wear a yellow sapphire and a diamond in the same setting. Venus is an enemy to Jupiter."

Martin: Telling clients this must drive them crazy.

James: Not really. Basically, it arms them to deal logically with the situation and with overly dogmatic astrologers. When I prescribe gems, I tell my clients that they are receiving <u>my</u> views on gem prescriptions which are based as much as possible <u>on my experience</u>. I explain that I'm not infallible and like anyone else I could be wrong. But I have taken the time to check with clients to see which prescriptions work and which ones don't, and my clients report getting good results.

I also tell many clients (not all, but many) that in India the way people test gemstones is by taping one to their body for a day or two and observing how they feel and watching the news that comes to them while wearing the stone.

Martin: I've heard Indians say they do that.

James: By the way, if a client is upset because some other astrologer has a disagreement with my gem prescription, I explain what I've just told you and advise the person to return to that astrologer and ask point blank, "Which authoritative <u>astrological</u> scripture does your gem information come from?" If the astrologer doesn't admit he or she is only giving out personal opinions, or reveal that the information comes from a non-astrological source, he or she is lying or misinformed.

Martin: Are you actually saying that there is no *Jyotish* <u>scriptural</u> information about gems regarding size, color, quality, secondary stones, which finger to wear the stone on, whether stones can be worn together, whether to wear one in gold or silver, or whether a stone can be too large for someone?

James: That's right. The seers only mentioned which stone fits which planet. Period. And you need to grasp the ramifications of that fact.

Martin: Maybe they wanted each astrologer to use intuition for each client.

James: Maybe. I don't think we'll ever know what was on their minds. Now you have the knowledge and can help your clients deal with other astrologers with different opinions.

Martin: This also demonstrates why we have to trust our own experience rather than what some teacher says.

James: That's right.

Martin: What do you do when you see clients who wear stones that you think shouldn't be worn? Do you mention it?

James: I do. But I make sure that when I tell them I disagree with someone else's gem prescription that it is only my opinion. If I see what I think is a wrong stone on a client's finger, I ask the person, "Have you noticed any benefit from wearing that stone?" If it's a Mars stone and I think Mars should not be strengthened in that case, I ask that person, "Do you find that wearing that stone heats you up or makes you irritable or angry?" If they say, "No, actually it makes me feel strong or powerful," then I reply, "I wouldn't have prescribed that stone, but if it works for you then keep wearing it." There are also times when I think a stone might be good for someone but might also cause problems. (This usually occurs in the case of a malefic planet that needs help, but throws a fairly wide aspect onto another planet. It becomes a judgement call as to whether the planet being aspected is far away enough to escape serious harm.) In those cases, I advise the person to try the stone and see what happens.

Martin: And they test it by wearing it for a few days and seeing how it feels?

James: Exactly. If it has good effects, buy it. If the results are very mixed, leave it alone. When it comes to gems and everything else in astrology, we have to go by our experience. It's the only way. In the beginning, follow your teacher, but eventually all techniques have to prove themselves or they shouldn't be used. I've told you this about a thousand times now; you don't need to hear it again. I hope.

Now, let me give you some more personal views. Although gemstones are the most popular form of *upayes*, in my experience they are not necessarily the strongest.

Martin: Why are they so popular?

James: Because they're easy. Put on a gemstone and forget about it. All your troubles will go away and your life will be wonderful. At least that's what people think. My experience with gems is that they are extremely important, but when a planet or house is massively afflicted, a person should do more than wear a gemstone.

Martin: Like chanting a mantra or having *yagyas* performed?

James: Yes. I believe that mantra chanting and *yagya* ceremonies are the most powerful method to significantly alter karma. Basically, mantras and *yagyas* are a way of asking God or the Lords of Karma to intervene in your life and provide some grace in a particular area. (Note: All nine astrological mantras are given in *Appendix A.*)

Certainly I can tell you stories about putting on gems and having powerful reactions, but I don't believe gems will alter karma in the sense of making a terribly afflicted planet function <u>consistently</u> well.

Martin: But you do tell clients stories about gems that have had good effects in your life.

James: Definitely. I've worn stones that have produced excellent effects; but when it comes to alleviating significant problems in my life, mantras and *yagyas* are essential. I constantly receive phone calls from grateful clients who have successfully changed their lives through mantra chanting or *yagyas*. I rarely hear the same from clients who simply wear a gemstone.

I'm not trying to minimize the importance of wearing gemstones, but I think they need to be understood properly. In my experience, gems are wonderful but they are different from mantras and *yagyas*. On the other hand, if a client tells me he or she only has enough money for a gemstone or a *yagya*, I always advise buying the gemstone (after reminding the person that mantra chanting is free).

Martin: Why?

James: Because the gemstone will serve as protection as long as the stone is worn. It will help whenever the person has a period, subperiod, or sub-subperiod of the planet involved. The gem's effect, subtle though it is, lasts as long as the stone is worn. As for a *yagya,* there's no guarantee that a person will get God's grace. That depends on the person's karma and God's reaction. Also, the traditional recommendation for a seriously afflicted planet in a person's chart is to have the *yagya* performed <u>twice a year for about four years</u>. A person who has one *yagya* performed *may* receive a miraculous effect, but that doesn't mean the planet is going to suddenly function normally in all its significations. It takes a series of *yagyas* done over a <u>period of years</u> to truly ameliorate a planetary affliction. But I'm ahead of myself. First let me tell you a good gemstone story and then I'll explain how I was taught to prescribe gems. After that, we'll talk about mantras and *yagyas*.

Before my Jupiter *dasa* began, I bought my twelve-carat yellow sapphire. I got a huge, extremely high quality stone because in my chart Jupiter is aspected by Saturn and Mars <u>to the degree</u>. When I run the Jupiter-Saturn *dasa bhukti*, it puts me in a very precarious situation. Worse yet, Jupiter rules the 8th house, which has to do with longevity and accidents. Well, during the first few days of holding onto the yellow sapphire (I had neither purchased nor set the stone yet), I began to have psychic experiences.

Martin: Because Jupiter rules your 8th house?

James: Yes, the house of intuition. On the second day I carried the stone,

I got a call from a German publisher who wanted to publish my first book in German and pay me $10,000 to do it! That may not sound like a huge sum of money, but if you ever write an astrology book, you'll find that if someone offers you a $10,000 advance you will leap for joy, believe me.

Martin: How does this relate to the yellow sapphire?

James: Jupiter rules the 11th house of my chart — the house of major desires. From the time my Hindu astrology book was first published, one of my biggest desires was to have it printed in German. I always felt that Germans would do extremely well with *Jyotish* because the German culture appreciates attention to detail and because most Germans I know are meticulous about rules and regulations.

Martin: Which is critical in astrology.

James: Exactly. So for about seven or eight years after my book came out, I used to send sample copies to German publishers every year. After years of rejections, I realized they weren't interested and stopped sending them books. Well, as soon as I put on the stone, I got the call about the book offer. I hadn't contacted a German publisher in years and suddenly one contacted me out of the blue. It was pretty obvious that the stone had an effect. <u>Large high quality</u> stones can produce some great effects, no doubt. I've seen that happen to many people.

Martin: Yet you believe that wearing a gem isn't as powerful as chanting a mantra or having a *yagya* performed?

James: I believe that the purpose of a gem is somewhat different from mantra chanting and *yagyas*. I believe that a gemstone serves as a protective measure and as a kind of "booster." As important as it is to wear astrological gems, I would not expect a person with a seriously afflicted 9th house to suddenly have consistently good effects with his or her father or with religious teachers (9th house significations) just by wearing the stone of the 9th house ruler. And I think it's patently absurd to let a client who has a fallen planet in the 7th house or a fallen 7th house ruler think that by wearing the stone of that afflicted planet that he or she is going to suddenly have a happy marriage.

Martin: And you're saying that if that person chants mantras or has *yagyas* performed, he or she could have a happy marriage or happy love relationships?

James: I've seen it happen. I've seen people's lives dramatically improve through chanting mantras and performing *yagyas*, and not just in very isolated cases. By the way, I'm not saying that wearing a gemstone couldn't avert some great danger in a person's life. Yogananda mentions how this works in his book <u>*Autobiography of a Yogi*</u>, and I respect him. But if I see a client facing a dangerous period, you bet your life I am going to recommend mantra chanting or a series of *yagyas* for that person.

Now let me give you the guidelines I use for gemstones. Remember, these are my opinions, my findings. For everything I say about gems, there is some astrologer out there who will disagree. At some time or other, I have heard someone disagree with everything I'm about to say.

Martin: But there must be general agreement about *some* of this stuff, no?

James: Of course there is, so I'll let you know what is agreed on by the vast majority of astrologers and what is controversial. Here are four main points.

1. ***Gems should be natural.*** They should not be dyed, treated, or chemically altered. This is traditional wisdom. I know there are some people out there prescribing gems who say that a man made stone works just as good as a natural stone. But that is not traditional, and in my *experience* it's untrue. I've tried man made stones and I've never felt any effect from them.

2. ***Gems should be high quality.*** They don't have to be flawless, but they must be very high quality or they won't produce good effects. This is traditionally accepted by astrologers. There are some who say that flawed stones actually produce bad results, but I don't believe that. In my view, flawed stones just don't do any good.

3. ***Gems should slightly touch the skin.*** They can be worn in a necklace, bracelet, or ring.

Martin: But generally speaking, a gem can be worn anywhere?

James: Yes.

Martin: What about astrologers who advise using palmistry? They say to wear a Jupiter stone on the Jupiter finger and a Mercury stone on the Mercury finger, and all that.

James: I think it's totally irrelevant. The point of a gem is to have the essence of a particular planetary energy on your body. Whether wearing it on a particular finger boosts the effect, I can't say authoritatively. I know my mentors never mentioned it, and my reaction to the idea is that it's kind of silly. Not bad, but kind of like a game. If it pleases you to wear a stone on the palmistry finger, by all means do so. But I wouldn't go out of my way about it. It's certainly not something the ancient sages ever instructed in their writings.

4. ***Stones should be large and a person should not wear a***

bunch of little "chips" that add up to a large amount. In the West, the traditional recommendation is that a stone should be <u>at least</u> two carats (I don't know if there is any agreed-upon size amongst Indian astrologers). When astrologers say two carats, they generally mean "in the vicinity of two carats." A stone that is pure but only one-and-three-fourths carats will obviously work fine.

Martin: So, *around* two carats is good?

James: Yes. Now, if a planet is very afflicted or if a person says they want to boost a planet's influence tremendously, I recommend a very large stone. That means five or six carats, or bigger. The bigger the stone the bigger the effect. That is traditional thinking.

Martin: Could a stone be too big?

James: I don't believe so. But there are times when I will strengthen a malefic planet that desperately needs help, but happens to throws a *fairly wide* aspect (fifteen or twenty degrees or more), and I don't want to strengthen that planet too much for fear it will harm that nearby planet. In those cases, I stick to one- or two-carat stones.

Of course, I have met astrologers who think that a stone should never be more than three or four carats. They say that in the same way a small dose of medicine is good, too much is harmful. But those astrologers are rare, and their thinking is <u>not</u> traditional.

Now, when it comes to telling clients what size of a stone to wear, you must be careful. Quite often, people will take an astrologer's size recommendation as the gospel truth — as if there is a magic size for each recommendation. If you tell such a person to get a five-carat stone, he or she will turn down all four or six carat stones, no matter how wonderful. So you have to make your clients understand that the size you recommend is not exactly set in stone, no pun intended.

Martin: What if the person can't afford the size of stone I recommend?

James: That happens a lot, which is why I'm telling you to make sure you let your clients know that they don't have to get the <u>exact</u> size you recommend. If you tell some clients to buy a five-carat pearl and all they can afford is three carats, some will buy nothing thinking that only the five-carat stone will work.

Martin: That's crazy.

James: I know. But how are your clients supposed to know that unless you educate them? If a person can't afford the stone you recommend, he or she should either get a smaller stone or a secondary stone.

Martin: How small can they get and still get a good effect?

James: That's a judgement call, but I tell my clients that if they can't get a stone near two carats, they should buy a secondary stone. Here's a list of the secondary stones I use. Remember that secondary stones were not mentioned in ancient texts and therefore different astrologers may prescribe different ones. Sun — <u>high quality</u> red garnet (not a ten dollar red garnet); Moon — moonstone; Mercury — green tourmaline or peridot; Venus — white sapphire, danburite, or any natural white stone; Jupiter — yellow beryl; Saturn — blue tanzanite (avoid blue topaz, most of which were originally white stones that turned blue when heated); Ketu — any form of cat's eye that's cheaper than chrysoberyl. Or turquoise.

Martin: You didn't mention Mars and Rahu.

James: I don't know any secondary stone for Mars, and red coral is cheap enough anyway. And to be honest, I've never heard of a secondary stone for Rahu. I know there are lots of different kinds of hessonites that astrologers prefer, but they are all in the hessonite family.

Martin: What are your rules for prescribing gems?

James: First, I'll tell you two rules that I know are traditional. This doesn't mean there aren't a few astrologers who will disagree, but I'll explain what is agreed upon by the vast majority of Indian astrologers.

Rule one: *Always wear the stone corresponding to the birth planet (the ascendant ruler).*

Martin: Even if that planet is a malefic, and even if that malefic planet is tightly aspecting some other planet?

James: Yes. We're speaking about the <u>chart ruler</u>. It is the planet that will have the most impact on a person throughout life and it should <u>always</u> be strengthened in order to boost confidence, well-being, and the ability to gain recognition.

Rule two: *always wear the gems of the dasa (or* bhukti*) planet.*

Martin: No matter what?

James: No matter what. If you want the *dasa* to go better, you strengthen that planet and then remove the stone after the period <u>if you feel it will cause harm when the *dasa* ends</u>. By the way, you can always strengthen the *bhukti* planet as well if you like. Most people don't, but if the subperiod planet is in very bad shape, I do sometimes tell clients to strengthen it even though it means getting rid of the stone after that short period.

Now, everything I've just told you is traditional, as far as I know from my experience in the field. Most of what I'm about to say now is subject to debate.

Martin: But you're going to tell me how you were taught?

James: I'll tell you two more rules which I was taught and have found from experience work well regarding natal planets. I've already told you about wearing the gem of the *dasa* or *bhukti* planets and the ascendant ruler. The following statements apply to planets that are not running their *dasa* or *bhukti* and are not ruling the ascendant.

1. ***I never strengthen a malefic planet like Sun, Mars, Saturn, Rahu, or Ketu unless that planet needs help and is not aspecting any other planet*** (or that planet is the ascendant ruler or running its *dasa* or *bhukti*). That means if I see a fallen Sun in Libra, I may strengthen it as long as there is no other planet in Libra or Aries (the sign opposite the Sun in Libra).

2. ***I will always consider strengthening a benefic planet like Venus, Jupiter, Moon, or Mercury if it is afflicted.*** And if I recommend the stone of a benefic planet because that planet is running its *dasa*, I tell the person to keep the stone on for the entire life if he or she wants.

Martin: Even if it is a functional malefic — a planet ruling bad houses?

James: Yes. And this is where the biggest disagreement among astrologers arises. There are many astrologers who believe that if a person strengthens the 12th house ruler, that person will experience negative 12th house effects. The 12th house rules accidents, problems, and losses. Well, I vehemently disagree with that assessment. I don't believe that stones work in that fashion, and it certainly hasn't been my experience. If you strengthen the 12th house ruler, you will get 12th house benefits.

Martin: You mean better spiritual experiences?

James: Yes. And better bed pleasures, better experiences in remote foreign countries, and less debts and expenses. This isn't something I'm going to try to prove to you. It's just the way I was taught and the way I see it. And I can tell you from experience that wearing stones that rule bad houses don't cause bad effects.

Most astrologers simply accept what their teachers have said about wearing gemstones. So when they say that you shouldn't wear stones of functional malefics and you shouldn't wear a stone that is an enemy to your ascendant ruler and you shouldn't wear a yellow sapphire and a diamond together because those planets are enemies, it's because that's what they were taught. Most astrologers I've met have never even considered that everything we say about gemstones is our speculation. They haven't given much thought to the fact that the ancient seers said nothing about how to wear gemstones.

Of course, I'm not beholden to what the ancient seers said.

Martin: That's for sure.

James: But I've experimented with gems, and I've worn stones that are functional malefics in my chart without any problem or negative effect. I've worn stones that were enemies to my ascendant and I've worn several stones in one setting, without experiencing any harm.

If you ask most of the astrologers who go by all the rules I disagree with, whether they have ever experimented with how to wear stones, my guess is that ninety-five percent will say "no" if they're truthful. They simply rely on what they were taught. That's understandable, of course, but it's not good enough in a field with so much disagreement. And if you think there wouldn't be so much disagreement if we only accepted the teachings of sages, then you need to read the writings of those sages because even they disagree. Understanding that fact should be essential to anyone's approach of *Jyotish*.

Martin: Are the only stones you avoid the gems relating to natural malefic planets?

James: That's right. I won't advise wearing a stone for Sun, Mars, Saturn, Rahu, or Ketu, unless that planet is running its *dasa* or that planet is the ascendant ruler.

Martin: And sometimes you'll strengthen a malefic if it needs it and doesn't throw any tight aspect onto another planet?

James: That's right. But, I would use my intuition and judgement for each situation. I might not want to strengthen Mars or Saturn, even if it needed help, if it happens to be aspecting a sensitive house like the 7th (marriage) or the 5th (children).

As far as wearing stones, they can be worn together or separately. When someone tells you that stones can't be worn together, which some will, remind them that *navaratnas* are quite popular. A *navaratna* is an amulet that contains all nine planetary gemstones, with the largest stone being placed in the middle of the others. That large stone should be the gem of the ascendant ruler.

Martin: You're not bothered by the friendship scheme when prescribing gems? You don't care whether planets that you strengthen are friends or enemies?

James: I've told you before and I'll say it again, in my experience the friendship scheme is either very overrated or simply misunderstood. The natures of the planets (benefic or malefic) come first, and the purpose of the friendship scheme is simply to determine which planets welcome other planets in their houses. Venus, Moon, Jupiter, and Mercury are so good-natured that they would never go out of their way to hurt other planetary beings. These are kind, well-behaved beings who simply try not to associate with those they do not like. If an enemy to Venus, Jupiter, Moon, or Mercury occupies one of their houses, that enemy planet does not function well because it has not been invited, is not welcomed, and does not receive the grace of the host. That's all.

Martin: I knew that, but I wanted to make sure. Some astrologers are very dogmatic about friends and enemies.

James: I know they are. As always, there are different opinions, and I suggest that you experiment and come to your own conclusions.

Martin: I've also heard that some astrologers like to strengthen the good planets in a chart rather than the afflicted ones. Do you always strengthen the afflicted planets?

James: My habit has always been to find the afflicted planets in a chart and strengthen them, unless those planets are natural malefics that may harm planets they aspect. If a <u>malefic</u> planet is afflicted, I advise mantra chanting or *yagyas* for that planet, because those methods will <u>not</u> cause harm to other nearby planets.

The question of whether to strengthen the well-disposed planets in a chart or the afflicted ones is an interesting one. Some astrologers look in each horoscope to find a planet that is giving a person benefits in life and then they strengthen it so the person gets even *greater* benefits. They will often strengthen a planet that rules the 5th or 9th house because those are considered good planets for the chart.

Martin: You mean like strengthening Venus if a person has a Gemini or Virgo ascendant?

James: Exactly. Or the astrologer will advise strengthening the Moon for a Scorpio ascendant because the Moon rules the 9th house in that chart. The 9th house rules luck, so strengthening it increases the person's luck.

Martin: And you're saying that if a person has a very strong Moon, Mercury, Jupiter or Venus that is already giving good results, some astrologers will strengthen that planet so it gives <u>more</u> good results?

James: Yes. I've never prescribed gems that way, but there's nothing wrong with that method. I think it's a personal philosophical choice that each astrologer has to make. I used to think that the method of strengthening well-disposed planets or planets ruling excellent houses rather than damaged planets was absurd, until one day I had a realization when I was fertilizing my fruit trees.

Martin: Your fruit trees?

James: You know I have about thirty fruit trees in the back yard. Well, when I planted them, they were all about the same size. But after a few years, some of the trees have grown tremendously and some have barely grown at all. I noticed that it's been my habit to give extra care to the trees that seem to have problems.

Martin: That makes sense.

James: Yes, it makes sense. But one day I was running out of fertilizer and realized I would have to choose which two trees would get the rest of my batch. My instinct, of course, was to fertilize my lemon tree and blood orange tree, both of which were growing so slowly I felt like I was watching paint dry. Then I suddenly thought, "Why should I waste the fertilizer on trees that won't give fruit for years when I could fertilize my mango trees which already give fruit and will give *more* if I fertilize them?" So as you can see, either method has its merits.

Martin: But you still mainly focus on afflicted planets when prescribing *upayes*?

James: Yes, but that's just my personal choice. You have to decide for yourself which path to take.

Martin: A minute ago you said that you won't strengthen a malefic planet that happens to be afflicted because making it stronger could hurt the planets that it aspects. Why do you say that chanting a mantra or having a *yagya* performed for a malefic planet won't cause harm to the planets that the malefic planet aspects?

James: First, let me tell you that I will go to my death wondering why God set up a system where strengthening one planet with a gem hurts another planet. I know the logic and reasoning of how it works, but I still find it truly absurd.

Regarding your question, the practice of mantras and *yagyas* is quite different from wearing gemstones. The purpose of wearing a stone, as I see it, is to have the essence of a particular planetary energy on our body so we receive its powerful vibrations. If we are subtly feeling the vibration of Venus all day long, for example, that has to have a significant effect, right?

Martin: That makes sense.

James: And if we are feeling the vibration of Mars all day long, and Mars aspects some sensitive planets in our chart, that could hurt those other planets somehow.

Martin: So far, I understand.

James: Well, mantras and *yagyas* are a completely different phenomenon. When we chant a mantra or perform a *yagya*, we are simply imploring God or a particular Lord of Karma to give His or Her grace. And if that grace is given, the problems associated with the particular planet involved are ameliorated or fixed, and no one gets hurt. It's a win-win situation.

I've heard other astrologers say things like, "Oh, you mustn't pray to Mars because Mars aspects Venus, and Venus will get hurt," and, "You can't pray to the Sun because the Sun is an enemy to your ascendant ruler, Venus." To me, these statements are so absurd I barely know how to address them.

Martin: How can praying to a god possibly hurt anything?

James: It can't! If the Sun in your chart is afflicted, it means you have misused the Sun's energy — the Sun's principle — in a past life and are now paying the price by suffering in the realms and significations of the Sun. Praying to the Sun through mantra chanting or *yagyas* is your way of saying to the Sun, "I know I have misused your energy and I'm sorry. Can you possibly bestow your grace on me and lessen the suffering?"

The whole point of a predictive form of astrology is to see a person's good karma and bad karma *and then be able to do something about it*. This is, by far, the most important purpose of astrology.

Martin: Every chart has afflictions, so why bother looking at karma if you can't fix it?

James: That's the point. Also, I know that there are some astrologers who believe that only an enlightened guru should prescribe mantras and *yagyas*. This is another ridiculous concept in my view — as if there is such a thing as praying to a wrong planetary being! If a person has problems with children and should be praying to Jupiter (*karaka* of children) or the planet ruling the 5th house, but the astrologer makes a mistake and tells the person to chant the mantra of the ruler of the 7th house, at worst the person begins having better love relationships. If the person has *yagyas* done for Saturn instead of Jupiter, the worst that can happen is that the person starts having better career results and benefits relating to the houses ruled by Saturn in the horoscope.

Martin: Some astrologers think that by giving a person a mantra they are taking responsibility for the person's evolution.

James: Perhaps, but I don't know where they get that idea from, since the astrological mantras and *yagyas* have nothing to do with *moksha* (enlightenment). These astrological mantras and *yagyas* strictly relate to worldly karma. Their purpose is simply to fix the problems and alleviate the suffering that humans experience. Which brings me to another point.

If you practice for spiritual disciples, about one out of three people will tell you that they believe they don't have to do mantras or *yagyas* because they have been told by their guru that their bad karma is being ameliorated through their *sadhana*, their spiritual practice. This is pure nonsense and it gets my goat because Indian gurus should know better. Even enlightened gurus constantly get karma back, unless they chant mantras or perform *yagyas* to change the situations. I've seen bad karma come back to gurus.

Martin: What do you tell these disciples?

James: I explain what I just told you, and I say that what the gurus mean is that when bad karma comes back to someone who is meditating and constantly evolving, that person may be *less upset by the bad karma coming back*. But the karma still comes back. There's no question about that.

Martin: So, if the person who is meditating or practicing some *sadhana* is about to have a period of accidents, financial loss, or marriage disruptions, the problems still occur but the person doesn't care so much?

James: Exactly. You have to explain to these people that if they want their worldly life to work better, the astrological mantras and *yagyas* are the methods to use.

Martin: I see. I have another question. If a person has a planet or house that is terribly afflicted, or the person is entering a bad *dasa-bhukti*, is it better to prescribe mantra chanting or a *yagya*?

James: They're pretty much the same. If the person has the money for *yagyas*, it's easier and perhaps more reliable because you're hiring priests who are good at what they're doing. But if a person doesn't have the money, mantra chanting is the way to go. Or, if the person has a very afflicted Jupiter or 9th house, dealing with religious priests may be distasteful.

Now, some people don't like chanting mantras. I've gotten scores of phone calls from people who chanted mantras and got miraculous results. But some people enjoy chanting, while others would rather pay priests to do it for them. So, that's a personal choice. Whenever I chant mantras, I prefer meditating on them silently.

Martin: You mean mental repetition?

James: Exactly. Mantras can be chanted silently or out loud. I prefer doing them silently. Chanting out loud often tires me out, while meditating on mantras is very relaxing. Also, I've heard that meditating on mantras is more powerful than chanting them out loud. But, to a large extent it's a personal choice.

Anyway, you certainly have to appreciate how important *yagyas* are. Do you know about the Bhrigu astrology readings that are done in India?

Martin: Where the astrologer reads what Bhrigu wrote thousands of years ago?

James: Yes. Maharshi Bhrigu was a great seer (or a God) during *Satya Yuga*. According to Indian philosophy, there are four *Yugas*, or "spans of creation" that occur cyclically. *Satya Yuga* is the greatest and most enlightened of the four, and during that age people live for many thousands of years.

Martin: We're in *Kali Yuga* now.

James: That's right. *Kali Yuga* is known as the "age of quarrel," where people live very debased lives. Well, during *Satya Yuga* Maharshi Bhrigu wrote down the horoscopes of every person that would <u>ever exist,</u> and these horoscopes which are now on palm leaves have been passed down from parent to child for generations. (I am aware of the oddity of this statement, but everything about Bhrigu readings defies the imagination. I can only suggest that what I am saying about Bhrigu readings will make sense after you have had one.) If you go to Hoshiarpur, India, there are four brothers who are Bhrigu readers. (Note: One of the brothers has died and his wife now does the readings.) You can also get Bhrigu readings in other parts of India, but the readers are more difficult to find.

When you see how accurate Bhrigu was about your life, past and future, you'll be absolutely amazed. In the <u>main</u> reading, Bhrigu talks about many of your past and future lives (Sometimes a person may only receive a partial reading that only deals with a few present issues). I should mention, though, that the accuracy of a Bhrigu reading depends to an extent on the interpreter. Bhrigu wrote his horoscope delineations in Sanskrit, which has to be translated into Hindi, and then English. Sometimes, a bit of accuracy is lost because of this.

Martin: What does this have to do with mantras and *yagyas*?

James: Well, having a Bhrigu reading is a great experience when you realize that thousands of years ago someone predicted with <u>startling accuracy</u> what would happen in your life. But the most important feature of the reading is that Bhrigu tells you what sins you committed in a past life that are causing current suffering, and exactly which *yagyas* you should do to fix the problems. Other than the accuracy of readings, the most consistent factor is the recommendation of *yagyas*.

Martin: Everyone needs *yagyas*?

James: Or mantras. But there is a note of caution about Bhrigu readings. Most people find that the information given is nearly one hundred percent accurate *up to the time of the reading*. The predictions about one's future are not quite so accurate.

Martin: That makes no sense. The entire reading occurred thousands of years ago. Why should the second part of the reading be less accurate?

James: I believe it has to do with the interpreter. Bhrigu wrote his interpretations in Sanskrit, which is not an easy language to interpret. One word can have several different meanings. Therefore, the interpreter's skills come into play.

Martin: Then why would the information about a person's past be accurate but not his or her future?

James: Because the interpreter uses intuition when trying to interpret the Sanskrit phrases. It's easier to intuit what has already happened to a person than to see the person's future. In my Bhrigu reading, I was told I would eventually have a large *"sanstha."* Well, one man translated this to mean a hotel or restaurant. Another said an orphanage, and another said an astrology school. Since I have very little desire to open an orphanage, restaurant, hotel, or astrology school, I've asked lots of Indians for their interpretation of the term *sanstha*.

Martin: What do they say?

James: An organization or a spiritual ashram of some sort. Some of Bhrigu's predictions that seemed strange when I heard them have already come true.

Martin: Really?

James: Bhrigu said I would do political astrology, which seemed very unlikely. Well, a few years after the Bhrigu reading, I got a call from <u>The Mountain Astrologer</u> magazine asking me to write an article on the presidential candidates. It came out of the blue, completely unexpected. I never would have initiated something like that on my own.

Martin: That's impressive.

James: Bhrigu also gave intimate details of my first marriage and divorce. He said my second marriage would be to an astrologer, which Vashti is. He said I would write astrology books, travel to India, and that I am perfectly suited to be an astrologer. He also said that I would combine *Jyotish* with spiritual life, which I take to mean my involvement with prescribing mantras and *yagyas*. I've been a huge proponent of mantra chanting and *yagyas* for years, while so many astrologers ignore them. The truth is, if I didn't have a way to help alleviate people's suffering with mantras and *yagyas*, I wouldn't want to read people's charts.

I want to mention some important points about *yagyas*. First of all, the *yagyas* done in the West are usually small — one priest chanting for one hour. This kind of *yagya* can be obtained in any Hindu temple you can find. The only time I recommend such a small *yagya*, however, is if a person is in a crisis and needs one immediately. Or, if the person can't afford a big *yagya*, the one-priest *yagya* is good because it usually costs $100 or $150. But whenever possible, I prefer large *yagyas*. I know of one organization called

Biswa Kalyan, that is located in a town called *Nabadwip*. They do large *yagyas* that consist of about twenty priests chanting for seven days, for about eight hours a day. Remember, this is a *yagya* specifically for the person ordering it.

Martin: As opposed to?

James: There are some *yagyas* (also sometimes called *pujas*) that are done for groups of people that will not have nearly the same effect as one that is done specifically for one person. Anyway, the large *yagya* cost about $750 (in 2000). There is also a smaller *yagya* that consists of about ten or twelve priests chanting for three days, for about eight hours a day that costs about $450. I've dealt with this organization for years and my clients have gotten excellent results from them. The man who organizes the *yagyas* is named Yves DeCarie and he lives in Canada. His phone number is (450) 463-3636. Or you can look at his website: www.yajna.com.

Yagyas can be done anytime. For example, if Venus is afflicted in a person's chart, the person doesn't have to wait until massive suffering occurs in a Venus period or subperiod. My advice to a person with an afflicted planet is to fix that planet as soon as possible.

Martin: Even as a child?

James: Absolutely. In fact, the three day *yagya* is essentially a child's *yagya*. If a person is under the age of eighteen, I recommend a three day *yagya*. If an adult can't afford a seven day *yagya*, that person should do a three day *yagya*.

Martin: Does that work?

James: You bet your life it does. The first *yagya* I ever did for my mother (she's had about six or seven done by now) lasted three days and it was miraculous. For a period of about a month, she was exhausted and didn't have the strength to even leave her apartment. I actually thought she was dying (she was in her mid-seventies at the time). I got her a three day *yagya* because I was scared to have a seven day *yagya* done for her.

Martin: Why?

James: I know now that my fear was completely silly, but my mother's life has been so tragically difficult that I thought that a big *yagya* might put her completely out of her misery.

Martin: You mean kill her?

James: Yes. You'd have to know how bad her suffering has been to understand. Anyway, I got her the small *yagya* and then called her on the phone about two or three days after the *yagya* to see if she felt any better.

Martin: What happened?

James: Every time I called, I got her answering machine! She hadn't left her apartment for a month and now every time I called I got her answering machine. Then I got really scared! A day or two later, she returned my calls and do you know what her exact words were? "If you want to call me, call at 8:00 in the morning or 11:00 at night." I couldn't believe my ears. I asked her what was happening and she said, "I have so much energy. I'm going shopping, I'm going swimming, I'm going out with friends." That was a typical *yagya* effect, when the *yagya* results are strong. *Yagyas* aren't always this effective, but when they are, they are miraculous.

Another point: *yagyas* usually have more noticeable effects when you do one for a planet running its period or subperiod. That doesn't mean you should wait for the period or subperiod to occur before fixing a planet with a *yagya*. It's far better to avert danger before it happens. I'm just letting you know that a *yagya* usually gives more noticeable results when you have it performed in that planet's *dasa* or *bhukti*.

I've also noticed that the more afflicted a planet is, the less likely a person is to notice the effects.

Martin: Could a person's karma be so bad that mantra chanting or performing *yagyas* won't help?

James: Unfortunately, yes. Consider someone like Hitler. Do you think that after being so evil that he can escape the bulk of his suffering just because he suddenly wakes up and prays to God? There are charts that you'll see where the karma of a planet or a house (or in some extreme cases an entire horoscope) is massively afflicted, and you'll wonder whether the person has any hope of getting help. This brings me to the next point.

Never, never, never try to determine who should be told about gems, mantras, and *yagyas* and who shouldn't. I learned this very early on in my practice. In my early days, I had no access to *yagyas*, so all I could prescribe for someone who needed more than a gem was mantra chanting. Well, I read a chart for a woman who didn't appear to have a spiritual or metaphysical bone in her body. I knew that my job was to prescribe gems, mantras, and *yagyas*, but I felt ridiculous telling this Midwestern housewife to chant a mantra. But what was I going to do, tell her go off and just suffer some more? I gave her the astrological mantra that I felt she needed and sent her on her way.

Martin: What happened?

James: She called me about two months after the reading to say that her and her husband's lives began to turn around the day she began the chanting. Their lives had been dramatically falling apart when she came to me. Remember this story. Don't ever discriminate about who you think will chant a mantra or consult a priest for a *yagya*. That's not your job. Your job is to tell <u>every</u> person how to get help. Period.

I have a five minute cassette tape where I've pronounced all the mantras slowly and clearly, and at the end of each person's reading, I transfer that five minutes of tape onto their cassette. Everyone gets the mantras, and everyone gets Yves' (the *yagya* organizer) phone number.

Martin: What if clients tell you they're not interested in mantras or *yagyas*?

James: That happens once in a while. Those people get the recommendations too. I tell them that they don't have to act on the recommendations, but it's my job to give them. I do this because many times people will reconsider later on, when they hear their tape. This particularly happens if I predict a terrible period, say, two or three years away. When that period occurs and the suffering starts for real, it's fun to watch the person suddenly change his or her mind.

I once gave a mantra to a man who needed help with some very afflicted planet. Months later, he called to say that he loved the results so much he wanted to know if there was a mantra that could help his finances. I gave him the mantra for the ruler of the 2nd house and wished him luck. About six or eight months later, he called to say his salary had doubled and asked me to give him all nine mantras. So you see, the mantras work just as well as *yagyas* for many people. But even though I could tell you success story after success story, lots of times people do *yagyas* and the results are not at all noticeable or dramatic. That doesn't necessarily mean they're not working, but it does mean that the person may be somewhat disappointed that the results aren't more pronounced.

In my chart, Venus and Jupiter are extremely afflicted. I've done many *yagyas* for Venus and nearly every time I do one I get sick (due to a purification process) during the seven days it's going on. Venus rules my 1st and 6th houses — the houses governing health. I don't usually see dramatic results when I do a Venus *yagya*, but as the months progress, the effects *slowly* begin to manifest. I've done many Jupiter *yagyas* and I'm always somewhat disappointed during the *yagya* and a week or two after. But again, as the months pass, I notice that the significations of Jupiter and the houses it rules slowly get better.

Martin: Have you done *yagyas* for planets that are not so afflicted in your chart?

James: Yes, and I almost always get noticeably positive results quickly. I get great results from Moon *yagyas*. My Moon is in a "mixed" condition because it is in the 12th house, which is bad, but it's so bright it gives some good natal results as well. I've done large Moon *yagyas* twice and gotten excellent results both times.

I also did a Mars *yagya* a few years back, when I was in Rahu-Mars *dasa-bhukti*. That was a bad period because whenever a planet is *tightly* opposite Rahu (e.g. conjunct Ketu), the results are very rough. I was having all kinds of friction with people and lots of near accidents in my car. Mars occupies the 4th house, which rules cars.

Martin: Why were you having friction with people?

James: Even though Rahu occupies my 10th house and Mars occupies the 4th, there have to be some 7th house effects because these *dasa* and *bhukti* planets are 7 houses away from each other. So I kept attracting aggressive and annoying people.

Martin: Does that mean that anytime a person runs a Rahu period and Ketu subperiod, they will have some 7th house effects because Rahu and Ketu are always seven houses away from each other?

James: Yes. Many people get married in Rahu-Ketu periods. Or they enter an important relationship. Not everybody, of course. But many people do. Anyway, as soon as I did the Mars *yagya*, I stopped having so many difficulties.

I have one more thing to say about *yagyas* and mantras before we move on. If I see a very bad period for a person coming up many years down the road, I tell the person to work on the afflicted planet involved <u>before</u> the period arrives and then <u>during</u> the afflicted period.

Let's use your chart as an example. Let's say I notice you entering a Jupiter-Mars period and subperiod five years from now. This is hypothetical, of course. I know you're nowhere near a Jupiter *dasa*.

Martin: My Jupiter-Mars period would be terrible because in my chart Jupiter is aspected by Mars <u>to the degree</u>.

James: Exactly. So I would advise you to chant mantras or perform *yagyas* for Jupiter (the afflicted planet) two or three years <u>before</u> the period begins, so that the period would not be so bad. And I would advise you to do Jupiter mantras and/or Jupiter *yagyas* throughout the entire period as well. On top of that, I would advise using common sense. Common sense means not trying to conquer the world in a terrible period. It means taking it easy until the period ends.

Martin: Would it be good to go meditate somewhere or live in the country until the period is over?

James: It would. I tell clients in a bad or dangerous period to just try and make it through the period without taking on any more stress than necessary. That's the best a person can do in a very bad period.

Now I want to move onto a new subject.

Martin: Wait. You haven't yet told me how people should chant mantras and exactly how you prescribe *yagyas*.

James: For mantra chanting, I advise buying a strand of 100 or 108 beads, and that's how you count your chants. Usually, Westerners will chant 100 or 108 (108 beads is called a *mala*) times per day. That generally takes about fifteen minutes. When I meditate silently on mantras, I avoid beads. I just meditate on the mantra for fifteen or twenty minutes each sitting.

Mantra chanting should be kept as consistent as possible. So, if you chant in the morning at, say, 8 AM, then you should chant every day at that time. I also advise <u>starting</u> the chanting on a bright Moon that is waxing (getting bigger). I never start anything when the Moon is dim or waning. Try to start chanting about a week (or a few days) before a full Moon <u>on the day ruled by the planet</u>. So, if you're chanting for Venus, you start on Friday, about a week before a full Moon. For Saturn, start chanting on Saturday, just before a full Moon. That's just the <u>starting</u> day. After that, chant seven days a week. The duration of chanting is a judgement call, but I tell my clients to chant a planetary mantra for at least six months or more.

If a person is in a terrible *dasa*, I advise chanting for the entire period or for six months at a time. That means you chant for six months and stop, and then half a year later you start the chanting again.

Martin: What about *yagyas*?

James: Regarding *yagyas*, if I'm trying to strengthen a planet long-term (in other words, if I'm trying to fix a <u>natal</u> problem), then the traditional recommendation is to have a *yagya* performed for the particular planet every six or nine months — for about four years.

Martin: So, in my case with my heavily afflicted Jupiter, you would advise having a *yagya* performed for Jupiter twice a year for about four years?

James: Yes. Actually, the ideal scenario would have been for you to do these *yagyas* as a child, when the *yagyas* could have been small (three days). Once you are an adult, the *yagyas* should be seven days. But, there's one very important qualification. If you can't afford seven-day *yagyas*, then the three-day ceremonies should definitely be done. I have seen three-day *yagyas* work miracles as often as the bigger ones.

I always advise a person in a rough period or subperiod to do *yagyas* <u>before</u> the bad period arrives and then every three or four months (or more if you like) during the rough period. This is very important, because if a person has worked on a planet before the bad period arrives, it significantly lessens the hardship. And, I definitely would continue the *yagyas* (or mantra chanting) throughout the afflicted period, that's for sure.

Now, I want to talk briefly about a different subject. Do you have any more questions about mantras and *yagyas* and gems?

Martin: No.

James: Good. I want to give you some advice about the practice of astrology. Unless you are financially independent, it's important to develop a side venture to bring in money while you practice. The reason for this is that astrology is somewhat of a burnout profession. As a career, it's quite similar to therapeutic massage.

Martin: People burn out after practicing massage for five or ten years. It requires too much physical energy.

James: Exactly right. In the case of astrology, it takes too much psychic energy. The process of talking to clients for an hour or two at a time, day in and day out, takes an enormous toll after some years. If you speak with almost any seasoned astrologer who has been making his or her living doing chart readings alone, that person will tell you that astrology is unduly demanding in the long run. Are you aware of the fact that enlightened yogis don't have to eat or drink if they remain in silence? They say they can actually live on sunlight unless they begin talking. That's how much energy talking requires.

So, there are two factors to dealing with this burnout problem. First, you should have a schedule that allows for periods of regular rest. Some astrologers work for three weeks every month and then take a full week off. Some work nine months and then take a three month vacation. So, you have to find some way.

Second, you should try to develop a side income so that as you get older you won't have to pay all your bills from chart readings. I meet far too many middle-aged astrologers who are so burned out it shows in their bodies.

Martin: They gain too much weight?

James: Yes. They gain too much weight because astrology is such a mental and sedentary profession. Another reason this issue is so important is that the long term depletion of energy that occurs is hard on your spiritual evolution. If you're serious about pursuing enlightenment, having your energy constantly drained is a serious drawback. During my Bhrigu reading, I was told that I have "the perfect karma" to be an astrologer. Well, I must tell you that after about ten years of practice even I began to find doing readings day in and day out extremely tedious.

Many astrologers develop horoscope interpretation printouts to help pay their bills or they write astrology books. Unfortunately, astrology books don't produce great profits. They mainly help generate publicity, which bring in more and more clients.

Martin: And that doesn't help.

James: Please don't get me wrong, now. Astrology is a wonderful profession that gives some great spiritual benefits as well a tremendous sense of joy from the service you provide. It's also a way to be your own boss. But after many years, astrologers typically start to feel like they don't have a life of their own. The phone is constantly ringing and people constantly need your help.

Most clients you will see are fine, but there are always some difficult, needy people. And the more overworked you are, the more they can get to you. I was talking with Dr. David Frawley (author of <u>Astrology of the Seers</u>) recently, and he has a humorous term about the rough clients. He calls it the "ten percent rule."

Martin: Ten percent of clients are difficult?

James: That's right. David has noticed that ten percent of all clients are difficult, no matter what. And I completely agree with him. Again, please don't misunderstand me. Astrology is a fun profession. It's also miraculous and awe-inspiring, to say the least. But I am advising you <u>at the start of your work</u> to begin thinking about developing a second way to bring in money. Maybe a metaphysical bookstore, a health food store, or some other side venture. It's just a suggestion that will make your life as an astrologer a lot easier and more enjoyable as you get older. So, take the advice for what you think it's worth.

Martin: It sounds important. And it makes me want to look more closely at my 11th house – the house of gains and profits through side ventures.

James: Good point. Now, onto another subject. In our very first class when I analyzed the *muhurta* chart for this project, I mentioned that I would talk about my wedding *muhurta*.

Martin: I remember that.

James: So let's talk about *muhurtas* for a bit, and then I'll show you why we got married late at night on a Tuesday. I'll also talk about compatibility charts.

First of all, it's not so easy to find a truly good marriage chart. The truth is, I usually only see a few good marriage *muhurtas* per year.

Martin: Really? Why?

James: Well, aside from finding a good chart, there are so many conditions that need to be avoided. I never want to begin <u>any</u> endeavor within a day or two on either side of the new Moon (dark Moon). Preferably, I want a very bright Moon. I never want to begin any endeavor on a waning Moon if I can help it. This requirement alone cuts out two weeks of every month. I will, however, use a waning Moon if I <u>have to</u>, but *only if the Moon is very well-aspected by benefic planets.*

I also would not let a person enter a marriage, or any contract, when Mercury is retrograde.

Martin: That occurs three times a year, for about three weeks at a time.

James: That's right. So there's another nine weeks every year that are useless. For a marriage *muhurta*, I can't possibly use a date when Venus (planet of love) is retrograde. This happens once every two years, for about 40 days at a time. I also can't use a date when Venus occupies Virgo, its fallen sign, which occurs about once every year-and-a-half for four or five weeks.

Martin: And you wouldn't want to use the months when Venus occupies Scorpio or Aries, the signs opposite Venus' own signs.

James: You're getting the picture. Now, as if these constraints aren't enough, there are three or four week periods when Venus is conjunct Mars or the Sun, or aspected by some other malefic planet. I would never start a marriage when Venus is afflicted.

Martin: Or when the 7th house is afflicted, right?

James: Of course. The 7th house and the ruler of the 7th house have to be in good shape. And the ascendant, which is the essence or nucleus of a chart, needs to be well-disposed as well.

On top of all these concerns, there's the matter of other planetary afflictions. Should anyone get married when the Sun is tightly conjunct or opposite Saturn?

Martin: That would cause limitations and restrictiveness, wouldn't it?

James: Of course. How about choosing a day when Jupiter is conjunct Ketu or tightly aspected by Mars? These placements would harm religious compatibility as well as luck in general.

Martin: This sounds impossible.

James: Well, it's is difficult. Finding a <u>perfect</u> chart is impossible, so certain compromises are made. The *muhurta* for my marriage was excellent, but it certainly had some planetary afflictions. I would like to have avoided certain features within my marriage chart, but Vashti and I had already waited a long time and we weren't willing to wait another 9 or 10 months.

With marriage *muhurtas* you do the best you can, and if the chart feels good <u>on the whole,</u> you go with it. If not, you wait. But, it's easier telling a client to wait. It's very hard when you're planning your own marriage.

Martin: So, what did your marriage chart look like?

James: The date was January 26, 1993, at 10:50 P.M., in Boca Raton, Florida. It's a good *muhurta*, but not completely problem-free.

Before we analyze the chart, here's a list of some astrological concerns I use when choosing a wedding *muhurta*:

1. The Moon should be bright and waxing (getting bigger) if possible.

2. The 7th house and the 1st houses are the most important. They should be very well-disposed by occupying and aspecting planets, including the ruling planets.

3. The most important planets for a marriage chart are Venus (love), the Moon (because *Jyotish* is a lunar-based system), and the ascendant ruler (the essence or nucleus of any chart).

4. The "feeling" of the chart, in terms of love and romance, should be as positive and harmonious as possible.

5. According to the late B.V. Raman (the most famous astrologer and most prolific astrological author in India), there should be no planets in the 8th house. Raman felt that even one 8th house planet in a marriage chart would cause too much suffering.

6. Any positive connections between the 1st and 7th houses would increase harmony between husband and wife.

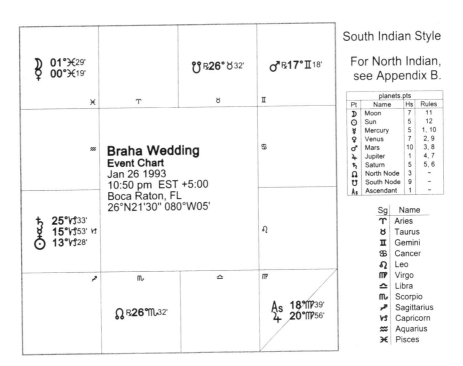

As you can see in my wedding *muhurta*, we were able to achieve most, though not all, of the desired features. Let's look at the Moon first. The Moon is waxing, but is actually not bright at all. In fact, the Moon is only about three days past its darkest point. The reason I was willing to use a chart with a Moon just beginning to gain strength was because the Moon was so well-aspected. Notice that the Moon is conjunct with benefic Venus, and Venus lends even better vibrations than usual because it occupies Pisces, its exaltation sign. On top of this, the Moon-Venus conjunction is incredibly tight — within a degree-and-a-half, which is great. The Moon is receiving an aspect from benefic Jupiter, and Jupiter is aspecting its own sign — Pisces.

Martin: This is great.

James: Yes, I think so. This is an extraordinary 7th. Can you see the romantic and harmonious love energy a 7th house like this would bring?

Notice that the ruler of the 7th house, Jupiter, occupies the 1st house. This makes a strong connection between the 1st and 7th houses (husband and wife), which is great for married life. Normally, I would not want the ruler of the 7th house to be in a bad sign (Virgo is the sign opposite Jupiter's own sign, Pisces, and is therefore detrimental). But I'm not too bothered by this placement because Jupiter is aspected by two benefic planets, Moon and Venus. I know Venus is aspecting Virgo, its fallen sign, but on the whole I like Jupiter's placement. One of the main reasons I like it is because of *Chandra lagna*.

Martin: Moon ascendant.

James: That's right. From the vantage point of the Moon, Jupiter occupies the 7th house. That's just one more positive 7th house effect to throw into the mix.

Now let's look at the drawbacks of this *muhurta*. The first negative is that malefic Saturn aspects the 7th house. This is a harmful aspect that we certainly didn't want. I wouldn't have accepted that aspect if it weren't for the fact that the 7th house is otherwise phenomenally strong.

Martin: What do you think the aspect will cause?

James: A certain amount of restrictions, limitations, and karmic conditions. We'll both have to make compromises within the marriage.

Martin: What else is new?

James: On the other hand, it's possible that Saturn's aspect could lend some staying power to the marriage. I wouldn't go overboard in that assessment, because I would definitely prefer that Saturn <u>not</u> aspect the 7th house. But the *possibility* of some good is there.

By the way, I wouldn't have been able to live with Saturn's aspects on the Moon and Venus if the aspects had been close *by degree*. Saturn's aspects occur within about twenty-four and twenty-five degrees of Moon and Venus, which will not cause extreme damage to them.

The second dilemma of this chart is the ascendant, which happens to contain a mixture of very positive and negative energy. The 1st house is strong because benefic Jupiter occupies the 1st house. Even though Jupiter is poorly placed by sign (Jupiter in Virgo), the effect is that Jupiter's benevolence in the house is not <u>as good</u> as it would be in some other sign. This is still a major benefit for the 1st house.

The bad news, which is quite serious, is that the ascendant ruler (Mercury) is terribly harmed. Mercury is hemmed in by malefics, combust the Sun, and aspected tightly by Mars.

Martin: Mercury is definitely afflicted.

James: Well, let's see you try to find a perfect marriage chart! Compromises always have to be made somewhere, because there is no such thing as a perfect chart — <u>ever</u>. But the 1st house is not completely afflicted. Jupiter occupies the ascendant, and two benefics — Moon and Venus — throw aspects onto the 1st house. That's why I said the ascendant is a mixture of extreme positive and negative energy.

Martin: I have a question about *muhurta* charts. How significant are they? If two people have poor compatibility or if one of the partners is not very healthy in love relationships, does the good *muhurta* make the marriage work? Does it turn things around for the couple?

James: I don't think so. But I can't answer the question with certainty because I'm not in the habit of choosing marriage charts for people who have terrible compatibilities. My opinion is that there are many factors that go into creating a good partnership, a good marriage. Ideally, you want to choose a good *muhurta* chart <u>and</u> marry a moderately healthy partner with whom you have a harmonious compatibility chart.

For compatibilities, I use two different methods. Both come from Western astrology, but will work whether you use a sidereal zodiac (the zodiac used in Hindu astrology) or a tropical one. A composite chart is where you take the midpoints of planets of both people to draw a horoscope. In other words, if the man's Venus is in one degree of Aries and the woman's Venus occupies one degree of Libra, then in the composite chart Venus would be placed in one degree of Cancer — the exact middle of one Aries and one Libra. The ascendant and all planets are calculated that way, and that comprises the composite chart. The composite chart reveals how the couple functions and whether they can get along or not. Although you can use this method as a Hindu chart, using traditional Hindu methods, I would advise using Western astrological aspects (squares, trines, sextiles, and so on) because there's so much important information to be gained.

Martin: What's the synastry chart you mentioned?

James: Actually, it's not a chart. It's simply noticing where one person's planets fall within the other person's chart. In other words, if my Venus occupies ten degrees of Virgo, it is not good if my partner's Saturn occupies, say, eight or nine degrees of Virgo. That would mean that when I am trying to be loving, artistic, and fun-loving, my partner would be inhibiting and restricting my experience of those realms.

Martin: But if your partner's Moon was near ten degrees of Virgo, there would be a great connection in the love area?

James: Exactly. And conjunctions are not the only aspects used. All Western aspects apply (for detailed descriptions of Western aspects see my book *How To Be A Great Astrologer*). Astrologers have their own preference of which is better to use for compatibility — the composite chart or synastry. I use them both, but greatly favor the composite chart. If you want to read about the composite method, get Robert Hand's book *Planets In Composite*. In any case, if I had to choose between a good *muhurta* or a good compatibility chart, I'd rather marry someone with whom the compatibility, the intrinsic harmony, is strong.

While we're on the subject of compatibility charts, I need to warn you about something. There is a Hindu compatibility method called the *kuta* system that is inappropriate for Westerners to use. It's inappropriate because it doesn't work for Westerners. In this system, many features of the man's and woman's horoscopes are analyzed for compatibility, and each factor within the system results in a certain number of points. If the number of points is high, then compatibility is said to be strong. If the number of points is low, then compatibility is weak. The problem is that the system doesn't work at all for Westerners because it was designed for *ancient Indians*.

Westerners use compatibility charts to find a partnership with *domestic harmony and tranquility*. We look to compatibility charts to see if we will be able to get along with a partner without too much friction, arguments, disagreements, and so on. We also want to know that our feelings of love and affection for a spouse will endure and that our marriage will last. The *kuta* system has nothing to do with these things.

Martin: What is it for?

James: A lot of things. Wealth, luck, having children, sexual compatibility, longevity, compatibility of castes, general welfare, and having enough food to eat. What the *kuta* system does not address is romance, passion, and whether a couple can get along or not. When a Westerner gets into a relationship, he or she wants to know "Will we fight, will we argue, will we remain close?" These things are not addressed by *kuta*. (Note: The *kuta* system mainly addresses ten considerations, one of which is "harmonious compatibility" of the partners. It is, however, quite possible for that feature to be completely weak, or low in points, while most other features are strong, or high in points. Thus, a Westerner who has a high total point number may believe incorrectly that he or she will achieve harmony in marriage. Even if the "harmonious compatibility" points are high, a Westerner should not necessarily assume that his or her marriage will be happy or smooth because of it.) They aren't addressed in India because Indians ensure that married couples will achieve a significant degree of domestic harmony simply by having parents arrange marriages for their children. In other words, parents choose a partner for their child who comes from the same general background.

Martin: I get it. That guarantees that the couple shares the same basic value system?

James: Yes. And that creates the kind of harmony necessary for marriage. It doesn't mean the couple won't argue, but the *essential* goals, ambitions, ethics, morals, religious customs, and approaches to life will be similar. That takes care of many potential problems, obviously.

Martin: Why aren't Indians concerned with the same kind of compatibility as us?

James: You have to understand that Indians live very differently from Westerners. They live in extended families and in very close knit communities. This helps enormously when a couple is not getting along all that well, which definitely occurs. If Westerners marry and don't get along, the pressure to divorce is enormous because there is no "buffer" to take one's mind off of the suffering. In India, a person who doesn't get along well with his or her spouse spends more time with siblings, cousins, uncles, and so on. The life is more communal and the person isn't constantly thinking about his or her joyless marriage. I know this sounds strange, but that's how Indians manage to stay married when they're in less than wonderful relationships. Speaking of which, God help you when you do a chart for an Indian in this country who is in a bad marriage. Divorce is so alien to them, they'll suffer endlessly rather than divorce. Although they are as pained as anybody by a marriage that is unhappy, they don't divorce. They simply don't consider domestic harmony as the end all and be all of marriage, like Westerners do.

Another point here is that when the *kuta* system was designed, Indians didn't concern themselves with romantic love and passion. That was not a priority. Tell a Westerner who comes for a compatibility chart not to be concerned with passion, romance, and affection. See how far you get.

Martin: You never use the *kuta* system?

James: I've had no interest in it since I found out how badly it worked for Westerners. Over the years, I've done lots and lots of horoscope for disciples of different spiritual groups. It seemed that every time I met a person who had *kuta* compatibility work done, he or she would either say that the points of the compatibility were high and the relationship was disastrous, or the points were very low and the relationship was wonderful. I heard this over and over. It wasn't until I talked with an Indian astrologer about the poor results the *kuta* system was generating in the West that I understood the reasons. Don't forget what I've told you. The *kuta* system not only doesn't work for Westerners, it gives people false information.

Martin: With regard to the *muhurta* you chose for your marriage, have you noticed concrete results from it? Did it help your relationship?

James: Yes. Our relationship became even more romantic than it had been before our wedding. If you think about Moon <u>tightly</u> conjunct exalted Venus in the 7th house and aspected by Jupiter, you can see why.

I also find that my wife and I are great friends as well as being romantically linked. That's because the Moon, which occupies the 7th house, rules the 11th house — the house of friends.

On the negative side, our marriage has been "heavier," or more serious than I expected. All the planets in the sign of Capricorn caused that. Vashti and I work together and some of the lightheartedness of our daily lives has disappeared. But the romance and sweetness is always there.

As much as I hate to say it, this is our last session. If there's anything that you're burning to ask, do it now. I know we haven't discussed astrological *yogas*, but that would make an entire book and I'm not the person to teach that. I don't use *yogas* extensively.

Martin: But you do use them. You mention them occasionally.

James: I probably only notice about twenty or thirty. There are actually thousands of them. In India, some astrologers rely more heavily on *yogas* than natal analysis and some rely more on natal analysis. I suspect the best way is to use both. But it's difficult, and actually somewhat rare to find astrologers who excel in both.

Martin: Even in India?

James: Even in India. Astrologers usually get fascinated by one or the other.

Martin: Well, I still have a very hard time when I see a chart with a stellium of planets in one house. Could you say something about that?

James: Okay. Let's take a hypothetical chart and I'll show you how I analyze it (see next page). This isn't anyone I know. It's just a time and date when a stellium of planets were all in the sign of Cancer in the 5th house. This chart has *Kala Sarpa Yoga*, by the way, but let's ignore that for now. I just want to show you how I would analyze the chart in terms of so many planets in one sign. First of all, there is a *yoga* (its name escapes me) that says that whenever there are four or more planets in one house, the person will be spiritual. That's about the only thing I can tell you that applies to every chart with a stellium. After that, it's simply a process of natal analysis using everything I've taught you so far. No tricks, no magic — just *Jyotish* logic.

Regarding the fact that there are lots of planets in the 5th house of this chart, do you think that makes the 5th house powerful?

Martin: Not necessarily. That depends on the nature of the planets in the

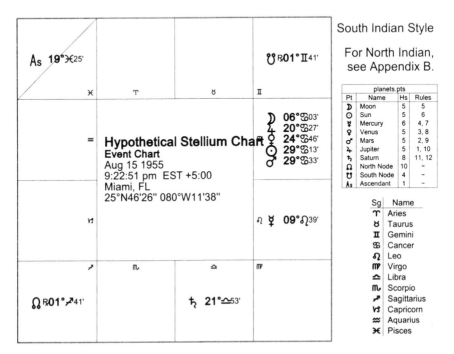

house, and especially the house ruler, and whether those planets are afflicted or well-disposed.

James: Exactly right. You've passed the first test regarding stellium charts. In this case, the 5th house ruler is the Moon, which occupies its own sign (Cancer) *and happens to occupy the earliest degree of any planet in the house.* Remember when I told you that the planet in the earliest degree of a sign/house containing a stellium *generally* has the biggest impact? To a large extent, the Moon is the key to understanding the stellium in this chart.

Now before we go any further, I have to tell you that this is one heck of a mixed 5th house. This is the kind of chart that makes my eyes go cross and causes me to consider drawing a *prasna* chart for the moment of the client's appointment.

Martin: That lets you know what's on the person's mind and why he or she is coming to you, right?

James: Right. Now, what makes this chart incredibly mixed is not the fact that there are some good planets in the 5th house (Moon, Jupiter, and Venus) as well as some bad planets (fallen Mars combust the malefic Sun). If that were the only complexity, I would say that the 5th house would function more on the positive side because the 5th house ruler and earliest planet in the stellium is the well-disposed Moon. And both Moon and Jupiter are well-placed by sign (Jupiter is exalted) in the 5th house. That means the 5th house would give generally powerful results and the person's life would largely center around 5th house affairs. Problems, however, would definitely be expected during Sun and Mars periods and subperiods.

Martin: Would those problems be severe?

James: Absolutely. But the person would *generally* enjoy 5th house significations, as well as 11th house significations.

Martin: Why 11th house?

James: Always remember that whenever you see a stellium of planets, those planets will aspect the opposite sign/house that they occupy. That makes the opposite house both important and prominent in every case. Don't forget that.

What makes this chart so complex is the fact that Saturn aspects the 5th house. Even benefic Venus and exalted Jupiter, which appear so well-disposed, are aspected *tightly* (within a few degrees) by malefic Saturn. And the aspect occurs in the sign of Cancer, a sign that doesn't like Saturn energy. The all-important Moon is also aspected by Saturn, which causes some problems and some restriction, but at least the aspect isn't incredibly tight. So you see, Saturn has thrown a big monkey wrench into the situation. Therefore, this chart is very hard to interpret with any certainty. As I told you in an earlier class, it takes an awful lot for me to consider drawing a *prasna* for the moment of a client's appointment. But I would probably draw one for this person.

Martin: This 5th house is basically a wild card?

James: Pretty much. But despite that fact, there's still a lot we can determine by using basic *Jyotish* techniques.

For one thing, there's a strong chance the person would favor 11th house matters more than 5th house matters. This is because the 11th house is aspected by so many planets while the 11th house ruler, Saturn, occupies its exaltation sign. I know Saturn is in the 8th house, a bad house, but because it's exalted it is clearly well-placed.

Also, we know for sure there will be severe problems with the houses ruled by the afflicted Sun and Mars, as well as the planetary significations of Sun and Mars.

Martin: Does the person have problems with everything connected to the 2nd, 6th, and 9th houses?

James: Yes. And the person will most likely have difficulties with father and government (Sun), and his or her bloodstream and temper (Mars), among other things.

As for Jupiter and Venus, and everything they rule (planetary-wise and by house rulership), the person will feel great *potential* in the areas ruled by those planets, but *manifesting* that potential will be an uphill struggle for an entire lifetime. Jupiter and Venus have some strength because they aspect each other tightly, but the benefits are weakened because they receive Saturn's tight aspect. I would strongly urge the person with this chart to strengthen Venus, Moon, and Jupiter with mantra chanting and *yagyas*, as well as gemstones.

Martin: Do you think the person would feel compelled to speculate or get involved with children (5th house significations)?

James: Yes, but I would advise against the person speculating for him- or herself. A career as a stock broker would be okay, but if the person gambles or speculates there will enormous ups and downs. Speculating would not be a good choice.

Regarding the strength of the 11th house, I would advise the person to try and make lots of money from side ventures. Actually, I advise anyone with a weak 2nd house and a strong 11th house (both of which this chart contains) to make money from side ventures. Or to make money that comes in large sums.

Martin: What does that mean, "money that comes in large sums?"

James: Businesses like real estate bring in occasional large sums of money. So do businesses where very high-priced items are sold. These are good for people with strong 11th houses. The person may not bring in much money regularly, but when the cash does flow it flows big.

Martin: What would you say about this person's children?

James: Not much. I wouldn't say much because I couldn't be certain. The 5th house is definitely a wild card. There could be several children, or there could be no children. There is a chance of no children because of Saturn's extremely tight aspect thrown onto Jupiter, the *karaka* of children. With a chart like this there could be some children, as well as some abortions or miscarriages. To know a person's situation with children in a case like this would take massive psychic ability. I do think a person with this chart would have a strong bond with children because the Moon is fairly well-placed in the 5th house. And the person would enjoy spending a lot of time with children, *if* he or she decided to have them.

Martin: What about career?

James: Going by the natal chart alone, without looking at the *dasamsa*, I would strongly advise the arts. Not because the 5th house rules art in general, however. Notice that the 10th house (career) ruler, Jupiter, is closely conjunct Venus — the planet of art, which happens to rule the 3rd house (house of art). Notice also that the 3rd house ruler, Venus, is closely conjunct exalted Jupiter which expands Venus' strength. The fact that the 5th house is energized by so many planets is also going to help with the arts.

Martin: But what about the fact that Venus and Jupiter are aspected by Saturn in the sign of Cancer, a sign that hates Saturn energy?

James: That means that the career is not going to be as easy or successful as it looks. But the arts are still the biggest likelihood of a career. Let's see how subtle you can get in your predictions. Do you have any feeling for what kind of art is the most likely for this person?

Martin: It's very hard to tell, James. The 3rd house rules music, dance, and drama, and it looks better-disposed than the 5th house, which rules painting and crafts. But I would really just be taking a wild guess.

James:. Here's where learning <u>every single meaning of every single house</u> comes in handy. Dancing is the greatest likelihood, because the 11th house specifically rules dance.

Martin: That's right. You said that the 11th house rules dance, just as well as the 3rd house.

James: I wouldn't bet all my money that the person would become a professional dancer, but it would definitely be one of the first things I mention. At that point, the person would either say, "I love dancing, but it's only a hobby," or, "Yes, I'm a professional dancer." Because the 11th house is strong, the person might also be very interested in group activity.

I'm not going to go over the rest of the chart because you should be able to do that yourself by now. The main thing is to tell the client with this chart what you can with <u>certainty</u>.

Martin: Like how Mars and the Sun are afflicted, as are the houses they rule (2nd, 6th, and 9th)?

James: Yes. Be careful in predicting 9th house problems, though. Remember that Jupiter aspects the 9th, which will give some good effects and render the house mixed. This is a spiritual chart, by the way. Look how Jupiter aspects the Pisces 1st house. Even Mars' aspect on the 1st house, which is bad, confirms an interest in higher knowledge because Mars rules the 9th house. Also, the two spiritual planets Jupiter and Saturn aspect the all-important Moon. And the 12th house (*moksha*) ruler is exalted. This is a person who will definitely follow some sort of spiritual path. Just remember that when you analyze a stellium, the task is to look at each individual factor separately. How are the houses disposed? How are the house rulers? How are the planets doing? What are the tight apsects involved? The main problem that astrology students have with stelliums is that when they see one, they freeze. Don't do that. Take your time and follow basic *Jyotish* logic and you'll do fine. Anyway, I guess that's enough for now.

Martin: I really and truly appreciate what you've taught me James. If I ever write a book, there's going to be a huge acknowledgment to you.

James: It's been my pleasure, Martin. You've been a great student, as I knew you would. You've asked excellent questions that are really going to help the students who read these transcripts. Who knows, maybe we'll do this again sometime. There's so much we haven't talked about. Bas.

FINAL SUMMARY

Throughout the text you have just read, I have done my best to share my personal experience with Hindu astrology. *Jyotish*, however, is a truly vast field and the need for exposure to <u>various</u> expert opinions is essential. Ever since I began teaching *Jyotish*, I have intermittently been asked by students on their way to India, "Who should I study with when I am there?" My advice has always been the same — if you are going for many months, find several different teachers to learn from. Travel widely and have your own horoscope interpreted by every *jyotishi* you can. When an astrologer is extremely accurate, ask if he or she will teach you. Bring many charts from home (of friends whose lives you know very well) and during the lessons let that astrologer demonstrate his or her predictive ability. Bearing in mind that every astrologer has his or her own distinctive talents, learn what you can from that teacher <u>and then move on to someone else</u>.

What you will inevitably find is that when it comes to *jyotish*, no one person knows it all. Even enlightened gurus are not infallible when practicing astrology. One astrologer will be extraordinarily gifted at predicting minute details, while another can look at a chart and instantly see the "big picture." One astrologer will know exactly how to fix a person's problems through *upayes*, while another will be able to tell a client every little detail about his or her karma in love relationships. One astrologer will be expert at predicting the future, while another will excel in analyzing the natal chart. And on and on it goes.

Your task in making use of the information given throughout this text, as well as in learning from any astrology teacher, is simply this: to discriminate and discern whether the astrological predictions and analysis are <u>accurate</u>. Although this sounds easy, for many students it is not. One of the greatest obstacles to predictive accuracy is the tendency toward gullibility. Too many astrologers and students accept the teachings of scriptures and teachers without thorough testing and objective analysis. This problem is exacerbated by the fact that astrology is an intuitive art. I have several times been dazzled by an astrologer's remarkable prediction about some area of my life, only to experience profound disappointment when that astrologer could not give a <u>reasonable and logical</u> astrological explanation. The havoc created by this phenomenon is great. Because of the vastness of our field, we astrologers must <u>forever</u> remain open, innocent, and genuinely interested in new techniques and teachings. We must also, however, remain deeply skeptical, picky, and discriminating. Make no mistake, the task is enormous and not for the faint of heart. Further, students must be on guard not to blindly accept astrological precepts simply because a teacher has shown several examples where a particular technique works well. Some techniques only work ten or twenty percent of the time, but students are not shown any examples of the technique failing miserably.

I am pleased with the teachings in this book and the fact that I could address many controversial *Jyotish* issues. As mentioned in the <u>Introduction</u>, I am more confident of the teachings in this book than in those of my earlier works because the more practice I have had, the more I have learned and the more accurate I have become. It is up to you, however, to determine which of my teachings work for you and which do not. It is up to you to seek out teachers who disagree with some of my assessments and hear their side of the truth. Remember this: *Jyotish* is a vast and infinite field and <u>no one teacher has a corner on the truth</u>. There is plenty of room for different opinions, different methods, and different approaches. Even the ancient astrological seers who were considered enlightened often disagreed on certain *Jyotish* features. That there are many paths and many masters is truer for astrologers than for any other profession!

May you find the techniques and teachings that allow you to become the best astrologer possible. May you make a powerful and profound difference in the world. And may you share <u>all</u> your findings with fellow astrologers. Godspeed and God Bless — All glories to Lord Sri Ganesh. Hare Krishna. Jai Guru Deva. Jai Ma. Mahalakshmi namah. Jai Mata Kali Durga.

Gratitude to helpful teachers: H.W.L. Poonja (Papaji), Maharishi Mahesh Yogi, Ramana Maharshi, Neem Karoli Baba, Paramahamsa Yogananda, A.C. Bhaktivedanta Swami, Michio Kushi, Werner Erhard, Sondra Ray, Maharshi Bhrigu, R. Santhanam, P.M.Padia.

Devotional Shiva mantra – *Om Namah Shivaya*

Mantra for healing abilities – *Om Hreem Kleem Krishnaya Govindaya Gopijan Vallabhaya Swaha*

Durga mantra (Mother Divine) – *Om Aim Hreem Kleem Chamundaye Veechay*

Maha Mrityunjaya mantra (for serious illnesses) – *Om trambakam yajamahey shoo-gandi push-tee var-danam oordvar roo-kumey bandanam rityoor ra-makshee mam-roo-tata*

Gayatri (highest daily meditation) – *Om bhur bhuvah svah tat savitur varenyam bhargo devasya dhimahi dhiyo yo nah pracodayat.*

Greatest spiritual books I have read in the last two decades

<u>Enlightenment is a Secret</u> by Andrew Cohen (www.andrewcohen.org)

<u>Nothing Ever Happened</u> by David Godman (Extraordinary three-volume autobiography of Hindu saint H.W.L. Poonja)

APPENDIX A:
HINDU ASTROLOGY FUNDAMENTALS

This Appendix is divided into seven main sections. *The Art and Practice of Hindu Astrology* talks about Hindu astrology at primarily an intermediate level. This Appendix covers all of the basics so that readers new to the topic may quickly bring themselves up to speed without having to buy a separate primer. For a comprehensive yet easy to understand introductory textbook, see James Braha's *Ancient Hindu Astrology for the Modern Western Astrologer* (1986).

Section I.
The Meanings and Symbols of the Planets

The Sun ☉: Dignity, confidence, willpower, ambition, one's father, government, eyesight, power, authority, the soul, ego, physicians, rubies, copper, Sunday

The Moon ☽: Emotions, feelings, general well-being, one's mother, females, agriculture, nurturing in childhood, the mind, common sense, memory, breasts, brain, menstrual cycle, cooks, nurses, the public, masses, silver, pearls, Monday

Mars ♂: Courage, heroic deeds, aggressiveness, assertiveness, ability to fulfill one's desires, siblings, sports, landed property, mechanical skills, computer work, builders, designers, engineers, surgeons, mechanics, the military, soldiers, policemen, war, general, commanders, rulers, accidents, violence, fires, cuts, burns bruises, temper, arguments, fights, weapons, guns, energy, passions, sex, medical operations, the blood, muscular system, bone marrow, Tuesday, red coral.

Mercury ☿: Intelligence, education, learning, teaching, speech, poetry, confidence, communication, writing, drawing, books, papers, publishing, conscious mind, intellect, commerce, trade, business, humor, wit, astrology, math, nervous system, lungs, intestines, nerve disorders, brain diseases, short journeys, writers, astrologers, secretaries, scholars, Wednesday, green emerald.

Jupiter ♃: Money, wealth, prosperity, luck, fortune, opportunity, religion, philosophy, children, long distance travel, faith, devotion, spirituality, wisdom, truthfulness, morality, charity, benevolence, compassion, foreigners, meditation, astrology, law, legal affairs, liver, allergies, thighs, optimism, speculation, gambling, one's Guru or religious teachers, bankers, lawyers, judges, ministers, Thursday, yellow sapphire, yellow topaz.

Venus ♀: Marriage, love matters, romance, comforts, luxuries, jewelry, wealth, prosperity, happiness, beauty, vehicles, conveyances, sensuality, passion, sexual desire, art, dance, music, drama, actors, artists, musicians, reproductive system, venereal diseases, silver, diamonds, Friday.

Saturn ♄: Longevity, death, misery, adversity, sorrows, restrictions, denial, delays, discipline, responsibility, accidents, chronic diseases, authority figures, elders, leadership, ambition, wisdom born of experience, humility, honesty, sincerity, spirituality, non-attachment, asceticism, organization, form, structure, paralysis, teeth, bones, construction work, carpentry, tedious work, mining, wood, coal, steel, iron, ascetics, monks, hermits, Lord Shiva, blue sapphire, Saturday.

Rahu ☊: Insatiable worldly desires, great worldly benefits, Science, dullness, laziness, sense gratification, ignorance, gomed or hessonite (honey colored form of agate).

Ketu ☋: Asceticism, non-attachment to worldly desires, natural healing methods, healing diets, *moksha* (enlightenment), psychic ability, tendency to go unnoticed or be invisible to others, spirits, astral forces, cat's eye or chrysoberyl.

The Meanings of the Houses

The First House

A *dharma* house, connected to life purpose; the personal self, ego, appearance, head, character, disposition, well-being, ability to gain recognition, self-esteem, confidence, self-love, health, birth, early childhood, start in life.

The Second House

An *artha* house, connected to money matters; money, finances, education, knowledge, writing, writers, teachers, counselors, speech, foul language, imagination, family life, domestic happiness, face.

The Third House

A *kama* **house, connected to desires**; One's own efforts and adventures, siblings, daily desires, courage, bravery, ambition. Fine arts of music, dance, and drama. Actors, dancers, singers, managers, public relations, advertising, computer work, mechanical skills, letters and magazines (but not writers).

The Fourth House

A *moksha* **house, connected to final liberation**; Mother, happiness and contentment, the heart, emotions, and passions, fixed assets, land, buildings, real estate, comforts, luxuries, cars, boats, planes, conveyances, academic degree, endings, close of life.

The Fifth House

A *dharma* **house, connected to life purpose**; Children, the mind, intelligence, *poorvapunya* (rewards or credit due from last incarnation), speculation, gambling, investments, love affairs, romance, kingship, government, rulers, politicians, spiritual techniques, mantras, religious practices or rituals, morals, good deeds, charity, merit, fine qualities, integrity, humility, ability, religious-mindedness.

The Sixth House

An *artha* **house, connected to wealth matters**; Health, illness, disease, enemies, competitors (seen and unseen), foes, jealous people, daily job, service, detail jobs, service jobs, restaurants and caterers, appetite, subordinates, tenants, maids, employees, litigation, tendency to be charged in court cases.

The Seventh House

A *kama* **house, connected to desires**; The spouse, married life, all partners, sexual passions, residence in foreign countries, courts, veins and loins.

The Eighth House

A *moksha* house, connected to final liberation; Life, longevity, means of death, experience of death, wills and legacies, insurance benefits, joint finances, partner's money, alimony, ability to receive partner's wealth, sexual strength, reproductive system, venereal diseases, sexual attractiveness, chronic and long-term illnesses of any kind, occult subjects, secretive matters, intuition, accidents.

The Ninth House

A *dharma* house, connected to life purpose; The father, luck, fortune, solutions to problems, religion, philosophy, faith, worship, a person's guru, spiritual teachers, elders, travel—long journeys, wisdom, higher knowledge of all kinds, higher education, law, performance of good deeds, charity, virtue.

The Tenth House

An *artha* house, connected to wealth matters; Career, professional activities, the *dharma* or life purpose, fame, honor, status, worldly power, holy pilgrimages, good deeds, activities which benefit society, authority figures, eminent persons, government officials.

The Eleventh House

A *kama* house, connected to final liberation; Major goals, ambitions, and desires, opportunities, eldest sibling, gains and profits by any means (wealth), sudden financial fluctuations, supplemental monies, wealth from sideline jobs or sudden ventures, legs and ankles, dancing.

The Twelfth House

A *moksha* house, connected to final liberation; Expenditures, expenses, *moksha* (enlightenment), self-realization, final liberation, salvation, the bedroom, bedding, pleasures of the bed (sexual pleasure), "unknown places" (remote, spiritual countries), hospitals, prisons, ashrams, confinement, hearing, the left ear, vision, the left eye, feet, anus, waste, debt, misfortune, experience with thieves and robbers, secret enemies.

Section II.

Exaltations and Falls

In Hindu astrology, planetary exaltations and falls work in much the same way as Western astrology. However, there are two main differences. First, Mercury is considered exalted in Virgo and fallen in Pisces, whereas Western astrology gives the exalted and fallen placement as Aquarius and Leo, respectively. Second, the Hindus have narrowed down the <u>exact degrees</u> of exaltations and falls. They are follows:

	Exalted	Fallen
Sun	10° ♈	10° ♎
Moon	03° ♉	03° ♏
Mars	28° ♑	28° ♋
Mercury	15° ♍	15° ♓
Jupiter	05° ♋	05° ♑
Venus	27° ♓	27° ♍
Saturn	20° ♎	20° ♈
Rahu	♍	inconclusive
Ketu	♍	inconclusive

(Note — Rahu and Ketu are considered to be in their <u>own</u> signs when occupying Gemini.)

Planets approaching their highest degree of exaltation gain in power and reach their peak of strength in their highest exaltation degree. Planets that occupy exaltation sign degrees beyond their highest exaltation function clearly better than average but are no longer exalted. The same is true for fallen planets. Those planets that approach the lowest point of the fall get weaker and more afflicted the closer they get to the most extreme degree of their "fall." If a planet occupies its fallen sign but is beyond the utmost degree of fall, it functions poorly but is no longer technically fallen. It therefore causes less damage then if in a degree preceding its fallen extreme.

Exaltations and falls are extremely important in Hindu astrology, especially if the planet involved is in a degree close to its positive or negative extreme. *Dasas* or *bhuktis* of exalted planets are significantly strengthened, and a person's life increases in fortune and benefit during such a planetary period. Likewise, during a *dasa* or *bhukti* of a fallen planet a person may have unending problems until the period ends. As always, rulerships, aspects to planets, and other natal birthchart factors must be taken into consideration.

Rulerships

In Hindu astrology, rulerships are monumentally important, perhaps more important than planets in houses. Rulerships are the connections each planet makes with the house or houses it owns or "rules." For example, Venus governs Libra and Taurus, and therefore in a chart Venus rules the houses occupied by those signs. Mars governs Aries and Scorpio, and therefore Mars rules the houses containing those signs, and so on.

♓ ♃	♈ ♂	♉ ♀	♊ ☿
♒ ♄			♋ ☽
♑ ♄			♌ ☉
♐ ♃	♏ ♂	♎ ♀	♍ ☿

Rulerships and planets in houses are the essence of Hindu astrology. Birthchart analysis based upon them produces consistently accurate results. This differs from the Western system where rulerships and planets in houses are very important but function so inconsistently that astrologers must search among a multitude of house systems to find one that produces relatively dependable results. (I certainly do not mean to disparage Western astrology. It is simply my experience that Western rulerships and planets in houses are far less reliable than those in Hindu astrology and that the most profound features of the Western system are the sign meanings — Aries, Taurus, Gemini etc. — and the astrological aspects — the squares, trines, oppositions, etc.)

Benefics or Malefics By Virtue of House Rulerships

In Hindu astrology, planets carry with them a benefic or malefic influence by virtue of the houses that they rule. This is an extremely important principle that affects not only natal chart interpretation but also the effects that planets have during their *dasas* and *bhuktis* (periods and subperiods). Indeed, the positive or negative nature of a planet by virtue of rulership is one of the first conditions to consider when attempting to determine the effects of a planet natally, in its *dasas* and *bhuktis*, and in the aspects it throws. Malefic planets (Mars, Saturn, and Sun) when ruling "good houses" become what are called "functional benefics" (or temporal benefics). While retaining their fundamentally harmful nature functional benefics also carry with them **SOME** ability to do good. Benefic planets (Venus, Jupiter, Moon, and Mercury) that rule "bad houses" become "functional malefics," which means that while producing good effects they simultaneously cause **SOME** damage.

GOOD & BAD PLANETS FOR EACH ASCENDANT BY VIRTUE OF RULERSHIP			
Asc.	Best	Good	Bad
♈	♃	♂☉	♀☿☽♄
♉	♄	☿♂☉	♃☽
♊	♀		♂☉♃♄
♋	♂	♃	☿♀♄
♌	♂	☉	☿♀
♍	♀		☽♂♃
♎	♄	☿♂♀	☽☉♃
♏	☽	☉♂♃	☿♀
♐	☉	♂	☿♀♄
♑	♀	☿♄	♂♃☽
♒	♀	♄♂☉	☽♃
♓	♂	☽	♄☉☿♀

PLANETARY COMBINATIONS FORMING RAJAYOGAS	
♈	☉♃
♉	♄
♊	♀☿
♋	♂
♌	♃♂
♍	♀☿
♎	♄
♏	☉☽
♐	♂♃
♑	♀☿
♒	♂♀
♓	☽♂ OR ♃♂

Planets not listed as good or bad for each ascendant are considered neutral by virtue of their rulership.

The most auspicious houses in a horoscope are the fifth and ninth (the ninth is considered the best house and the fifth comes next). These houses are called *trikonas* or trinal houses, and they bestow enormously beneficial energy wherever their influence is felt. Planets that occupy the fifth or ninth house becomes strong, powerful, and able to function in their most positive way. For example, if Venus is in the fifth or ninth house, Venus' significations — art, beauty, love, etc. — are strengthened because Venus occupies such a good house. If Mars is in the fifth or ninth house, the significations of Mars — sports, physical energy, mechanical ability, etc. —

flourish. Also, the houses that are ruled by planets <u>occupying</u> the fifth and ninth houses (in the above cases, the houses that Venus and Mars rule) become strong and favored.

More important, planets that rule *trikona* houses carry tremendous positivity and bestow their beneficence onto the houses they occupy and the planets and houses they aspect. (In Hindu astrology, planets actually aspect houses. This is explained in the section titled "Aspects.") In other words, if the ruler of the fifth or ninth house occupies the second house (money), then the person's financial conditions are strengthened, even if the ruler of the fifth or ninth house happens to be a malefic (Mars, Saturn, or Sun). Furthermore, the aspects that the fifth house ruler and ninth house ruler throw onto other planets and houses are beneficial, even though the planet throwing the aspect may be a malefic and therefore **simultaneously** throws some harmful energy.

The business of functional benefics and functional malefics is a basic premise of Hindu astrology, but beginners who are reading about Hindu astrology for the first time should not expect to completely absorb this material now. For now, the main points to understand are that in Hindu astrology the best houses in a chart are the fifth and ninth, and the worst houses are the sixth, eighth, and twelfth, which are known as *dusthanas* or grief-producing houses. Of the three bad houses, the sixth is slightly less bad because it also known as an *upachaya* or growing house (the exact meaning of *upachaya* is "increasing.") This means that although a planet occupying the sixth house is wrecked, the affairs relating to that planet can gradually improve if the person works hard on the problems indicated.

The ancient Hindu astrological sages actually considered many more rules when determining functional benefics and functional malefics. (For those who are interested, some basic rules are included at the end of this chapter.) For example, consider that in the case of Gemini ascendant birthcharts, Venus rules the twelfth house, a *dusthana* or bad house, as well as the fifth house, a wonderful *trikona*. Further, Saturn for a Gemini ascendant chart rules the ninth house, the best house of a chart, while also ruling the terrible eighth house.

Follow the graph on page 381, which presents the conclusions of the ancient astrological seers, and note that for a Gemini ascendant, Venus is judged to be the best planet for the chart, by virtue of rulership (the best planet for a chart by virtue of rulership is called the *yogakaraka* or union-maker). Notice that Saturn for a Gemini ascendant falls under the category of bad planets, not because it is a malefic by nature, but because after considering all the intricate, detailed astrological rules and formulas, Saturn is deemed to be carrying malefic energy by virtue of the houses that it rules. When trying to predict the effects any planet (and its periods and subperiods), it is important to note whether the planet is a functional benefic or functional malefic. Furthermore, if the planet happens to be the *yogakaraka* (the union maker or best planet for the ascendant — i.e. Venus for Gemini, Jupiter for Aries, Saturn for Taurus, and so forth as noted in the graph on page 381), then the effects will generally be extra powerful and positive unless that planet is extremely afflicted (by sign or house placement, or because it receives harmful aspects thrown by malefics). This point cannot be overemphasized. *Yogakarakas,* even when occupying their fallen sign, produce some significant benefits.

Regarding the graph on page 381, if a planet is not listed as good or bad, this means it is considered neutral by rulership. For example, look at the good and bad planets for Virgo ascendant. Only four planets out of seven are listed. Three planets, Sun, Mercury, and Saturn are missing. Thus, these planets are neutral. This means that the Sun and Saturn, as natural malefics, simply carry their usual harmful energy with no supplementary positivity or negativity by virtue of house rulerships. Similarly, Mercury, because it is also considered neutral in this case, carries only its usual positive energy without any additional positive or negative force. (Technically speaking, Mercury is actually considered a neutral planet by nature, not a benefic. It is considered neither masculine nor feminine and is said to be extremely adaptable, taking on the positive or negative nature of the planets it is aspected by. In practice, however, Mercury only casts good aspects and causes good effects to the houses it occupies. Therefore, even though technically neutral, Mercury behaves in a benefic way. But because it is technically neutral, which makes it the most adaptable of all planets, Mercury's *dasas* and *bhuktis* are much more affected by the benefic or malefic aspects Mercury receives. As an example, Richard Nixon's presidency was destroyed during a seventeen-year Mercury *dasa* that began in November, 1970. Mercury is conjunct in the same degree as malefic Mars, and Nixon was brought down by the press, college students, the intelligencia, tape recordings, and his own lying — all Mercury significations.)

One last point. A special condition called a *rajayoga,* or royal union, occurs when two planets that both rule good houses form a conjunction in one house of a chart. (See the right hand column of the graph on page 381.) (Remember that in Hindu astrology conjunctions and aspects always occur within a thirty-degree orb. In other words, if Mars is two degrees of Leo, and the Sun is twenty-eight degrees of Leo, a conjunction exists.) A *rajayoga* is one of the best astrological indications possible, and the house containing the two *rajayoga* planets flourishes tremendously. The three or four houses ruled by the two planets forming the royal union also prosper. *Rajayogas* and other special planetary unions can be created in a great many different ways. (Ancient Hindu astrological scriptures contain literally thousands of good and bad astrological *yogas* or unions.) The *rajayogas* that are listed on the far right side of the graph on page 381 are the most fundamental ones based upon rulership conditions. Please note that for birthcharts with Taurus, Cancer, and Libra ascendants an automatic *rajayoga* exists, because in these charts, one planet rules two very good houses. For Taurus, Saturn rules the ninth and tenth houses. For Cancer, Mars rules the fifth and tenth houses. And for Libra, Saturn rules the fourth and fifth houses. All of these planets are malefics by nature that rule *kendras* and *trikonas* (angular houses and trinal houses). Never underestimate the power and beneficence of planets involved in *rajayogas*.

Some Rules Which Form Rulership Table

KENDRAS (angular houses) — 1st, 4th, 7th, & 10th

- Benefics which rule *kendras* take on negative energy and the ability to do harm.

- Malefics which rule *kendras* take on positive energy and the ability to do good.

- Lords of *kendras* are powerful. Of them, the lord of the 1st is weakest, the lord of the 4th stronger, the lord of the 7th stronger still, and the ruler of the 10th strongest.

- Planets in *kendras* are powerful, and they are prominent influences in a person's life.

TRIKONAS (trinal houses) — 5th and 9th

- Any planet ruling a *trikona* is auspicious and carries the most postive energy with it.

- Trikona lords are so auspicious that they produce great benefits even when they simultaneously rule evil houses.

- Planets posited in a *trikona* house flourish, as do the houses they rule.

- The lord of the 5th is not quite as powerful as the lord of the 9th.

☞ *Note* — Some astrologers consider the ruler of the 1st as a trikona and a kendra lord.

UPACHAYAS — 3rd, 6th, 10th, & 11th

Upachayas are growing houses where planets gain in strength throughout a person's life, and conditions indicated by the house can improve in time and effort.

- Any planet ruling an *upachaya* house takes on negative energy, through not of an intense nature, and may cause slight harm.

- Malefics in *upachayas* give excellent results.

- Benefics in *upachayas* give good results and are not particularly enhanced or benefitted by the house energy.
- Of the *upachayas*, the 3rd is the weakest and the 11th is the strongest.

☞ *Note — the 10th house is an upachaya house in terms of its nature and behavior, but for lordship purposes it is considered a kendra.*

NEUTRAL HOUSES — the lords of the 2nd, 8th, & 12th

- Give good results if they are conjunct with a benefic planet. (In practice, Indian astrologers do **NOT** follow this advice except perhaps for the lord of the 2nd. **Practically speaking, the 8th and the 12th destroy all of their associations.**)
- Planets posited in the 2nd house are not greatly influenced one way or the other, unless by aspect or sign placement.

DUSTANAS (evil houses) — 6th, 8th, & 12th

- Any planet ruling a *dustana* carries negative energy with it and causes destruction where it is posited.
- Any planet posited in a *dusthana* is ruined, as are the houses it rules.
- The 6th house and its ruler are the least malefic of the *dusthanas*, especially since the 6th is a growing house where conditions may improve.

MARAKAS (Death-inflicting planets) — the rulers of the 2nd and 7th houses.

- The houses of life are the 8th and the 3rd (the 3rd being the 8th from the 8th). The 12th is known as the house of loss. The 12th from the 8th house is the 7th; therefore, the 7th takes on an evil influence to life. The 12th from the 3rd is the 2nd, and it also becomes destructive.

☞ *This matter is an extreme subtlety, and concern over **marakas** should be delayed until the astrologer is highly experienced in Hindu astrology. The most obvious effect occurs when both **marakas** are posited in the same house. In such a case, there may be an evil effect which is otherwise astrologically undetectable. Most astrologers use the **marakas** to determine the time of death, because many people die in a period or subperiod of a **maraka**. However, this is a very <u>complicated</u> matter, and there must be other strong afflictions to the planet in question for a death to occur. Also, **marakas** are more ominous during <u>old age</u>, when death is most likely.* **Young and middle-aged individuals need not be** *concerned about dasas of marakas.*

Section III.
Planetary Aspects

Astrological aspects in Hindu astrology function somewhat differently than those in the Western system. There are no such things as squares, trines, oppositions, sextiles, and so forth. Each planet has certain houses that it aspects and if a planet happens to occupy the house being aspected, then that planet also receives an aspect:

- **All planets aspect the seventh house (opposite) from themselves.**
- **Mars aspects the fourth, seventh, and eighth houses from itself.**
- **Jupiter aspects the fifth, seventh, and ninth houses from itself.**
- **Saturn aspects the third, seventh, and tenth houses from itself.**
- **Any planet occupying a house that is being aspected is also aspected.**
- **Two planets in the same sign form a conjunction.**

The beneficial or harmful nature of an aspect depends on the nature of the planet throwing the aspect. The benefic planets — Moon, Venus, Jupiter, and Mercury — throw positive aspects onto other houses and planets. The malefics — Mars, Sun, and Saturn — cast damaging influences. On top of this, rulership factors must be considered (refer to graph on page 381). Benefic planets that rule good houses (i.e., the fifth or ninth) throw extra positive energy while malefics that rule good houses throw some good energy, along with their essential harmful forces. Benefic planets that rule *dusthanas* (grief-producing houses) throw malefic energy as well as their natural positive forces.

One of the most significant differences between Hindu aspects and Western aspects, a difference that many Western astrologers often find hard to grasp in the beginning, is that when two planets aspect each other, as they do in conjunctions and seventh house aspects (what Western astrologers call oppositions), one planet may benefit tremendously while the other may suffer tremendously. For example, if Venus is conjunct Saturn (Degrees are irrelevant in Hindu aspects. Therefore, if Venus is in the same sign as Saturn, a conjunction exists. Of course, however, the tighter the aspect by degree, the more intense the effect), then Venus is terribly harmed by Saturn's malefic energy. However, Saturn's condition flourishes because it receives Venus' extremely beneficial energy. As another example, take a case where Jupiter occupies the fourth house while Mars is in the tenth house. Because all planets aspect the seventh house from themselves (their opposite) Jupiter aspects Mars while Mars aspects Jupiter. However, this does not constitute an "opposition" as in Western astrology because oppositions in Western astrology are difficult or "challenging" for both planets. In Hindu astrology, Jupiter is damaged by receiving Mars' harmful rays, but Mars becomes powerful and very happy because it is aspected by benefic Jupiter. This is the way Hindu astrology aspects work.

Another important feature about aspects is that whenever a planet aspects a sign that it rules or the sign of its exaltation or fallen placements, the results are altered for better or worse. For instance, if Jupiter aspects the fourth house and that house happens to be Pisces, the sign that Jupiter rules (in Hindu astrology, ancient rulerships apply because Uranus, Neptune, and Pluto are not used), then the aspect is much more beneficial than usual. If the Moon aspects Taurus, the house of Moon's exaltation sign, then that house is exceptionally strengthened. If Mars throws an aspect onto its fallen sign, Cancer, then the harm to the house of Cancer is far worse than if another house received Mars' ordinary malefic energy. Furthermore, any planet occupying Cancer would also be harmed by the Mars aspect much more than usual.

In the case of malefics aspecting their own or exaltation signs, this matter of "special" aspects is a subtlety requiring practical experience to properly grasp. Certain houses simply cannot fully integrate malefic energy, no matter how much additional benefic energy the malefic planet may carry. Specifically, the houses representing people are the most sensitive in this matter. These houses are the first (the person himself or herself), the third (all brothers and sisters except the eldest), the fourth (mother), the fifth (children), the seventh (spouse), the ninth and tenth, (either of which may signify one's father. In South India, the ninth represents the father because in that part of India the father also functions as the guru — which is a ninth house matter. North Indian astrologers see the father from the tenth house. In my own practice, I have seen certain charts where the ninth house unequivocally represents the father and others where the tenth house takes this honor), and the eleventh house (the eldest sibling, not older but eldest).

Let us first consider the case of a malefic planet aspecting its own house where that house does not signify a person. If Mars aspects the second house and the second house happens to be Aries or Scorpio (Mars' signs), the aspect will cause only good effects for money. However, if Mars aspects the seventh house, the house of marriage, and that house happens to be Aries or Scorpio, there will be good effects regarding the spouse, but there will also be serious damage to the relationship with the spouse. The seventh house is too sensitive an arena for Mars energy. In this case, the spouse would likely be powerful, successful, assertive in a good way, and beautiful (or handsome) or exceptional. However, there would still be arguments or fighting in married life.

As another example, if Saturn aspects the third house and the third house is Capricorn, Aquarius, or Libra (Saturn's own or exaltation signs), then the person might have a younger brother or sister who is Saturnian in a positive way. That sibling might be disciplined, responsible, highly evolved, successful, or an authority in his or her field. But the relationship with the sibling would suffer, and there would be very few siblings (or none) because Saturn bestows its restrictive nature onto the third house. As I state repeatedly throughout this text, positive influence does not cancel negative influence. There are many realms of life where a person experiences some extreme good and some extreme bad. Mixed birthchart influences are the astrological explanation for such conditions.

Most ancient Hindu astrological texts say that Rahu and Ketu, the "shadowy" planets, have no ability to cast aspects. However, there is a school of thought, based upon the writings of the sage, Parasara (the originator of the system we are using), that Rahu and Ketu cast negative glances onto the fifth and ninth houses from their natal placements. Although most Indian astrologers I have met do not use the aspects, after years of research I have found that sage Parasara was correct and the aspects should be noticed.

Regarding predictions for *dasas* and *bhuktis*, Planetary aspects influence both the quality and content of them. For example, if a person enters a Moon dasa and the Moon is closely aspected (close by planetary degrees) by Saturn at birth, then during that ten-year period, the person will be more serious, disciplined, and organized because of Saturn's aspect. The period will also be difficult, tedious, and frustrating because Saturn, as a malefic, seriously harms the Moon. If, in this case, the Moon occupies the fifth house, then the problems and frustrations during the dasa center around fifth house significations. There will also be problems relating to the house that the Moon rules, the house of Cancer. As another example, if Mercury occupies the second house and is tightly aspected by benefic Jupiter at birth, the seventeen years of the Mercury period will bring great financial gains or educational benefits (both Mercury and the second house rule education and literary endeavors in Hindu astrology). During this dasa, the person will also feel more interested in God or religion than usual because of Jupiter's intrinsically spiritual nature. The houses that Mercury rules will also flourish because Mercury is so well-aspected.

The aspects that I have listed are considered "full" or 100% aspects, and these are ones used by all practicing Hindu astrologers. There are, however, aspects called three-quarter aspects, one-half aspects, and one-quarter aspects, which most astrologers simply ignore. I will, however, include these aspects for reference purposes.

Aspects of Secondary Importance

- **All planets aspect the third and tenth houses from themselves with a one-quarter effect.**

- **All planets aspect the fifth and ninth houses from themselves with a one-half effect.**

- **All planets aspect the fourth houses from themselves with a three-quarter effect.**

Using only the full aspects, which are listed in the beginning of this chapter, let us now consider Lord Rama's chart. Lord Rama was a Hindu avatar who was so great that every planet in his chart except Mercury and Rahu is exalted or in its own sign. Despite Rama's greatness, his father died before full adulthood because Saturn aspects the Sun, and the aspect is a worse one than usual because Saturn throws its harmful energy onto Aries — the sign where Saturn is fallen. Rama's father's died, the story goes, of a sudden heart attack after Rama's mother announced that their child was destined to leave home in order to serve God.

South Indian Style

♓ 9th ♀	♈ 10th ☉	♉ 11th ☿	♊ 12th ☋
♒ 8th			♋ 1st Asc. ☽ ♃
♑ 7th ♂	Lord Rama		♌ 2nd
♐ 6th ☊	♏ 5th	♎ 4th ♄	♍ 3rd

North Indian Style

Lord Rama chart (North Indian Style): Cancer ascendant with Moon and Jupiter in 1st; Mercury in 12th (Gemini); Saturn in 4th; Sun in 10th; Venus in 9th; Mars in 7th; Rahu/Ketu on 6th/12th axis.

Lord Rama's Full Aspects

- ✓ Moon aspects the seventh house.
- ✓ Moon aspects Mars in the seventh house.
- ✓ Jupiter aspects the fifth, seventh, and ninth houses. The aspect to the seventh house is not as beneficial as usual because Jupiter aspects Capricorn, its fallen sign.
- ✓ Jupiter aspects Mars in the seventh house, aspecting its fallen sign, Capricorn.
- ✓ Jupiter aspects Venus in the ninth house — an excellent aspect because Jupiter aspects its own sign, Pisces.
- ✓ Saturn aspects the sixth, tenth, and first houses. The aspect to the tenth house is an especially bad one because Saturn aspects its fallen sign, Aries.
- ✓ Saturn aspects Rahu in the sixth house.
- ✓ Saturn aspects the Sun in the tenth house — in Saturn's fallen sign, Aries.
- ✓ Saturn aspects the Moon and Jupiter in the first house
- ✓ Rahu throws no aspects. (According to sage Parasara, Rahu aspects the tenth, twelfth, and second houses of Rama's chart.)
- ✓ Mars aspects the tenth house and the Sun in the tenth causing some good and some bad because, on the positive side, Mars aspects its own sign, Aries, but on the negative side malefic Mars throws harmful aspects.
- ✓ Mars aspects the first house and the Moon and Jupiter in the first house, aspecting its fallen sign, Cancer.
- ✓ Mars aspects the second house.
- ✓ Venus aspects the third house, aspecting Virgo, its fallen sign).
- ✓ Sun aspects the fourth house and Saturn, aspecting the Sun's fallen sign.
- ✓ Mercury aspects the fifth house.
- ✓ Ketu throws no aspects. (According to Parasara, Ketu aspects the fourth, sixth, and eighth houses of Rama's chart.)

Section IV.
The Two Zodiacs

There is a fundamental difference between the zodiac used in the Hindu system (sidereal) and the one used predominantly in Western astrology (tropical). A zodiac is an imaginary circle in the heavens, inside of which the Sun, Moon, and planets travel in their orbits. In order to plot the positions of the heavenly bodies, it is necessary to determine a starting point within the circle. To construct a starting point, it is necessary to establish a reference point, some kind of fixed element to be used as a backdrop to the ever-orbiting planets, the Sun, and the Moon. Herein lies the difference between the two zodiacs. The sidereal zodiac uses as its reference point the positions of "fixed stars" — stationary star clusters which have no motion whatsoever. In other words, the sidereal zodiac is calculated by determining the positions of the planets and the Sun and Moon in relation to a stationary point in the sky, a particular "fixed star" cluster, which is delegated as the first degree of Aries. Aries then becomes the first of twelve 30* zodiac "signs" (portions of space) making up the 360* zodiac.

The tropical zodiac uses an entirely different, but equally fixed, reference point. For measuring purposes, it uses the equinoxes (the relationship between the Sun and the Earth which creates the four seasons: the Spring Equinox, the Summer Solstice, the Autumnal Equinox, and the Winter Solstice). The starting point of the tropical zodiac, also called the first degree of Aries, is determined by the spring equinox — the first day of spring. Each year when spring arrives, the position of the Sun within the imaginary circle establishes the first degree of Aries. All other planets are then calculated in relation to the Sun. This works well because the Sun moves approximately 360 degrees in one year, the same number of degrees in the zodiac, and because the first day of spring occurs at the exact same time each year (even though our yearly calendar makes it seem to vary by a day or two). Tropical astrology is not based upon a fixed position in the heavens, as is the sidereal zodiac. It is based upon an undeviating, similarly fixed, atmospherical condition called the four seasons — specifically, spring.

For thousands of years there has been confusion and disagreement as to whether both zodiacs are legitimate and if so, which one is preferable and produces the most accurate results. Astrologers who have studied and practiced both systems, USING THE TROPICAL ZODIAC FOR WESTERN ASTROLOGY AND THE SIDEREAL FOR HINDU ASTROLOGY, almost always conclude that both work because they have experienced accurate results from both. (It is possible that the information gained from tropical or seasonally-based, astrology, may relate somewhat more to a person's psychology and behavior than events and circumstances.) Unfortunately, most astrologers are not expert in both Hindu and Western astrology and have therefore confronted the question of the two zodiacs only from a theoretical perspective.

Most people, astrologers and astronomers often included, unfortunately, overlook the fact that the zodiacs are based on different principles and have different reference points for determining the first degree of Aries. Therefore, when the first degree of Aries in the tropical zodiac differs from the first degree of Aries in the sidereal system, it is assumed that one zodiac is incorrect. This is not the case. The problem is exacerbated by the fact that there is a consistent mathematical relationship between the two zodiacs so that the first degree of Aries in the sidereal zodiac is always a perfect mathematical formula away from the first degree of Aries in the tropical zodiac. This can also make it appear that the two zodiacs are based upon the same reference point but that one zodiac has somehow been miscalculated.

The mathematical difference between the two zodiacs — specifically the difference between the first degree of Aries in the tropical zodiac and the first degree of Aries in the sidereal zodiac — is known by Hindu astrologers as the *ayanamsa* (pronounced aya-nam-sha). The *ayanamsa,* though able to be precisely calculated for any single moment, is a moving figure. For example, in 1900 the difference between the first degree of Aries in the tropical zodiac and the first degree of Aries in the sidereal zodiac was twenty-two degrees and twenty-seven minutes. In 1970, the *ayanamsa* was twenty-three degrees and twenty-six minutes — a difference of approximately one degree. This motion of approximately one degree per seventy-two years between zodiac starting points, describes the "precession of the equinoxes." The precession of the equinoxes is a perpetual, though extremely slight, tilting of the earth.

In present day, the way astronomers arrive at the starting point of the sidereal zodiac is by using the calculated positions of the tropical zodiac and then taking into account the movement of the precession of the equinoxes. Because the starting points of the zodiacs are always moving apart from each other (within a circle), there are times when the starting points coincide. Therefore, astronomers try to determine exactly what year the first degree of Aries was the same in both zodiacs. From there, they simply begin to subtract approximately one zodiac degree for every seventy-two years and thus arrive at the current sidereal first degree of Aries. There are slight disagreements amongst certain astronomers as to the exact year that the zodiacs coincided. But the Indian government has sanctioned the work of N.C. Lahiri, and it is therefore his *ayanamsa* which is most widely used for astrological purposes. My experience in trying different *ayanamsas* (There are about three or four popular ones. They produce differences of only two or three zodiac degrees different from Lahiri's), is that Lahiri's *ayanamsa* is the accurate one. Hindu astrology texts generally offer a few different ones so astrologers are free to choose for themselves.

In trying to come to terms with the two zodiacs, please consider that different techniques often produce the same results. Different spiritual paths lead to the same enlightenment. There is good reason that tropically-based Western astrology has endured for thousands of years in the West and sidereally-based Hindu astrology has endured in the East.

Section V.
The Chakra — the Birthchart

There are two prevalent Hindu horoscope formats, one that comes from South India and one from North India. The designs have no effect on the results and are simply a matter of tradition. The South Indian method is somewhat more popular in India, and that is the one taught in this book. For those who use the North Indian method, I will include both chart formats of the horoscopes that are analyzed in this text. But, for now, beginners should go by the South Indian method and completely ignore the North Indian chart, which is approached in an entirely different way.

Contrary to the Western birthchart, where the houses are fixed (if the chart were a clock, twelve o'clock is the tenth house and nine o'clock is the first house) and signs rotate, in the South Indian chart the signs are fixed and houses rotate. In other words, zodiac signs always fit the same squares (the top left square is always Pisces and the bottom right square is always Virgo) and house numbers rotate. The first house, whichever square it might be, is denoted by a diagonal line within the square. Another difference from Western astrology is that the chart flows in a clockwise direction rather than counterclockwise.

Chart with Pisces Ascendant

♓ 1st	♈ 2nd	♉ 3rd	♊ 4th
♒ 12th			♋ 5th
♑ 11th			♌ 6th
♐ 10th	♏ 9th	♎ 8th	♍ 7th

Chart with Cancer Ascendant

♓ 9th	♈ 10th	♉ 11th	♊ 12th
♒ 8th			♋ 1st
♑ 7th			♌ 2nd
♐ 6th	♏ 5th	♎ 4th	♍ 3rd

As for the "house systems", there are two that are generally used in India. One is older and more traditional and the other is somewhat more contemporary. The older method is the one used in this book. This is the "equal house" system, meaning that if the first house begins at ten degrees Capricorn, then all other houses begin also at ten degrees (i.e., second house starts at ten degrees Aquarius, third house at ten degrees Pisces, and so on). In the traditional Hindu chart system, the degree of the house cusp is completely irrelevant. This means that although the first house may begin at twenty-five degrees of Scorpio, even a planet in two degrees Scorpio occupies the first house. This differs from Western astrology in that all planets in degrees less than the ascendant will occupy the twelfth house. In typical Western house systems, the first house may start at the middle of one sign and continue until the middle of the next sign (e.g., from three degrees Leo to three degrees Virgo or from twenty degrees Gemini to twenty degrees Cancer). This does not happen in the traditional Hindu equal house system (It does occur in the contemporary Hindu chart method, but that is not the method we are using.)

To put it simply, planets in the second SIGN from the ascendant occupy the second house. Planets in the fifth sign from the ascendant, occupy the fifth house. The ascendant degree is irrelevant in positioning the planets (the ascendant degree is not insignificant in other ways — only in terms of determining the other houses).

Drawing the Chart

In order to transform a Western birthchart (calculated with tropical zodiac) to a Hindu one (that employs the sidereal zodiac), all that is necessary is to subtract the *ayanamsa* the figure that accounts for the precession of the equinox or tilting of the earth, from the positions of the ascendant, the planets, and the North and South Nodes. (Uranus, Neptune, and Pluto may be disregarded as these are not used in ancient Hindu astrology.)

The precession of the equinox moves approximately 50 1/4 seconds per year. Given below are some *ayanamsas* during the twentieth century.

LAHIRI AYANAMSAS DURING THIS CENTURY

January 1, 1900 22° 27'59" January 1, 1960 23° 17'54"

January 1, 1910 22° 35'51" January 1, 1970 23° 26'21"

January 1, 1920 22° 44'43" January 1, 1980 23° 34'31"

January 1, 1930 22° 52'40" January 1, 1990 23° 43'14"

January 1, 1940 23° 01'21" January 1, 2000 23° 51'11"

January 1, 1950 23° 09'34" January 1, 2010 24° 00'04"

In order to determine approximate ayanamsas for years in between the ones listed above, use 50 1/4 seconds per year (but remember that the precession moves *approximately* 50 1/4 seconds per year. Therefore, your final calculation for the *ayanamsa* will be close but not exact). As an example birthchart let us use the chart of Richard Nixon. See the chart of his birth data on the following page.

Nixon was born in 1913, three years after the 1910 *ayanamsa* of 22° 35' 51". Therefore, add 50 1/4 seconds for each of these three years:

50.25"	22° 35' 51"
x 3	+ 2' 51"
-----------	------------------
150.75"	22° 38' 42"
Divide by 60" = 2' 51"	

The final figure, **22° 38' 42"**, is an approximation of the *ayanamsa* (because, as already mentioned, the precession moves *approximately* 50

1/4"). The exact *ayanamsa* was **22° 38' 31"**. For our purposes, we will simply use **22° 38'**.)

EXAMPLES

The Sun: **19° ♑ 24' = 289° 24' minus 22° 38' = 266° 46' = 26° ♐ 46'.**

The Moon: **20° ♒ 08' = 320° 08' minus 22° 38' = 297° 30' = 27° ♑ 30'.**

Rahu (North Node): **07° ♈ 15' (add 360° since 22° 38' cannot be subtracted from 07° 15')= 367° 15' minus 22° 38' = 344° 37' = 14° ♓ 37'.**

For those who wish to quickly transpose Western charts into their Hindu sidereal counterparts, there is an easy way to do this that produces APPROXIMATELY ACCURATE Hindu birthcharts. The technique is a simplified way to make zodiac subtractions and works well for all planets and ascendants except those that occupy twenty-two or twenty-three degrees of a sign. During the entire twentieth century, the *ayanamsa* is approximately twenty-three degrees, so that is the figure to subtract from the ascendant, planets, and the nodes. Subtracting twenty-three degrees from planets located between twenty-four degrees and thirty degrees is simple. Subtracting twenty-three degrees from, say, ten degrees (or any figure below twenty-three degrees) becomes confusing. To make the calculation easy, just add seven degrees to the figure (in this case, add seven to ten) and then subtract a sign. This works because seven and twenty-three equals thirty, the number of degrees in each sign.

Chart 1
Richard Nixon
Male Chart
Jan 9 1913
9:35 pm PST +8:00
Yorba Linda, CA
33°N53'19" 117°W48'44"

Sg	Name
♈	Aries
♉	Taurus
♊	Gemini
♋	Cancer
♌	Leo
♍	Virgo
♎	Libra
♏	Scorpio
♐	Sagittarius
♑	Capricorn
♒	Aquarius
♓	Pisces

		planets.pts		
Pt	Name	Sg	Long.	Lat.
☽	Moon	♒	20°♒07'22"	−03°37'
☉	Sun	♑	19°♑24'08"	−00°00'
☿	Mercury	♑	00°♑01	+00°11'
♀	Venus	♓	03°♓29	−01°21'
♂	Mars	♐	29°♐45	−00°33'
♃	Jupiter	♑	01°♑40	+00°13'
♄	Saturn	♉	27°♉29 ℞	−02°04'
☊	North Node	♈	06°♈11 ℞	+00°00'
☋	South Node	♎	06°♎11 ℞	+00°00'
As	Ascendant	♍	17°♍24'59"	+00°00'

For example, the Moon in Richard Nixon's Western chart is

approximately twenty degrees of Aquarius. Therefore, to find the sidereal position of the Moon, add seven degrees to twenty and subtract a zodiac sign. The result is twenty-seven degrees of Capricorn. Remember that this is only a quick way to gain an approximate Hindu chart and cannot work for planets occupying a degree near the *ayanamsa* (twenty-two or twenty-three degrees during twentieth century births). The exact figures of such planets as well as the exact *ayanamsa* are necessary in order to determine whether such planets fall in the final degree of one sign or the earliest degree of the next sign.

COMPUTER CHART SERVICE
FROM WHICH YOU MAY ORDER HINDU CHARTS WITH DASA BHUKTIS
Astro Communications Services Inc.
P.O. Box 34487
San Diego, Calif. 92163-4487
1-800-888-9983

Section VI.

Dasas and Bhuktis

The *dasa* system of prediction is one of the greatest features of Hindu astrology. Although transits are also used in *Jyotish* in a slightly different way than Western transits, it is the *dasas* and *bhuktis* that produce the great predictive accuracy for which Hindu astrology is famous. *Dasas* and *bhuktis* are periods and subperiods during which a person's life is affected by, or corresponds to, the attributes and significations of particular planets. The first *dasa* of a person's life is based upon the zodiac sign and degree position of the Moon in the natal horoscope. *Dasas* last from six to twenty years. The longest *dasa* is that of Venus (20 years) and the shortest is that of the Sun (6 years).

The Sun	6 years	**Saturn**	19 years
The Moon	10 years	**Mercury**	17 years
Mars	7 years	**Ketu**	7 years
Rahu	18 years	**Venus**	20 years
Jupiter	16 years		

One may be born at any point during a *dasa* and from then on the *dasas* follow the order listed above. For example, one may be born into the final six months of a sixteen-year Jupiter *dasa* after which begins the nineteen-year Saturn *dasa*, and then the seventeen-year Mercury *dasa*, and so on. Or, a person may be born in the third year and fifth month of a Venus *dasa*, after which comes the six-year Sun *dasa*, ten-year Moon *dasa*, and so on.

Dasas, which show the overall picture of a person's life for such long periods of time, are then broken down into *bhuktis*, which give more detailed information about shorter intervals within the *dasas*. As an example, a person may be in a sixteen year Jupiter *dasa* which, if Jupiter is powerful and well-aspected in the natal chart, indicates that person will have wonderful gains, benefits, and happiness in the realms of life governed by Jupiter and the houses that Jupiter rules. If, however, the person enters a two-year Moon *bhukti* (subperiod) within the sixteen-year Jupiter *dasa* and if the Moon is weak, afflicted, and badly aspected, then the person suddenly begins to encounter various problems in the areas signified by the Moon and the houses the Moon rules. The good effects of the sixteen-year Jupiter *dasa* are still in effect, but the person's happiness and benefits cease while he or she endures obstacles or difficulties.

Over forty *dasa* systems exist, of which only two are widely accepted as consistently reliable. These two are called the *Vimshottari* and *Ashottari* (pronounced vim-show-tree and eh-show-tree) systems. Because the *Vimshottari* system is the most consistently accurate, it is the one most widely used and the one taught in this book. All *dasa* examples in this text are calculated according to the *Vimshottari* method.

According to Hindu philosophy, the normal span of human life would be 120 years in a physically and spiritually healthy world, without the excessive stress, strain, pollution, and mental unrest of present day life. Appropriately then, the combined duration of all nine *dasas* totals 120 years. Uranus, Neptune, and Pluto, being unseen in ancient times, are not part of the *dasa* system. The nine *dasas* include the original seven planets (including Sun and Moon) and Rahu and Ketu (the North Node and South Node). The order of the *dasas* is as follows: Sun, six years; Moon, ten years; Mars, seven years; Rahu, eighteen years; Jupiter, sixteen years; Saturn, nineteen years; Mercury, seventeen years; Ketu, seven years; Venus, twenty years.

The same scheme exists for the *bhuktis*, and they also follow a set order. The first *bhukti* of an *dasa* is the same as the *dasa* planet. For example, in a Moon *dasa* the periods and subperiods run like this: Moon-Moon, Moon-Mars, Moon-Rahu, and so on. In a Sun *dasa*, the periods and subperiods are as follows: Sun-Sun, Sun-Moon, Sun-Mars, and so forth.

Calculating a person's *dasas* and *bhuktis* is a time-consuming process and is subject to human error. I therefore recommend either buying a Hindu astrology program or mailing away to an astrological computer service (listed in the section titled "Services" at the end of this book. Those who wish to learn how to calculate *dasas* and *bhuktis* may purchase my first book <u>Ancient Hindu Astrology for the Modern Western Astrologer</u> (See Services).

Dasa-Bhukti Fundamentals

There are many factors to consider when analyzing *dasas* and *bhuktis*. In fact, there are so many that to list all the subtleties and nuances would be overwhelming to beginners. Normally, one learns *dasas* after possessing a working knowledge of natal Hindu astrology. Because this section is meant to serve as an introduction to the possibilties and benefits of Hindu predictive astrology, only the most necessary information is presented here.

Planets Are Benefic or Malefic by Nature

BENEFICS — Venus, Jupiter, Mercury, Moon (waxing and bright is much more benefic than waning and dim)

MALEFICS — Mars, Saturn, Rahu, Ketu (North and South nodes), Sun (Sun is a hot star and burns anything in its way)

Hindu astrology is different from Western astrology in that it is more simplistic (not necessarily easier, but more simplistic). Houses are either benefic or malefic. Planets are either good or bad. If a planet is aspected by Venus, Jupiter, or other benefics, it flourishes. Planets aspected by malefics suffer. Unlike Western astrology, aspects are not called squares, oppositions, trines, and sextiles, though they may be comprised of the same specifications. Aspects in Hindu astrology are good or bad depending on the planet throwing the aspect. For example, if Venus is opposite Saturn, this is not called an opposition as it is in the Western system, and damage is not done to both planets. Venus is harmed because it is aspected by malefic-natured Saturn. On the other hand, Saturn becomes tremendously powerful and well disposed because it is aspected by benefic Venus.

In analyzing *dasas*, it is crucial to determine the dasa planet's natal condition. This is done by examining such fundamental birthchart factors as the *dasa* planet's sign and house placement, the houses it rules, and the aspects it receives (whether benefic or malefic) from other planets. The most common mistake beginners make is expecting wonderful results from a Venus or Jupiter *dasa* or *bhukti* simply because these are benefic-natured planets. Or, predicting terrible results from a Saturn, Mars, or Sun *dasa* or *bhukti* merely because these planets are malefic by nature. This is not how *dasas* and *bhuktis* work. The critical factor is the overall natal condition of the planet involved. For example, if Venus, a wonderful benefic, is "fallen" by sign position (in Virgo), in the eighth house (a *dusthana* or grief-producing house), conjunct with Mars, and aspected by Saturn, the twenty-year Venus *dasa* for this person would be horrific because Venus in this example is terribly afflicted. So, the person's love life would suffer, he or she would have illnesses involving the throat, thyroid, or reproductive system, and the person would have serious problems with women. Furthermore, the areas of life signified by the house Venus occupies as well as the houses Venus rules (the houses of Taurus and Libra) would also seriously deteriorate. On top of all this, life in general would be rough, painful, and difficult. On the other hand, if a person enters a nineteen-year *dasa* of malefic Saturn but Saturn is very well disposed, the person could expect good results. For example, if Saturn rules excellent houses (in Hindu astrology the best houses are the fifth and ninth and the worst are the sixth, eighth, and twelfth), and it is aspected by Jupiter and a full Moon, the person would definitely prosper. The person could expect significant career advances and leadership opportunities, and his or her organizational skills would increase. Also, the significations of Saturn's house position as well as the houses Saturn rules (Capricorn and Aquarius) would flourish. Clearly, the condition of the *dasa* or *bhukti* planet is more significant than whether the planet is benefic or malefic by nature.

While the overall condition of the *dasa* planet indicates the positive or negative effects of the *dasa*, it is the significations of the *dasa* planet and the significations of the houses that the *dasa* planet occupies and rules that reveal the exact areas of life to be affected. For example, Mercury rules education, writing, learning, the mind, the nervous system, and the lungs and intestines, among other things. If one enters Mercury *dasa* and Mercury is strong and well disposed, the person may happily return to school and enjoy all kinds of new information and psychological realizations. Life would be enjoyable and the person would succeed because of his or her alertness, mental clarity, and increasing intellectual dexterity. If, however, Mercury is afflicted natally, then in the Mercury *dasa* the person suffers from nervousness, mental problems, or depression. The person would also have problems in schooling and upsets with teachers, writers, and the press. The person might suddenly develop bronchitis or intestinal problems.

In another example, if the person enters a Venus *dasa* and Venus is well-placed and well-aspected natally, then the person begins to have happy love relationships, enjoyments with music and drama, and he or she might receive many gifts of art or jewelry. Also, the houses Venus rules would benefit. If, in this case, Venus rules the fifth and tenth houses, the significations of the fifth and tenth houses flourish and the person's fame (tenth house) increases and the person will have good luck with investments and children (fifth house). It is crucial to analyze the significations of the *dasa* or *bhukti* planet and its house position and house rulerships.

It is common for beginners to make mistakes when trying to analyze dasas and bhuktis because of making predictions based solely on the nature of a planet and the house it occupies, while ignoring the houses the planet rules, the houses that planet is intrinsically connected to. For example, consider a person who has a Taurus ascendant entering a seven-year Mars dasa. What will be the results if Mars occupies its exaltation sign (Capricorn) in the ninth house and is very well disposed because it receives beneficial aspects from Jupiter, Venus, or a bright Moon? Of course the person will become temporarily energetic, ambitious, and aggressive because that is the nature of Mars. The person is likely to travel to far off countries on and off for seven years because Mars occupies the ninth house (travel) and is so well disposed. The person will gain higher knowledge from gurus and religious teachers during the entire Mars period. And certainly the person's luck may increase dramatically (the ninth house rules luck in Hindu astrology). In addition, however, the person stands a good chance of getting married soon after the dasa begins or at least sometime within the seven years of Mars dasa (especially during a favorable bhukti). Why? Because Mars rules Scorpio and for a Taurus ascendant birthchart, Scorpio comprises the seventh house, the house of marriage. The person may also have some of the greatest spiritual experiences of his or her life and enjoy "remote foreign countries" such as India, Africa, Israel, etc. because Mars rules the twelfth house (Aries) and the twelfth house governs enlightenment and remote foreign countries, among other things.

Some examples within the lives of famous living people to illustrate the importance of rulerships in dasa prediction are as follows: 1) Al Gore, who has a Cancer ascendant, watched his son get struck by a car during the worst bhukti of a Mars dasa. Mars, in his case, is very afflicted and rules the fifth house, the house of children. 2) Robert De Niro, who has a Gemini ascendant, has enjoyed great fame during Mercury dasa. Mercury occupies the third house in his birthchart (in Hindu astrology the third house rules music, dance, and drama) and is extremely well aspected, thereby giving great artistic success during the dasa. Fame was forthcoming because Mercury RULES the first house, the ability to be recognized and appreciated. 3) Robert Duval, who has a Pisces ascendant, won his academy award in Jupiter dasa, Saturn bhukti. Saturn occupies the tenth house (career success and fame) and Jupiter RULES the tenth house. Jupiter also rules the first house (ability to be recognized, promoted, and so forth).

Listed below are some of the general manifestations likely to occur during dasas and bhuktis of planets ruling or occupying the twelve houses. It is difficult, however, to make an absolute statement about whether house rulers carry more weight than planets in houses. The best explanation I can make about the issue is that a house ruler is like the structure of a building while planets in a house are like the furnishings. Tom Hopke in *How To Read Your Horoscope* gives the analogy that house rulers are like landlords while planets in houses are like tenants. In my own practice, I place slightly more importance on house rulers.

Please remember that planets always rule two houses, except for the Sun and Moon, which rule Leo and Cancer, respectively. Therefore, in most cases, dasas or bhuktis involve effects generated by three different houses, the two houses a planet rules and the house that planet occupies. For example, if a person with a Scorpio ascendant enters a enters Jupiter dasa and Jupiter occupies the ninth house and is very well aspected, then there are three fundamental benefits that the person gains. The person will probably travel a great deal and enjoy religion, philosophy, and higher knowledge because Jupiter is posited in the ninth house. The person also makes a great deal of money because Jupiter rules the second, and he or she has wonderful experiences with children or investments because Jupiter rules the fifth house.

Western astrologers should bear in mind that while most house meanings are the same in Hindu astrology as they are in the Western system, some are very different. Those that differ significantly are marked with an asterisk.

Dasa or Bhukti Results of a Planet <u>Ruling or Occupying</u> the First House

IF POWERFUL, WELL-PLACED, AND WELL-ASPECTED:

☺ Fame, recognition, promotions, awards

☺ Good health, general well-being

☺ Improvement of one's appearance (face lifts, nose jobs, etc.)

IF WEAK AND AFFLICTED:

☹ Deterioration of status

☹ Weakening confidence

☹ Poor health, bodily harm (through accidents or otherwise)

☹ Head ailments

☹ Negative reactions from others

☹ No support of nature

Dasa or Bhukti Results of a Planet <u>Ruling or Occupying</u> the Second House

IF POWERFUL, WELL-PLACED, AND WELL-ASPECTED:

- ☺ Financial gains, monetary rewards
- ☺ Enjoys happy and fruitful family life* (includes marital harmony)
- ☺ Successful educational pursuits*, writing ability*, teaching ability*, benefits from lecturing activities*.

IF WEAK AND AFFLICTED:

- ☹ Money problems, loss of wealth
- ☹ Deterioration of family life* (includes marital disharmony)
- ☹ Educational difficulties*, problems in literary endeavors*
- ☹ Throat problems, ailments of the right eye.

Dasa or Bhukti Results of a Planet <u>Ruling or Occupying</u> the Third House

IF POWERFUL, WELL-PLACED, AND WELL-ASPECTED:

- ☺ Tremendous energy, lots of courage, great adventures
- ☺ Ability to fulfill daily desires*
- ☺ Benefits and happiness from brothers and sisters
- ☺ Success in the fine arts of music dance and drama*
- ☺ Enjoyment of entertainment*

IF WEAK AND AFFLICTED:

- ☹ Disturbances and suffering on account of brothers and sisters
- ☹ Loss of desires and ambitions*, weak energy*, lethargy*
- ☹ Inability to fulfill daily desires*
- ☹ No enjoyment of entertainment*
- ☹ Problems in artistic endeavors (specifically music, dance, and drama)*
- ☹ Ailments involving arms or lungs, problems with hearing (especially the right ear)

Dasa or Bhukti Results of a Planet Ruling or Occupying the Fourth House

IF POWERFUL, WELL-PLACED, AND WELL-ASPECTED:

- ☺ Happiness from mother, mother becomes successful
- ☺ Obtains new home, obtains land
- ☺ Successfully moves to new city or country
- ☺ Obtains cars or other conveyances*
- ☺ Obtains jewelry and all kinds of other comforts* (stereos, computers, televisions, etc.)
- ☺ Enjoys contentment and happiness*
- ☺ Success in gaining academic degrees*

IF WEAK AND AFFLICTED:

- ☹ Problems with mother, mother suffers intensely
- ☹ Disturbances inside the home, problems with houses
- ☹ Problems with cars*
- ☹ Suffers from lack of happiness and contentment*
- ☹ Difficulty gaining comforts* (jewelry, stereos, televisions, etc.)
- ☹ Problems in obtaining academic degrees*
- ☹ Heart ailments*

Dasa or Bhukti Results of a Planet Ruling or Occupying the Fifth House

IF POWERFUL, WELL-PLACED, AND WELL-ASPECTED:

- ☺ Childbirth, success with children
- ☺ Financial gains through investments and speculations
- ☺ Successful endeavors in the arts of painting or crafts
- ☺ Abundant fun and pleasure, help and benefits from benefactors* chanting of mantras*, practicing spiritual techniques*
- ☺ Mental clarity and power*, mental happiness and optimism*

- ☺ "Kingship" or political power*
- ☺ Comprehension and realization about one's destiny*
- ☺ Benefits relating specifically to one's *poorvapunya* or past life credit*

IF WEAK AND AFFLICTED:
- ☹ Troubles or suffering on account of children
- ☹ Losses through speculations and investments
- ☹ Unfavorable endeavors in painting or crafts
- ☹ Unable to have fun and pleasure
- ☹ Mental suffering including depression and confusion*
- ☹ No desire to practice mantras and spiritual techniques*
- ☹ Loss of political power*
- ☹ Miscellaneous problems relating to one's *poorvapunya* or past life
- ☹ Credit or debt* (i.e the person reaps specific negative effects of bad actions done in past lives)
- ☹ Confusion about one's destiny*
- ☹ Stomach ailments*

Dasa or Bhukti Results of a Planet <u>Ruling the Sixth House</u>

IF POWERFUL, WELL-PLACED, AND WELL-ASPECTED:
- ☺ Improvement of health, healing ability
- ☺ Success and happiness at daily job
- ☺ Overcomes enemies and competitors*

IF WEAK AND AFFLICTED:
- ☹ Health problems relating to exact nature of planet ruling (or occupying) the sixth house (i.e. Venus = throat, Mars = bloodstream, Jupiter = allergies, and so forth)
- ☹ Difficulties in daily work
- ☹ Suffers on account of enemies and competitors*
- ☹ Charged in court cases*
- ☹ Various difficulties and obstacles* (for no reason except that the sixth house is a *dusthana* or bad house - this is

explained further on)
- ☹ Intestinal problems

Dasa or Bhukti Results of a Planet <u>Ruling or Occupying</u> the Seventh House

IF POWERFUL, WELL-PLACED, AND WELL-ASPECTED:
- ☺ Likelihood of marriage
- ☺ Happy love relationships
- ☺ Dealings with the public
- ☺ Expansion in business*

IF WEAK AND AFFLICTED:
- ☹ Marital problems or divorce
- ☹ Unhappiness in love
- ☹ Few opportunities for marriage
- ☹ Becomes romantically involved with unfavorable or unhealthy partners
- ☹ Ailments involving the genitals
- ☹ Problems in business

Dasa or Bhukti Results of a Planet <u>Ruling or Occupying</u> the Eighth House

IF POWERFUL, WELL-PLACED, AND WELL-ASPECTED:
- ☺ Interest in astrology or psychic phenomena
- ☺ Visits to astrologers and psychics, interest in occult arts
- ☺ Increase of intuition
- ☺ Beneficial spiritual or mystical experiences
- ☺ Financial gains from "unearned means" (lotteries, wills, legacies, insurance companies and so forth)
- ☺ Monetary rewards from spouse or other partners

IF WEAK AND AFFLICTED:
- ☹ Problems with joint finances

- ☹ Difficulty paying or receiving alimony
- ☹ Inability to receive money from wills and legacies
- ☹ Accidents and assorted obstacles* (for no other reason than the fact that the eighth house is a *dusthana* or grief-producing house, as explained further on)
- ☹ Reproductive ailments

Dasa or Bhukti Results of a Planet <u>Ruling or Occupying</u> the Ninth House

IF POWERFUL, WELL-PLACED, AND WELL-ASPECTED:

- ☺ Enjoys travel to other countries or far away places
- ☺ Obtains a guru or spiritual teacher
- ☺ Becomes interested in religion and devotion
- ☺ Benefits from philosophical and spiritual teachings
- ☺ Favorable experiences with the father* (for some individuals, the ninth house represents the father - for others the father is seen through the tenth house)
- ☺ Increase of general luck and fortune*

IF WEAK AND AFFLICTED:

- ☹ Travel plans are cancelled, endures hardships while traveling
- ☹ Problems with gurus and religious teachers
- ☹ Deterioration of faith and devotion
- ☹ Inability to gain higher knowledge
- ☹ Obtains faulty or erroneous higher knowledge
- ☹ Problems with father*
- ☹ Ailments involving the thighs

Dasa or Bhukti Results of a Planet <u>Ruling or Occupying</u> the Tenth House

IF POWERFUL, WELL-PLACED, AND WELL-ASPECTED:

- ☺ Career expansion, career success
- ☺ Obtains awards and honors, increasing status and fame

- ☺ Increasing influence on the world
- ☺ Performs benevolent acts for society
- ☺ Benefits from authority figures and government officials
- ☺ Holy pilgrimages*

IF WEAK AND AFFLICTED:
- ☹ Career downfall
- ☹ Professional problems
- ☹ Confusion about one's dharma (life purpose)
- ☹ Problems with authority figures and government officials
- ☹ Ailments involving the knees

Dasa or Bhukti Results of a Planet <u>Ruling or Occupying</u> the Eleventh House

IF POWERFUL, WELL-PLACED, AND WELL-ASPECTED:
- ☺ Financial gains and profits* (including but not limited to side ventures)
- ☺ Makes new friends, benefits from friends
- ☺ Engages in group activities, forms his or her own group
- ☺ Abundant opportunities
- ☺ Realization of major goals and ambitions
- ☺ Benefits and successful experiences with eldest sibling*

IF WEAK AND AFFLICTED:
- ☹ Financial losses* (including but not limited to side ventures)
- ☹ Loses friends, suffering on account of friends
- ☹ Problems with groups
- ☹ Scarce opportunities, misses opportunities
- ☹ Confusion about one's major goals
- ☹ Inability to fulfill major goals
- ☹ Problems or suffering on account of eldest sibling*,
- ☹ Ailments involving the ankles.

Dasa or Bhukti Results of a Planet <u>Ruling or Occupying</u> the Twelfth House

IF POWERFUL, WELL-PLACED, AND WELL-ASPECTED:

- ☺ Interest in obtaining enlightenment or final liberation, spiritual growth, Powerful experiences of enlightenment
- ☺ Enjoyment of meditation
- ☺ Enjoyable seclusion or confinement in a monastery or ashram
- ☺ Obtains bargains* (the twelfth house rules debts and expenses - the positive side of debts and expenses is bargains)
- ☺ Travel to remote foreign countries* (for a Westerner remote countries means places like India, Nepal, Africa, Israel, and so on)
- ☺ Enjoyment of "bed pleasures*" (positive sexual experiences)

IF WEAK AND AFFLICTED:

- ☹ Encounters unexpected debts and expenses*
- ☹ Hard to experience spiritual growth or enlightenment*
- ☹ Problems with "bed pleasures*" (sexual enjoyment)
- ☹ Travel plans to remote foreign countries are cancelled*
- ☹ Problems in remote foreign countries* (for Westerners this means places like India, Africa, Israel, Nepal and so on)
- ☹ Confinement in a prison or hospital, disturbances caused by "secret enemies"
- ☹ Problems on account of thieves and robbers*
- ☹ Assorted difficulties and problems* (for no other reason than the fact that the twelfth house is a *dusthana* or grief-producing house, as explained further on)
- ☹ Ailments involving the feet
- ☹ Problems with hearing and sight* (specifically the left eye and left ear)

Section VII.

Gemstones, Mantras, and Yagyas

Because Hindu astrology is so predictive, it would be absurd for the system not to include definitive methods to alleviate karmic difficulties that appear in one's birthchart. After all, what is the point of knowing that a life-threatening *dasa-bhukti* is ahead if one does not have the means to alter the problem? Hindu astrologers are famous for their *upayes* or antidotes to planetary afflictions. The most common methods that are used are gemstones, mantras, and *yagyas*, which I will briefly describe. The gemstones for the planets are:

The gem for the **Sun** is **red ruby**.

The gem for the **Moon** is **Pearl** (**moonstone** is a secondary stone).

The gem for **Mars** is **red coral**.

The gem for **Rahu** is **hessonite**.

The gem for **Jupiter** is **yellow sapphire** (**yellow topaz** is a secondary stone).

The gem for **Saturn** is **blue sapphire**.

The gem for **Mercury** is **emerald** (**tourmaline** is a secondary stone).

The gem for **Ketu** is **chrysoberyl**.

The gem for **Venus** is **diamond** (**white sapphire** is a secondary stone).

Although ancient astrological seers explained which gemstones are related to which planets, they were unspecific about how to prescribe the gems. Thus, astrologers differ on their use. There are, however, some commonly agreed on viewpoints. The two most traditional recommendations are that a person should wear the gemstone corresponding to his or her birth planet permanently and wear the gemstone corresponding to each *dasa* temporarily. The birth planet is the planet that rules the ascendant or first house of one's horoscope. For example, a person with a Scorpio ascendant should wear the stone of Mars (red coral) because Mars rules Scorpio. A person with Sagittarius should wear the stone of Jupiter (yellow sapphire) because Jupiter rules Sagittarius. (Westerners beware that these recommendations are ONLY TO BE PRESCRIBED FOR ONE'S HINDU BIRTHCHART CALCULATED BY THE SIDEREAL ZODIAC. Wearing a wrong stone can be harmful and destructive.) By wearing the gemstone of one's birth planet, a person strengthens confidence, self-esteem, support of nature, and the ability to gain recognition. Everyone should wear the gemstone of their birth planet.

Aside from wearing the gem of the birth planet, a person should wear the stone for the current *dasa*. During the six years of the Sun *dasa*, wear the stone for the Sun (red ruby). When that period ends, take off the red ruby and replace it with the stone of the next *dasa* — the Moon (pearl), and so on. The stone that corresponds to the dasa strengthens the *dasa* planet, causing it to give the best possible effects. If the dasa planet is powerful, well-aspected, and well-placed, and well disposed, wearing the dasa gemstone makes the period even more beneficial. If the *dasa* planet is weak or afflicted, wearing the *dasa* gemstone lessens potential damage.

The effects of gemstones are subtle. But they are profound enough for most sensitive individuals to notice a positive difference in their lives. Gemstones can also be worn to strengthen afflicted planets unrelated to one's birth planet or one's *dasas*. They may also be worn to strengthen beneficial planetary influences, thereby creating even more good fortune for a person. Determining which planets can be strengthened without harming other birthchart features, however, requires expertise in Hindu astrology and beginners should consult an expert. As mentioned before, wearing the wrong gems causes negative effects. (See Class Nine for full details on how to prescribe gemstones.)

Gemstones should be natural, of very high quality, and should not be heated, dyed, and chemically altered. The stones should touch the skin, if possible. As a general rule, most astrologers advise wearing stones that are two carats or larger. If this is not possible, one should consider purchasing a <u>slightly</u> smaller gem or a "secondary" stone — a stone which is similar in color and chemical properties to the traditional gem (since the effect of secondary stones are weaker, the size should be increased). Size and quality are crucial. <u>Do not expect an extremely flawed stone or several tiny stones that add up to two or three carats to have a positive effect</u>. This point cannot be overemphasized.

Perhaps the most powerful *upaye* of all is called a *yagya* (also spelled *yagna*). A *yagya* is a religious or spiritual ceremony performed by a Hindu priest in order to alleviate karmic difficulties. It is a kind of offering or sacrifice in which a priest appeals to the planetary beings or the forces of nature (or the gods) for grace and intervention on behalf of the person requesting the *yagya*. During the *yagya*, the priest lights a fire, burns incense, and throws rice, and ghee (clarified butter) into the flames. This symbolizes the burning of negative karma from the past so the person may be relieved of the most intense influences of past destructive actions. During the *yagya*, the priest continuously chants astrological mantras. Astrological mantras are Sanskrit prayers which entreat higher evolutionary beings to remove obstacles in the person's life.

Yagyas are extremely powerful and should be prescribed during a *dasa* or *bhukti* that is difficult or life-threatening. *Yagyas* can also be done during good periods to help fulfill heartfelt desires or to remove unrelenting impediments in life). I have had several *yagyas* performed during rough periods and can attest to their force and efficacy. *Yagyas* can be obtained by calling any Hindu temple in the U.S. or India that employs a Hindu priest. (Some temple addresses are given on page 430.) There are many kinds of *yagyas* that are available. There are *yagyas* for wealth, childbirth, removal of obstacles, family happiness, acquisition of a spouse, and so on. For the purposes of ameliorating a difficult period or subperiod, the *nava graha* or nine-planet *yagya* is usually recommended because it is both effective and easily affordable. Most temples (currently) ask for a donation of around $150 for the two-hour ceremony, and more for three- or seven-day *yagyas*.

Another very important point: much of what causes a *yagya* to work is the subtle power of the mantras being chanted. As the priest chants and chants, his consciousness naturally transcends to finer levels of creation. It is on these subtle levels of nature that a person's karma can be altered. Therefore, it is crucial that the priest perform his chanting uninterrupted. Because *yagyas* are performed in the Sanskrit language, Hindu priests will sometimes interrupt the *yagya* in order to explain to a Westerner the symbolism or meaning of what is happening. This can have a weakening effect and, as much as possible, should be avoided. I therefore recommend asking any questions about the *yagya* before or after the ceremony and explaining to the priest clearly and firmly that there should be no interruptions during the *yagya*. This point cannot be overemphasized.

It is preferable to be present with the priest during the *yagya,* but if this is impossible, a *yagya* can be performed in absentia with fine results. I recommend sending a photograph to the priest, explaining the nature of difficulties you are having or what kind of results you are seeking and perhaps sitting in meditation or prayer while the *yagya* is performed (even though the yagya may take place hundreds or thousands of miles away). Some priests want to know your birthday and birthtime so they can ascertain your birthchart *nakshatra*. (The zodiac is divided into twenty-seven *nakshatras* or "lunar mansions" consisting of thirteen degrees and twenty minutes each.) It is a good idea to have the *yagya* performed on the day that relates to the afflicted planet. For example, if the problem concerns the Sun and your Sun is afflicted, then have the *yagya* performed on Sunday. If the problem is with the Moon, have the *yagya* performed on Monday. The rest of the days are as follows: Mars — Tuesday, Mercury — Wednsday, Jupiter — Thursday, Venus — Friday, Saturn — Saturday.

Another way to heal afflicted planets and difficult *dasas* and *bhuktis* is to chant (or meditate on) astrological mantras. These are the same mantras that the Hindu priest performing a *yagya* chants, although the priest chants all nine planetary mantras as well as other traditional mantras. Using mantras may be uncomfortable for some Westerners, but I have included them in this text for those who are interested. In my astrology practice, I have prescribed astrological mantras for people with afflicted planets and many who have tried chanting (or meditating on) them have reported that their lives were dramatically altered for the better. The planetary mantras and their prescribed number of repetitions are as follows:

PRONUNCIATION OF ASTROLOGICAL MANTRAS

☞ *Note: The number of times a mantra should be chanted does not have to be done in one sitting. About 100 can be chanted in fifteen minutes.*

Mantra for the Sun — to be chanted 7000 times.

PRONUNCIATION

Japa koosooma sankarsham kashya-peeyam mahajuteem, tamoreem sarva pahpagnam pranato smee deevahkaram.

Let us chant the glories of the Sun god, whose beauty rivals that of a flower. I bow down to him, the greatly effulgent son of Kasyapa, who is the enemy of darkness and destroyer of all sins.

Mantra for the Moon — to be chanted 11,000 times.

PRONUNCIATION

Dadee shanka tusha-rabam ksheero-darnava sambhavam na-mahmee shasheenam somam samboor mookuta booshanam.

I offer my obeisances to the Moon god, whose complexion resembles curds, the whiteness of conch shells, and snow. He is the ruling deity of the soma rasa born from the Ocean of Milk, and he serves as the ornament on top of the head of Lord Shambhu.

Mantra for Mars — to be chanted 10,000 times.

PRONUNCIATION

Daranee garbha sambootam vidyut-kahntee sama-prabam koomahram shaktee hastam-cha mangalam prana-mam mya-ham.

I offer my obeisances to Sri Mangala, god of the planet Mars, who was born from the womb of the earth goddess. His brilliant effulgence is like that of lightning, and he appears as a youth carrying a spear in his hand.

Mantra for Mercury — to be chanted 4,000 times.

PRONUNCIATION

Preeyangava guleekash yam roopeyna prateemahm budam sowmyam sowmya goon-peytam tam boodam prana-mahm mya-ham.

I bow down to Bhudda, god of the planet Mercury, whose face is like a fragrant globe of the pryangu herb, and whose beauty matches that of a lotus flower. He is most gentle, possessing all attractive qualities.

Mantra for Jupiter — to be chanted 19,000 times.

PRONUNCIATION

Deva-nancha rishee-nancha gurum-kanchan shaneebam boodee bootam treelo-keysham tam na-mamee brihas-pateem.

I bow down to Brihaspati, god of the planet Jupiter. He is the spiritual master of all the demigods and sages. His complexion is golden, and he is full of intelligence. He is the controlling lord of all three worlds.

Mantra for Venus — to be chanted 16,000 times.

PRONUNCIATION

Heema-kunda mri-nala-bam deyt-yanam para-mam gurum sarva-shastra pravak-taram barga-vam prana-mam mya-hum.

I offer my obeisances to the descendant of Bhrigu Muni (i.e. Venus), whose complexion is white like a pond covered with ice. He is the supreme spiritual master of the demoniac enemies of the demigods, and has spoken to them all the revered scriptures.

Mantra for Saturn — to be chanted 23,000 times.

PRONUNCIATION

Nee-lanjana sama-basam ravee-putram yema-grajam chaya-martanda sambootam tam na-mahmee sanee-charam.

I bow down to slow-moving Saturn whose complexion is dark blue like nilanjana ointment. The elder brother of Lord Yamaraja, he is born from the Sun-god and his wife Chaya.

Mantra for *Rahu* — to be chanted 18,000 times.

PRONUNCIATION

Arda-kayam maha-viryam chandra ditya veemar-danam seeng-hee -ka garba sambootam tam rahum prana-mam mya-ham.

I offer my obeisances go Rahu, born from the womb of Simheeka, who has only half a body yet possesses great power, being able to subdue the Sun and the Moon.

Mantra for *Ketu* — to be chanted 17,000 times.

PRONUNCIATION

Palasha-pushpa-sankasham taraka-grahu masta-kam rowdram rowdrat makam goram tam keytoom prana-mam mya-ham.

I offer my obeisances to the violent and fearsome Ketu, who is endowed with the potency of Lord Shiva. Resembling in his complexion the flower of a palasa plant, he serves as the head of the stars and planets.

Mantras should be started at an auspicious time. Begin mantra chanting on a waxing Moon, when the Moon is bright, not dim. Also, begin on the day that relates to the planet being propitiated. Start chanting (or meditating on) a Jupiter mantra on a Thursday, Venus on a Friday, and so on. These instructions apply ONLY TO THE COMMENCEMENT OF CHANTING. Once you start using a mantra, use it seven days a week, at the same time every day.

Most Westerners chant 108 repetitions (one *mala*) per day, which takes about fifteen minutes. Of course, more *malas* can be done if time allows. Mantra repetitions is are counted by using a strand of beads. In India, 108 *tulsi* or *rudraksha* beads are strung together along with a protruding bead called the guru bead. As each mantra is chanted, the person moves to another bead until he or she has chanted 108 mantras.

To Obtain 3-Day or 7-Day *Yagyas* - Biswa Kalyan Foundation. Mr. Yves Decarie - ph (450) 463-3636 Website: **www.yajna.com** For temples where one-hour *yagyas* can be obtained, see *Services* (page 429).

Friendships Between Planets

In Hindu astrology, planets have friends, enemies, and those which are considered neutral. Generally, Rahu, Venus, Saturn, and Mercury are friendly to each other, while Jupiter, the Sun, the Moon, and Mars welcome each other's presence. While Rahu is included in the friendship scheme, Ketu is not. A planet occupying an enemy sign functions **slightly** worse than usual because it is not welcomed in the house. A planet occupying a friendly sign functions **slightly** better than usual because it is welcomed. Planets in friendly or enemy signs are not of huge significance and are nowhere near as important as planets that are exalted, fallen or in their own signs.

Above are two horoscope forms showing in which signs each planet is welcome or unwelcome. If a planet is not in a sign in either chart, it is because that sign is a <u>neutral</u> influence to the planet. Some astrologers use friendships to judge aspects, gemstone and mantra prescriptions, and much more. In my view, this is not an accurate use of the friendship scheme. **The friendship scheme is only meant to be used to determine whether a planet is welcome in another planet's house**. See Page 86 for full details.

APPENDIX B

This Appendix provides charts in the North Indian style. They are listed in the order in which they appear in the main text.

Book Muhurta
(See page 16)

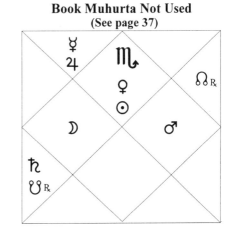

Book Muhurta Not Used
(See page 37)

James Braha's Rasi
(See page 48)

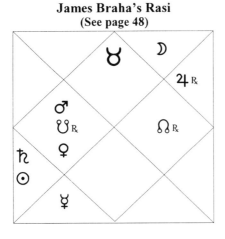

Martin Timmons' Rasi
(See page 50)

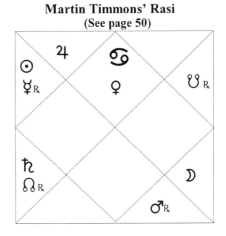

Martin's Dasamsa
(See page 58)

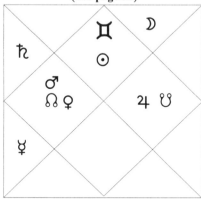

Rajesh Naz's Rasi
(See page 67)

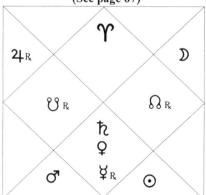

Ram Das' Rasi
(See page 72)

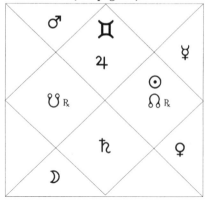

Roberto's Rasi
(See page 111)

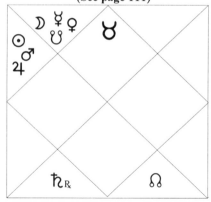

Bill Clinton's Rasi
(See page 124)

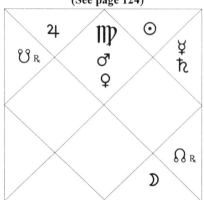

John F. Kennedy's Rasi
(See page 133)

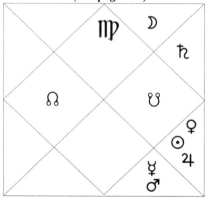

Appendix B: North Indian Style

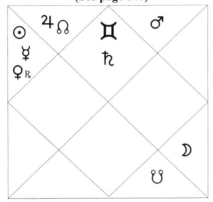

Robert de Niro's Rasi
(See page 140)

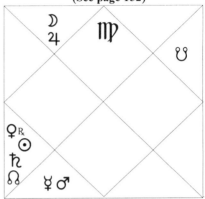

Hank Aaron's Rasi
(See page 152)

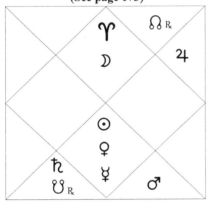

Kerry's Rasi
(See page 173)

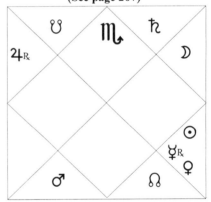

Fidel Castro's Rasi
(See page 207)

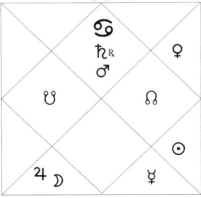

Al Gore's Rasi
(See page 208)

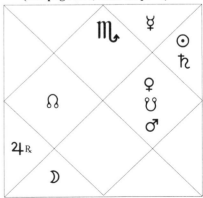

James' Karakamsa
(See page 214; Rasi on p. 48)

Martin's Karakamsa
(See page 215)

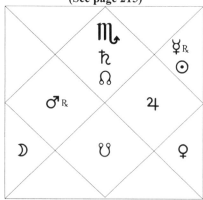

Vashti Braha's Rasi
(See page 224)

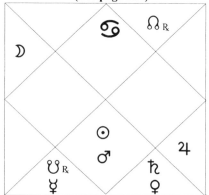

John Lennon's Rasi
(See page 227)

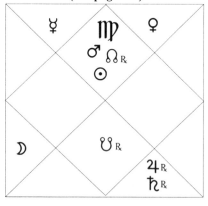

Lennon's Rasi, Pisces ASC
(See page 228)

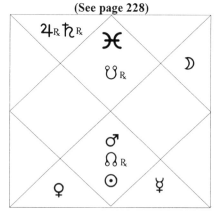

David Stockman's Rasi
(See page 249)

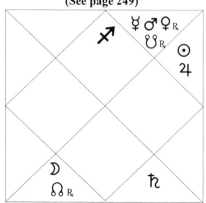

Deborah's Rasi
(See page 259)

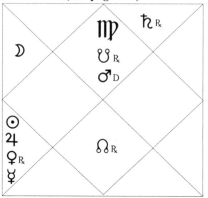

Appendix B: North Indian Style

Deborah's Navamsa
(See page 259)

Henry's Rasi
(See page 272)
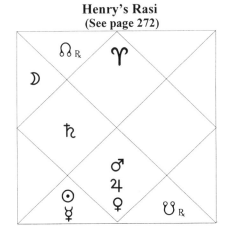

Henry's Dasamsa
(See page 275)
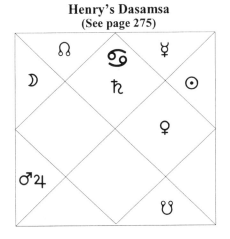

Henry's Navamsa
(See page 281)
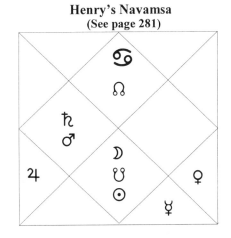

John's Rasi
(See page 285)
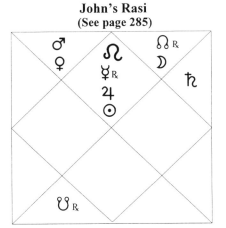

John's Dasamsa
(See page 286)
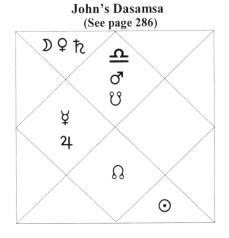

John's Navamsa
(See page 291)

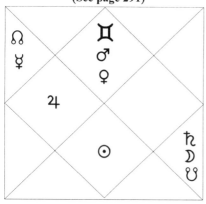

Annie's Rasi
(See page 294)

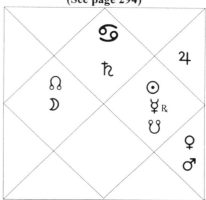

Annie's Dasamsa
(See page 298)

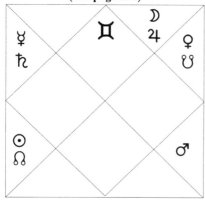

Annie's Navamsa
(See page 305)

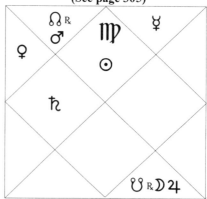

Al Pacino's Rasi
(See page 310)

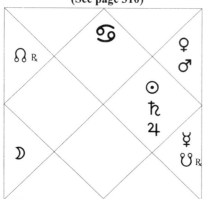

Werner Erhard's Rasi
(See page 315)

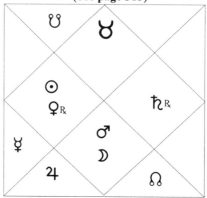

Appendix B: North Indian Style

Chuck's Rasi
(See page 317)

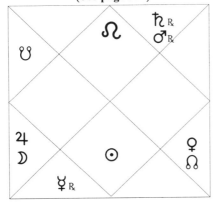

Francis Ford Coppola's Rasi
(See page 319)

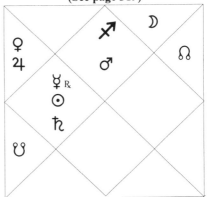

James Braha's Rasi
(See page 321)

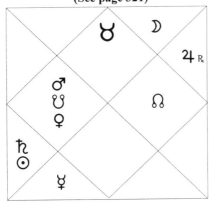

James Braha's Navamsa
(See page 321)

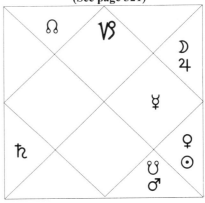

Jack Nicholson's Rasi
(See page 325)

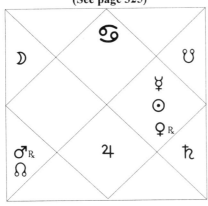

Albert Einstein's Rasi
(See page 326)

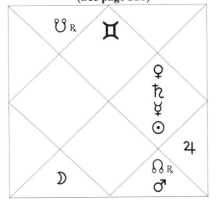

Mick Jagger's Rasi
(See page 326)

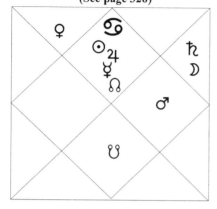

Man with Thyroid Problem
(See page 328)

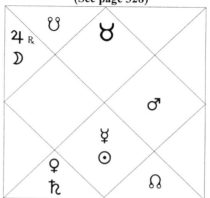

Orson Welles' Rasi
(See page 331)

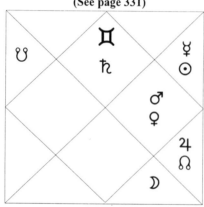

Man with Career Problems
(See page 335)

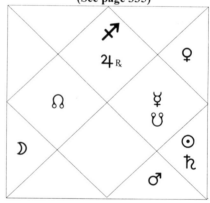

Braha Wedding
(See page 361)

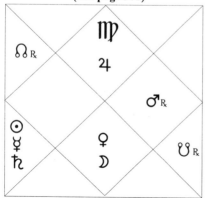

Hypothetical Stellium Chart
(See page 367)

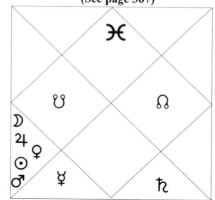

GLOSSARY

Artha - Money matters; One of the four functions of human life according to Hindu philosophy.

Ascendant - The 1st house in a horoscope. Same as ascending or rising sign.

Atma - The soul.

Atma-karaka - The astrological indicator of the soul. There are two in each horoscope. The Sun is one, and the planet occupying the latest degree in the horoscope is the other. The *atmakaraka* reveals strongly ingrained tendencies and affinities.

Ayanamsa (pronounced "aya-nahm-sha") - The figure to be subtracted from the tropical (Western) zodiac to arrive at the sidereal zodiac used in Hindu astrology.

Benefic - A planet which by its essential nature gives fortunate results, i.e. Venus, Jupiter, the Moon, and Mercury when unaspected by any malefic.

Bhava chart - a chart that does not use the "whole sign" house system. In a *bhava* chart, the ascendant degree is considered the middle of the 1st house. Planets that are within fifteen degrees of either side of that degree are taken to be in a particular house. Planets before or after that point are considered to be in an earlier or later house.

Bhukti (pronounced "booktee") - Planetary subperiod within a *dasa* or major period. There are 9 *bhuktis* (1 for each planet) in each *dasa*.

Chandra lagna - Moon ascendent. The procedure of delineating the horoscope using the Moon sign as the 1st house.

Conjunction - Two planets occupying the same sign (and therefore having an effect upon each other).

Combustion - A debilitating condition occurring when any planet other than the nodes is found within approximately eight degrees of the Sun.

Dasa (pronounced "dah-sha") - Period of time during which a person's life is under the influence of a particular planet. There are forty known *dasa* systems, the most popular one being the *Vimsottari* - the one used in this text.

Dasamsa - The one-tenth divisional chart, specifically relating to a person's career.

Dharma - Way of life. Duty. One's proper action or work in the world. One of the four functions of human life according to Hindu philosophy.

Dristhi - An astrological aspect.

Dusthana (pronounced "dush-tana") - One of three misery-producing houses, that is, the 6th, 8th, and 12th.

Jyotish (pronounced "joe-tish", <u>NOT</u> "joy-tish") - Hindu name for astrology.

Kama - Desires. One of the four functions of human life according to Hindu philosophy.

Karaka - Astrological indicator, e.g. the Sun is the *karaka* of the father.

Ketu - The Moon's descending or South Node.

Kujadosha - Mars affliction. A condition spoiling married life. Also called *magaldosha* and *manglik*.

Lagna (pronounced "lug-na") - Ascendant or 1st house

Lord - The planet connected to a house by virtue of rulership. Same as house ruler.

Malefic - A planet which by its essential nature causes harm.

Mangaldosha - Same as **Kujadosa**.

Moksha (pronounced "moke-sha") - Enlightenment, salvation, final liberation, nirvana, state of eternal freedom.

Muhurta - A chart drawn for the beginning of a project to ensure that the undertaking goes well.

Nakshatra - Lunar mansion. There are twenty-seven lunar mansions that comprise thirteen degrees and twenty minutes each. Each *nakshatra* has its own positive or negative effects and its own particular qualities.

Natal - Pertaining to the horoscope based on the exact time and place of birth.

Navamsa (pronounced "nah-vahm-shah") - The 1/9th divisional chart specifically relating to marriage. The most important of all the sixteen *vargas*. Used by all astrologers alongside the natal horoscope.

Neecha - A planet in its fallen sign, i.e. the sign where a planet functions the worst and produces misery.

Neechabhanga - A special planetary yoga which, when it occurs, cancels the negative effect of a fallen planet.

Panoti Yoga - A method of determining whether each two-and-a-half year period within the seven-and-a-half year *Sade Sati* period will go well or badly.

Parasara system - Most popular system of Hindu astrology and the one taught in this text. Named after the great sage Parasara.

Parivartana Yoga - Mutual reception or two planets that exchange signs.

Poorvapunya - Specific credit from past-life efforts destined to appear in this lifetime.

Prasna (pronounced "prushna") - Horary astrology. A method whereby a person puts a specific question to an astrologer and a horoscope is drawn up to give the answer.

Rahu (pronounced "rah-hoo") - The Moon's ascending or North Node.

Rajayoga - Royal union. An extremely favorable condition which occurs when the lords of two auspicious houses join together in one house.

Rajayoga-karaka - Royal union indicator. A planet which, because of the two good houses it rules, has the same effect as a planetary union. For example, whenever the lords of the 9th and 10th houses join together, a rajayoga is formed. Saturn is therefor a *rajayoga-karaka* for Taurus ascendent because it rules both the 9th and 10th houses.

Rasi - A zodiac sign or constellation. The natal horoscope is referred to as the rasi chart.

Sade Sati (pronounced "sah-dee sah-tee") - A mistakenly dreaded seven-and-a-half year period when Saturn transits the house before the Moon, the house containing the Moon, and the house following the Moon. *Sadi Sati* can be either good or bad.

Shiva (pronounced "Sheeva") - One of the three main Hindu Gods. The God of destruction.

Sri Pati (pronounced shree pahti) - A house system used in Hindu astrology that differs from the ancient "whole sign house" system. In *Sri Pati*, the ascendant <u>degree</u> is the <u>middle</u> of the house.

Upachaya (pronounced oo-pah-cha-ya) - A 'growing' house, where the significations of a planet improve or grow stronger as time goes on. The 3rd, 6th, 10th and 11th houses. The only houses where malefics produce good results.

Upaye (pronounced "oo-pah-yay") - Antidote (to a planetary affliction), e.g.

wearing a specific gemstone will neutralize the negative effects indicated or caused by a harmful planetary condition.

Varga - One of the sixteen divisional charts based on fractions of each sign in a natal horoscope.

Vishnu - One of the three main Gods of the Hindus. The God known as the great maintainer or preserver.

Yagya (also spelled **yajna**) - A Hindu ritualistic ceremony where many priests chant mantras to heal an afflicted planet in a person's horoscope. *Yagyas* are also performed to help a woman conceive, to obtain a spouse, and to ensure the success of an endeavor.

Yoga karaka - Union indicator. The best planet for a horoscope because of its house rulership, i.e. a planet which, because it rules good houses, gives beneficial results, wherever it is placed, regardless of its essential nature.

SERVICES OF JAMES BRAHA AND HERMETICIAN PRESS

James Braha
Hermetician Press
P.O. Box 195
Longboat Key, Fla. 34228

Website www.jamesbraha.com
E-mail brahas@earthlink.net

All orders can be made through e-mail (using credit cards MC/VISA/DISCOVER) or postal mail using James Braha/Hermetician Press address above.

Books by James Braha

Ancient Hindu Astrology for the Modern Western Astrologer, $21.95
How To Be a Great Astrologer; the Planetary Aspects Explained, $19.95
How to Predict Your Future; Secrets of Eastern and Western Astrology, $22
Astro-Logos; Revelations of a Hindu Astrologer, $9.95
The Art and Practice of Ancient Hindu Astrology, $29.95

Add $1.50 per book for shipping and handling.

James Braha Eastern & Western Astrology Computerized Birthchart Report
Beautifully bound, 60+ pages, full text by James Braha includes full interpretations of Hindu planets in houses, Hindu *dasa* and *bhukti* periods for 15 years, transits of Western "outer planets" for 3 years, Western natal astrological aspects, South Indian Hindu horoscope with *dasa-bhukti* periods, Western horoscope. $45.

Hindu Full-Life Birthchart Interpretation by James Braha
In-depth analysis of natal Hindu horoscope and future *dasa* and *bhukti periods* (with full astrological explanations). 60 to 90 minutes long, given by phone and recorded on cassette tape. Includes gemstone recommendations, mantra and *yagya* prescriptions, as well as transits, progressions, and *dasa-bhukti* periods and subperiods. More in-depth for next 3-4 years. For details, call James Braha at (941) 387-9101, or call directory assistance for James

Braha in Longboat Key, Florida.

Hindu Astrology Software – Haydn's Jyotish
Calculates all 16 *varga* charts, *nakshatras, dasas, bhuktis,* and sub-bhuktis. Includes options for English or Sanskrit, North or South Indian chart formats, and explanatory comments on planets and houses (Note: This is not an interpretive program). Extremely user friendly. DOS PC or MAC. $110.

American Council of Vedic Astrology (ACVA)
One of the purposes of ACVA is to promote Vedic astrology in the West through their yearly conferences and certification programs. For more information, contact Dennis Harness at (520) 282-6595.

Excellent Horary Astrologer
Lee Lehman – (321) 728-2277 (answers questions based on William Lilly's 16th century techniques).

To Have Large *Yagyas* Performed in India
For 3-day or 7-day *Yagyas* performed in India, contact Yves DeCarie – (450) 463-3636, or visit his website www.yajna.com

Temples Where One-hour Yagyas Can be Obtained

Sri Shirdi Sai Baba Temple
3744 Old William Tell Highway
Pittsburgh, Pa. 15235
Ph. # (412) 374-9244, (412) 823-1296

Hindu Temple of Greater Chicago
12 South 701 Lemont Road
Lemont, Illinois 60439
Ph #. (630) 972-0300

Gemstone Information
Jay Boyle 1-800-559-5090   See www.astrologicalgem.com

Catalogue of Hindu Astrology Texts, Chanting Beads, and Deity Pictures
21st Century Books
401 N. 4th St.
Fairfield, Iowa 52556
Phone 1-800-593-2665

Computer Calculated Hindu Charts With Dasa-Bhuktis
ACS - Astro Communications Service
PO 34487, San Diego, Calif. 92163-4487   Phone 1-800-888-9983